HOW JIMMY WON

BY KANDY STROUD

HOW JIMMY WON

The Victory Campaign From Plains to the White House

WILLIAM MORROW AND COMPANY, INC.

NEW YORK   1977

Printed in the United States of America.

1   2   3   4   5   6   7   8   9   10

Library of Congress Cataloging in Publication Data

Stroud, Kandy.
   How Jimmy won.

   Includes index.
   1. Presidents—United States—Election—1976.
2. Carter, Jimmy, 1924-   3. Presidents—United
States—Biography. 4. Carter family. I. Title.
E868.S86   973.926′092′4 [B]   77-1344
ISBN 0-688-03153-6

BOOK DESIGN   CARL WEISS

To My Beloved Frank, who made this year of personal growth possible, who held hearth and home together, supported and encouraged, turned disappointment to laughter, and who never once complained.

To My Dearest Parents, Kathryn and Andrew Shuman, who offered love and prayers.

And to My Blessed Children, Brooke and Lindsay, who understood.

Thank you.

CONTENTS

INTRODUCTION

PRESIDENT JIMMY CARTER was born into a privileged world surrounded by poverty. He grew up with blacks as friends and self-made millionaires as relatives, an aristocrat in the midst of twentieth-century slavery. His father was a segregationist, his mother the radic-lib of her day.

Part of him was naval officer, Sunday-school teacher, scholar, engineer, liberal, businessman, conservative. Primarily, he was a politician. And those of us who covered him found him the most complex and interesting of our time. His enemies said he was consumed with selfish ambition, a ruthless opportunist who would change his politics to further his climb to the top. Yet his ambition was not only for himself, but for others. He said to me once, "I feel like I have a certain amount of talent and ability and one life to live and I don't want to waste it. I'd like it to be meaningful to myself and the people around me. I just don't like to feel any potential stretching of my mind or my heart has been neglected."

He has an existential dimension. He defines and creates himself in action, and insists to this day that he is still growing. His solutions are pragmatic. Yet there is optimism in his growth and in his approach to problems.

He is like very few men who seek worldly power, an alienated man. He is shy—"isolated and withdrawn sometimes," he admits. And so are some of his closest friends, like John Pope and Charlie Kirbo, and his wife, Rosalynn. He finds fraternal situations often difficult to cope with. He prefers the privacy of his home and the security of his family to the world of men's clubs and cocktail parties. He often cloistered himself in the womblike solitude of his compartment on Peanut One, and his forays to deal with the press were often characterized by small give-and-take and sarcasm.

He is a moral, even a holy man, devout in his prayers and his Christian pursuits, a man dedicated to Christ and His gospel, and yet he is a politician trapped in the venal and compromising snake pit of American politics. That is part of his conflict. He has done things other liberal politicians and many human beings would be ashamed of. He did not oppose the Vietnam war until almost the end. He proclaimed an "American Fighting Men's Day" which was really a Lieutenant William Calley day in Georgia. He peddled himself as a racist in his 1970 gubernatorial campaign against Carl Sanders. He spoke sympathetically of racists Alabama Governor George Wallace and Lt. Governor Lester Maddox. He criticized Sanders for having once barred Wallace from a scheduled speaking engagement in Georgia by refusing to permit the use of a state building for the speech. He visited a private segregated school in the Piedmont region of Georgia and told backers for thirteen south Georgia counties at a rally in Tifton not to "let anybody, including the Atlanta newspapers, mislead you into criticizing private education."

And yet he announced the day of his inauguration as Governor, "I say to you quite frankly that the day for discrimination is over." As Governor his track record in race relations was superior. He appointed blacks to major state boards and agencies. He placed blacks on the Board of Paroles and Pardons, in the State Welfare Department, and on the State Board of Regents. When he came into office, there were three blacks serving on major boards and agencies. There were fifty-three when he left. The number of black state employees increased under his aegis from 4,850 to 6,684. He selected a young black patrolman to be the security guard who accompanied him on his travels around the state; he even took the guard into his home, and into his then segregated church. He proclaimed January 15, 1973, Martin Luther King Day, to honor the slain black leader. And above the advice of some of his closest aides he hung King's portrait in the state capitol. He had taken a stand against prejudice in his own community of Plains in 1965 when he and his own family were the only ones to stand up and be counted in a vote for the admission of blacks to his church. For that, he was boycotted, his children were beaten, their cars were pelted with stones and rocked by groups of youths. He finally overcame when eleven years later, Carter in his first act as President-elect persuaded the people of his hometown to reverse their 1965 edict and to open the doors of their church to all who wished to worship there.

He was a changeling who matured late. He was once a young man whose dreams were only of the seas and of self, a military man who built weapons of war and destruction, whose eyes were finally opened to the needs of others. But he relinquished his career on the water and thrust himself into the tilling of earth. And the seeds of his

Christian faith, which had fallen on fallow ground, flowered as did his spirit and concern for others. In the land he found himself and his purpose. He directed his search for power to the service of mankind.

His politics fit no simple category. He could be conservative on abortion and welfare reform and taxes, and simplifying the federal bureaucracy, liberal on programs like National Health Insurance, Day Care, ERA, cutting the defense budget. Like Robert Kennedy, he became a new kind of liberal, leapfrogging over the old liberalism he thought to be obsolete, unworkable, divisive. He questioned the old shibboleths of welfare and federal paternalism. He was more interested in a manageable bureaucracy, an America back at work, with financial and judicial equality for the poor as well as the rich.

Above all, he was misunderstood. Being Southern, he would be, and being rural Southern, he would be even more so. "What are you doing working for some red-neck cracker peanut farmer from Georgia?" a sophisticated Maryland liberal had said to a friend of mine who decided to work for Jimmy Carter's campaign in 1975.

Being a born-again Bible-toting Baptist in an ever more Godless world did not help to explain him either. Agnostics disdained him. Catholics suspected him. Wasps despised him. And all accused him of using his religion, if not to convert the world to Christ, or to move the Vatican to Plains, then certainly for his own political gain.

Snobbism accounted for part of the lack of understanding. A farmer could not possibly comprehend complex international issues of nuclear proliferation, global confrontation, détente, the hidden mechanisms of the CIA, Arab boycotts, a crumbling world financial structure. A peanut farmer could not be fit to welcome with white tie and tails a leader such as Leonid Brezhnev or the Shahanshah of Iran to the marble and silken halls of the White House. Or for that matter appreciate opera. And a politician with no further experience than one term as Governor of a small state and a stint as state senator representing a red-neck, Wallace constituency could not be equipped to serve as leader of the free world.

An outsider with no Washington connections or political IOU's could never hope to be elected, no less fit in, or cope with the political expediency of Presidential politicizing.

And yet, on November 2, 1976, James Earl Carter, Jr., was elected the thirty-ninth President of the United States.

PROLOGUE:
FIRST IMPRESSIONS

IT WAS EIGHT O'CLOCK one dazzlingly clear Saturday morning in April 1974. Atlanta was ablaze with azaleas in a thousand different shades of pink, purple and red. And beneath a brilliant blue sky on the stone steps of the red brick million-dollar Governor's mansion that looked like a backdrop for *Gone With the Wind* stood a slight, sandy-haired man with a smile that seemed too large for his small face, a smile that registered around intense blue eyes in a profusion of wrinkles and crow's feet. He wore faded jeans, a Wrangler jacket and tattered sneakers, both hands were thrust in his hip pockets and he looked more like the gardener than the Governor. I was surprised to find the Chief Executive of Georgia, whom I expected to be the epitome of Southern sophistication, in his peanut clothes. I had heard about his habit of walking around his house barefoot and I inquired about it. The famous Carter grin widened until the edges of his mouth practically touched his ears. "Ah put on mah shoes foh y'all."

Carter was greeting Washington reporters who had flown to Atlanta to cover Betty Ford, then the wife of the Vice President. Mrs. Ford's Southern mission was to officiate at the opening of a project known as Arttrain, railroad cars converted into a moving museum designed to bring the old and new masters to those who had no access to culture, no less Modigliani or Renoir. And that day Carter's wife, Rosalynn, was to ride in a motorcade through Atlanta with Mrs. Ford, then accompany her to the Arttrain site for ribbon-cutting ceremonies. Since the excursion was going to absorb six or seven hours, I asked the Governor what he planned to do with his day. "Baby-sit," he stated matter-of-factly. "Amy, my six-year-old daughter, has planned a schedule. First we're going to the movies. Then we're coming home to watch *Sesame Street* and the cartoons. Then we're going to McDonald's for a hamburger. Then we're going swimming."

It seemed rather refreshing that this new breed of Governor who had made the cover of *Time* magazine, a man who in a few short years as Georgia Governor had carved out a reputation for himself as a harbinger of the New South and a politician to watch, was actually taking Saturday off to ramble around Atlanta with a six-year-old vixen who had planned his day, not vice versa.

I had actually met Carter the evening before, but that morning's memory of the casual denim-clad peanut farmer juxtaposed against the elegant setting of his colonial manse, one of the most beautiful Governor's mansions in the country, whose antique-filled interiors equaled, if not surpassed, the White House, is indelible.

The night before had been more formal. The wealthy barons of Atlanta stood in a receiving line to shake hands with the Second Lady of the Land and to sup at a highly polished twenty-foot-long mahogany table groaning beneath the weight of silver candelabra, huge silver tureens steaming with hot hors d'oeuvres and gleaming platters laden with fruits and artichokes. Carter, again, was outside on the steps of his pillared home, meeting and greeting his guests, while keeping an eye on Amy, who cavorted irrepressibly about a fountain surrounded by yellow tulips. I took the opportunity to catch Carter in a free moment. We talked at some length about Watergate and Richard Nixon. Carter, who had heretofore been supportive of Nixon's Vietnam policies, did not spare the razor's edge. "In two hundred years of history, he's the most dishonest President we've ever had. I think he's disgraced the Presidency. I'm a longtime Nixon-hater from way back. I lived in California when he ran against Helen Gahagan Douglas." Carter said he did not think Nixon would resign. "It's not in the nature of that man. He'll be impeached. I think the evidence is there . . . the accumulated impact of a dozen different culpable acts."

We talked about Ted Kennedy and Gerald Ford, and Carter, who had already secretly laid out his Presidential game plan, said, "I think Kennedy is the leading man in the party today. He could have the nomination if he wanted it," but he also wagered that "in a Kennedy-Ford race, Kennedy would lose." Word had filtered through Washington circles that Carter, an ambitious man who sought second spot on the ticket with George McGovern in 1972, might have an eye on the Vice Presidency again in 1976. But Carter shook his head. "I wouldn't go after it. You have to sidle up to people and I don't like that." Back in 1972 at the Miami Convention, Carter's lieutenants, Peter Bourne, Jerry Rafshoon and

Hamilton Jordan, had ill-advisedly urged Carter to nominate Scoop Jackson. His subsequent efforts to secure the veep position with McGovern were considered ludicrous by McGovern's forces. It was at that convention, Carter aides say, they decided to aim for higher stakes.

But Carter denied that his ambition went beyond Plains. He intended to retire from office in November, finish his work traveling the country as Democratic Campaign Chairman and then go back to Georgia, and run his peanut business.

He seemed anxious to talk about his hometown, "Population six hundred eighty-three, three hundred fifty blacks, two hundred whites. My daughter, Amy, attends public school there. There are thirteen blacks in her class and only ten whites. We send her there because she wants to go there, and because her mother and I want her to go there."

Carter went on about his town—"Both my wife's and my families have been there since the 1700's." He talked about how he worked in the peanut fields, and Rosalynn worked every day keeping the books for the business. He made a strong point about the boycott against him as a result of his family's lonely fight for civil rights in the Sixties. "My wife, my sons and I were the only ones who stood up in the Plains Baptist Church several years ago and defended the rights of black people to attend that church."

Little did I realize at the time that this was all a dress rehearsal of the same material he would use in his Presidential campaign, and a condensation of the book he was then writing about himself. It was also a concerted effort to be quoted. As Hamilton Jordan advised Carter in a seventy-two-page memo, in order to gain the national name recognition needed for a Presidential race, it was imperative to attract as much media attention as he could, and to do so as soon as possible. Almost everything he said that night appeared in Clare Crawford's article in *People* Magazine.

I left Atlanta with a vivid impression of Carter as a politician who was somehow different from the others, a man who was both down to earth and sophisticated, accessible though guarded, friendly yet reserved, casual but disciplined, and above all human.

The next time I saw Jimmy Carter he was about to announce his candidacy for the Presidency of the United States. What transpired between that meeting in April 1974 and Carter's announcement of his candidacy is interesting in retrospect.

From 1970 to 1973 my husband, Frank, a pediatrician, had

worked as the medical director in the Comprehensive Health Services Division in the national office of Office of Economic Opportunity (OEO). Among the many bright and dedicated young staff members was Mary King Broadhead, a program analyst for a number of health programs in poverty areas around the country, including one in Atlanta, Georgia. Mary, who had played an important role in the civil rights struggles of the Sixties, had brought her skills and experience in community organization and consumer participation into the health program planning and development world of OEO. There she quickly earned a reputation for toughness, perseverance and political savvy. For that reason, one of her assigned programs became Atlanta Southside Comprehensive Health Services, Inc. As with most federally funded health programs, local political forces began to take sides, with Emory University, local elected officials, and the poor all in different corners. Mary quickly found an understanding ally in Dr. Peter Bourne, a British-born, American-educated psychiatrist who had become well known through his published works on the mental stresses and drug usage of the Green Berets in Vietnam. Bourne was now the Mental Health Services Director for Atlanta Southside and had put together one of the most innovative and imaginative programs seen anywhere in the United States. Through the use of special training programs he had originated in the center, talented lay members recruited from within the poor community had been taught to work in groups or on a door-to-door basis with the depressed patient, the drug user, the alcoholic and others ravaged by the stresses of poverty. Many of the counselors were rehabilitated alcoholics and drug addicts themselves and their effect was often greater than that of a professional social worker or psychologist. Bourne's vision was that of a community reaching out to help itself, recognizing the impossible nature and expense of any program that relied on college degreed or certified professionals.

It was this very program that brought Bourne to the attention of Rosalynn Carter, who, as First Lady of Georgia, was looking for a meaningful way to make a contribution in her role as Governor's wife. She chose mental health as her field and Bourne as her advisor. Through Rosalynn, Bourne subsequently became the State Director of Mental Health for the Department of Human Resources and a close associate of Jimmy Carter's. By the time Carter returned to Plains, Bourne and Mary King, who had both since been divorced from their respective spouses, had been dating and were engaged.

Bourne was called to the White House to serve on President Nixon's Special Action Office on Drug Abuse. He used his Washington base to help launch Jimmy Carter's presidential campaign through his contacts with the press.

After they were married, the Bournes' home became Carter's Washington pied-à-terre. He continued to stay with them during his trips to the nation's capital throughout the campaign until November 2, when he was given Blair House as President-elect. Mary King also became a close advisor of Carter's, serving him in the field of health and women's rights.

Bourne, at Carter's behest, had long been trying to convince me and dozens of other reporters of Carter's political assets. During the primaries in 1972 I covered George McGovern on a trip to Atlanta where the Democratic candidate spoke to a rally on the steps of the statehouse. Bourne found me in the crowd and told me, in the shadow of the statue of Thomas Edward Watson, that Carter wanted to be Vice President. Nixon's Southern strategy had been extraordinarily effective, he said, and to win in '72 the Democrats needed someone who could help carry the South. Carter was a popular Southerner, a new face, a Kennedyesque figure. "And he wants it," Bourne said with the certainty that anything Carter wanted he could have by snapping his fingers. We had dinner that night with columnist Rowland Evans, and Evans got an earful of Carter too. Bourne was convinced Carter was a man destined to play a crucial role in the future of American politics.

The first time I can remember Bourne's mention of a 1976 Carter candidacy was just an hour after George McGovern's acceptance speech at the 1972 Democratic National Convention in Miami. It was four A.M. and a group of us had collapsed in a sleazy little Miami Beach restaurant for breakfast. Bourne predicted that McGovern would lose the election and made the outlandish statement that Jimmy Carter would be elected President in 1976. Most of us chalked off the remark to battle fatigue from the struggle to make Carter Vice-Presidential nominee and an overdose of hero-worship.

Over the next two years there was much saber-rattling for Carter in our occasional encounters with the Bournes. "Jimmy and Rosalynn are going to be in town this weekend." . . . "We'd love to have you meet Jimmy and Rosalynn when they're in town next time." There was a spate of invitations to dinner, which finally materialized in March of 1974 when we rendezvoused at the Sea Catch, a restaurant in the Fairfax Hotel. What was planned as a simple reunion turned out to be another hefty dose of public relations for Carter.

He was, Bourne said, one of the most unusual men he had ever known or had the privilege to work for, an "absolutely fantastic individual." He was a nuclear physicist, an engineer, a Naval Academy graduate, a businessman, a voracious reader. Yet he was hip—he was into Bob Dylan's music and often invited the Allman Brothers rock band over to the Governor's mansion for drinks after they were through with a gig in Atlanta. Barefoot and blue-jeaned, he would sit up, drinking with them until three or four o'clock, then work an eighteen-hour day. I should go to Atlanta to interview him for *Women's Wear Daily*. (I was Washington correspondent at the time.) I should meet him. I should know him. "It would make a great story. He might be President someday." We were both politely attentive and titillated but unmotivated. A remote Southern Governor President?

Many Democrats were convinced that 1976 would be Hubert Humphrey's or Ted Kennedy's year. Kennedy had been approached in 1968 after his brother Robert's death, but the overwhelming despair that consumed him prevented a try that year. In 1972 McGovern surprised the party with his primary successes and ended Kennedy's chances as did Chappaquiddick but 1976 was a distinct possibility. Kennedy wanted to be President some day, he told me, and although he had made a public statement declaring that his decision not to run was irrevocable, many Kennedy associates were certain Kennedy could be convinced he was needed for the country's sake. If not on the top of the ticket, then in second place with Hubert Humphrey at the helm.

In March 1975 I wrote a cover story for *New York* Magazine pronouncing that hidden mechanisms were in motion, and Kennedy was running. Clay Felker, the publisher, agreed with me. "Everybody's saying it," Felker said, and he conceived the title: "Is Teddy Running? Do Birds Sing in the Morning?" The thesis was that the Democratic party would field a platoon of candidates, all of which would probably kill each other off, and Kennedy would emerge like the Phoenix, out of a brokered convention. But Bourne smiled and with the air of a disciple predicted that Jimmy Carter, "you wait and see," would be President.

I had one of the first stories on Carter's intention to declare his candidacy entitled "The South Rises Again" which ran in *WWD* on October 3. Carter came to Washington to address the National

Press Club on December 11 and announced his candidacy two days later. I had arranged an interview with him timed to run with the announcement. It was not easy to interest my editor, Mort Sheinman, in the story. "Carter?" Sheinman laughed. "Running for President? Nobody's ever heard of him. It's a joke. Go ahead and do the interview, but keep it short." He wouldn't guarantee space.

I met Carter the morning of December 12 in the lobby of the Hotel Washington. He was wearing a dark blue suit, his handshake was firm, and he seemed extremely gentle and friendly. We sat side by side on a small bench in the gloomy hotel lobby and talked for about forty-five minutes.

With his elbows on his knees, and his hands folded under his chin, Carter talked about why he wanted to run for President. He felt he was just as "qualified" as anyone, and listed his credentials—peanut farmer, businessman, scientist, nuclear engineer. As Governor of Georgia he had established an excellent track record in the environment and the field of mental health and prison reform. He had initiated zero-based budgeting and completely reorganized the agencies.

Had he considered the possibility of a Kennedy candidacy? "Yes, I just had a long talk with him yesterday. I spent two hours with him and he reaffirmed that his withdrawal from the race is irrevocable. I believe him." Carter said he had an advantage over all the other potential candidates. He had free time. His term as Governor would soon expire and he would be able to devote full time to running. The other candidates would be encumbered by Senate, House, or gubernatorial responsibilities. They would be limited in the number of primaries they would be able to enter. He on the other hand would enter them all and fight to the finish. "I'm in to stay." He also had energy and stamina for a long race. "I'm used to a twenty-hour day. I'm up at six-thirty every morning and I go to bed at twelve or twelve-thirty." And he had been collecting political IOU's as Chairman of the Democratic Campaign Committee, had crisscrossed the country that summer making friends he could count on in a campaign. And money? "I hope to raise five hundred thousand dollars in Georgia, then build my campaign with individual contributions of no more than one thousand dollars."

Rosalynn appeared. She looked more like a missionary than a Governor's wife in a severely tailored suit and very short hair. She seemed less enthusiastic than Carter about campaigning. "Sometimes I say, 'Oh, I just want to go home.' But I never thought about

Jimmy's not running. Of course I worry about him working so hard, but he's happiest that way. And I know he'd make a good President. He's always had the interests of the people at heart. He's never done anything for his own benefit."

That afternoon Jimmy Carter spoke to the National Press Club. He spoke of a loss of integrity, "acceptance of mediocrity, subservience to special interests, and an absence of vision and direction." Several noted how much he looked and sounded like Robert and John Kennedy as he gestured with pointed finger. "Our government can express the highest common ideals of human beings—if we demand of it standards of excellence. . . .

"For our nation—for all of us—the question is, 'Why not the best?' "

Carter formally announced his candidacy that afternoon in Atlanta, but for months, the Carter cortege seemed to drop out of sight.

It was almost a year later and we were having dinner one fall evening at the home of another former Atlantan, Dr. Tom Bryant. Bourne was my dinner partner. "What ever happened to your candidate?" I teased. "There hasn't been much about him in the newspapers. Is he still running?" A slightly amused grin crossed Bourne's face. "I'll bet you that Cahtuhh," he said in his soft British accent, "is going to surprise everyone in the primaries and will win the nomination." I bet him that Carter would never come close even to winning the New Hampshire primary. Bourne accepted the bet.

On January 29, 1976, after Carter had swept the Iowa caucuses and was favored to win the New Hampshire primary, I had lunch with Bourne at the Sans Souci restaurant. "I told you." He smiled. This time I listened.

Bourne explained how it all happened, and the part he played in Carter's decision to run. He had been impressed from the moment he met Carter and thought of him as Presidential timber. By 1971, when he saw Carter's disillusionment with the hordes of Presidential candidates who stopped in Atlanta and stayed at the Governor's mansion, he began to think the possibility of a Carter candidacy might not be so farfetched. During one trip they took together, he broached the subject. "We had been to Washington where Carter testified before one of Senator Ed Muskie's committees on intergovernmental regulations, and on the way back we were talking about Muskie's qualities. He was interested that Muskie was the front-runner at the time. It surprised Carter because he was most unimpressed with Muskie, who just didn't strike him as that Presidential. It was part of the process of realizing his own talent and of building his self-confidence. He thought that if this guy can get to be President that it was not too farfetched for him. I asked him then if he'd ever thought about running himself. He said, 'No, but if I ever do, I'd run the way I ran for the Governorship, four years flat out.' I assumed he was thinking about it. But we didn't discuss it again for a long time. I had it in the back of my mind for the next year. I thought about it a lot. Around Christmas, 1971, I was reading *Nicholas and Alexandra,* a very inspiring book about the czar. Nicholas was a very popular czar even though he was a great oppressor. He had a great feeling for what Russia was all about. And it reminded me of Carter because Carter understands the mood of this country more than anyone I've seen. I thought it presumptuous of me to talk about it then. I wanted to wait for a more opportune time, for some signal or indication that he was interested. Then when the whole Vice-Presidential thing happened in Miami in 1972, when he let us push him for Vice President and didn't try and stop us, I knew he must have an eye on it. Morris Dees and Pat Caddell had forced him to look at some polls that showed McGovern would do better with a Southerner on the ticket and he had seemed interested. But after the whole effort collapsed at the convention, I spent a few hours one night in a bar in Miami with his son Chip. I said, 'I think your father shouldn't waste his time with the Vice Presidency. I think he should run for President himself.' Chip agreed." The Friday after the McGovern nomination Bourne and Hamilton Jordan sat sunning themselves by the pool at the Doral Hotel discussing "what a screwed-up situation it was to try and get someone on the ticket and how demeaning the whole thing was, and we talked about Carter running for President next time."

The following week Bourne sat down and composed an eight-page memo to Carter.

He gave me a copy of that memo at lunch.

MEMORANDUM

TO: GOVERNOR CARTER
FROM: PETER BOURNE
DATE: July 25, 1972

I waited a couple of weeks to write this memo to be sure the euphoria and pandemonium of Miami was not clouding my objectivity. However I feel my observations are substantially valid, and I hope you will not feel my suggestions are too blunt.

The events in Miami further convinced me of the truth of a number of points:

1) Party reforms as well as the climate in the country have politicized segments of the population who have never previously been involved in the political process and the resulting coalition which is unique will have a lasting impact on the party for at least the next ten years. I do not think it will make very much difference whether McGovern wins or loses. The kinds of people who were delegates in Miami are in the political process to stay and they have enough political sophistication not to invest all their hopes for change in one campaign or one person's candidacy. The old politicians who think that once McGovern is defeated it will be politics as usual are dead wrong and do not understand the social forces at work in the country. . . .

3) The people who will win the big prizes are going to be increasingly the people who are willing to take risks, particularly in terms of hazarding existing power bases. One can take moderate and compromise positions on issues and remain a successful, respected, secure politician, but one will not get the big apples. McGovern is only one example of this. If a Southerner is ever to get the Democratic nomination for President he is going to have to go out on a limb, risk the loss of a substantial block of Southern support and hope (which I think is true) that Southern attitudes are now increasingly moving towards the national mean.

4) If the McGovern ticket loses, the field will be extremely open in 1976. . . . At this point I do not think Kennedy will ever be President. He appears to have diminished ambition for national office, both because of the very real concern about assassination and the major problems in his personal life. Both he and his wife seem to be drifting from one emotional crisis to another, he has repeatedly handled stress poorly, and in fact has never been tested by a knock down drag out campaign.

There is a new crop of very attractive potential candidates. Jay Rockefeller particularly stands out to me as someone to watch. However most of these people will be waiting until 1980 or later.

Even if McGovern wins the present political scene is sufficiently unstable that it would be a terrible mistake to count on an authentic eight year term.

5) Despite what we see as the extensive favorable press coverage

that you have received I realized in Miami that we have been rather provincial and that very few people elsewhere in the country either knew who you were or very much about you. Regardless of people's political position those who knew anything about you identified you with three issues, your inauguration speech, your position on busing (mostly misinterpreted), and the "Stop McGovern movement." To really make a national impact and get more recognition with a significant percentage of the population, press coverage has to be frequent, and repetitive particularly on affirmative issues.

6) While it has been repeatedly proven that it is almost impossible to strategize for the Vice Presidential nomination I felt the lack of clearly planned and executed strategy in Miami pointed up an area that you need to radically change in the future. In retrospect it is clear that they had written off the possibility of a Southerner very early and by not clearly campaigning as did Governor Lucey you saved face when you did not get it. However, this was more by luck than anything else.

I think you really understand what is going on in the country in a way that most people on the national scene do not. I also believe that you have certain unique qualities which if adequately exploited would make you a major contender for the Presidency in 1976. However I believe that to do so you have to begin making the right moves now. These include:

a) Making a definite decision within the next few months as to whether you are going to make the national scene or not. . . . Unless you would be satisfied with a career in the Senate, it seems like an extremely poor base for anything else at this point.

b) If you do decide to seek the Presidency in 1976, I think you have got to do several things. First you have got to begin now to develop a carefully planned strategy developing a base throughout the country. Senator Jackson failed to do this, probably in part because he never made a full commitment and never had the real will to win. Second I think you have got to take a very hard look at some of the issues, and realize that once you have made the decision to compete nationally you have to take positions that will alienate a lot of people in the South. George Wallace went about as far as you can go using the South as a power base and proved that it can not be used to get you anything more than a powerfully registered protest vote.

c) If McGovern campaigns in Georgia and if a respectable organization is developed for him in the State I do not see how you can lose by strongly supporting him. There are also ways of doing it that could be turned enormously to your advantage.

d) To begin developing better recognition you might consider immediately beginning to write some articles for national publications, or even writing a book to be published before you go out of office. You could easily obtain the assistance of a professional writer to help you do this. It would not only get you better known, but would enhance your image nationally as a more substantial person. I think also you should hire someone now (privately, without state funds) who can relate to people at the national level, developing the necessary groundwork perhaps without even being formally identified as working for you. They should work not just in Washington but around the country.

e) Despite what I said about Kennedy I feel that his influence is going to remain critical and no one can draw you better into the nation's spotlight with a positive image than he can. I think you should try to get him to visit Georgia and try to foster a personal relationship with him any way you can. If he is willing to do it.

f) I also feel it is important to have one or two people, either Senators or Governors who are willing to make a commitment to you to serve as trusted negotiators and operatives for you. They have to be people who are realistic enough not to still see themselves as having competing ambitions with you. Again Senator Jackson would seem to fit this as long as he is not so unrealistic as to hold any hope for himself in 1976.

g) You need to begin developing extreme expertise in a number of key areas, so that you can be a leading spokesman on them nationally. There are many possibilities including health care, and the environment, although the latter will probably not become critical until the '80s. There are many possibilities, but once you have determined one or more issues there should be a systematic effort to promote you nationally as a leading spokesman on them.

Beginning two years from now if you do not run for the Senate, you should capitalize on the image you have created particularly by such things as writing a book and go on a protracted nationwide speaking tour including fund raising for the party. In that way you will develop a strong committed and obligated constituency throughout the country; you will also be able to capitalize on your greatest asset—your personal charm. The more people you can meet around the country during that year or so without overtly campaigning the stronger you will be when you are ready to go for real.

There are several other possibilities I would suggest to you, but despite appearances to the contrary, I am rather hesitant to give unsolicited advice. No Southerner has captured the Presidency because he has not been willing to take the drastic step away from traditional Southern politics that is necessary. What is critical is the psychological and emotional decision to take the risk and to run for the Presidency to win whatever the eventual outcome might be. I hope you will consider it and I think you can win.

The memo proved to be the first crucial step in Carter's decision to run. It was to be later followed by another memo from Hamilton Jordan, who became Carter's campaign manager, which further detailed the Georgia Governor's strategy.

Carter read the Bourne memo, took it home and showed it to Rosalynn, and after a few weeks Carter, Jordan, Jerry Rafshoon, who became Jimmy's media expert, and Landon Butler, a future political coordinator, met one night in shirt sleeves in the family room of the Governor's mansion. "We've come here," Jordan began, "to explain to you what will happen with your future." It was clear Carter had made up his mind to run. He detailed a research staff to study delegate selection rules, agreed to lure David Broder, the *Washington Post* political columnist, to Atlanta for an interview, organized a group of twelve advisors to meet with him every two weeks.

Then the strategy began to form. It involved understanding the complex delegate selection and federal election finance rules, reading every book that had ever been written on Presidential campaigning. "We studied the delegate selection rules backwards and forwards. I don't think the others did. Our strategy involves exploiting that. A lot of the candidates don't understand the money problem. They're already operating on the verge of bankruptcy. Shriver, for example, started off with a big fanfare. Now the staff is down to ten and they're only being paid on an 'as needed' basis. The money is tight on the Bayh campaign too. You have to use your resources in a terribly planned way. We know that. We've made it clear to even our ablest supporters that we won't pay them. Even Ham Jordan, our campaign manager, won't be paid much.

"Psychological momentum was crucial. Iowa, for example, was

politically vital. That gave him a leg up. We understand the kind of issues that can backfire on us. Like the one-thousand-dollar welfare thing McGovern put out in 1972. We knew how to position Carter on the Democratic National Committee so he could go around the country building relationships with Democrats. Carter helped Strauss get the chairmanship too back in 'seventy-two after Florida. We pushed the McGovern people out and consolidated around Strauss. So Carter got the position he wanted. Strauss didn't like Carter really. He tried to block us, but people kept saying what a fine job Carter was doing. Still, he's not close to Strauss. He's been cold to us for a long time."

Bourne also talked about the kind of man he perceived Carter to be—an "organization man," punctual to the point of fanaticism, a "meticulous planner," a man who cared deeply about his staff and therefore exacted tremendous devotion from them, a "religious man" who reads the Bible every night, a "highly disciplined man," a man with "great stability and resources of emotional strength . . . one of the most put-together people I know. He'll give the race his one hundred percent commitment and he doesn't intend to lose."

PART

I

JIMMY CARTER'S WORLD

CHAPTER 1

PLAINS: COUSIN HUGH AND UNCLE BUDDY

ONE AFTERNOON I WAS TALKING to Carter about how many Americans felt discomfited that they did not know or understand him.

Carter replied: "I don't see myself as mysterious. I think people try to make a mystery out of me. But most observers feel that they can get to know me more as they meet my family, my mother, as they talk to Billy and as they get to know Rosalynn, and as they live a few days in Plains . . ."

There is only one way to travel to Plains, which is not on the map but lies 115 miles from the Florida border, and that is by automobile . . . There are no airports, no buses, and no longer any passenger trains. It's a two-and-a-half- to three-hour drive from the Atlanta airport, one hour from Columbus and forty-five minutes from Albany, Georgia. Only a single-lane, tortuous highway makes its way to Plains. Route 180 S winds through south Georgia like some overused black ribbon, snaking its way through mile after mile of swamps dotted with the stumps of ancient trees, patchwork pecan orchards, and verdant forests of scrawny pine contrasted with brick-red clay. And there is nothing on the road to Plains except poverty. Except for an occasional tin-roofed, wood-windowed, ramshackle hut, where blacks rock in chairs on crumbling porches and watch the traffic go by, civilization seems to have vanished. The dwellings of this anachronistic region are camouflaged in spring by a riotous profusion of dogwood and azalea, but in winter, their somber poignance stings the eye like acid.

This is mean country, where gun-totin' and Bible-preachin' go hand-in-hand and where little has changed in two hundred years except that the blacks who eke out a living here are supposed to be free. From the look of things, they are not much better off than they were two centuries ago.

Union prisoners were once shunted down this way in 1864. Between two hundred and three hundred men died every week for over a year, and their corpses were tossed into mass roadside graves to dry and shrivel like so many peanuts in the searing Georgia sun.

As Jimmy Carter puts it, "South Georgia is different."

But suddenly from a desolate highway one is in the middle of a town surrounded by stately white Victorian homes with green roofs, gingerbread trim, and gracious verandas, houses that are quite pretty and proper and spacious, peopled no doubt by the proprietors of many of the shacks along the way, but nevertheless, for a first-time visitor, an oasis after a long lonely ride.

"Downtown" Plains is a shock to outsiders. Certainly to a native New Yorker like myself . . .

Fifty-four miles from Columbus, nine miles from Preston, and nine miles from Americus, the scene of severe racial disturbances during the 1960s, Plains, no larger than a fraction of a New York City block, is a movie-set town. It looks more like a cardboard backdrop for Matt Dillon's *Gunsmoke* or *The Last Picture Show* than the home of James Earl Carter, Jr., President.

The main business district remains as it was in 1904, a tiny string of eight stores, nestled beneath an overhang supported by wooden poles that once served as hitching posts. Just around the corner, to the right, the black ghetto begins—a strand of dilapidation and decay, and souls steeped in cheap alcohol, loitering in late afternoons on tilted wooden porches.

It was March 1976 when I first arrived, well before Jimmy Carter seemed a certainty for the Democratic nomination. The town was desolate and deserted, the storefronts in disuse and disrepair. The first two from the left belonged to Carter's competitors, the Williams family, and served as dingy storage space for bags of fertilizer and seed. One has now been converted into a make-a-quick-buck souvenir shop, the other to a Peanut Museum. The next consisted of a warehouse containing the spillover from Hugh Carter's antique store and a conglomeration of old Carter family belongings. Now it is a makeshift headquarters for the press—a sea of telephones, tables and white styrofoam cups half filled with cold black coffee and doused cigarettes.

Next came another old warehouse, later the lime-green and white Back Porch Café, the only sit-down restaurant in town.

In March, not so much as a french fry was available for a hungry visitor to Plains. The closest eatery was located some two hundred yards down the main highway—a roadside stand some six feet wide with a dirt drive and an archaic barbecue pit out back, stoked now and then by an aged black who spent most of his day on a wooden chair waiting for the meat to sizzle.

At the Williams' Fina gas station, just a few hundred yards from Billy Carter's Amoco station, neither the telephone nor the facilities worked very well. The attendant, a blond, wavy-haired youth of nineteen with quizzical eyes, said that half the town stands with the Carters, the other half against them. "But even them that hate him would tell you they love him now." The anti-Carter half, he claimed, resented Carter for having ignored Plains when he was Governor, for not putting through a four-lane superhighway, for paving the road near his house and nowhere else—things like that. Basically, he said, the town was economically divided between the Williamses—his employers—and the Carters. Rivalry had and always would exist. Both families were in the peanut business in a small town.

The Carters have a visible monopoly on Main Street, at least. If all of Plains is two hundred yards long, then one hundred yards of that belongs to the Carters, including six peanut warehouses, a cotton gin and a liquid fertilizer silo to the left of the shopping district, plus three storefronts on Main Street, compared to the Williams' two. The Carters also own most of the farmland in and around Plains, some thirty-two hundred acres.

The Tuesday I arrived, the town was sleepy, silent and cold. Main Street was devoid of pedestrians and cars, save for one—mine. One feeble black woman in a long skirt and using a cane, hobbled slowly and painfully down the cement walkway.

Blanton's Barbershop was closed and a sign on the window read, "Open next Saturday." Barber Blanton, also the mayor of Plains, had not only official duties to occupy him, but a full-time job as a control-tower operator at the airport at Albany.

The depot, a large white clapboard building next to the railroad tracks that sliced through the town, was abandoned and badly in need of a paint job. Later it would be rejuvenated with a fresh coat of white and green paint and pressed into service as the most bustling campaign headquarters in the country. By November, over 70,000 visitors had signed its guest book or paused to obtain an autograph or a snapshot of Jimmy Carter's mother, Miz Lillian, who stationed herself in a wooden rocker every day. "Jimm-eh asked me to."

Except for a massive red, white and blue billboard: "Plains, Georgia—Home of Jimmy Carter Our Next President," it seemed the entire community had come to a grinding halt a century ago.

Turner's General Merchandise Store, a cavernous, dusty structure with peeling and crumbling walls, was obviously the town meeting place that day, and several women were seated on wooden folding chairs around an old gas heater warming themselves and discussing the box of abandoned puppies at their feet.

There, amid the bolts of fabric, mops, brooms, potatoes, thirty-foot fishing poles for catching white perch on the Chattahoochee River, lawnmowers, Hee-Haw overalls, shoes and pipe fittings, they gossiped about the biggest news in town—their hometown boy, Jimmy Carter, was running for President. Vera Robinson, who worked at Turner's, said everyone in town was excited. Business had picked up a bit with the influx of tourists, and the Secret Service had been in buying up bib overalls and work shirts in an attempt to blend into the scenery as townies rather than feds. Mayor Blanton's wife, who had bicycled over to "pass the time of day," planned to open a gift shop that would feature souvenirs, including plaster maps of Georgia and placques of Jimmy Carter's face. When I went to try on a pair of blue jeans, I found a Confederate flag hanging in the "dressing room," a corner of the store separated from the retail area by a battered curtain.

Three doors down, Carter's Antiques, a rambling old place owned by Jimmy Carter's first cousin Hugh, was a maze of old bottles, books and furniture ranging from a ninety-five-dollar soda fountain table and chairs to a fifty-dollar brass coal scuttle with blue and white porcelain handles (made in Iran), Victorian rockers and wicker couches. There was not a customer in sight. Plains, with its mostly black population, did not seem like the most likely locale for an antique store. Yet, according to Alton Carter, Hugh's father, better known as "Uncle Buddy," who shuffled out from the rear of the store with a friendly Southern greeting, Carter's Antiques was a booming business. Buddy, a snaggle-tooth octogenarian with a tuft of white hair, a perky face and jolly blue eyes, said, "It turns over ten thousand dollars sometimes twice a month and brings in close to a quarter of a million dollars annually." Hugh Carter does most of his trade with dealers who come from miles around for the weekly auctions and buy in quantity. While I was there, one dealer from Florida picked up four hundred dollars' worth of wicker furniture. Another dealer purchased $1,500 worth of merchandise.

"It's just a hobby for me," said Hugh Carter, a freckled, taller and slimmer version of his dad, who was working on his income taxes at a counter in the back. "I started the business a few years ago just to give mah daddy something to do," he continued, looking up from his work, his Carter eyes exaggerated by a pair of gold-rimmed spectacles. "Daddy's eighty-seven, but he comes to work every single day."

Jimmy Carter's cousin's major occupation, and the source of most of his income, is raising worms, red wigglers to be exact. Hugh started the business back in 1945 after he returned from the war in Germany and found he could corner the market with Plains tradesmen who shut down every Wednesday afternoon and just went fishin'. Carter started off with crickets but discovered worms easier to breed ("They're self-propagating. Each worm is both male and female and they just love each other") and more lucrative. Today he boasts "the World's Largest Worm Farm" and sells fifty thousand to one hundred thousand worms a day at $6.95 per thousand to fishermen, zoos, schools and other worm farmers from coast to coast. He also peddles How to Raise Worms books and boxes of worm-aerated soil at ten dollars per fifteen pounds. "There's only one comparable worm farm I know of," said Uncle Buddy. "It's in Denver and it makes over a million dollars a year." Hugh Carter will not reveal his annual take. "But I make a lot of money," he grinned. In fact, he ships so many red wigglers he brags that Plains acquired a "second class" post office, a status only granted to towns with populations of 25,000 or more.

While Hugh rolled up his sleeves and helped the two dealers load their trucks, Uncle Buddy offered a tour of the town and the worm farm in his 1962 Ford.

Uncle Buddy was born in Arlington, Georgia, the eldest of four sons. His second brother was Jimmy Carter's father, Earl. When Alton was sixteen and had only completed the seventh grade, their father died and Alton had to go to work to support the family. In 1919 he opened a general merchandise and dry goods store on Main Street in Plains, known as the Carter Mercantile Company, and later sold horses and mules as well. His brother, Earl, went to work too, buying up farmland and opening a peanut and insurance business. "Earl made a lot of money. Everything he touched turned to money. He made three or four times as much as I did. When he died he had close to a million dollars in the bank and over four thousand acres of property. He was one of the wealthiest men I ever knew," said Buddy.

As we drove, Uncle Buddy pointed out the sights—a brick schoolhouse on the left where Amy Carter attends classes. "Used to be a nigguh school, but then they put all the nigguhs and whites all together and now there's twice as many nigguhs as is white folks. I don't like the nigguhs much, but we put up with 'em though. They's sorry as they can be now. Can't get one to work."

A field of corn. "Here's a pretty good story," he said, pointing out the window and nearly driving us off the road. "When I first came here in 1904 that land sold for sixteen dollars an acre. Last year it sold for four hundred and fifty dollars an acre."

We drove two miles from Plains through Archery, an area peppered with poor black dwellings scattered on rich farmland, past a tidy yellow clapboard farmhouse—"This is where Jimmy and his family came to live from the time he was a little boy until he went away to college," past the Carter family graveyard and "the nigguh cemetery over there." The Carter cemetery is a patchwork of perfect white gravel graves held in check by cement borders and surrounded by manicured greens. Connected to it, but separated by a row of slender trees, is the black graveyard, a desolate, unplanted mud slide of a hill dotted with toppling tombstones like pulled teeth tossed on a mound. "Why separate?" I asked. "We won't let 'em be buried with us," Alton muttered.

"This is Archery Church over here," he continued, nodding at a simple white picturebook structure. "Nigguh church. No, Jimmy didn't go to a nigguh church. They still go separately. Ain't no nigguhs go with the white folk. White folk go to the Baptist Church uptown. Don't allow no nigguhs. Wouldn't let 'em in. Never have. Never will." The membership of Carter's Baptist Church voted November 14 to end their 1965 ban on the admission of blacks to worship services and church membership.

"Now they had a nigguh college right down in there somewhere," Uncle Buddy said, gesturing at a thicket of trees on a hillside, his raspy voice almost inaudible beneath the din of the old engine. "But the bishop died and the nigguhs were movin' out and they just kind of let it go down."

When I asked him to describe the current attitude of whites toward blacks in Plains, Uncle Buddy replied, "They think there's a place for 'em, but they'd still like to see 'em stay in their place. But they don't hate 'em. Just don't associate with 'em that's all, 'ceptin' sometimes. Like when Earl died, his nigguhs went to the funeral. All two hundred of 'em. Jimmy? He don't worship with 'em neither, but he considers 'em folk. He's more liberal with the nigguhs than anyone else down here."

The old black car rumbled past the large white clapboard house on Main Street that Alton bought for $6,000 back in 1922 (now worth $35,000 he proudly estimated), past the one-level brick house where Miz Lillian spends her time when she's not at her Pond House, and down a winding dirt road to Hugh Carter's worm farm. A sign tacked to a tree in the driveway announces, "World's Largest Worm Farm." Out back behind a sprawling, typically suburban brick home ("Worth sixty thousand dollars," said Buddy. "Built every bit of it hisself out of worms"), behind a greenhouse filled with giant orchids and mammoth geraniums cultivated in worm-rich soil, behind a figure-eight-shaped swimming pool, loomed what looked like a mass grave. Row after row of long cement troughs sprawled in orderly ranks like giant sarcophagi, filled with manure and millions of worms.

"Who picks the worms?"

"Nigguhs," said Uncle Buddy. "Hugh's got four nigguhs that haul 'em out, working all the time."

On the side of one trough sits a solitary black woman with scrawny, pencil-thin braids cascading below her waist. She is bent, digging in the manure with thick, hard hands. Rusty tin cans, each packed with a hundred red wrigglers, are lined up behind her on the edge of the worm bed. "Mary" digs worms eight hours a day, five days a week, averaging 40,000 worms a day. For her labors she is paid thirty-five cents per thousand worms, or roughly sixty dollars a week. Mary has supported four sons for fifteen years on that salary. "I ain't got no husband. We're separated," she says, never looking up.

Her sons are grown now, except for one twenty-year-old boy in the Marine Corps, so her work is almost done. "No, I never get tired of it," she adds, her hands moving swiftly, mechanically. "But one of these days I gonna take mah money and left."

The antique store was tomblike when we returned. The two dealers had driven off with their purchases and Hugh Carter was back at the counter working at his books.

Hugh Carter is an expansive man, gregarious, and instantly likable. A rural Midas with a shiny freckled face, he can spin yarns for hours at the same time he is polishing silver candlesticks for Saturday's auction or running the adding machines, calculating his earnings. It is apparent after several hours of conversation why he and Jimmy Carter were inseparable as children. Apart from the fact they are first cousins. Hugh had what Carter lacked—height and extroversion.

He also possesses a hefty dose of the family vanity, a trait that causes the likes of Miz Lillian to shake her head and sigh, "Oh, Hugh! Did he say that?"

Hugh takes pride in his many accomplishments. Besides his lucrative worm, souvenir and antique enterprises, Hugh leads the church choir every Sunday in purple robes and keeps the church records, which he will produce from beneath the counter at any given moment, quoting dates of marriage, birth, death, and baptism for anyone willing to listen. "My dad was baptized August 12, 1912, my mother May 14, 1925. Jimmy was baptized in 1935, there is no date. The clerk forgot to record it. Earl Carter died July 22, 1953." And like cousin Jimmy, Hugh also reads the Bible every day.

"I'm a state senator too. I'm pretty well known around the state myself," he says, puffing with hubris. "Lot of people say if it was not for Hugh Carter, reorganization would have failed. I held the respect of my fellow senators and got them to vote for Jimmy's bills. Maddox would call 'em . . . he presided over the senate . . . and he'd say, 'Don't vote for this bill or you'll lose your chairmanship.' Well, we spoke our heads off and we passed ninety-seven percent of the bills. I got along with Maddox fairly well. He told me one day, 'Senator, you have your job and I have mine,' but he understood I was fighting for Jimmy and he respected my position as a floor leader and the fact I had the power of the Governor's office behind me. We whipped him on every hand."

He also had a major hand in Jimmy Carter's 1970 gubernatorial race. And although Miz Lillian calls him an arch segregationist, he disavows having suggested Carter run a subtly racist campaign. "I didn't handle his strategy. He made all those decisions himself," says the man who claims to know Jimmy Carter better than his own brother.

Hugh Carter has pulled up a wicker rocker and we are sitting by the old electric heater try to fend off chilblains in his great, hollow, freezing-cold store.

"We were always religious. We'd go to Sunday school at ten A.M.

and preaching service at eleven and Sunday night we'd go to training union for an hour. You got to open the door and let Christ come into your life. Christ is the center of life here. He's the center of Jimmy's life. Jimmy's always witnessing."

(Hugh is one of nine deacons who opposed allowing Reverend Clennon King, a black minister from Americus, to enter the Plains Baptist Church and supported the original 1965 resolution banning blacks and "civil rights agitators" from the Plains Baptist Church.)

"We're real simple people. This is a very rural community, but the Carter family has always been a family of leaders. Each and every one of us. My brother Don is an editor with the Knight newspapers. My daddy was mayor here for twenty-six years and a county commissioner. Jimmy's father was in the state legislature when he died. All of us have been officers in the armed services. And all three of my children have Master's degrees.

"Our families set the example for us. They did not drink or smoke, they taught us the value of a dollar, took us to church, made us mind. I attribute our moral lives to this. This upbringing as Christians with Christ foremost in our lives has contributed to our success in becoming leaders. We're hardheaded, we Carters, but it's worked to our advantage. We have always known what we wanted. [Gloria Carter Spann says Hugh Carter always wanted to make money.] Right now, Jimmy wants to be President and I think he's going to be President, because he's the kind who'll work twenty-two hours a day if he has to."

CHAPTER / 2

BROTHER BILLY

"BILLY'S GROWN UP a lot in the last few years," says a close family friend. "He's not as nervous as he used to be. I think for the first time in his life he's felt needed by his family."

The first time I saw Jimmy Carter's baby brother, Billy, he was "just settin'" on a couch at the peanut warehouse, takin' it easy. It was 8:30 A.M. and he was inhaling clouds of cigarette smoke. He would draw in the smoke with his mouth wide open, then expel it, puffing out his cheeks like a chipmunk, the same way his father, Earl Carter, used to. Earl Carter smoked three packs of Home Runs a day. Billy smokes four packs of Pall Malls.

His blue work shirt sloped gently outward over a carefully cultivated good-ole-boy beer belly and cascaded into his blue jeans. Meeting a stranger, he flashed his dazzling set of Carter ivories and when he smiled his eyes almost disappeared for the million crinkles around them. Jimmy Carter, who is fifty-two and thirteen years older than his brother, told me Billy looks just like their father, Earl . . . short and squat . . . "Daddy was only five foot seven, . . . but to me, with thirty extra pounds, Billy looked just like a swollen Jimmy Carter."

Billy's wife, Sybil, a friendly, broad-shouldered blonde, considerably taller than Billy, with pale blue eyes and short wavy hair, was at work behind the counter, and like everyone else in town, it seemed, marking figures in an accounting book. She was wearing white slacks and a pale blue smock and smiled when she spotted a visitor. "Hey! How'rr eeeyew?" she drawled. "Things are slow this time of year," she explained as though I had expected to find gnomes feverishly mixing peanut butter in vats. "Waitin' for the land to be ready for plantin'."

She offered coffee and we sat around and talked in that quiet front office as though nothing was happening in the outside world, particularly not a Presidential campaign.

While Sybil leaned over the counter narrating her story, Billy, who walks everywhere with great urgency, attended to the farmers who drove up with queries about seed peanuts or fertilizer.

Sybil was born in Eufaula, Alabama, the daughter of a barber. Her father moved his family to Plains after her grandmother died so they could be near her grandfather and care for him. They were poor and Sybil had to begin working at fourteen. On Saturdays she worked in the Carter grocery store where her mother clerked during the week. Holidays she worked in the administrative offices of Belks Department Store in Americus. She married her lifelong sweetheart, Billy Carter, when she was sixteen and he seventeen and they ran off together the day after Billy finished Marine boot camp. "There was none of this down-on-your-knees stuff. He just gave me a ring." Sybil laughs with an infectious high-pitched giggle, and, like Billy, hoots at her own lines. Neither family approved of the union, least of all Jimmy Carter and Miz Lillian. "But we're living proof that you can be married at sixteen and last twenty-six years happily."

Almost immediately Billy Carter was sent overseas and Sybil, pregnant with their first child, Kim (who was eighteen months old before Billy saw her for the first time), went to live with her mother and father. It was not a difficult move. The only furniture Sybil and Billy owned was a television set and a baby bed. "I often think back and say, 'Good Lord, how did I ever do that!' I was just a baby at the time myself." Another melodious giggle.

Sybil did not work for ten years while five of her six children were growing. It was 1964 before she began helping Rosalynn and Jimmy in the warehouse during peak peanut season. But when gubernatorial campaigning began, Sybil gradually assumed all of Rosalynn's bookkeeping duties. She has worked ever since because she feels Billy needs the help, because she is proud to be a part of the business, and mainly because she wants to. "Jimmy said to me once when I was complaining about something during peanut season, 'Don't knock it. It's your bread and butter. Besides, you don't know how lucky you are that Billy and I let you and Rosalynn work.' And I thought, Huh!? LETS us work?"

Sybil earns just enough to pay for the maid who cares for her house while she's gone, but calls working at the warehouse "a picnic." That is, with the exception of the months from August to October, when peanuts are harvested, dried and sold. Then her job becomes a nightmare. During those days the entire family works twenty-four hours straight. Often Billy is at the warehouse seven weeks at a time, rarely going home except to shower. "He'll work all night. Sometimes just sleep three hours on the couch in the office. Sometimes he'll come home at midnight or one A.M. all covered with red dirt. All you can see is his eyes. He'll clean up and I'll get out of bed and fix him a hot meal. Then he'll go right back to work." Jimmy Carter used to switch off with Billy every thirty-six hours. It's no wonder he has the stamina the other candidates lacked, says Sybil. "He's worn the Secret Service into the ground. They say they just can't keep up with him."

Billy is the proverbial "good ole boy," as Southern as sawmill gravy and hominy grits. An ex-Marine with a blue Ford Bravo pickup truck, a cooler full of Pabst Blue Ribbon, a CB radio, bright orange leisure suits, a gas station, and a proclivity for strong bourbon and Pall Malls, Billy has a reputation for telling it like it is. "Yes, I'm a real Southern boy," he has been known to say. "I got a red neck, white socks and Blue Ribbon beer."

Thirty-nine-year-old Billy considers himself the one exception to the Carter eccentricity. Billy said once on an interview program: "My mother went into the Peace Corps when she was sixty-eight. My one sister is a motorcycle freak, my other sister is a Holy Roller evangelist and my brother is running for President. I'm the only sane one in the family."

Throughout the campaign Billy came to be more popular with the tourists than Jimmy. "People like Billy better'n Jimmy," says one gas station attendant at Billy's Amoco stand. On some sunny Saturdays when Jimmy is in town, the wait for gas at Billy's pumps can be thirty minutes or more. The customers don't want the Green Stamps. They want Billy, want to touch him, to tell him they admire him for refusing to put on fancy airs. "They appreciate a man who doesn't think he's better than they are just because his brother is running for President."

The press corps liked Billy. Reporters voted Billy the best

softball player of the year in a questionnaire that was passed around Peanut One the last few days of the election campaign. In Plains, cameramen and TV technicians gathered at Billy's service station to shoot the breeze with him, cuss each other in jest, and borrow another brew from the Crown Prince of the Beer Cooler. Billy was one of the few bright spots in the colorless landscape of Plains and the humorless cast of Presidential politics. He achieved stardom, cult status even, on the red-neck hit parade along with Burt Reynolds and Elvis. He won himself the devotees of Spiro Agnew when he had to be restrained from pounding a photographer when his gas station caught fire. George Wallace, when asked what he thought of Jimmy Carter, said Jimmy was his third choice for President. His first choice was himself. When reporters asked him who his second choice was he said, "Billy Carter." "Made me feel pretty good," says Billy.

One problem is, however, that despite his outward happiness, Billy seems to drown whatever insecurities he may have incurred as the younger brother of an immensely successful man in a daily deluge of Pabst Blue Ribbon. Sometimes bourbon. One reporter who went to Plains to interview Billy was warned about his cavernous capacity for brew which has earned for him the nickname, "Castiron," a name he proudly adopted for his CB radio handle. The reporter popped Pabsts with Billy until he confessed that his vision was blurring badly and he finally had to pour out his beer in the parking lot when Billy wasn't looking.

Billy went out to campaign for his brother during the Wisconsin primary, but would usually end up half in the bag. At one afternoon rally in Green Bay, while Jimmy talked about the need for tax reform, Billy, barely able to stand, listened stage right, leaning against a wall in his orange suit, a silly grin on his cherubic face. "I've been out having a few beers with some of the Udall workers," Billy chuckled in his nasal staccato. Peanut Billy had also been out helping Udall volunteers hang posters. "They were really good people," said Billy. The night of the Wisconsin primary, when Mo Udall won his short-lived victory, Billy appeared in the ballroom on the Marc Plaza Hotel in Milwaukee to bestow a giant hug and kiss on Ella Udall's cheek. "Some of my best friends are Carter people," Ella winked.

Most of that night Billy swilled bourbon down so fast he could hardly put one foot in front of the other. Dot Padgett, a longtime Carter worker, was sent to minister to him, to restrain him from staggering into people and burning them with his cigarettes, planting kisses on strange women or bear-hugging female reporters. Billy successfully eluded Dot and ended up drinking in the Bombay Bicycle Club downstairs in the Marc Plaza Hotel until well past two o'clock.

Daily, during the Democratic convention, Billy was most often found sneaking beers (with approval) from the NBC headquarters at the Americana Hotel. And the night of the election, television viewers watched Billy weaving his way past the gas pumps, sporting a beatific you-ain't-seen-nothing-yet grin.

The Sunday after the election Billy could not bear the heavy influx of tourists in his little town. "Used to be at ten o'clock on Sunday morning, you could walk out onto Main Street and take a leak and nobody would see you," he said. "Last Sunday there must have been two thousand damned tourists here. I couldn't stand it. I went off to the bootlegger, bought me a fifth of Jim Beam, drove around the rest of the day and got good and drunk." Nevertheless, Billy Carter runs the family peanut farm and warehouse with an iron hand and regards his stewardship of the Carter family business interests as his contribution to his brother's campaign, for it freed Jimmy to concentrate full time on politics.

Billy works hard at his job starting at five A.M. and ending at five P.M. six days a week, and is considered a no-nonsense, tough, shrewd, highly successful businessman who has built the family enterprise into a highly profitable venture. "I made more money for the business than Jimmy ever did," he says.

But once the doors of his warehouse close at five o'clock, Billy heads for his service station across the street to jaw with the boys and to toss down as many as a dozen beers. In effect, Billy Carter is the town saloon keeper. Because there is no white bar in Plains, only the black Skylight Club, Billy's Amoco serves as the town tavern, at least until seven P.M. when the station closes and everyone goes home to supper. And Billy usually outguzzles everyone in the joint.

It was partly because of Billy's lobbying for a beer license for his service station and his frequent inebriation ("I drink nine beers by midnight") that Billy lost his seat on the city council after one term and lost the race for mayor several years ago, and again right after his brother became President-elect.

His drinking saddens his mother, Miz Lillian. "Billy drinks too much," she admits. "He's a wonderful boy and he's really my favorite son. But he drinks too much. Jimmy never tells him off for it and neither do I. But he does."

But if Billy smokes too much, drinks too much, stutters a bit and suffers from insomnia, it may be understandable in the light of his upbringing.

Billy was the baby in the Carter family. Daddy's boy. Earl Carter's favorite. While Earl was severely stern with Jimmy, he spared the rod with Billy. "Daddy used to say he did the best he could to raise the rest of us and failed completely," says his sister Gloria. "So he was just going to enjoy Billy. And he did. He just loved him."

While Jimmy had to work in the fields, stacking peanuts, plowing the land, hauling water, Billy never did. "I was the baby," Billy grins. "Besides when I was twelve my father was already a big farmer, and we moved to town, so I worked at the warehouse some, but I never did work on the farm. I had a horse though and Saturdays I'd ride the farms to check things out."

"Buck Shot," as Earl Carter called his second son, was only six or seven when Jimmy Carter left for college and the navy. For the next seven years he grew up like an only son. He went everywhere with his father, even to the state legislature in Atlanta when Earl Carter served as state senator.

Yet somehow over the years, in spite of Billy's special-son status, Jimmy seemed to preempt Billy at every turn. Jimmy was the model student at Plains High School, while Billy—twenty-fifth in his class of twenty-six—was forced to leave for disciplinary problems. "I had to go to military school for one year. The principal said I couldn't come back. I didn't get along with the principal." Billy grins. "He used to drink a few beers in high school," a friend recalls. "He was a lot more rowdy than Jimmy. A hell of a lot more rowdy. And he was never a student."

While Billy was the one most interested in politics, and with his outgoing personality seemed a natural to follow in his father's footsteps, it was Jimmy who moved from the school board, to the state senate, to the Governor's mansion to the White House.

But if there was one rub that hurt more than any others, it was having his one special role usurped by his older brother. "Daddy expected Jimmy would be CNO and he expected Billy to run the warehouse," says Gloria. When Earl Carter died, Billy, fourteen at the time, felt ready to assume the responsibility. But Jimmy returned from the navy and not only filled the shoes that were being readied for Billy, but became a surrogate father.

Resentment built up for the "stranger" who was suddenly father and master in Billy's life. Rebellious, Billy ran off to the Marine Corps with his sixteen-year-old bride, seeking happiness as a military officer, coincidentally the role Jimmy had abandoned. But four years of Marine discipline convinced Billy he was "not cut out for that kind of life." He quit and came home to work in the peanut warehouse for a year. He tried college after that, lasted two and a half years at Emory, but "flunked English five times," and with a wife and four small children packed into one tiny apartment, decided the plight of a student was no bed of roses either. He dabbled in construction, sold paint in Macon, Georgia, and finally settled into the family business. With no college degree, no self-confidence and less money, he had few career options. He sold the land his father left him, bought himself and Sybil a house and went to work for Jimmy driving a manure spreader.

Although Billy has run the business efficiently and built it up over the last six years while his brother was Governor and Presidential candidate, the business may never be his. Billy only owns a small percentage. The certificate of registration dated April 11, 1922, No. 129-25-02182 that hangs on the warehouse wall features the name "J. E. Carter, Jr., et al." Jimmy and his mother, Miz Lillian, own controlling stock, and it is expected the enterprise will eventually pass to Jimmy's son Chip. The filling station is Billy's only possession.

When Billy's gas station caught fire in the summer of 1976, Jimmy and others tried to restrain Billy from rushing to the scene of the conflagration with the fear that the thousands of gallons of gas beneath the ground would explode momentarily. "Let it go, Billy," Jimmy cautioned. "No," Billy refused. "It's all I've got."

Trapped by circumstances, Billy seems at times riddled with hidden resentment. One morning walking along the railroad track after he had shown me through the peanut-shelling warehouse, Billy kicked at the ground. "You can have this town. I wouldn't give you anything for it." All he ever wanted to do was get out, he said.

His mother says, "Billy is always the first person Jimmy wants to see when he returns to Plains. They spend hours walking in the woods and fields. They need each other." Although Billy claims to have "a good working relationship" with Jimmy, a strain exists. When asked what they have in common, Billy snaps, "Peanuts."

Jimmy and Billy spent mostly media time together during the Presidential campaign. Every time he came home Jimmy walked over to inspect the warehouse between six and seven in the morning, where he and Billy would sit on the counter, sipping coffee and posing for the photographers who took pictures through the window.

But they rarely talked about politics. "I very seldom discuss politics with him. I follow Jimmy real close. I'm interested. I read all the clippings from the paper. I see him every time he comes home, but I don't ask him much except how's he doing in one state or another."

If they do not discuss politics it is with good reason. Billy has voted in the Republican column most of his life. "I voted for Eisenhower and Nixon. I never voted Democrat except for Lyndon Johnson. Jimmy's more liberal than I am." Still he told me in the spring of 1976, "He has better qualities than John Kennedy, even if I didn't vote for Kennedy. And I think he'll be President. He's been working longer and harder than anyone else and he's better organized. He runs his own campaign. He's on top of everything. Even traveling he knows what's going on. He's like his own campaign manager."

Billy and Jimmy Carter seem worlds apart philosophically, spiritually and even physically. While Jimmy prides himself on self-discipline (one hundred push-ups every morning; he does not smoke and gave up drinking during the campaign) Billy overeats, overdrinks, oversmokes and underexercises except for an occasional game of soft ball. While Jimmy follows the straight and narrow, Billy's been in jail twice, he told the *Washington Post*. "I did time in South Carolina for speeding. And I went to jail in Daytona Beach for drinking in public—nothing serious though." While Jimmy struggles to attend church and even taught Sunday school throughout the campaign, Billy gave up going to church long ago. "I didn't like it. Bunch of damned hypocrites down there at that Baptist Church." While Jimmy and Rosalynn send their daughter, Amy, to the integrated public school in Plains, Billy pulled his children out of the local school system and sent them to Buena Vista, thirty-five miles away. "My next to youngest went to grammar school in Plains, but she was the only white in her class when it first started. I pulled her out and put her in a church school in Americus. I'm not an integrationist." When Jimmy Carter brought his black state trooper to the house, Billy admits, "It was very hard for me at first, that was the first black that was ever in our house." Billy admits he inherited his father's prejudice. "The first year in school I wouldn't ride the bus and I wouldn't be in the school play with a black kid." The blacks of Plains are quick to admit that Billy still treats them like second-class citizens. In the black nightclub, both bartender and customers will attest to the fact that Jimmy's brother is "an out and out racist." Said the bartender, "He's gotten worse recently," although some who work in his employ, like Joe Streeter, say that Billy is quick with a handout. "If you need some money he'll let you have it right quick. He's just like his father." However, the handout is the fastest way to step into an even more subservient position with the Carters, said one black in Plains, "The best way to stay on their good side is not to ask for money."

If there is one distinct trait the brothers share, besides a noticeable set of ivories, Caribbean-blue eyes and a lack of height, it is a love for reading. Billy may have flunked English in college, but he now devours books by the bushel. "There's nothing else to do around here." His warehouse is piled high with paperbacks and he may dip into five, six, as many as eight books at a time, although, if you ask he probably won't remember the titles. "Billy's probably much better read than I am," Jimmy told me, "and yet he still has the demeanor of someone not advanced in the concept of public affairs." An insomniac, Billy often begins his reading at two-thirty in the morning and plows through history, biography, mysteries and mostly cowboy books until five. A trip to the bookstore may produce a bill as high as seventy dollars says Sybil, "For paperbacks!" Billy also read five or six newspapers a day in the beginning of the campaign, a habit that rapidly diminished. "There are more goddam lies that have come out of Plains," he grumbles. "I don't believe a goddam thing I read anymore. Now I look at the headlines and the editorial pages and that's it. It takes me fifteen minutes to read the five papers."

For diversion, Billy usually heads for the Americus Moose Club, an exclusive drinking establishment described by its membership brochure as "A patriotic organization that demands unquestioned loyalty to the government and profound respect for its flag." He often drives to Americus to lunch at the Best Western Motel and Saturdays he sometimes goes fishing with the good ole boys in the mountains of north Georgia. In hunting season he shoots deer, and once a month or so he and Sybil drive to Albany, Georgia, for parties. "We used to go to the Moose Club in Americus for square dances. I can do it, but I don't like it."

He rarely takes time off. A week at Christmas, the Fourth of July and maybe a few peanut conventions here and there. The family vacation last year was a trip to Disney World in Orlando, Florida. "What I like best," says Billy, "is running a peanut sheller."

Billy Carter's maid, Johnnie Mae Streeter, and her husband, Joe, one of Billy's peanut shellers, live just off Main Street in the black section of Plains about a block from the Carter warehouse. Their home consists of a wooden shack with a corrugated aluminum roof, a dirt yard and spaces between the wallboards so wide a pencil would fit between them. They pay twenty-five dollars a month to rent it. The house has no indoor toilet, no phone, no air conditioning, no running water. Curtains separate the three bedrooms from the living room and the kitchen. The Streeters have fourteen children. Now only six live in the house. So each three share a double bed and Johnnie Mae and Joe have their own.

When I stopped by the Streeter house, Johnnie Mae and Joe were just coming home from work and four of their children were returning from school. Momentarily the humble little shack was a beehive of activity and motion. "Turn the light on, Joe." The light was a bare lightbulb overhead from which a colored string dangled. We sat in the living room in the stifling heat of the late summer afternoon. A picture of John Kennedy and a color television set were the two elements of decor. When I asked for a glass of water I was escorted to the kitchen, a small area between two bedrooms. The Streeters had two stoves (they bought one when the other stopped working) and a tiny sink from which no water flowed. Well water sat in three large buckets on top of the nonfunctioning stove. I ladled some into my glass.

As we talked, Johnnie Mae unbuttoned her dress to cool herself. What she missed most about her old home, Johnnie Mae said, was indoor plumbing. The Streeters had lived in a better house until a few years ago when the landlord raised the monthly payments to one hundred and nine dollars and they couldn't make a go of it. They had to move. Her biggest outlays are for clothing and food. It costs her forty to fifty dollars a week to feed eight people. It was worse when all fourteen children lived at home. But she is resigned. "It's me and the Lord and somehow He always provides."

The Carters provide too, although not as well. Joe makes only two thirty-five an hour shelling peanuts for Billy Carter when the minimum wage is two sixty-five. He works eight hours a day, five days a week, "six during peanut season."

Johnnie Mae makes two dollars an hour doing housework for Billy and Sybil Carter and cleaning their office downtown. Neither she nor Joe has had a vacation in over a year. "I got five days last summer. What did we do? Stayed home, watched TV, went to ball games and fixed the kids' clothes," she said cheerfully. "Ain't never been nowhere. But maybe someday." "I never had no problem with 'em," says Joe. "Mr. Earl. He was all right. He was a very rich man with a big plantation. Gave a lot of people work. He was a very busy man, but I remember when my first wife was sick and in the hospital he came to the door and said, 'How you gettin' long, Joe? I know you must miss your wife very much. Let me know if there is anything I can do to help.'" Joe never cared much for Earl's brother, Alton, commonly known as "Uncle Buddy." "He always called me 'nigger.' He'd say 'Hey, Nigger! Come here, Nigger!' and I'd say, 'I ain't no nigger. Mah name's Joe Streeter.' He still called me Nigger."

Joe Streeter got laid off as a grapefruit picker a few years back. He was riding high then, making two hundred dollars a week. When he got fired he didn't work for a while. But Billy Carter gave him work when he needed it. "And he never pushes me around. He says 'Joe, would you do this?' And he looks out for me. He'll say 'Joe Streeter, don't you go up there, please' if a place is too high." Johnnie Mae is fond of Billy. "If he promises you a thousand dollars he'll give it to you." She appreciates the fact too that all Billy and Sybil's children "have to pull their own load." She admits they work her hard. "They work so they expect you to work."

Joe thinks Jimmy Carter will make "the best President who's ever been in the White House. He's a good man. He knows both poor whites and colored folk. He knows what it is to work for a living. I've never known him to deceive anyone."

Johnnie Mae concurs, "I've never known him to deceive anyone." And anyone who works like he does knows the hard life of a working person.

CHAPTER 3

SISTER RUTH

HAD IT NOT BEEN FOR Ruth Carter, perhaps Jimmy Carter would not be President today. It was his younger sister who helped to heal him spiritually from his sense of failure after his defeat by Lester Maddox in 1966.

Carter had reached his lowest ebb. "The problem in my life that had been created by that 1966 loss was the fact that my life seemed to be without purpose and that I was overly concerned about the defeats, that I had lost an interest in other people, individually, to a great extent, that I didn't get any sense of accomplishment when I achieved success and I felt like my religious beliefs were shallow and just a matter of self-pride. And Ruth and I had a long walk and it was a very important conversion for me . . ."

Not that that one walk in the woods with Ruth in itself changed his life, but it was, nevertheless a major factor in his search for meaning, and his desire to make a total commitment to religion and to others.

After Carter lost to Maddox for Governor, he walked with Ruth in the woods and asked, "You and I are both Baptists, but what is it that you have that I haven't got?"

Ruth replied, "Jimmy, through my hurt and pain I finally got so bad off I had to forget everything I was. What it amounts to in religious terms is total commitment. I belong to Jesus, everything I am." He said, "Ruth, that's what I want." "So we went through everything he would be willing to give up. Money was no problem, or friends, or family. Then, Ruth asked, 'What about all political ambitions?' He said, 'Ruth, you know I want to be Governor. I would use it for the people.' Ruth said, 'No, Jimmy.' "

It was there that Jimmy Carter was "born again," a phrase that was to win him the support of millions of evangelicals in America. "I found a new life," he told a close friend.

As part of his rebirth Carter became associated with part-time missionary work. He spent nearly a year traveling to Pennsylvania and New York with a Baptist missionary tour.

According to Ruth, she got Jimmy back on the political track.

Ruth Carter had been through a similar conversion herself. At twenty-nine she realized that her own sense of guilt and frustration and failure was traceable to her childhood. She writes in her book, *The Gift of Inner Healing*:

I first became aware of my feelings of rejection when I was married at the age of nineteen. To that point my emotions were pretty "normal," but the problem was there, buried inside me. When I moved into the demanding adult relationship of marriage, I found myself terrifyingly unprepared.

My understanding and healing began with the questions: What was your relationship with your father and mother? What was your childhood like?

My father had been dead for seventeen years, and I remembered him as the most wonderful, the most beautiful man I had ever known in my life . . . in fact, the only perfect human being.

He adored me . . . worshiped the ground I walked on . . .

My father had always loved me deeply, but his way of expressing that love was not altogether healthy. He had given me everything I had ever wanted. "Ruth," he used to tell me, "you are the most wonderful person in the world."

I had been raised to believe that I was God's gift to the world, the most beautiful child ever born. I was led to believe that I was the most talented, the most gifted of persons. I grew up thinking I was the queen of the universe.

Because of my sheltered and protected life, I never really learned about the outside world. Because my father did not want me to be hurt, I was protected from many experiences that would cause suffering or pain. Although I lived on a farm in south Georgia, I never saw an animal born. Relatives passed away, but I was spared the pain of ever attending the funerals. I never had to endure the creative but often painful conflict of making a decision of any importance.

At home I had played with the black children on the farm. I never knew until I became an adult that there had been an unwritten law, spawned by centuries of prejudice, that the white children must be allowed to win all the time. So every game I ever played throughout my entire childhood, I won. I was best at kick the can, fastest in any race, and I always caught my friends immediately at hide-and-seek. I grew up believing that I was the most gifted, most loved person in the world . . .

To fall short of number one in any area of life registered as unbearable failure.

Ruth Carter, Earl and Lillian Carter's third-born child, was the family princess. An A student with the face and disposition of an angel, she could do no wrong. Her father adored her. In fact, there was a time just before Ruth married that she was her father's constant companion—date—if you will. On Saturday nights Lillian would often stay home while Earl and his teenage daughter would go dancing at the Elks Club in Americus with John Pope and his first wife, Marjorie.

Looking back on her own childhood, Ruth says she was a "flirtatious, spoiled Southern Belle who thrived on being loved. My father overindulged me, which conditioned me to think I was the best, then my mother didn't overindulge me. That made me feel rejected, even though I now realize she was just treating me normally. But if you can imagine, every person I met in my whole life who didn't overindulge me, I thought didn't love me," she told Myra Mac-Pherson of the *Washington Post.* "Well, I lived in a world of rejection. You can stand it as long as you blame it on others. And so I had bad neighbors, a bad husband, a bad minister, bad friends." At nineteen she dropped out of college and married a teenage beau from Americus, Bob Stapleton, a young veterinarian, and moved to Fayetteville to save the marriage "because every time I had a problem I would run nine miles to home." She became an overcontrolling mother of her own three children and readily admits that she scarred them out of her own insecurities. She's now "working things through." But before that, she went the painful route from deep depression, hating herself and everyone around her, to psychotherapy. Her psychiatrist told her there was little he could do for her. Finally she came to grips with the fact that the problem was inside of her. Then she found Jesus.

Ruth's solution to her midlife crisis was a total commitment to Jesus Christ, a commitment that grew and developed into a full-time international ministry of "inner healing," a ministry that combines the principles of psychology and spiritualism. Across the country and around the world from communist colleges to Catholic charismatic groups, she invites Jesus to heal the emotional wounds of the "inner child" of one's past. Calling on her audiences to close their eyes and relax, she asks the Lord to enter their imaginary world.

Some psychologists scoff at her technique. Other detractors call her a "psychotherapist without a license." She has been denounced as an "antiscripture witch disguised as the angel of light" by some fundamentalist ministers.

I flew to Fayetteville, North Carolina, in March to see what this unusual self-made minister was like and to talk to her about her methods.

Because my plane developed engine trouble, I arrived eight hours late for our appointment. Ruth was about to go out for dinner with her husband, but she delayed and then finally canceled her plans and stayed to talk. She stretched her Southern hospitality to the extreme and was gracious in spite of the inconvenience.

Ruth neither looks like a witch nor a full-time evangelist. I expected a spooky, severe, nunlike woman with horn-rimmed glasses and a giant diamond crucifix around her neck like Jeane Dixon's.

Instead I found a soft-spoken, well-groomed, warm and delightful woman. Ruth, forty-six, is a chic buxom blonde, pale-blue-eyed mother of three, with gold hoop earrings and diamonds on both hands. She wore a cream-colored blouse and gray slacks and looked more like a Junior Leaguer than a preacher.

She and her husband, Bob, a tall, pleasant man who only appeared for an instant and then vanished for a nap, live in a rather affluent section of town. Their home is comfortable, not ostentatious, with standard but expensive furniture, a largely unused but attractive living room and a long, narrow library that ran the length of the rear of the house lined with leather-bound books and religious tomes of every variety. Two armchairs faced each other by a wall of windows and I started to sit in one. "No, you sit there," said Ruth. "That's my chair."

The Stapletons also own a home in Portugal on a cliff overlooking the ocean, where they vacation three weeks a year, and a country cabin on a lake not far from the Fayetteville airport, which Ruth calls her "Walden," because Thoreau was her favorite author. Ruth often goes to her Southern Walden after many days on the road preaching, to regroup, sort out a problem or to pray. It is there her conversion to Christ took place, as well as her sister, Gloria's.

With stockinged feet propped on the edge of her chair, Ruth talked about her conversion. It happened around the time she turned thirty. She had become a typical suburban wife, bored with her book club-garden club routine. "I was a doer, but I was exhausted from doing." Like her brother Jimmy, she says, "All of a sudden nothing satisfied me." She had very little communion with her husband, and less with her children. "And I didn't even know I had a problem."

She went on a retreat with some friends for a week and prayed for help; came home, packed herself up and moved with her children to her cottage for three months of contemplation. Her husband commuted every night. At the end of that quiet period, with no garden clubs and book clubs to distract her, she returned determined to serve Christ, although she didn't know how.

First, she decided to finish college. She had attended Georgia State College for Women, but dropped out at nineteen in her junior year to marry Bob Stapleton. College was counterproductive, she says. It had been her first time away from home and she "goofed off" mostly. This time she studied hard. She majored in religion and English and went on to get her master's degree in teaching.

Ruth was fired from her first job. "I was teaching English in a high school and the principal thought I was spending too much time counseling students. If I saw someone had a problem, I would take them off to the side and talk to them about it. I had been through this new experience where I had found the answer to the problems in life, so if a kid had parents who were alcoholics, I'd go out and talk with the kid. Finally the principal came to me and said 'Ruth, you have to decide if you're going to teach or preach.' I said, 'I'm going to preach.' I was so shy I couldn't even give an oral report, and I panicked, but the preparation in that school had been really good." She had also been attending a Bible class daily during her lunch hour at Fort Bragg and when the chaplain there went to Vietnam, he asked her to fill in. She jumped at the chance.

Her idea of a missionary was a plain-looking schoolmarm in long skirts. "I let my hair go to its natural color, tied it back, took off my makeup and put on dark clothes. The first time I arrived to teach the pastor said to me, 'My gosh, what happened to you? Go back to your old self so people can identify with you.'" She did.

Ruth taught there for five years, and taught another Bible class on the side. Monday nights she held prayer meetings at her house. People began to turn to her for solace. "If a child drowned, or someone died, the wives at Fort Bragg came to me as their pastor." Gradually, invitations came from around the state asking her to speak at ashrams and even Catholic retreats. Today she teaches all over the United States and abroad. She's published one book, entitled *The Gift of Inner Healing,* and was working on another, that dealt with "how to apply the principles of Jesus to daily life."

According to Ruth, there are five root causes of adult emotional suffering and negative behavior imprinted on the personality in the early years of life—fear, frustration, guilt, inferiority and loneliness or rejection. "They are all basically caused by lack of sufficient love," she says.

Her "technique" for dealing with such problems is what she calls "creative imagination," that is, "using creative imagination to re-create a positive experience where there's been a negative." Her approach differs from psychiatry, she says, because "Only the Holy Spirit can move back into these areas and remove the scars." She cites an example in her own experience.

She had literally hated her husband for not being present at the birth of two of her sons. One time he was absent because he had the flu. Another time he fell asleep when she went into labor. "I harbored resentment for years."

Eventually she tried her "technique." "I relived the moment and conjured up the emotion. I cried bitterly. I hated him for not being there. Then I re-created the moment with Jesus. In my imagination I heard Bob saying, 'Being with you is more important than anything.' I saw him taking me into the doctor's office and putting me into my hospital bed after the baby was born and getting me all covered up. Then I invited Jesus in Perfect Love. I said, 'O.K. Jesus, let your love move over the whole experience.' And I can claim by faith that He moved back into the moment and that moment was changed. The past is closed to everyone but Jesus."

She says it is irrelevant that the facts were different. "Facts are immaterial. It was my resentment that had caused the problem. The emotion was what I dealt with. I relived the emotion, and brought Jesus in. There was nothing but joy. I could feel the negative being consumed. Yes, it's being childlike, it's a childlike imagination, but

Jesus told us, 'Unless you become like little children you will not enter the kingdom of heaven.' "

Another experience she often conveys to the various groups she teaches is the trauma she and her husband suffered with one son who experimented with drugs. His life was out of control, his room always looked like it had been hit by a tornado. Nothing seemed to work. Ruth and her husband finally went to an evangelist and sought advice. He told them to put the problem in the hands of the Lord and let Jesus heal it. Two weeks later the son came to them, apologized and told them he was mending his ways. Ruth calls it the power of Jesus.

Psychiatrists take different views of both cases. One Catholic psychiatrist says the treatment is healthy and highly respected. One Washington psychiatrist calls the "technique" Band-Aid treatment. "If she had problems with her husband over his not being there for the birth of the children, I would tend to think that that was just a manifestation for something deeper seated in their relationship that she had just tended to focus on that one experience. I would ask a lot of questions about their relationship and find out what other moments she recalled that rankled and caused resentment. But I would also tend to suggest as a psychiatrist the same thing the evangelist did, that is to lay off the kid for a while, not to constantly be after him. It's entirely possible that's what brought him around. I would also try to go back and see if there was any resentment against another person in her life, like a parent. Perhaps her husband was repeating some of the things that a parent did that grated on her."

In fact, in her faith healing Ruth does delve into the patient's childhood. She not only tries to show parents that "any mistakes they made with their children can be redeemed in Jesus," she tries to go back and find "why they projected certain fears and guilts on their children, and usually it has been projected on them from one of their parents. If a person suffers from loneliness, you often find a parent rejected them. If a person suffers from fear, perhaps they were threatened as a child that they had to make all A's. If a parent disciplines his child by threatening, sometimes it's a deeply repressed fear of failure, fostered by a parent of their own."

It sounded as if she were speaking of her own father and her brother Jimmy.

CHAPTER 4

SISTER GLORIA

JIMMY CARTER CALLS his sister Gloria, who at forty-nine is closest to him in age, "an unorthodox person. She likes to be unorthodox and she has a startling way of bringing an unexpected question forward or a fresh idea."

Ruth Carter, the evangelist, calls her sister "different."

Miz Lillian calls Gloria, "The one I go fishing with."

And I call Gloria a motorcycle/Jesus freak.

She can most often be found peeling down the dirt roads of Plains on a Honda 500, decaled with butterflies, wearing a black leather jacket and jeans hand painted with butterflies.

But she can also be found ministering to a friend in spiritual need at a prayer group she started in Americus, serving members of the press at Faye's Bar-b-que Villa, painting butterflies or flowers on her clothes, writing a book containing all her mother's letters from her Peace Corps days in India, balancing the family farm books, or just cooking rabbit for her husband, Walter Spann, on the large copper stove in her kitchen.

When I first met Gloria she had never been interviewed before She reveled in privacy. She had withdrawn since the campaign began, stayed close to home and refrained from heading uptown where she would be pummeled with questions about Jimmy. She had even taken to grocery shopping as far away as Columbus, where no one would recognize her. But one day in March she consented to an interview.

We sat by the kitchen window at a table covered with oilcloth, and talked for four hours over a dozen cups of coffee and what seemed like a hundred cigarettes. She was dressed in white slacks and a blue work shirt liberally sprinkled with hand-painted blue and pink petunias and, while we talked, she kicked off her shoes and stretched out her bare feet on a chair, while Amy Carter cavorted in the back yard, darting in occasionally for another Pepsi or a spoonful of banana pudding.

From that time on, Gloria became my Plains den mother. Whenever I came to town her door was always open and Gloria was always there ready to offer a glass of iced tea, to sit on her front screened-in porch smoking cigarettes and commiserating about the campaign. She liked to shoot the breeze off the record. "Put your notebook away," she'd always say. More than anything she liked to laugh. If you were hungry she'd quickly produce lunch—sometimes tomato and mayonnaise sandwiches on white bread or corn on the cob or dinner—maybe a cheese sandwich. She kept some bourbon stowed away in a kitchen cabinet if you were interested.

Usually Miz Lillian, making her daily rounds, stopped by with her brown poodle ("What-a-Bitch," says the matriarch), to pass the time of day or to ask Gloria to join her for dinner at Faye's Barb-que Villa. One day they talked about Gloria's birthday present to her mother—a six-pack of ninety-nine-cent canned martinis, which they had shared the night before. "I had one and a half last night," said Gloria. "I came home absolutely stoned. I couldn't even eat dinner."

Gloria was as refreshing and spontaneous as her brother Jimmy was studied and programmed, as humble and self-deprecating as her mother was narcissistic, and every bit as intelligent, spunky, capable and funny as the whole family put together.

I did not recognize her from descriptions I had heard. Carter's friend John Pope said she had once been considered "The prettiest and sexiest girl in all of Sumter County. She was absolutely beautiful." In the *Gale,* the yearbook from Georgia Southwestern College which Gloria had attended for two years, she was indeed extremely pretty—with long golden curls, peach skin and a sparkling smile. Strength of character and determination were written on her face, and in spite of her light frame, she looked sturdy from hours of practice as a member of the all-star basketball team.

But the thirty years that had passed since then had exacted their toll. Her long blond hair had darkened to brown striated with gray, and was cropped just below her ears. ("I used to have long hair and permanents, but I cut it all off. It's been wonderful. I've never had to refuse an invitation to go anywhere because of my hair. I don't have to worry anymore about my motorcycle helmet messing it up. And Walter and I can stop and swim in a river anytime we want. But I'm afraid short hair won't look right with the formal gown I'm going to wear to the Inaugural Ball. So I'm letting it grow. I just hope it will be long enough by next January," she was already saying in March of 1976.) Gloria wore no makeup, except for a little lipstick. Her beauty was in her transparent-blue Carter eyes, full of light, good humor and warmth. They focused so intently on a listener that one imagined they must detect every flaw, idiosyncrasy and neurosis in the person with whom she is talking. She punctuated her every sentence with a smile, but her face bore the imprints of more than smile lines. Years of despair over a bad first marriage and a mentally disturbed child had left an indelible mark. Her once-lovely face was now wizened from years of worry covered over by smiling to hide the pain.

She would not talk about the pain. She would only say, "Look, I'm lucky to be able to stand up and walk and get through the day."

Gloria was always the gregarious, outgoing, fun-loving leader of the family. Full of spunk, she loved athletics, especially baseball and basketball. An A student through high school and college, she was considered the best-looking woman for miles around—"a heart-breaker," says a friend. "She could wrap men around her little finger and then drop them in front of others." Intense and energetic, she sometimes drove her brother, Jimmy, up a wall. He recalls she once so infuriated him that he shot her rear end full of pellets with a BB gun.

At Georgia Southwestern she studied journalism, was associate editor of the student newspaper, editor of the yearbook, a member of the dramatic club, and a crack player on the all-star basketball team.

By the time she graduated, at seventeen, she was what her father hoped she would be—educated, polished, motivated. She was perhaps overqualified for the tiny, unsophisticated town of Plains. She stood out like a rose among thorns. Had she gone away and established a life for herself elsewhere, she might have made a better future for herself, but the family ties were too thick and the roots too deep to leave. She was at once freed from the cloying boredom and mediocrity around her, and yet bound to it.

To find a suitable man to match her wits and personality was next to impossible. The numbers were stacked against her. Men were scarce in Sumter County (there were only five in her graduating class) and good men scarcer still. Although with her brains, personality and looks she could have had any man she chose, Gloria, like Rosalynn, fell in love with a uniform. Everett Hardy, better known as "Soapy," a former soda jerk from Americus, returned home in 1945 wearing his Air Force blues and captured Gloria's heart. "She could have married anyone," says a friend, "but she wanted Soapy." They ran off the first week of December 1945 and married.

Romance quickly faded. Marriage with Soapy Hardy was an endless series of Air Force bases, parties and drinking. All the partygoing created a problem for Gloria and her husband, she told friends.

Four years later she stepped off the bus in Plains with her young son Willy, or "Toady" as they called him, and her luggage—one dress in a brown paper bag—and ended the marriage.

Gloria had to work to make ends meet. She attended business school and got a job as a secretary/bookkeeper in Americus by day. In the afternoons she worked in the family warehouse. She became an expert in farm taxes and so proficient in her trade that in time she was keeping the books for more than a dozen plantations in the district.

While she worked, Mrs. James Knight kept her hyperactive son. Mrs. Clarence Dodson recalls "Toady" as a "darling little boy, a lovely child when he was four, five, six and seven." Others remember him as severely disturbed from the day he was born. Those who will talk about him say he craved a father's love, others say he never knew the distinction between right and wrong.

Gloria met Walter Spann, a farmer, on Christmas eve 1949. "We had three hundred and eleven dates and never had a cross word." They were married in 1950. She hoped the presence of a father figure would provide the missing ingredient in her son's life. It did not. Although Walter Spann adopted the boy, friends remember that Willy was never close to him or anyone else. He grew into a worse and worse disciplinary problem. He broke into a store when he was a teenager, and Gloria had to sell a piece of her farmland to raise the bond to get him out of jail. Jimmy Carter gave him work, but he would always steal a truck or a car and run off. One time he took Billy Carter's car and abandoned it in a ditch somewhere in North Carolina. He got into everything from drugs to homosexuality.

Gloria sent Willy from one psychiatrist to another, but nothing seemed to stem the problem. After he flunked out of a public school in Plains, they sent him to a military academy and finally to a special school for emotionally disturbed children, which Gloria helped to build with her own money and land. "He was beyond help," says a friend. "He never had any respect for anyone trying to help him . . . not his mother, not the family, no one. Finally, a psychiatrist told Gloria just to let him alone." She did. In 1968 he went to California where he is now serving time for armed robbery committed while under the influence of drugs.

Through it all, Gloria blamed herself. "Anyone who has an emotionally ill child thinks it's something wrong with them. I became an emotional and physical wreck."

In 1960 when Willy was fourteen and she finally realized she and her husband had "absolutely no control over him," Gloria sought solace by escaping to her sister, Ruth's, cabin in North Carolina and it was there that she was, "I hate to say born again. It's so tacky. But that's what happened. I elevated my relationship with Christ. I absolutely fell in love with Jesus."

She was reading when it happened. Not a religious book, but a book of radio tapes by a woman from South Africa named Gertrude Keehn. "Somewhere in that book it said, 'If you are an emotional and physical wreck, how can you expect to solve your problem alone? For sixty seconds, just give your problem to God and let Him worry about it.' It hit like a bolt of lightning."

Gloria says for all her Bible-school training, all her strict Baptist upbringing she "had never really believed in God before. If you had asked me if I were a Christian I would have said yes, but everything was learned by rote, not lived. I had been so self-centered. I thought I could handle everything myself, but this time I said, 'I don't know if you are real, but if you are God, I am going to give you my son.' It was the first time I've ever been truthful with God. It put everything in a whole new perspective. I began to realize that God is nothing but love and I'm his favorite child." Two weeks later she went on a prayer retreat and "cried and cried and cried." From that point on "I was able to get on top of my problems. And I've been on top ever since. 'Put the past under the blood, leave the future to God and get walking.' That's the way I live now. I don't worry about anything at all. I know God will answer all my prayers even if I don't always see the manifestation of the answer. I have problems, but I know they always turn out for the best. 'In everything give of yourself, for this is the will of the Lord Jesus concerning you.' If something terrible happens now I see it as an act of the directed will of God and therefore I can accept it. I might get mad at God, but I have this knowledge and faith and I can go on.

"I learned to see man as an expression of God's personality. I learned that even some of the most unloving people are worthy of His love. If He can love me, He can love anyone. We are all holy vessels of the spirit of Christ. I learned if you can follow in God's obedience then you don't have to follow any other human being. So did Jimmy. If Jimmy had followed what others told him, he wouldn't be where he is today."

To Gloria, following "In God's obedience" meant quitting her job, spending more time with her son and being a farmer's wife. She had never really wanted to work, she says, and like her sister, Ruth, she blamed her father for making her feel she had to work to be anyone at all. "My father had always wanted me to work. He had a horror of a girl not being able to earn a living. He wanted us to be more than factory workers. But I didn't want to work. All my life I just wanted to marry a farmer like Walter and not worry about anything except if it rained. My father owned this house and rented it out. It was my dream to live in it someday."

Instead she had been working eighteen hours a day. And when she wasn't working, she was praying.

Gloria's newfound faith had quickly become fanaticism. She channeled all her frustrations into prayer and eluded the reality of her problem by running off two or three times a year to week-long retreats, leaving her husband at home to fend for himself and to find fun with friends instead of with her.

In 1969 she attended her last retreat. "It was glorious, as it always was," she says, particularly because she was in a monastic setting where no one questioned her and no one knew that her son was sitting in a California jail. But she realized that her faith had run amok. It was pure escape and an easy one too. "I was so sweet and holy in a love-filled setting." She decided it was more of a challenge to reinforce her beliefs without the brace of a retreat.

"I hated it. I couldn't stand it. I finally admitted to myself that I loved Walter more than anything. And since all love comes from God, there was nothing wrong with devoting my life to him. So I became a full-time housewife. I became absolutely free to be exactly what I am. I didn't have to feel intimidated anymore by trying to be perfect, trying to make myself an example so others would have nothing to criticize. I simply became the person I am. And now I am perfectly at peace with myself. Of course everyone in the family is so dynamic. They throw up their hands and say, 'She's just a housewife.' But they have to admit I'm happy."

Miz Lillian is one of those who throws up her hands. "It's a shame she doesn't work. She's so terribly capable. And so in demand. She could have any job she wanted. But she wants to be with Walter. They're very happy. Besides, she doesn't have to work anymore. He's been very successful. And for them, money is no object."

(Walking through the simple white clapboard farmhouse, it is hard to believe money is no object for the Spanns. The small yellow parlor behind the screened-in porch is decorated with circa 1940 furniture, including a desk usually cluttered with the books she keeps or the biography of Miz Lillian she is writing. The house is immaculate, but often a clothesline will be strung across the bedroom with a pair or two of Walter's bib overalls hanging up to dry. Aside from a small library containing an encyclopedia and a variety of religious readings, there are no valuable objets d'art, no antiques, no paintings, no photographs.)

Unlike her evangelist sister, Ruth, Gloria does not feel her conversion presupposes a life of preaching and witnessing in public. She is happy to practice her own brand of Christianity at home. She calls herself "a practical Christian." Her smallest actions, whether they involve making a bed or a meal, or answering the phone, are a form of prayer. "Christ said, 'Whatsoever you do to the least of my brethren you do also unto me.' So if I make up a bed, I make it so if Jesus should come, it would be ready for Him. If I cook something, I do it with love and devotion, and if I answer the phone, I say to myself, 'O.K. someone wants to speak to me,' so I try to have a pleasant hello instead of a growl that implies I'm busy, what do you want!"

She also keeps up a running correspondence with a friend, Norman Grubb, a British-born Bible teacher and past secretary of the Worldwide Evangelization Crusade, who lives with his wife, Pauline, in Fort Washington, Pennsylvania. When Grubb found out that I often went to visit Gloria on my many trips to Plains this year he sent me one of his books, *Who Am I?*, inscribed, "I was so glad to hear of your link with my dear friend, Gloria, and that as Gloria knows the secret of Christ in her, so do you also." In August, after an appearance by Rosalynn Carter on a nationwide interview program, *Meet the Press*, Grubb wrote to Gloria, "Rosalynn was a magnificat. Such a testimony to Christ . . . Christ lives in Jimmy, is in Jimmy. You see Christ through the Carters. You are Jesus in Gloria."

Gloria's work for the past seventeen years has been minimal, mainly volunteer. "I just piddle around." She laughs. She belongs to the local garden club. She drives to Columbus once a month for a prayer luncheon and to Americus now and then to attend a prayer group she founded. She audits the books for the town of Plains and helps friends with their income taxes. For two years she taught ball-point painting—which is exactly what it sounds like—an art that requires no brushes, the paint comes out of a ballpoint tube. She had never painted before, but became intrigued with the concept of painting with tubes at a church fair, took a correspondence course and became an instructor. She taught every Tuesday in the Plains High School, at Buena Vista and at Southland, Georgia, and in her own home five nights a week. She even taught the black state championship basketball team, and painted shirts for all the black motorcyclists in town, never charging for her services.

One moment that gave her great pleasure came when she was teaching an adult black woman to shade a daisy. "When she finished she put her head on the table and cried. She said, 'I knew I could do it. All my life I knew I could paint if someone would just show me. I'm going home and paint, paint, paint.' That kind of experience satisfies the soul more than collecting a paycheck."

Gloria gave up teaching when Walter Spann finally put his foot down. "He got tired of walking over paints in the living room. And he didn't like me working every night." He also got tired of finding black people, whom Walter calls "nigguhs" too, in his living room.

In Gloria's house Walter is the boss, and Gloria has no complaints. To her ERA and women's liberation can be hanged. "I just love the way men work," she sighs. "In the late afternoon I see Walter come in dirty and tired. I think the least a wife can do is be there and have a happy home and nice house.

"I can't wait for you to meet Walter," she says, her eyes brightening like electric lights. "He's so gorgeous. I'm so in love with him." Walter appears for lunch, stalking in the back door in overalls and brogans, a handsome, fifty-one-year-old blondish-gray man with eyes like sea water, and a pleasant disposition. Although he does not converse extensively, he seems a peaceful, smiling man and one who knows he is in charge of his domain. Walter is country. Interested in farming, not politics, especially not Jimmy Carter's campaign. He was too busy to care. And besides, he is a Republican.

Friends say he is jealous of Jimmy Carter's success; that he secretly detests his famous brother-in-law. Spann just laughs.

Even so, he frowned on Gloria's involvement with her brother's Presidential efforts, which must have caused Gloria considerable heartache. Gloria with her entire family had participated to help get Jimmy elected to the state senate. "We were all there at the courthouse during the deposition [concerning vote fraud] and we were all out at the polls handing out leaflets." And she campaigned statewide fourteen hours a day, seven days a week for Jimmy in his 1966 and 1970 gubernatorial races. "Walter was not wild about the schedule." She grins.

Friends say rather than do anything that would "upset Walter," Gloria did little more for the Presidential campaign than write letters to friends asking for support, keep Amy when Miz Lillian was unable to, and make one trip to Florida with the Peanut Brigade.

She was not present at Miz Lillian's victory street dance the night Jimmy Carter won the Ohio primary. ("You know me," she said, laughing.) She did not attend the Democratic National Convention to see him nominated. ("I was in the hospital having a D&C," she said later. "But I didn't tell Jimmy till he called to ask where I was.") She watched the convention from her hospital bed, alone. Walter Spann never watched any of it. "He couldn't have cared less," Gloria says.

Walter Spann's only involvement in the campaign was a get-rich-quick scheme, selling square-inch plots of land billed as Plains peanut land for five dollars a piece to thousand of citizens in thirty-seven states. Jimmy Carter was never consulted in advance and frowned seriously on the action.

Since Walter Spann is retired, they take many vacations. They weekend at their country cabin on a nearby lake, take frequent Sunday-afternoon motorcycle trips, go skiing at Christmas and are prone to spur-of-the-moment vacations. In 1975, on only a few hours' notice from a friend, they packed their bags and left at 4:30 A.M. for Alaska. They were gone thirty-one days in their Chevy pickup truck, camping out in state parks along the way. The same year they motorcycled three hundred and fifty miles to Daytona Beach and Key West, Florida, and on another trip cycled through the Blue Ridge and Shenandoah mountains.

Gloria realizes that a motorcycle is "a dangerous machine," but has no fear except when huge semitrucks hurtle past her on super-highways at incredible speeds. She was instrumental in urging the passage of a Georgia law requiring cyclists to be licensed and over the age of sixteen.

What do folks in a small Southern town say when she buzzes by on her Honda? "Well." Gloria laughed. "At first there were some unusual stares, but now they just say, 'There goes Gloria.'" She doesn't care what others think anyway. "My doctor says it's great. It keeps me feeling young."

CHAPTER 5

AMY AND CHIP

ONE OF CARTER's favorite lines during the campaign was, "Rosalynn and I had an argument for fourteen years, and I won." Amy was long in coming into the Carter life, however not for the reason Carter states. She was not merely the happy resolution of an argument. Amy's entrance into the world was delayed because twelve years after the birth of their youngest son, Jeff, a large tumor on Rosalynn's ovary was found to have impeded conception. After the tumor was removed, the doctors told the Carters they could have another child. They prayed for a daughter and got Amy.

Amy is the apple of Carter's eye. It is said the first thing he does when he returns home, no matter how late the hour, is to make a beeline for Amy. "Coming twenty-one years after we were married, she's very special to us," Carter told me. "She gives a fresh aspect to our family life. She's been like a separate family for us."

When I first laid eyes on Amy, she was skipping barefoot across the flagstone path leading to her father's motel room in Orlando, Florida, the night of the Florida primary. A female Huckleberry Finn, her waist-length, strawberry-blond hair streamed behind her. Her freckles were more prolific than ever from the tropic sun. She seemed oblivious to the myriad of newsmen gathered at the door and sheepish with those who tried to converse with her. She answered queries in monosyllables or ignored them completely. When Carter made his victory speech close to eleven o'clock, Amy cavorted behind him on the stage, still barefoot.

The next time I saw Amy was in Plains. She was staying overnight with her Aunt Gloria because Miz Lillian had the flu, and was

eating a cheese sandwich in the kitchen. Like her father, Amy requires some getting to know, but once known, she is an enchanting
blithe spirit with a megaton of charm and the family's tantalizing
eyes. We sat on the couch in Gloria's living room that evening and
chatted a bit. Amy told me she didn't like the campaign all that well
because she missed her parents so much and was very lonely. "I wish
I could go with them." But she was willing to forgo a normal family
life for a while. Why? "Cuz he might win," said she. Did she want
to live in the White House? "Suuuuuure!" Amy smiled. Why? "Cuz
it's so beeeeg! Just like the Governor's mansion only beeeger!" Amy
separated all her sentences with an irrepressible musical giggle that
ran the scale from middle to high C. "And Mommy promised that
when we move to the White House I can have a cat, a dog and a
rabbit and go to an all-girls' school." In Plains Amy attends an integrated public school and Carter talked throughout the campaign
about continuing her public-school education in Washington. After
the election it was decided she would attend the integrated Stevens
school. Why did she want to go to an all-girls' school? "Cuz girls are
more fun. They like to giggle and whisper in class. Boys aren't any
fun. They just sit there. They won't even pass notes in class."

What did she like to do when her mommy and daddy were home?
"Help Daddy make breakfast. He makes grits, then he breaks a couple of eggs into that and adds some cheese and it's yummy." What
did she want to be when she grew up? "A pilot. I flew in a private
plane to Atlanta with Daddy once and the pilot let me fly it. It was
so easy. Pull the wheel back and it goes up. Push it and it goes down."
Does she have a boyfriend? "Yeah, Scott Robertson. He sits next to
me in class. And we go roller-skating every Friday night. I used to
have another boyfriend, and he's jealous because I don't like him
anymore. He says the only reason Scott likes me is cuz muh daddy's
going to be in the White House. But he's just saying that cuz he's
jealous."

Amy is spoiled not only by her daddy, in whose eyes she can do no
wrong, but by her grandmother, Miz Lillian, who cared for her while
the Carters were campaigning. "Amy's mah life, mah heart," Miz
Lillian says. And she often proves it with candy. Amy is rarely seen
without a sucker of some kind in her mouth. And in her parent's
absence, she developed a whopping sweet tooth.

One time early in the campaign, when I was the only reporter in
town and had my six-year-old daughter, Brooke, with me, I took
Brooke and Amy roller-skating at the rink in Americus. When Amy

wasn't barreling around the wooden floor at a forty-five degree angle going eighty miles an hour, her arms half extended like little chicken wings, she was dipping into her little red purse which contained: one chocolate bar, half a dozen packages of Carter peanuts, a brownie, several kinds of suckers and some raisins. She devoured them all with gusto and washed them down with a Dr Pepper.

After skating we stopped at a diner for a snack and Amy absorbed a hamburger, french fries, a Coke and a piece of chocolate cake. Rosalynn told me she was worried about her daughter's consumption of sweets, but didn't know exactly how to control it in her absence. Carter banished Coke from the house.

That night Amy took along her pets, Twirly and Whirly, two fuzzy caterpillars she had lovingly incarcerated in an Old Maid card box and stashed in her purse along with her hoard of candy. Every third or fourth spin around the rink, she would skate over to where she left her purse, stopping herself by lunging into the guard rail, open the card box to inspect Twirly and Whirly's condition, stroke them lovingly with her forefinger, and skate off. In a three-hour period she never rested. She once removed her skates and pleaded to play the pinball machines. "I have quarters," she said, plunking two into an electric tennis game. "You can pay me back." She didn't forget to ask later for her quarters.

After skating three hours straight, Amy was still full of bounce and go. "Watch me clog," she said, sashaying off down the sidewalk performing one of the most complicated pieces of footwork I have ever seen. Clogging is a combination of tap dancing and folk dancing, and Amy, it turns out, is a champion clogger, and has danced with a group called the "Little Generals" all over the state of Georgia.

And she was most solicitous of her caterpillars. They had been in the card box for too long she felt, and walking to the car took them out for a stroll along the window sill of a furniture store. Amy thought Twirly must be either Whirly's mate, "or maybe Mamma, cuz he's so faaaat!" The last time I inquired, Amy had given her caterpillars their freedom in the back yard "cuz they were spinning cocoons."

The back yard is where Amy's trampoline sits and one day when we were filming for NBC she gave us a demonstration of her acrobatic skills. Amy can do front flips and back flips and carry on like a member of the circus. She can also sew with a sewing machine, play the piano well and ice skate.

With the exception of her extroversion and her sense of humor, Amy is a duplicate of her father both in mind and body. She looks like a strawberry-blond miniature Jimmy, and, like her dad, barely has to study to make a straight A average. She can rapidly devour books five years above her own grade and is gifted with her father's retentive memory as well. Eleanor Forrest, her Sunday-school teacher, recalls one Sunday morning when she asked Amy fourteen questions on the last lesson the class had had. "She didn't get one wrong, and she hadn't studied. She remembered it all from the Sunday before."

She shares her father's drive to succeed in business. After the Ohio primary, Amy set up a lemonade stand with her next-door-neighbor's sons for which she charged scalpers' prices. The first day she charged ten cents a glass for red, green or lemon Kool-Aid, but soon jacked the price up to a quarter when she found newsmen on expense accounts would pay it. She would also vary her prices according to whim. One morning, when Carter toured the peanut fields for the television cameras, he decided to pay a visit to Amy's stand. When she saw him approaching, surrounded by a cloud of press, she charged up the road, leaped into his arms and whispered into his ear. Carter threw back his head and guffawed. "She told me, 'If they take my picture I'll only charge 'em a dime. If they don't they'll have to pay twenty cents!' "

Amy was successful with her small business too. "The first day I made five dollars. The second I made nine dollars and today I made seventeen," she bragged. "Come on," she called to her friends. "Let's count the money." Later Amy added tuna fish sandwiches to the menu and earned even more.

One day, NBC cameraman Earl Wells asked Amy if she owned a Frisbee. "Yeah," said Amy. "How much do you want to pay me for it?" Wells told her he'd give her twenty-five cents an hour. "Well, how am I going to know when an hour's up?" "Oh, I know," said Amy, dashing into the house and producing an egg timer. At the end of the afternoon after several games with his camera crew Wells absentmindedly tossed the Frisbee in the back window of his car. Soon Amy tracked him down with her egg timer. "Somebody owes me four dollars," she said.

Chip Carter, who looks like his father did as a young man, is the only Carter son who lives in Plains. Chip, twenty-six, and his wife Caron, live in a mustard-yellow trailer on the quiet end of Main

Street diagonally across from the depot. "In the third mobile home from the post office," he is fond of saying. They paid eight thousand dollars for it with Chip's savings. It has air conditioning, wall-to-wall carpeting, a guest room with flowered bedspreads, a dining area the size of most breakfast nooks, a smaller bedroom used as a den, a rather sizable bedroom with a double bed and a huge dresser, and a large living room dominated by a giant color TV. Out back sat a rusty, dilapidated jalopy Chip was restoring for their second car.

When I dropped by their trailer one hot, gnatty, Georgia after-noon Chip, barefooted, with his work boots beside him, was stretched out in a Naugahyde recliner, glued to the cartoons.

"If he got poor grades when he was a kid he was deprived of TV, so he's become a TV addict," explained wife Caron, a dark-haired beauty who resembles a young Rosalynn. "He just sits there and stares at that television by the hour. He doesn't even hear you if you're talking. There's little communication. I tell him if we ever get a divorce, I'll take J.B. [Their tiny black mutt, who almost took a hunk out of my leg one day when I opened the door unannounced] and I'll leave the trailer and the TV for you."

Relaxed and friendly Chip confirms he has become a boob-tube freak, although he is not sure the habit derives from deprivation as a child. Nevertheless he was denied it. "If you got one grade below what you normally got, Dad wouldn't let you watch for a week. Two grades and you couldn't watch for two weeks. The news didn't count. We always watched the news, but the cartoons went." Since Chip was always falling behind in his grades, he missed a lot of cartoons. He's making up for it today. (Cutting off TV was not his father's only method of discipline. He also administered swift justice with the swat of an AK fraternity-initiation paddle, or worse, the psychological torture of promising to punish the next day. "I just remember I got one whipping for smoking when I was ten or twelve," says Chip, now a chainsmoker. "Dad hated smoking. He forbade us to smoke in front of him. I never did till I got in an auto accident and was on pain-killers. I smoked in front of them after that." Willy Spann, Gloria's son, claims he was kicked out of Jimmy Carter's house for smoking.)

Nevertheless, for all his TV watching, Chip claims to be an avid reader too. Like his father, Chip says he reads several books at a clip, sometimes reading until 2:30 or 3:30 in the morning. That way he polishes off five or six books a week. He borrows books from his father's library, mostly, and the day I came he was reading Patrick Anderson's (his father's speechwriter's) book, *The President's Mistress*.

Reading was a ritual in the Carter household. Everyone read, constantly. "Sometimes Dad would read us poetry, or explain passages of Dylan Thomas to us." Everyone came to the dinner table in work clothes "at six o'clock sharp or else" with something to read and thought nothing of reading throughout the meal. The whole meal? "Yeah. What's the matter with that? Don't you do that?" asked Chip. I told him I thought it might stifle communication, but he said the family never had any trouble talking to each other. "We talked if we wanted to."

Carter would help his sons with their problem homework. Chip's greatest trouble was Latin. "He'd study my book and then teach it to me. Then he'd expect me to read it and translate it. In the eighth grade it was my worst subject, but I ended up with a B. My first week in college, he read all my textbooks—history, English, biology, everything, so he could ask me questions all year long."

Carter's diligence did little good. Chip dropped out of Georgia Southwestern College after a year. Although he is proud to have received the highest score in a national achievement test, he "just didn't study" at college. "I just didn't want to." In 1968 he went back "and got good grades" and then dropped out again. "He just didn't organize his curriculum," says Caron, who has her master's degree in Early Childhood Education. "He took things he wanted to, like political science and history. He almost has a double major in history and political science." "He'll finish," says mother Rosalynn. "One day before the campaign he said he was going back to Georgia Southwestern, not because he thinks it's important, but because he might run for office and it would look better if he had a degree."

Chip was more interested in working. Chip and his brothers had only received meager allowances from the age of five through the age of ten—"Five cents per year of age," after which they were expected to do their share in the family warehouse after school. Chip's job was tagging bags of peanuts, for which he received two dollars and fifty cents a week. "That was a lot of money in the Sixties. You could buy a lot of Coke for your friends with that."

By the time he was in college, working particularly in politics seemed preferable to studying. One year he worked in his father's campaign, another year, after Carter became Governor, he worked in his office. Another year he sold men's suits at Sears. Now, he does manual labor on his father's farm, spreading fertilizer, driving the tractor trailer, working in peanuts, and expects to run the business someday.

What about girls? His father was lenient about dating, according to Chip. The boys started dating at fifteen or sixteen, as soon as they were able to drive. They were expected home by twelve midnight or one A.M., and were only asked to knock on their mother and father's door "to tell them we were in." "It's funny. When Jack and Judy come down to spend a weekend and stay at the house, they still knock on Mom and Dad's door to let them know they're home." "Dad was shocked when I married Caron," says Chip. "I had always dated really hippy girls, and here I went and married a farmer's daughter from Hawkinsville. I must say, though, he never said anything about my girl friends. He always liked everyone I brought home."

Caron laughs that Chip had been "dating every girl who walked up the steps of the Governor's mansion, taking advantage of being the Governor's son. When I met him, I was working in the Governor's office, but I didn't pay any attention to him. I didn't want to like him because I didn't want him to think I liked him just because he was who he was. Maybe that's why he liked me." They never dated anyone else after their first date. "I remember we went to the Governor's mansion. All the other girls he had dated had wanted to go upstairs and talk to his mother and father. I didn't want to go upstairs. He knew I liked him just because he was himself." Caron liked Chip because he was "outspoken," "daring," and "different." "The first time I met him in the Governor's office he was wearing blue jeans, boots, a denim shirt, a tie and jacket. He was rebelling from here down." She laughs, drawing a hand across her waist.

"He was sensitive too about people who didn't have as much and he was so well informed about everything. He could talk about anything. He got me interested in politics. He made me aware of what was going on outside my own little world. He brought me out. If Chip's brothers, Jack and Jeff were A students while Chip muddled along with C's, D's and F's, he was the friendliest one, the best one with people." Says Caron, "He was the perfect one to run the family business and keep the farmers happy." Chip's the one-who's gotten to know the political world working in his father's gubernatorial campaign and in his office. When Carter was making his plans to run for President, Chip and Caron lived in a guest cottage behind the Governor's mansion. "We used to go over and sit in on all the meetings," said Caron, who has learned the art of politics as well as Chip.

Chip and Caron took off both separately and together to help in the 1976 campaign. They visited over forty states in the primaries alone, walking into stores, visiting homes, making speeches to schools and senior citizens homes, living on their campaign salary of five hundred dollars a month, even though Caron was in the early stages of pregnancy. "It's hard to grasp the magnitude of it," says Chip. "I was always all for it because I thought he could win if enough people got to hear him, he's so brilliant." And his own future? Politics. Chip smiles, pulls on his work boots and heads for his typewriter to work on a speech. "Yeah, I'll probably start on the Sumter County School Board someday."

But right now they'll have their first baby and live in the White House for a bird's-eye view of government.

PART

II

JIMMY
CARTER'S
WOMEN

CHAPTER 6

MIZ LILLIAN

"JUST TURN RIGHT at the road a little ways up from here, and keep going. You can't miss it," Gloria directed me to her mother's Pond House. To a New Yorker, accustomed to the numerical streets of Manhattan and the alphabetical streets of Washington, D.C., the small town of Plains and its environs are bewildering. Outside of Bond Street, Main Street, Church Street and a handful of other original names, there are no signs, lights, or house numbers in Plains. After several wild goose chases, I managed to find the right country road, but it was deeply rutted and puddled from the rainstorm the night before. It was like driving down an obstacle course on bivouac. Surely a jeep would have been more suitable than a rented Chevy Vega.

Past several hundred yards of shacks and sharecropper penury, I reached the Pond House. It looked like a Vermont ski lodge with all its glass, wood and angles—the only bow to twentieth-century flair in the anachronistic setting of Plains. It made even Jimmy's and Hugh Carter's expensive homes look commonplace.

The backdrop was like a Monet canvas. A still pond bathed in the reflection of weeping willows and blooming dogwood. The mystical silence was pierced now and then by a symphony of birds. I had hardly shut the car door when Miz Lillian emerged from her lair—a cathedral-ceilinged living room with a massive stone fireplace and glass wall overlooking the pond. It was where she watched the ball games and soap operas and read five hours a day. That day she was perusing Art Buchwald.

A more spry and erect seventy-eight-year-old I had never seen besides Rose Kennedy. And like the Kennedy matriarch she was intense, commanding, stately. She wore a neat blue polyester pant-suit and little flat white shoes. Her gossamer-white hair was perfectly coiffed, and everything about her spelled vitality. But she was like a coiled spring. Defiance was written on her unsmiling face. Royal defiance. Her arms folded like a barricade to her being. A queen bee guarding her hive. A verse sprang to mind:

> "It looked good natured, she thought;
> still, it had very long claws
> and a great many teeth,
> so she felt it ought to be
> treated with respect."

These were the first words out of her mouth: "I don't like women reporters."

REPLY: "Well, if you wish, I could leave right now."

MIZ LILLIAN: "Fine. Why don't you?"

There was not a twinkle of humor in her statement. Beneath the molasses-and-honey drawl seemed to lurk a razor. I panicked!

However, I like a challenge. I walked into the house and turned on my tape recorder. And after fifteen or twenty minutes, the teasing hostility subsided and Miz Lillian became a docile kitten, curled impishly in a turquoise armchair, pouring out the story of her life and her experiences in India. She was Ethel Barrymore, Greta Garbo and Bishop Fulton Sheen wrapped into one. Moreover, she was like her son, an enigmatic combination of conflicting facets—hard and soft, sharp and smooth, meek and proud, sophisticate and farmer's wife, saintly and salty, sweet and sarcastic.

At first she seemed to want to put down her interviewer, to embarrass, create a sense of discomfort, or was it theater?

The interview began like a duel. Asked to describe Jimmy Carter, she teased in her slow drawl, "That's a silly question. He's my son. I can't answer that." It bothered her to be asked what kind of Presidency Carter's would be. "My land! You're going to ask me the wrong thing directly. Why, it'll be so different. It will be wonderful." And she fussed when asked what motivated her to join the Peace Corps at sixty-eight. "Oh, mercy. I've been asked that again and again."

Miz Lillian says exactly what is on her mind. As one ninety-eight-year-old black Plains woman put it, "Miz Lillian is afraid of no man. She says what's bothering her, and shoot, if you don't like it, she ain't about to stop and ask you why."

I saw that side of her several times during the campaign.

On the night of the street dance she threw to welcome her son home after the last primary in June, Miz Lillian had been standing in the street with some 10,000 people for nearly seven hours. She was bone weary and exhausted from making conversation when the press entourage and "Jimmeh" pulled up to the depot. When a reporter asked her how she felt now that it looked like her son had the nomination locked up, she was not in the mood to consider the question and told the journalist to shut up.

One morning on the depot platform, Miz Lillian was joking with some of the television cameramen, when one of them teased her, "Miz Lillian, your son says he'll never tell a lie. Do you ever tell a lie?" "Yeah." She grinned. "I make up for Jimmy." When she saw a reporter taking notes, without even turning around she reached behind her and slapped the journalist's notebook to the ground.

In November, after the election, Miz Lillian was sitting in her rocker down at the depot signing autographs. It was just after the flap at the Plains Baptist Church over the admission of the black preacher, Clennon King, and the membership of blacks in general, an action Jimmy's first cousin, Hugh Carter, had vehemently opposed. Miz Lillian was infuriated with Hugh, calling him an "arch segregationist." When some tourists asked her to sign some T-shirts they had just purchased at Hugh's antique store, she flung them back. "He's not part of my family," she snapped. "I wouldn't sign anything from his store."

Betty Pope, a friend from Americus, says of Miz Lillian, "You never know when she's serious or kidding. She's very hard to read."

For example, one day when a reporter was interviewing Billy and Sybil in the peanut warehouse, Miz Lillian barreled in the door to talk to her daughter-in-law. "Go on, git the hell out of here," she said to the flabbergasted reporter. "I got things I got to talk to Sybil about." Sybil's mouth dropped open. "It's O.K. Sybil, we know one another . . . we're friends." She smiled at the journalist, batting her eyelashes.

Five minutes later she moved over to join the reporter and Billy and began to add her own opinion about Carter's extraordinary accomplishments in winning the primaries. "It's eerie. I never did think I'd get to see him be President, but about six months ago I started feeling positive and from then on I knew this would happen somehow. But now that it has, it's unbelievable." Seeing his mother ensconced, Billy seized the opportunity to take care of a matter of business. But as he rose from his seat, the Georgia matriarch flew at him. "Siddown Billy!" she commanded. "I'm your mother and I'm talking to you." Billy eased back down slowly with the expression of a four-star general who had just been ordered to clean the latrines.

"When she speaks they listen," Betty Pope says. They've found it easier just to go along with what she says. "Remember last summer when they had the big family fish fry? Well, John and I were going to have it at our farm pond, but Billy told us one day, 'We're going to do it out at the Pond House.' When we asked why, he said, 'Cuz Momma says . . .'"

"She's a very strong, gutsy woman," says John Pope. "She tells it like it is. She never hesitates."

Miz Lillian is also a Leo, born August 15, 1898, which according to *Linda Goodman's Sun Signs* means that she is a combination of arrogant pride and a sunny playfulness. Ms. Goodman says Leo rules "you and everybody else. It's best to humor him. Then he'll purr, instead of roaring and scaring you half to death . . . Even the gentle Leos are inwardly sold on their royal right to rule friends and family and peek out from behind the curtains for their chance on stage.

"You won't ignore the Lion for long in a group. He'll either get the center of the stage with dramatic statements and action—or he'll get it by pouting and sulking behind potted palms, until someone rushes over to ask what's wrong."

Miz Lillian does have an inclination to want to be the star of the show. She did not like it for example that "Miz Allie" (Smith), Rosalynn's mother, was stealing her spotlight. After all the favorable publicity Rosalynn had received, Miz Allie's face and name had also come to public attention. She, too, was being asked for her autograph. When a group approached Miz Lillian with a batch of leaflets that Miz Allie had just signed, she handed them back with the dictum: "I sign under no one's name but Jimmy Carter's."

The night of Carter's huge beer bash on a New York pier during the Democratic Convention, Miz Lillian stood ten minutes in the receiving line, then repaired to a chair off to the side, nursing a bruised hand, and complaining of fatigue. "I don't want to be interviewed," she whined at print reporters. "Ahm so tah'd." But when the TV cameras turned on her she revived quickly. She was suddenly on stage and performing like a pro.

When I was in Plains back in March for NBC, I had finished my interview with Miz Lillian and gone over to Jimmy and Rosalynn's. While we were filming in the back yard, Miz Lillian appeared unexpectedly and walked right into the picture with a handful of mail to hug and kiss Jimmy. She did not greet Rosalynn. Rosalynn just stood by expressionless while Mamma preened for the cameras.

There is little love lost between Rosalynn and Miz Lillian.

Carter writes in his autobiography that the biggest argument of his married life ensued over whether he would sacrifice his navy career and return to Plains. Carter writes of Rosalynn, "She did not, she protested, wish to go back to the restrictive life of our home in Plains, where our families lived and where our married freedom might be cramped or partially dominated by relatives, particularly by her mother or my mother."

"They were always telling me what to do," Rosalynn once told me. "Little things like 'Don't you think this dress should go to the cleaner's?' I was only eighteen when I was married, so they still thought of me as a child."

Some say the difference between Miz Lillian and Rosalynn is purely a difference in temperament, Rosalynn being serious and determined, Miz Lillian being fun and gay, with a lust for life. "I love Rosalynn," Miz Lillian told me, "but she's kind of . . . reserved." Miz Lillian seems to favor her daughter-in-law Sybil, an expansive, gregarious woman who loves to giggle.

Others say it's pure and simple competition for Jimmy's attention. "They're both Jimmy's women," says a friend, "and Miz Lillian doesn't think Jimmy pays enough attention to her."

Still others say Miz Lillian, who has always saved her son's letters and documents and sensed some divine mission in his future, never considered Rosalynn worthy of his journey toward the sun. "It's a typical case of mother not thinking any woman good enough for her son. Rosalynn's father was only an auto mechanic and her mother was a seamstress, and she thought Jimmy could do better," a family friend observes. When Jimmy began dating Rosalynn, Miz Lillian told him, "Jimmy, she's just a little girl. She's Ruth's friend." And she thought to herself, "My Jimmy is just so much more sophisticated than she is. He's been dating girls who are graduating from college, girls from New Jersey . . . this little girl Rosalynn is naïve." She tried to dissuade her son from pursuing the romance but her words fell on deaf ears.

Some say a feud developed over the family business. Jimmy and

Miz Lillian had bought the peanut enterprise from other family members at a time when the business was floundering; but as they built the corporation that processes peanuts, cotton, corn, beans and other grains and distributes fertilizer back to a profitable venture, it was Rosalynn Jimmy made his co-partner, not his mother. Observers say it rankled Miz Lillian that Rosalynn was making major decisions although she owned controlling stock.

Some say the feud grew so intense at one time that Rosalynn asked Miz Lillian to leave the house.

During Carter's term as Governor, Miz Lillian was losing the sight of one eye from cataracts and went to Atlanta for an operation. Afterward, she recuperated at the Governor's mansion, spending her time sleeping in a small, dark interior room and listening to "Ring Radio," a call-in talk show. "She really wanted to stay and be First Lady," says a Carter observer, "but the first time Miz Lillian raised her voice, Rosalynn told her, 'This house isn't big enough for the both of us. And I don't intend to leave.' Over the years Rosalynn has learned how to stand up to her strong mother-in-law, acquired an impenetrable shell so that Miz Lillian doesn't get to her. But they still don't socialize very much. Jimmy often visits his mother at the Pond House to have a meal with her. Rosalynn stays home." Says Jimmy, "Mother doesn't think I pay enough attention to her. She thinks I'm entirely too devoted to Rosalynn. I guess I have to learn to pay a little more attention to her."

In speaking of her mother-in-law, Rosalynn has learned to contain her feelings. Jimmy's wife merely says, "She had always been so sheltered and dependent on her husband, and she was very lonely after he died." Rosalynn denies any tension between herself and Miz Lillian, and emphasized instead what a big help Miz Lillian has always been with Amy, even if she spoiled her a bit.

Miz Lillian was born Lillian Gordy, in 1898, in Richland, a simple southwest Georgia town. Her family moved to Plains in 1921. She had eight blood brothers and sisters. Her father, the postmaster of Richland for thirty-two years, adopted two more children, and her grandmother moved in. "With thirteen of us around the table for supper, we had to learn that we couldn't always have an extra slice of bread just because we wanted it. Someone else might have a greater need." Her father interested her in politics and engrained in her an appreciation for blacks. The black bishop, William D. Johnson of the African Methodist Episcopal Church was a regular visitor to the Gordy house. The two men would sit and talk about the Bible and "the living Christ," and Miz Lillian recalls they would sit and crow in harmony:

"The King of love my shepherd is
Whose goodness faileth never;
I nothing lack if I am His
And He is mine forever."

Not only was Jim Jack Gordy "the biggest politician in this part of the world (even if he never did run for office), he kept up with politics so closely that he would tell you almost within five votes what the people who were running would get in the next election. And so he was very popular."

According to Carter, Gordy "was considered the most politically knowledgeable man in Webster and Stewart counties." In his book Carter writes: "For a while he lived near us in the Archery community, and he and Daddy kept the political scene thoroughly analyzed. Grandpa never ran for public office himself but was the postmaster during four Presidential administrations, and later was federal district revenue officer. This required nimble political footwork because at that time there was no civil service system. To the winners went the spoils."

Carter says, "My grandfather [Gordy] was an avid supporter of Congressman Tom Watson, who was a nationally known populist in his day. As postmaster in nearby Richland, Georgia, my grandfather had been the person who first conceived the idea of the rural free delivery of mail (RFD) and had repeatedly made his proposals to Congressman Watson to implement this idea through federal legislation. When this was finally accomplished, it was one of my grandfather's proudest achievements. When he was long past retirement age, Jim Jack had a doorkeeper's job at the state capitol just to be involved in the political life of Georgia."

Miz Lillian became a registered nurse and was working for the Wise brothers, two renowned general surgeons, who ran a sanitarium in Plains at the time she met Earl Carter, a farmer. They married in September 1923. Although friends remember that they were close and an unpleasant word rarely passed between them, their thirty years together was not always a smooth voyage.

While Earl Carter was a true conservative, Miz Lillian, Jimmy's mother, was considered a liberal. Although friends say she is not as radical as she makes out to be—"she still thinks blacks belong in their place"—she nevertheless ministered to their needs, tended to their wounds, delivered their babies and stayed up all night with their dying without accepting recompense.

Fanny Hill remembers how her only son once almost died of dysentery. "He began spilling blood. We couldn't even put a diaper on him. The doctor had given him up. He said he would be dead by morning, but Miz Lillian came over and gave him her remedy and the next morning he opened his eyes. He's still alive and I still have the baby syringe that she used. I will always keep it. She is a fabulous woman and raised the children to love everyone."

Asked what made her an integrationist living in the deep rural South, Miz Lillian shakes her head and utters a loud "Ooooooh-oo-oooh!" as though the word "integrationist" is still a red-hot term in Georgia. "I don't know. I've always had a feeling for the underdog. Right or wrong. And I guess it's the fact that I'm just different. I'm not in the same mold as some of the people I know. I'm just different."

She laughs that Jimmy recently called her "the most liberal woman in Georgia" on a TV interview show. "I said 'Jimmy you really put the mark of Cain on me. People have always known it, but they wouldn't say it.' "

One time when Jimmy was Governor they sat in Hank Aaron's box for a ball game in Atlanta. "I never liked Sammy Davis, Junior, and as we walked to our seats, Jimmy said, 'Uh-oh, Mother, look who's in the box.' It was Sammy. Well, we got to be good friends by the end of the night. He was so nice. He even kissed my hand. But when Hank Aaron hit the home run, Jimmy spun around and hugged me. Then Sammy spun me around and hugged me. And Jimmy said, 'Mother, look, the TV cameras are on. That's nation-wide TV.' And I thought, 'Uh-oh, liberal me!' "

Earl and Miz Lillian had four children—Jimmy, Gloria, Ruth and Billy.

Miz Lillian remembers her son Jimmy was "an ordinary little country boy," who milked cows and rode mules and fished with his friends. "The only difference was he was white and his friends were black." He was also an A student and bookworm. "I've never seen Jimmy sit down to breakfast without a book or a paper."

Little Jimmy rarely got in Dutch, she claims. "He never got into fights with other boys or pulled hair."

She had never really expected her firstborn to go into politics. Admiral was her dream for him. Although she plunged into his 1970 gubernatorial race with a vengeance, making over six hundred speeches around the state at the age of seventy-one, she was not in the country for his first gubernatorial race. "It almost broke her heart that she was not there when he lost," says her daughter, Gloria. Miz Lillian had gone to India to join the Peace Corps. She was sixty-eight at the time and "bored."

"I wasn't doing anything at home except fishing and reading. You know. You see how large Plains is. My husband and I had been social-minded, and after his death there was nothing to do except go to church, play a little bridge and go fishing."

She had always been extremely active in the community, a member of the garden club and the missionary circle, a nurse. She'd done everything there was to do. And after Earl's death "her world just fell apart," says Rosalynn. She took a job as housemother for A. K. fraternity at Auburn University where she remained for eight years until she "got nervous." "You can't get nervous with young boys." After that she ran a nursing home for a short time.

But with her vitality and good health, she refused to sit around the Pond House and mope. "I've never been one to give up on learning things and doing things." One night she saw the Peace Corps advertised on television and decided to try it as "a lark." "You know, to do something different." Secretly, she hoped her children would talk her out of such a wild venture. After she had stayed up until 1:30 A.M. filling out the application, she walked down to the office the next morning where Billy and Jimmy were working. "I said, 'Billy, do you and Jimmy love me?' And they knew I was going to stop them and ask them to come mow the lawn or something like that. Jimmy said, 'Momma, you know we love you.' And Billy said—don't you print this ugly word—'Momma, what in hell are you going to do now?'—Billy's different from Jimmy—and I said I'm going to join the Peace Corps. I knew it would be stopped right there. But if you ever saw two boys who let their mother down, it was Billy and Jimmy. They both said, 'Mother. You'll enjoy it.' They knew I was bored. They were delighted. It kind of floored me." She hoped her two daughters would dissuade her. "I hoped they'd say 'Mother, please don't go.'" But they encouraged her too. When Ruth pulled out her globe and asked where she would be in India because she would like to visit her on vacation, "I knew the die was cast. And I said 'Well, durn, is that all they think of me?'"

She went to the University of Chicago for nine months of intensive training and language study from seven in the morning till ten at night. She learned the Indian dialect, Marathi. She underwent psychological counseling. "You had to be perfect mentally and physically. My psychologist kept wanting to know why I wanted to go to a dark country with a warm climate, and leave my family and the things I had. One day he was trying to make me talk, and that was kind of hard for me to do then. I'm soft now, but in those days I just didn't tell my innermost secrets. I kept those to myself. My only intimate friend was my husband. I wouldn't tell the man why I wanted to go until one day he said, 'Miz Lillian, how is the integration problem in your part of the world?' and then I began to talk. And he said he knew the reason I wanted to go to India was my feeling that the South had been so terrible to minorities."

"Anyway, that's why I wanted to go. I wanted to be of service and to give of myself completely to people who didn't have anything. So I think that was pretty good. And I was so fulfilled. I was able to do everything I had ever wanted to do for the underprivileged and when I came back after two years I had such a grand good feeling of having given of myself entirely."

When she got to India, Indira Gandhi asked Miz Lillian and another woman her age to go into family planning. "I had never dreamed of going into family planning. Although I had been trained as a nurse, I hadn't practiced in forty years, so I hadn't even put it down on my application."

But she gave it a whirl. She went to the small town of Vikhroli, a few miles north of Bombay, where she stayed until her tour was completed. But she found the Indian people were more interested in her nylon hose than contraception. "They wanted to rub my legs and see how my stockings felt."

For three months she taught methods of contraception, but because there were no birth-control devices available, she had to recommend either continence or a vasectomy. The men laughed at her. "Finally, a nice, beautifully educated Indian man came to see me and told me, 'We like you. We've learned to trust you, but the illiterates do not trust you when you talk to them about giving up things and family planning. The only thing these people have is sex. A man works eight hours a day, walks two miles home and goes into his room with his wife and five children and they cook and eat and have sex in one room in front of the children. If you take sex away, they have nothing left.' And then I realized he was right."

Miz Lillian grew more and more frustrated by her failure—and depressed by the disease and poverty around her. "I saw people without a damn thing. Nothing. I saw kids picking wild weeds to eat because they had nothing else. One day the hot wind was blowing. It was during the dry spell. I had to walk a mile to work. My feet were blistered in the summer from the sun and almost rotted from walking in the water. I was outside the factory gates where I worked when I heard a rattling in the weeds. I thought it was a snake, but it was a woman all covered with vermin trying to scratch her way across the road to where there was a small trickle of water. Well, it frightened me to death. I ran back to my house and got food and water and threw it to her and tried to find someone to tell. I went to the factory office, which was a welfare station, to ask for help, but they just laughed at me. I saw a policeman, but he laughed at me, and I ran to the doctor's office, and he was a very blunt man. He said, 'Look Mrs. Carter, you can't change things in a few short weeks. Everyone here thinks you are a member of the CIA,' and I said, 'Well, I'm not.' He said, 'Look, that woman has infectious leprosy. Whatever you do, don't touch her and don't feed her. The leprosarium has put her out on the side of the road to die. They do that with terminal cases.'

"That broke me all to pieces. I never did go by her again. I went around the other way, but I got a little naked boy and what food I had I gave it to him to take to her. Later I hoped he ate it himself."

Despondent, she turned to prayer. "I'm not the dedicated Christians Jimmy and Ruth are. I'm my own sort of Christian, a liberal Christian, I guess. But I learned to pray for something to get me out of this little thing I was in. Every day after work I'd go up to the top of the hill where my home was and be homesick. I said, 'Lord, I couldn't have gotten here without you. You got me over here and if you don't do something I'm going to have to go back home. I can't stand to see all these things and not be able to do something about them.'"

The next morning she was asked to help out in the factory clinic to replace two men who had left because of illness. "It was the biggest miracle that ever happened to me.

"When I got there, no one was around but a sweeper, a little black boy, whose only job was to clean the public toilet with his hands. So I told this boy to cut my hair and he did. I had to wash and wash and wash to get the stink off. And I cleaned up the doctor's office and told God, 'If you let me work with the doctor, and be indispensable, I'll stay the whole two years and be satisfied.'"

Although her nursing skills had accumulated the rust of forty years of disuse, she had no choice but to restore them to working order. She gave seventy-five to one hundred injections daily, administered intravenous feedings, applied belladonna plasters, aided with vasectomies, examined eyes, ears, noses, throats, and ministered to lepers.

The conditions in the clinic were deplorable. Blood dried on the floor overnight. Needles went unsterilized. Vasectomies were performed without anesthesia. Medical supplies dwindled. More than two hundred patients who came through each day, including those with TB, were cursorily examined and sent home. Only factory workers were treated while the poor from the hills were barred outside the gates. In desperation she appealed to the millionaire-owner of the eight-factory complex where she worked. "I opened the door to his office and started crying. He said, 'Lilly, what's the matter? I thought you were so happy now.' I told him I would have to go home unless he did something about the poor. 'Won't you give us some money for medicines? Let the real sick ones from the hills come into the office.' He just said, 'No, no, no, no, no.' But I told him, 'I'm sorry. I can't stand it anymore.' " He finally consented to help if she could pay for the medicines.

Miz Lillian went immediately to the American embassy and wired her son to send her one hundred dollars. Cash in hand, Miz Lillian turned to the doctor for whom she worked to ask for a contribution. "He was a Hindi, and he loved flattery more than any man I know. I told him, 'If I get one of these diseases would you have a place to treat me? You know more than anyone I've ever seen.' I was building him up. I knew more than he did. He was an M.D., but he couldn't pass anything over here."

The doctor told her he couldn't do any more than he was already doing. " 'Well,' " said Miz Lillian " 'I'll have to resign. I'm going back.' I knew he couldn't do without me. I was the best free help he ever had."

He matched her one hundred dollars.

When the Parke-Davis pharmaceutical representative visited the factory clinic, Miz Lillian persuaded him to leave free medical samples. She fabricated an acquaintance with Mr. Parke and Mr. Davis. "I had no idea who they were, but I said I would write to both of them and tell them what good work he was doing. He left two cabinets full of medicine. I learned to steal and lie. I had to do it. I even stole the belladonna plasters. It was my Christian duty."

Lillian prevailed. By the time she left India at the age of seventy, she had established an American-style, completely sterile clinic with a full stock of medications. And she returned to the States with a sense of accomplishment.

Back home she continued her work for the clinic and for her son's campaign by making speeches on India around the state and sending her earnings back, yet she did not focus her attention on the poverty and squalor in her own town of Plains. The dilapidated shacks with tin roofs dotting the Plains landscape and providing the housing for most of the local blacks did not affect her. "India warped my ideas about feeling sorry for people here. The poverty I had seen in India was so great compared to what we have in the States.

"I don't see that kind of need around here. The poorest have so much and what they don't have they get in the form of aid from the federal government."

She left India seventeen pounds lighter, wearing an Indian dress and shoes with the toes sticking through. She had cut her own hair for two years, excepting the one coif from the sweep boy. "I was pitiful. It took forty-five hours to come straight through from Bombay. I could have stopped over, but I just couldn't wait to get home." With only eight dollars in her pocket, she couldn't afford a drink on the plane, and had to borrow money from the customs inspector for carfare from one airport to the next.

Her homecoming was a culture shock. The family was waiting to greet her at the airport with a brand new Lincoln Continental.

And beginning twenty miles outside of Plains, her grandchildren had plastered the trees every twenty feet with signs that said, "Welcome Home, Grandmamma."

Plains sported a poster too. "This is Plains, home of Grandmamma." Even her brick house was peppered with placards. "This is Grandmamma's kitchen, this is Grandmamma's bedroom."

A magnum of champagne, and her favorite culinary treats—chocolate cake, pimento cheese sandwiches and fried chicken—awaited her. She could not touch any of it. "My stomach had grown accustomed to Indian food."

The next day her sister was cooking her turnip greens, pork chops, and cornbread. "That's what I wanted." Rosalynn came by and said the family was planning to eat lunch at the pond. Lillian was moved by her daughter-in-law's thoughtfulness. "She's really nice. She's trying to be right." Reluctantly she tucked her turnip greens and chops in the oven and drove out to the site of the old pond house which had burned down before she left for India. All the way there signs read, "This is the way to Grandmamma's Pond House." When they arrived she was stupefied to discover the modern glass-and-wood structure. "I almost fainted. My children don't always love me that good, but that's because I had been away so long."

The Pond House, where so many high-powered meetings took place between Jimmy Carter and his economic and foreign advisors, and where Walter Mondale stayed when he came to Plains, is probably where Miz Lillian will spend most of her time during her son's Presidency.

Living in the village became practically impossible with thousands of tourists pounding on her town house door. Miz Lillian finally had to hang out a three-foot sign on her brick home that says: POSITIVELY NO VISITORS. And she finally collapsed and was hospitalized with fatigue after shaking tens of thousands of hands down at the depot.

But she can count on solitude at the Pond House. God knows, no one can possibly find it.

There she'll pass her days having coffee with Gloria, walking around the lake, raking her yard, fishing for brown bass, watching football ("Joe Namath's my hero"), hockey, baseball, basketball and the soaps, eating soup, and reading five hours a day.

She will not be any more of a Presidential advisor than she was in the campaign. "I never give Jimmy advice unless he asks for it, which is seldom." And even if she proffers it, he rarely listens, she claims. She wanted Governor Wendell Anderson for Vice President for example, "because he was so good-looking." Jimmy selected Walter Mondale. About the only serious suggestion she ever made to Carter was to play down the Godly passages in his speeches. "I told him to quit that stuff about never telling a lie and being a Christian and how he loves his wife more than the day he met her."

Her campaign role was limited to asking Jimmy for autographs and pictures for friends, signing millions of T-shirts and pictures at the depot, having dinner with reporters at Faye's almost every night and baby-sitting with Amy.

She doubts she will come to Washington except on rare occasions. "I'm worn out."

That is until she sees a TV commercial advertising for someone to run Jimmy Carter's Help for the Elderly Program with the stipulation, "Age is no barrier." Then the queenly matron will stride proudly with her loping gait into the airport and buy herself a ticket to the nation's capital.

CHAPTER 7

ROSALYNN

THE DARK-HAIRED WOMAN stepped on the toilet seat, stood on the toilet-paper holder, and with one mighty swing, hoisted herself over the top of the door and landed in the center of the ladies' room. Wonder Woman? No, demure, violet-voiced Rosalynn Carter, on her way to give a speech. "I was locked in," says Rosalynn, Governor Carter's wife at the time. "There was nothing else to do. The space under the door was too narrow and I was wearing my good suit and a corsage, so I had no choice but to go over the top. My only fear was that someone would walk in and find the Governor's wife scaling down the door in the Powder Room, but I had to do it. My philosophy is you do what you have to do. And I was determined to give that speech."

She was determined too, and angry, one night before the Florida primary when the mayor of St. Augustine did not show up for a Carter fund-raiser. "If he won't come to us, we'll go to him," said Rosalynn, forty-nine but still plucky. She ordered her staff car to take her down to city hall where the mayor was in the middle of a town meeting. Taking a deep breath, she squared her shoulders, thrust out her chin and stood firmly in the center aisle of the cavernous hall like a missionary facing the heathen. After ten or fifteen seconds, the mayor slid his glasses up his nose and squinted his eyes as he spotted the solitary figure. "Is that Miz Jimmy Carter? Come on up here, Miz Carter, and say hello." With a soldierly stride Rosalynn marched up the aisle, and, working her way along a twenty-foot mahogany table, shook every commissioner's hand and a few in the audience. Then, as silently as she came, she left. No one in her traveling party could quite believe the fragile Georgia magnolia had the nerve to interrupt a meeting of the City Fathers. "That was nothing," drawled Rosalynn with a grin of total satisfaction. "I've done it before in other cities. But the last time at least the mayor invited me to say a few words about Jim-meh."

Rosalynn Carter was equally resolute the night of October 8, when, knees quaking, she stood before an audience of two thousand in Washington's Constitution Hall, and with Maestro Leonard Bernstein conducting a full symphony orchestra, she narrated "A Lincoln Portrait" by Aaron Copland. Rosalynn had neither heard the score nor read the text until dress rehearsal, but she never missed a downbeat. "She read with incredible conviction, authority and general pizzaz," said Norman Scribner, director of the Choral Arts Society of Washington, which had taken part in the evening. "An amazing woman," Bernstein said later. Rosalynn Carter was just as amazed at herself. As she made her way through a sea of accolades after the performance she whispered to me, "Can you believe I did that?" "She's one tough lady," says Hamilton Jordan. "It's hard to imagine, but if one person wants him to be President more than Jimmy, it's Rosalynn."

True grit was not always the cornerstone of Rosalynn Carter's personality. A decade ago she could not give a speech, hold a press conference, entertain two hundred for dinner, blitz a shopping center with leaflets, or perform most of the other tasks associated with running for the Presidency. But this shy, soft-spoken Southern woman learned through sheer castiron willpower and the aid of her mate, "Jim-meh," that she could do anything.

Rosalynn Carter's story is more than a Cinderella rags-to-riches tale. It's a story of extraordinary personal growth. "She is someone who has taken advantage of every opportunity to stretch," says Mary Hoyt, her press secretary. "She's an innately intelligent woman who has taken every opportunity she has had to use her capabilities. She gets better at what she does and more sure of herself all the time. She has a very calm core. She's never moody. Everyone has this vision of her as very tough and selfless but she's really much more fun to be with. She's a very happy person with a happy disposition. The campaign is an incredible story of how two people just got in a car and drove from town to town and got in the newspapers and got on radio and TV. Her whole life has just been growing to this point."

I first met Rosalynn Carter when she was First Lady of Georgia, in the spring of 1974 when she and Betty Ford, then the wife of the

Vice President, rode through Atlanta in an open-topped car as part of a ceremony celebrating the opening of a cultural event. Rosalynn, in a blue belted coat, demurely waved a gloved hand at the crowds like a dutiful Governor's wife, stood in a receiving line, attended a ribbon-cutting ceremony, and made a pretty speech introducing Mrs. Ford. She seemed strong and self-confident but inconspicuous. Betty Ford was impressed and told an audience, "She has charm and all the ability any woman in political life needs."

Seven months later, in November 1974, I met Rosalynn in Washington for breakfast. Although she had become a private citizen, she had come to the nation's capital for a conference on mental health, her special interest as Georgia's First Lady. Rosalynn insisted on an eight o'clock breakfast so she would not have to miss any of the early morning meetings. Mary King, Lucy Bryant, wife of a prominent Washington public health physician who was Director of the Drug Abuse Council, and Mrs. Carter's assistant, Madeleine MacBean, joined us at the Shoreham Hotel coffee shop. The idea of the coffee which was arranged by Mary King was to generate further media interest in Carter who was to announce his Presidential candidacy one month later. Rosalynn impressed me as sweet, sincere, genuine, extremely pleasant and good humored, but painfully shy and unsophisticated. Her speaking voice was as soft as a camellia petal and her giggle was as dainty as a child's. But in spite of her outward timidity she boasted of her accomplishments in the field of mental health in Georgia and of her job as Jimmy's bookkeeper in Plains with a sense of liberated pride. She had kept the books at the peanut warehouse and helped to run her husband's business. As the wife of the Governor she had opened one hundred thirty-six mental health centers around the state. "I've always worked," she said. In her delicate way she was telling us she was not your average Southern Belle. She was a force to be reckoned with. She was somebody. Beneath that placid exterior lay a core of strength, ambition, determination, aggressiveness, political savvy and cunning that eventually earned her the nickname, "The Steel Magnolia."

Lucy Bryant, a native Georgian, recalls being sufficiently impressed with Rosalynn that morning that she decided to work for Carter when he announced. "I was touched that she had maintained her interest in mental health even though he was no longer in power, and I was moved by her gentleness and sincerity and her inner strength. She was so well put together I felt like I was talking to a woman who had gone West in a covered wagon and had lived to tell about it." That breakfast marked the beginning of a long correspondence, which Rosalynn kept up through even the busiest primary season. "She was always so thoughtful, especially when I was hospitalized for a back problem," says Ms. Bryant. "She called me from Florida to see how I was, and always sent handwritten notes. I wrote back and told her I was voting for Jimmy just to bring her to Washington."

The transformation that took place in Rosalynn over the next year was remarkable.

"You wouldn't believe her a few years ago. She was painfully withdrawn," says Lehman Franklin, a Carter associate from Statesville, Georgia. "She got better the years he was in the mansion, but the difference in her in the last year is astounding. The campaign really brought her out." Madeleine MacBean says, "I've seen her do things I never thought I'd see her do. She does anything she sets her mind to. She's become a pro in the last year."

"I am shy," Rosalynn admits. "I always have been. I used to be an introvert. I had no self-confidence. But you learn. Jimmy's given me confidence. He thinks I can do anything, and he's convinced me I can. The idea of campaigning was overwhelming to me at first. I had never even met a candidate, no less a President, when Jimmy first started thinking about running in 1972. I had only seen one President from a distance once when we were in the navy and Truman came to christen a ship. Then I met all the candidates in 1972. They came and stayed with us in the Governor's mansion. Most of them drank too much. They said they survived the campaign on alcohol. And none of them were as smart as Jimmy. I knew Jimmy would be a better President than any of them, but still I didn't like the idea of campaigning outside of Georgia. I remember when Jimmy wanted me to go to California, I didn't want to go. I didn't know anybody there, but he said, 'People are the same everywhere.' When I came home I said, 'You're right. People are the same.' The difference is, I can do it."

Carter helped his wife deal with her initial phobias about the campaign and taught her how to squelch the paralyzing fear that overwhelmed her. "The first primary was traumatic, but Jimmy taught me a long time ago that you just do the best job you can do. And you don't worry about things. You just develop a calmness about it. Jimmy says, 'Every single member of our family is doing all he can possibly do, and that's all you can expect.' " It was Jimmy who told her she could relax a bit on her dawn-to-dusk campaigning during the final stages of the race. "Jimmy said, 'We've done everything we possibly can, now just go out and enjoy the last three weeks of the campaign.' "

It was Jimmy who taught her to make notes on index cards and eventually to speak extemporaneously. When he was Governor, he had asked her to give a speech for him to the Georgia Mental Health Association. When she recoiled, Carter wrote out the speech for her word by word.

"I took that speech, and I practically memorized it. It scared me so much. But when I got up there, I was scared I'd lose my place. It was miserable."

That night Rosalynn put her foot down. "I just cannot do that anymore. Ever."

Instead of arguing, Carter sat down with her, gently praised her, stressed her assets, told her she could only do her best. "Why don't you do like I do," he said, "write down a few words as a memory device and then just get up and talk." She softened. She gave it a try. It worked. From that point forward, resolute Rosalynn rose before luncheons, speaking over the tinkle of glasses and bringing the dull hum of conversation to a halt with her smileful voice modulated to full pitch; she addressed Baptist and Jewish congregations, farmers in Iowa, retired citizens in Florida, groups along the railroad tracks in Pennsylvania, Ohio, Illinois, and never so much as glanced at a word. She spoke in simple declarative sentences sprinkled liberally with facts and figures and dramatized with pregnant pauses, fortissimos and pianissimos. There was no question but that by the end of the 1976 campaign she had become a better speaker than Jimmy.

Once convinced she had the ability, Rosalynn set about campaigning like a Sherman tank in a field of clover. She called it "a labor of love." There was nothing stand-offish in her approach. She searched out hard-hats on construction projects and called to men on ladders to come down and talk. She spurned ladies' teas and luncheons, opting for larger forums so she could bring the message of Jimmy Carter to the maximum number of people. She preferred shopping malls, churches, television and radio stations, senior citizen homes, day-care centers, airports, and factory shift lines which she blitzed with the boldness of a dive bomber and the charm of Scarlett O'Hara. "Gud Mawnin'. Ahm Miz Jim-meh Cah-tuh," she would say in barely audible mint julep voice. "Ah wont you to vote foh mah husband foi Prez-ee-dent." With that she would present them with a tiny plastic bag of Carter peanuts or a handful of literature.

Her day usually began at dawn. The first campaign trip I made
with her in February of 1976 we arrived at Florida's Sarasota airport
well past eleven P.M. Rosalynn spotted two pilots sitting and talking
on a couch. Before calling it a day she trotted over for one last
sales job. "I'm Miz Jim-meh Cah-tuh, and I hope you'll vote for
my husband for President." "My pleasure, Ma'am," one startled pilot
replied. Then she gave her little pitch to the man behind the ticket
counter.

Rosalynn's plane was only a three-seat puddle-jumper and there
was no room for this one reporter. Her pilot said he would return
in an hour after he had ferried Rosalynn and Madeleine MacBean
over to Lakeland. But Larry Olson, the pilot Mrs. Carter had just
greeted, was sufficiently smitten by Rosalynn that he rose to his feet
and offered his plane to fly me to Lakeland. "She impressed the hell
out of me," said Olson en route. "She just got herself two votes. That
personal touch was something. She showed that she cares about us.
She's a real working man's candidate. None of the other wives would
have done that. She was real forthright and aggressive. I liked that."

We arrived at Lakeland airport at midnight. Rosalynn was scheduled to shake hands at a factory shift change at four-thirty the next
morning, but she took time out to tell the locals who met us that
her traveling reporter needed accommodations.

Learning there was no hotel or motel in the area, she assigned a
Carter advance man to help. One stepped forward and offered to
move out of his apartment for the night. He would stay with a
friend. The apartment turned out to be the first-floor corner of a
large Victorian house with somewhat primitive conditions. There
were no rugs on the floors, no telephone, towels, or toilet tissue and
no heat. The bed had been stripped and the pillow was a soiled
pillow case stuffed with dirty linen. Rosalynn and her sidekick,
Madeleine MacBean, promised to be back for me at four-twenty A.M.
It was then one forty-five.

I was just dozing off when I heard water running. The bathroom
of the next apartment was just behind my head and a young couple
were making love in the shower. "Oh, David," the girl kept giggling,
"we've got to hurry. I told my mother I'd be home at eleven." The
water ran until two-thirty. I was still wide awake.

When Rosalynn and Madeleine MacBean arrived at four-twenty
A.M. the knock fell on sleeping ears. The next thing I knew someone
was trying to break down the door. It was five-twenty and Rosalynn
had returned a second time, already having been to one factory shift

and on her way to a hospital. "I like to get in a little campaigning before breakfast." She smiled serenely. She did not mention the fact that I had overslept and was still dressing when I fell into the car. "I'm used to seven hours of sleep but I can get by on four now. After a while it becomes routine. Your biological clock adjusts. The night of the New Hampshire primary I went to bed at three A.M. and got up at five and campaigned in South Carolina all day until eight P.M. Then I flew to Plains, went to a rally and never got home till midnight," she said proudly.

Rosalynn stood alone at the hospital entrance at the top of the steps clutching a bundle of green-and-white Carter pamphlets in her left hand, shaking hands with her right. More than two hundred doctors, nurses and orderlies filed by, largely ignoring her. "If one throws the literature back at me, don't be surprised. I've had that happen too," she said. "Good mawnin'. Ahm Miz Jimmy Cah-tuh. I wont you to vote foh mah husban' foh Prez-ee-dent. Ah need your help." Those who did shake her hand looked at her incredulously. "Are you really?" asked one. "Yes, I really am," Rosalynn said with a little smile. "Get all your friends to go to the polls." Turning to her companions she said, "I talk all day till my mouth hurts."

She became annoyed that morning at an advance man who suggested breakfast at a Holiday Inn where she was scheduled to hold an eight-thirty press conference. Rosalynn wanted to eat at a local spot where she could meet the "people." She selected "Jean's Place," a truck stop next to the Dixieland, Florida, post office, where green-and blue-shirted laborers were chainsmoking and guzzling black coffee. After she had ordered eggs and grits, Rosalynn slipped out of her booth and made her way back to the kitchen, greeted the cook and the dishwashers, then sashayed from table to table, singing the praises of Jimmy Carter in her soft drawl while the workers watched her in utter amazement. "I want you to vote foh mah husband foh President."

At the press conference only three reporters showed up at the Holiday Inn to question Rosalynn. She sat proudly in their midst explaining the Carter strategy, his waffles and weaves, his abandoned issues, his mistakes.

DEFENSE: "Yes, to be for a strong defense is a very conservative position and to be for a defense cut is a very liberal position. So it's a waffle, but he's always felt that way."

TAX REFORM: "Jim-meh wants to restructure the whole tax program so all working people would have to pay less. The average man would not have to pay as much, and the wealthier would pay more taxes. Tax experts have proposed this for a long time."

STRATEGY: "We considered certain states to be key. We felt since Jimmy was from Georgia, we had to show we could win in a different section of the country. Ah-wah was the first caucus state. We had to show we could win it. New Hampshire was the first primary and we had to show we could win in a New England state, so we worked hard and we won it. Florida was the next key state. If we won Florida, we could win Illinois. There is no one on the ballot in Illinois except us, Fred Harris, Sargent Shriver and George Wallace. Wallace is the only opposition. If we could beat him in Florida, we'd beat him in Illinois. North Carolina is the next week. North Carolina hinges on a Florida victory too . . .

"Our campaign is different than the others. We're campaigning in the whole country. In every primary. Every single other candidate has targeted key states in which he wants to do well. Udall concentrated all his time in New Hampshire and Massachusetts and Wisconsin. Jackson ran in Massachusetts and New York. We had no choice. Jimmy was not a national figure, so we had to go into all the states. But we have advantages. People are looking for a fresh face. Someone who can excite the country. We never had an association with the Washington scene, and I think people are going to take someone from outside Washington."

She was unperturbed by Carter's Massachusetts trouncing. "It did not upset me, considering the time we put in. You see, the Massachusetts primary was originally supposed to be in the late spring. They changed the date and we had already allocated our time to the other states. We didn't have time to wage a major campaign, whereas Jackson spent four hundred thousand dollars there, took out big full-page ads saying 'I'm against forced busing.' "

THE STEVEN BRILL PIECE ATTACKING CARTER IN *Harper's* MAGAZINE: "Steve Brill is called the Liberal hit man. He was hired by the ABC group (Anybody But Carter.) The article is all false. Brill said we removed things from the archives. But when Jimmy was elected we turned over all our records to the archives. The archivist even called us and said he wished everybody could be as thorough as Jimmy." What about the supposedly missing speeches from the 1970 campaign? "He never writes speeches. He only writes notes."

Eleven A.M. A shopping mall. Rosalynn has already handed out 495 brochures since six A.M.

"I like shopping centers best," she said en route. "You feel like you're doing more. A coffee break is a waste of time. At the most you get to meet thirty or forty people." Then she whispers out of earshot of her advance men. "I can go twice as fast when I'm alone. I can shake hands with twice as many people."

She targets a nest of shoppers in a drugstore. "You live in Illinois? Well, you can vote for him next week." . . . "You're Canadian? Well, I'll give you a leaflet so you'll know who he is when he wins." Hard-hats are soldering in a dark shell of a store under construction. Without hesitation, Rosalynn steps over debris, lumber, a nail keg, to shake hands and dispense Carter propaganda.

As she stalks through the shopping center, the expression on her face is as earnest as that of a Trappist monk.

Sparse. No frills. No airs. She wears sensible black pumps with low heels, a black-and-tan polyester dress. "Last summer I bought things I could pack and wash myself." Her hair is short, simple and coiffed by her own hands. Her jewelry is limited to a pair of inexpensive pierced gold ball earrings, a gold-plated rope necklace, her Annapolis gold-and-diamond engagement ring and wedding band; her makeup consists of a touch of lipstick and finely penciled-on eyebrows. Her nails are short, neat and unpolished. The perfect wife of the people's candidate. Nothing intimidating about Rosalynn. She is Everywoman.

At a cocktail reception at the Oehlschlaeger Art Gallery in Sarasota Rosalynn has changed to green polyester. It emphasizes her pallor. Rosalynn has been scrupulously avoiding the Florida sun because of her millionth allergy. ("I'm allergic to everything." She giggles. "Dust, pollen, cats, dogs, and I break out if I get in the sun. After sneezing and sneezing every morning I finally decided when Jimmy made up his mind to run for President, I would take the allergy shots." She still takes them every three weeks.)

Rosalynn gamely climbs to the top of a circular staircase and addresses a crowd of fifty tanned Floridians. She recites his string of victories . . . second place in Alaska and South Carolina, first in New Hampshire and in Iowa. She stresses the importance of the Florida primary; she makes them laugh with her quiet sense of humor. "I grew up in Plains, Georgia, population six hundred eighty-three. And everyone has ALWAYS known EVERYTHING about us." Then she waxes serious. "And Jimmy Carter has never had any hint of scandal in his personal life. I think he'll make a great President. That's why I'm here. I need your help."

They pepper her with questions about Jimmy Carter's position on foreign aid: "I don't know." About his position on amnesty: "He is for pardoning, not amnesty." About the difference between the major candidates in Florida: "Wallace is opposed to everything Jimmy stands for. Jackson has taken everything Jimmy said out of context. He's been in Washington for thirty-five years and his policy is, if one bill doesn't work, try another. Jimmy knows what it means to work. Jimmy's for a strong defense. He learned about defense from Admiral Rickover. He's a manager. He completely reorganized the bureaucracy in Georgia and made it work." About his foreign policy: "Jimmy has a background in foreign affairs. Over thirty foreign countries are represented in Georgia. He's traveled as a guest in many foreign countries and sat down with the leaders of those countries. He sat down with Golda Meir and General Rabin for half a day. They are now close personal friends. He went to Germany and Helmut Schmidt, who was foreign minister, sat down with us for half a day and discussed energy. Helmut Schmidt was appalled that the United States had no comprehensive energy plan. They had a five- or ten-year plan, that had been published in a book, and Schmidt promised to send it to us. I remember it took four months to arrive because they had to translate it into English for us. Jimmy also served in the Tri-Lateral Commission, which is a committee of experts from every field. They are all assigned problems to study and discuss like the world food shortage, international boundaries, and this has given him a wide picture of world problems and great resources to draw on. He has several very knowledgeable people he can call on for advice."

Her audience stood riveted to her words. They were touched by her fervor and moved by her devotion to her husband. She gave no hint she had said it all before. One black woman said afterward, "This is one woman who has worked with her husband side by side. She knows him." Said a woman named Edna Nottage, "She really sold him to us." Said Edna Reinach, "Impressive in her simplicity. It's so easy to speak in esoteric phrases. She keeps it simple without talking down to you." One Republican woman named Naomi Wertheimer was undecided but stated: "She's certainly a big asset to him. I might vote for him."

It has often been speculated that the forays of political wives into the campaign field have little if any effect. Rosalynn never accepted that. "I can call attention to Jimmy. Then when people hear his name again, they'll listen. I've studied his record as Governor and I know his positions on everything. I can explain them to people who might not understand or might have a question. And I can let people know that we're serious and doing all we can. I think that makes an impression."

And her dogged, eighteen-hour-a-day campaigning seemed to have an effect. One Illinois voter who had been leafleted and soft-soaped by Rosalynn while sitting quietly in the middle of a shopping center remarked, "It impresses me that Jimmy Carter's wife took the trouble to come over and talk to me. I wasn't going to vote in the primary, but now I think I will." Said one hard-hat after a handshake and some peanuts from Rosalynn, "Me and my wife were thinking of voting for him, but we were undecided. Now I know we will."

"I'm going to vote for him," said a surprised young waiter in an Orlando restaurant after a long chat with the candidate's wife. "Any man with a wife like that has got to be all right."

It was close to midnight that day, which had begun at four in the morning, and Rosalynn had not yet had dinner. But before she sat down to her steak and red wine at a roadside restaurant in Orlando, Rosalynn investigated the coat check room, discovered two potential voters and cornered them. "Wow! That's impressive," one was heard to say. "I think I'll vote for him."

Rosalynn shrugged her shoulders about the killing day. "I want Jimmy to be President. If I'm going to do this at all, I'm going to do a good job."

The night of the Florida primary, Rosalynn Carter sat in her suite at the Carlton House in Orlando watching the returns. The early projections showed Carter the winner. Yet when Jimmy arrived at seven-thirty from a long day of campaigning in North Carolina she said nothing except, "How was North Carolina?" "I thought he knew he was winning. He hadn't heard. Finally I put my sewing down and told him, 'We did it.' "

At nine P.M. in a suite packed with jubilant staff members watching returns on three TV sets, Jimmy and Rosalynn stood with their arms around each other's waists and kissed. "She played a tremendous part in this victory," Carter told me. "This was a state we went all out to win. We'd have no excuses if we lost. Rosalynn's been here for ten weeks. She went where I couldn't be. She magnified my presence greatly."

"I feel like the whole family did it," said Rosalynn, "and the Peanut Brigade. We had two hundred and fifty Georgians here for weeks, but we did it with the best candidate. We did all we could do and if we didn't win it, we weren't supposed to."

Important clues to understanding Rosalynn Carter emerged from a visit with her mother, Miz Allie Smith in Plains. Miz Allie lives four doors down on the left from the Carter warehouse in the beige single-level clapboard house with the gray painted porch. Allie Smith has lived in that same house for forty-seven years, since her daughter Rosalynn was sixteen months old.

When "Miz Allie" answered the front door it was startling to find another Rosalynn. Miz Allie and her daughter are look-alikes. They share the same high cheekbones that rise into perfect apples when they smile, the same doe-brown eyes accentuated by finely arched brows, baby skin, a slender build, well-turned ankles and a painfully shy personality. Rosalynn has overcome hers. Allie Smith has not.

"Rosalynn used to be very shy just like me. That's one thing that surprises me so," she began. "I never thought she'd be out making speeches like she is now. I don't know how she does it. None of the others in our family could go out and campaign. I think being married to Jimmy and having worked has made her more interesting and interested in other people," she says, as she shows a visitor into a humble but immaculate living room decorated in tones of yellow, gold and brown, and filled with healthy ferns and china knickknacks.

Allie Smith perches ramrod straight on the edge of a chair, her hands folded placidly in her lap like some once-wealthy dowager forced by fate to endure the hardships of poverty and small-town life. She is nattily dressed in white slacks, a blue polka-dot blouse, black patent shoes and does not look her seventy years.

She does not feel them either, she says, and admits she detests retirement. "I'd rather be working. I'm looking for a part-time job." Allie Smith had been postmistress of Plains for twenty years and only stepped down in January, 1976, because it was mandatory. She barely knows what to do with her time. She tools around town in her car, visits with her son Murray's children now and then, cares for Amy Carter some (although Miz Lillian seems to have a monopoly on Amy), and "crochets lots." For a while she served as postmistress of the Carter campaign, opening the small stacks of mail that arrived daily and sorting them into separate piles for her daughter and her son-in-law. But with the escalation of the campaign and the mountains of mail that inundated the Plains post office, she was replaced by a battery of volunteers. Then she spent only Thursday afternoons from one to five at the little depot headquarters next to the railroad tracks answering phones, folding letters and fixing packages of peanuts to be sold as souvenirs. "I liked it good enough," she said wistfully. She wished she could do more.

Allie Smith never knew much besides the little town of Plains. An only child, she was born and reared there and never left in seventy years except to visit relatives in the South and Midwest on rare occasions. Hers nevertheless was a "comfortable" childhood. Her father was a farmer who raised corn, peanuts and cotton on a five-hundred-acre farm just south of Plains, now owned by Jimmy Carter. "I didn't have to work much. Just did a few household chores. Sometimes I'd pick some cotton for fun. I got real lonesome lots of times. I didn't have anybody to play with till my uncle moved nearby with a daughter my age." Isolation from her peers and from city life bred an indelible bashfulness that still plagues her today.

Allie graduated from Plains High School, like almost everybody else in town, and studied home economics at Georgia State Women's College.

Two weeks after graduation she married Edgar Smith, whom she had known since ninth grade when he was her school bus driver. Smith, a garage mechanic, owned several small farms, including a sixty-acre farm within the city limits, and a three-hundred-and-five-acre farm on the outskirts of town which backed up to her father's property and which Jimmy Carter now rents from her. They produced four children—Rosalynn, Murray, Gerry and Allethia.

Murray Smith, "forty-nine, I reckon," has two master's degrees, one in science, the other in math, and teaches at Tri-County High School near Buena Vista, Georgia. Gerry, forty-seven, who has degrees in civil and industrial engineering, works for a steel company in Illinois. "I can't remember the name." Allethia, thirty-nine, lives in Ellenwood, Georgia, near Atlanta. A graduate of Georgia Southwestern, Allethia worked in banks in Americus and Atlanta until her first child was born.

Miz Allie's was a happy, uncomplicated life for more than a decade. She had plenty of household help to assist with the babies, the cleaning, washing and ironing. But Edgar Smith died of leukemia when Allie was only thirty-three years old and Rosalynn was barely thirteen, and the easy times abruptly ended. The four thousand dollar insurance benefits were enough to survive on for a short while, but after a year or two the payments dwindled. A monthly eighteen dollars and seventy-five cents covered nothing more than water and electricity, and Allie was forced to find work.

She had always sewed for the neighbors, but now she expanded her trade full time, making trousseaus, dresses, even men's clothing. She charged only five dollars for a man's coat. "I always said I charged too little." She laughs faintly. To increase her income, she worked part time in the grocery store and at the post office. Her sons contributed to the larder by delivering groceries for the market and packages for the drugstore. Rosalynn helped with the sewing and for a brief while shampooed heads at the local beauty parlor.

However, as the eldest child, Rosalynn had to fill in as surrogate mother. The long afternoons that Miz Allie worked, Rosalynn was in charge at home making her brothers and sister mind and keeping the household running smoothly. It was a large dose of responsibility for a young girl barely on the threshold of adolescence. "Those long afternoons we were by ourselves at home, Sister—that's Rosalynn—was old enough to know right from wrong and she kept us kids pretty straight," says Rosalynn's brother, Murray Smith.

There was not much fun in Rosalynn Carter's teen years. For a young girl with sparkle, verve, good health and intelligence, life was mostly sheer drudgery, wondering where the next meal would come from. Her mother, once a woman with affection and some happiness in her life, was nearly destitute, drained of her youthful effervescence, a dour, dutiful, hardworking figure whom Rosalynn admired for her devotion to duty but dreaded emulating.

Rosalynn was a blithe spirit. She loved to dance to the radio and to records. She was an excellent student, valedictorian of her high school graduating class. "She always made A's," says Miz Allie. "I remember how hard she studied. There was one subject she was having trouble with, so she'd have me wake her at five o'clock so she could study before school." At Georgia Southwestern College she was selected as social marshal, joined the Tumbling Club and the Young Democrats.

Rosalynn always strove to add a touch of style and fun in her rather drab existence. "I remember when she was fourteen or fifteen," says her mother, "she'd go to town, look in the store windows, draw the things she liked, and then have me make them for her." Later she made all her own clothes. Rosalynn would squirrel away her weekly five dollar carfare and skip lunch so she'd have enough

money for a movie now and then. The biggest event of her childhood was the coming of *Gone With the Wind* to the Americus
movie theater.

But like Jimmy Carter, the death of Rosalynn's father played an
important role in the shaping of her life.

Smith was an affectionate man and a good father. "I can remember how he would come into the house and put his arms around my
mother," Rosalynn told me one day. "And he would carry me on his
shoulders around the dining room table."

Edgar Smith was not a man with big shoes to fill, but he was hardworking and he had dreams for his children. He had wanted more
out of life for them than he had, and one Sunday morning he called
Rosalynn, Allethia, Murray and Gerry into his bedroom before they
went to church. He had been ill with leukemia for over a year and
he sensed the end was near. He told them, "My working days are
over." He also left them with a dictum: "I want you, all of you, to
go to college. I want you to have a better position in life."

Her father's words were a strong beacon but there was not much
encouragement at home. "My mother never pushed me or tried to
be an influence on me," says Rosalynn. "I just wanted her to do
right," Miz Allie recalls. "I wanted her to be a good student and
housekeeper and mother." Rosalynn wanted more. And yet her
goals were vaguely defined. She considered a career in interior deco-
rating, but two years at Georgia Southwestern were not enough to
provide that. She had always lived at home.

It was no wonder she fell head over heels in love with Jimmy
Carter, Plains' prize bachelor. He sprang from the town's aristocracy.
He had wealth, position, and a promising future. Actually Rosalynn
always had a crush on Jimmy Carter from the time he and his family
lived just a few doors down. "I used to think of any excuse to go to
Ruth's house," says Rosalynn. But Jimmy never noticed her. She
was just his little sister Ruth's friend, the teenager who used to sit
and listen to the *Hit Parade* on Saturday night and change the
names of the songs to the names of the different boys they knew. "We
idolized him," says Ruth Carter Stapleton. "We used to go out to the
Pond House to scrub and wax floors just because Jimmy was doing
it too." But Jimmy paid no heed.

He never noticed her "as a woman" until one night when he came
home from Annapolis, needed a date, and asked Ruth to call her.
"Rosalynn and I had been talking about her dating Jimmy," Ruth

told me, "but Jimmy was taking out another girl. I was so excited when I called Rosalynn to tell her he wanted a date with her. She wasn't even there. She had gone to a church party. I had to go get her." They ended up double-dating, going to a movie that night in the rumble seat of a car. "I don't know what made me fall in love with him. I just loved him," says Rosalynn. On their second date, according to Ruth, Rosalynn and Jimmy were sitting in the car in front of her house. When Rosalynn put her head back and looked at the moon, Jimmy said, "Rosalynn, I love you." She said, "Jimmy, I love you too." That was it. They wrote every day. They've never felt any different about each other.

Rosalyn had had lots of other beaus but when she started dating Jimmy Carter, she dropped them. Miz Smith leads her visitor to the room beside her bedroom where she keeps her laundry machine as well as a regular gallery of Carter photos. Among them is a framed snapshot of Rosalynn wearing a skirt and vest and open-toed shoes, cheek-to-cheek with a white-uniformed Jimmy Carter at Annapolis' June week. Both are grinning from ear to ear. "They didn't date very much. They had their first date before he went back to the Naval Academy one fall, another at Christmas, another in February, another in June and that was it. They wrote every day and they were married the July after he graduated. It was a very fast courtship."

It was in the navy that the process of growth for Rosalynn began. Jimmy Carter told me once during the campaign that Rosalynn "changed drastically" during their married life, as did he. In the beginning, he admits, "I was very domineering and demanding." Rosalynn laughs. "That means he made all the decisions." "I never thought of asserting myself or trying to do anything different. I was just happy having babies, going all over the world and feeling very independent to be away from home for the first time. But Jimmy was gone four days a week at sea. And I had to take care of everything. I just learned to assume responsibilities." She did things alone she never dreamed of doing, "like driving from Schenectady, New York, with three little babies all the way to Plains," or "finding an apartment without Jimmy along to approve. I learned that you just do what you have to do."

One major arbitrary decision Carter made, to leave the navy and return to Plains, snapped Rosalynn Carter abruptly out of her silent shell. She fought the decision to abandon ship with all her worth.

She was enjoying the carefree, glamorous naval life, the soft sandy beaches of Oahu, the rolling hills of upstate New York, the proximity to the Big Apple, and mostly, being severed from a double umbilical cord to both her mother and Miz Lillian. She wanted the honeymoon to last. She did not want to be stifled again.

And yet, returning to Plains proved to be a learning experience of major proportions for both Rosalynn and Jimmy. "I think the relationship really started when we returned to Plains," says Rosalynn. "After Jimmy's father died in 1953 we started to build his business back up. Jimmy loaded bags of fertilizer on the trucks. I weighed the trucks, started keeping the books for Jimmy, helping him, and as the business developed, he could come to me and say, 'Does this work, should we continue to do this in the business, should we continue to buy corn? Are we making any money on that?' and I could advise him. I worked hard. Sometimes I worked from six A.M. until eleven P.M. When he was away in the state senate I had nothing else to do."

She did more. She borrowed books from a friend who taught accounting and studied until she knew the subject backward and forward. "I was about to take the exam for CPA. If Jimmy hadn't run for Governor, I would have taken it. I love balancing books. I set up a good bookkeeping system, especially after the IRS investigated his father's taxes. We had to go through all his shoe boxes. That was a mess. I set up a special system so that would never happen again. I've always handled all our money. Both our salaries [she was paid three hundred dollars a month] went into a joint account. I keep the bank payments, write all the checks, do the income taxes, and the children's income taxes. When Jimmy needs some money I give it to him. He never has any," she laughs. (At every restaurant we stopped at during the campaign, Rosalynn was always ready with a twenty-dollar bill to pick up the tab.)

I asked her once whether she advocated that a mother should stay home until a child turned three, or whether she thought a mother could return to work soon after a child was born. "I hope she can." Rosalynn giggled. "Because I did. I worked until the day Amy was born, then I kept the books at home. I went back to the office when she was six months old. And I did more things with Amy when I was working than I would have if I had been home. We cooked together and we'd get out our sewing machines and sew together . . . I think so many women could work. There are so many frustrations they could overcome if they had a place to work as well as a place to leave their children. I know it's better for a woman to work and feel that she's contributing something. I can see it would have been very, very hard if Jimmy was out doing great things and I was home. It would be very tough on a marriage. I feel secure I guess because I've always been doing what Jimmy was doing. I think if I had been left out then I'd be very unhappy."

Just as she was determined to become an indispensable part of her husband's business life, she was hell bent on becoming his political partner as well. In the beginning she knew nothing and cared less about politics. She laughs as she looks back on her ignorance. "Politics was very unimportant to me. My mother was completely removed from it. She just worked all the time. I can remember one time she walked into the Peanut Warehouse and wanted to know who Earl Warren was. She had seen all these signs and bumper stickers saying 'Impeach Earl Warren,' but no one at the post office knew who he was. That's how completely removed we were in Plains from politics. I did not become interested until Jimmy and I got married. He was interested in what was going on in politics so I became interested with him. We were not actively involved, just very, very interested, particularly in Truman's campaign. I remember Jimmy was the only one in the sub school who was for him. But it was all new to me, living in Plains. I had never even seen a candidate."

Jimmy Carter never discussed his earliest political aspirations with Rosalynn. "I don't remember him talking about it at all. He had been appointed to things like the school board, and the library board, the hospital board, and the Peanut Growers Association, things his father had done—but they were always looking for people to do those things. I guess politics was in his blood. It was a natural for him. His grandfather was doorkeeper of the Georgia House of Representatives."

Rosalynn encouraged him to run for the state legislature in 1961. "Jimmy was on the school board and was trying to get a four-year college for Americus. But Bo Callaway was our regent and he wanted it in Columbus. I wanted Jimmy to run so we could get that college." She pushed him four years later to run for Governor. "Our leading candidate for Governor had a heart attack and he was running against Lester Maddox. Well, we couldn't just let Lester Maddox have it. Jimmy went to see different people to try and get someone to run against him but no one would. Ellis Arnall was running, but there was no way he could win. He was a minor candidate, so we felt like we had to do it."

Rosalynn was also one of Carter's earliest supporters for the Presidential race. Once she had met the 1972 Presidential candidates and deemed "Jimmy was smarter than all of them," she thought it a good idea for her husband to run. "Besides, Jimmy's term of Governor was up. And we had a really good business which his brother was running and we had the time to do it." After four years in the Governor's mansion she did not want to go back to Plains again.

She plunged into every race with gusto. During the senate race Rosalynn shunned active campaigning and handled all the campaign correspondence instead. While Jimmy stumped the state, Rosalynn stayed at home waiting for Jimmy to return with dozens of business cards. She would write to his newly made contacts to make sure they were properly thanked for their promises of political and financial assistance and filed away for future use. But following the 1966 and 1970 gubernatorial races, she shed her veil of timidity and struck out on the campaign trail. "The whole family campaigned," she proudly asserts.

Running a Governor's mansion was a new and terrifying prospect for Rosalynn Carter. She had never lived in a large home, particularly a million-dollar mansion worthy of *Gone With the Wind*, with a staff of fourteen. She had never entertained for two hundred. The prospect so haunted her that she finally gave in and called Mrs. Lester Maddox to see if she could give her some advice. "You see, I don't have any idea what goes on in a Governor's mansion. I've never been in one."

Mrs. Maddox helped her, but then told Rosalynn she had done all the cooking for company because she could not find a good cook. "She just scared me to death," Rosalynn says. She also called the wife of the German consul. "She had written books on gracious entertaining. She helped me. She taught me how to set a table, protocol and seating arrangements."

But once in the mansion, Rosalynn plunged in with her usual energy and found that she was up to the job, even if she did once serve the German ambassador collard greens for dinner.

Her Methodist perfectionism dictated her total involvement. She used the platform of Governor's wife to accomplish the things she wanted. "I could help with anything, I didn't even have to have any special powers. I could just ask somebody to do something and they did it. I never had one person turn me down. You can't imagine how many things there are to do, and to me it would have been a terrible waste to have been in that position and not do anything." She chose mental health and drug abuse as her field possibly because two members of Carter's family, Leonard Slappy and Gloria Carter Spann's son Willy Spann had been institutionalized for mental problems. Spann had a drug addiction as well.

(After a long day of touring mental-health facilities during the 1970 gubernatorial race, Rosalynn dropped by a Carter reception and decided to surprise Carter in the receiving line. "Hello, I'm Rosalynn Carter," she said, shaking her husband's hand. "I want to know what you're going to do about the deplorable condition of mental-health facilities in this state if you're elected." Carter rose to the occasion. "I'm going to do the very best job I can, and I'm going to put you in charge." He kept his promise, appointing her head of the Governor's Commission to Improve Services for the Mentally and Emotionally Handicapped. Under her aegis, one hundred and thirty-six mental-health centers sprang up around the state and are still functioning.) "I never worked so hard in my life, but I loved it."

She entertained legislators, businessmen and foreign dignitaries who came to Atlanta. "During reorganization we entertained two hundred fifty to three hundred people for dinner three times a week. I didn't have a housekeeper, and I ran the staff myself." She left the Governor's mansion proud of her social and political accomplishments, and more prepared to become the nation's First Lady. When I asked her if she were terrified at the prospect of running 1600 Pennsylvania Avenue, she replied, "No. I'm not afraid of it. I think I would be if I hadn't had the experience in the Governor's mansion." By 1976 she had not only learned how to be a gracious hostess but also had become a seasoned political pro with canny wisdom and a bottomless well of advice.

She could mix equally as well with the farmers of Iowa as she could with the millionaires of Manhattan.

She campaigned alone performing exactly the same tasks as the candidate himself, shaking hands at factory gates and addressing massive audiences. In April, where Jimmy Carter left off the Democratic National Committee whistle-stop train trip, she picked up.

Rosalynn considered it a duplication of effort to travel with her husband. "I have a lot to say and I feel if I just went with Jimmy, it would be a waste of time. I could be out meeting many more people and helping him. Sure I miss him and I love him very much. It's just that I want him to win."

During the campaign many people were "frightened" by Rosalynn Carter. They called her cold, tough, hard, calculating. They said she wanted to be President herself. That she made statements like, "When you get him, you get me." They charged her with undue ambition.

"Well," said Rosalynn, "I want him to be President to change the things that need changing and the more I become involved, the more I realize how much has to be changed. So instead of getting tired and backing out of the campaign and saying, 'I can't do it,' it makes me work even harder. And if that's ambition, I'm ambitious."

She became incensed if she were considered the typical campaign wife. One day when we were having lunch she said indignantly, "I called a labor leader to ask him to help us with something. And not only did he keep me holding for fifteen minutes but when he finally came on the phone he told me it would take a month for him to do what I asked him. How naïve did he think I was? I knew he could have done it in a couple of days."

She told friends she enjoyed discussing issues and making speeches rather than wasting her time at traditional ladies' functions and talking about home furnishings, campaign colors, fashion and food.

Fashion left her cold. "I have other priorities," she said. During the transition period while Inaugural Ball plans were being made, she was hounded by the fashion industry over her decision to wear the six-year-old ball gown she had worn when her husband was sworn in as Governor. Seventh Avenue sent a representative all the way to Plains with a questionnaire demanding to know why Rosalynn was "doing this to us." Rosalynn resented it. "I like the gown. It has very sentimental value and I'm going to wear it," Rosalynn said coolly. She dislikes shopping. In Georgia she had two fashionable stores, Cohen's and Jason's, send over boxes of clothes. She selected her wardrobe from what was in the boxes—usually drip-dry dresses she could wash herself.

Spartan Rosalynn rarely fit anything into her schedule that was not work-related. She neither smokes nor drinks anything but a little wine. "If Jimmy fixes me a Bloody Mary on Saturdays, I fall right asleep." She had neither the inclination, nor the discipline, she claimed, to keep a diary. She spurned daily exercise and took multi-vitamins instead. Unlike her husband, she found little room for reading anything besides issue papers. She hasn't seen a movie since 1974 and has only been out to dinner with Jimmy twice since the campaign began. She had little time for sorority either. Rosalynn told me she had no intimate girl friends with the exception of her social secretary, Madeleine MacBean, and her daughter-in-law Judy's mother, Edna Langford. "I've never had time for friends. I've always worked too hard. And I never was one for coffee klatches."

Personal questions left her cold. Once when we were traveling in a small Cherokee plane I asked what she would do if Amy were seventeen and having an affair. Her mood darkened. She turned away and looked out the plane window at miles of cloud banks. "I don't know," she said. Would she be surprised? "Of course," she replied, spinning around with flashing eyes. What would be her counsel? "I don't know," she said inaudibly. "I'd have to be in that situation before I'd know what I'd do."

Almost any discussion of things sexual jarred her. A lifetime of Baptist and Methodist training had left her somewhat prudish. Four-letter words were alien to her, and even the subject of homosexuality bothered her. "It offends me. I don't know why."

Rosalynn may act like a camellia, but she is as definite and strong-willed as an ox. Mainly, she did not want to be thought of as frivolous and she was most anxious to impress her seriousness of purpose and her important role as campaign advisor. "I have very strong opinions about everything. And I always let Jimmy know how I feel. He doesn't always react well to everything." Says Jody Powell: "She may be soft-spoken, but people tend to underestimate her. If you've ever been on the opposite side in a dispute, you've made a very serious mistake." Powell recalls the time Carter, as Governor, told reporters he did not think Rosalynn supported the E.R.A. Rosalynn exploded and took it upon herself to correct the misconception with the press immediately. "She straightened it right out, she didn't wait five minutes," says Powell. "She's an ever-present influence on his thinking. She's extremely strong-willed and has an acute sense of political judgment."

"There are very few things Jimmy decides that we don't talk about," Rosalynn said. "Jimmy has always asked my advice when there's been a big decision. I don't mean Angola or things like that. There are many things I don't know about, but when he was Governor he discussed the reorganization of the government with me and he appointed me to the delivery of mental-health services. I wrote the program and gave it to him. It was my white paper he accepted."

Rosalynn gave her advice sparingly, but when proffered it was usually accepted. It was Rosalynn Carter who intervened to make her husband back down on a position for which he had been soundly criticized—advocating the closing of the mortgage interest tax deduction loophole as a part of his tax reform scheme. "I rarely call him on the campaign trail," Rosalynn told me, "but I called him that time and told him people were upset by what he had said. I told him not to try and explain it, just be simple and say, 'I'm going to lower your taxes. I'm not going to take away your deductions.'" Carter did just that.

When Carter made his famous gaffe about "ethnic purity," which set off a storm of protest in the black community and nearly knocked the Carter candidacy out of the ballpark, he went into a funk and refused to talk to anyone for two days about it until Rosalynn called and convinced him to apologize publicly.

Watching the entire Republican convention on television Rosalynn was flabbergasted at the flagrant criticisms of Carter. "They kept saying he was going to be adding so many billions of dollars to the budget." Rosalynn turned to her husband and inquired in her mint julep voice, "Jimmy, you're not going to do that, are you?" He said "Of course not!" She said, "Well, we've got to get that message across to the people, because just watching the convention I would think you were going to add one thousand dollars to their income tax!" "I told him he had to be sure and let the people know that he did not intend to do that, that he intended to manage the government and would then have money for the services." Rosalynn made that the theme of her own campaign speeches.

Author James Dickey says of Southern women, "They're very loving and very affectionate but they really think their men are dependent on them. If their man is brilliant, they think he's brilliant because they've helped him be brilliant. Basically they think their men are weak and could never have gotten anywhere without their help."

Rosalynn felt that way about Jimmy's political career. "I had to manage the business three months a year when Jimmy was away in the state legislature. And I felt very, very important, because he couldn't have done it at all if I hadn't managed the business."

She does not give Carter the entire credit for being elected Governor. To her way of thinking she and her family were an integral part of his victory. "We've always worked together on everything. And we've always had a tremendous sense of accomplishment, like when Jimmy was elected Governor. It was not that Jimmy got elected Governor. It was that we all did. And when he was Governor, we all worked. The children worked. Chip helped in the afternoon after classes. Jeff and Jack both worked." She took it upon herself to get him elected President as well.

I once asked her during the grueling 1976 campaign why she campaigned five days a week, twenty hours a day, when most campaign wives, especially those with small children, just made occasional sorties and at a considerably more leisurely pace. Rosalynn smiled and shrugged, then giggled with her sidekick, Madeleine MacBean. "I don't know. Why do I do it, Madeleine? It's a labor of love. Besides, I won't have any regrets if he loses because I'm doing everything I can possibly do. If he loses I won't feel like I haven't done my share."

She prides herself on her involvement in the early strategy sessions of the campaign, as well as vice presidential, foreign policy and health meetings after the nomination. "I feel like I have some input." And she will not cease her participation in serious affairs as First Lady. Although she promises fun parties and occasional square dances, it would not be like Rosalynn Carter to remain in the family quarters of the White House and not occasionally drop by Cabinet meetings. She will lobby for a National Day Care program and direct her most serious efforts toward her ongoing interest— mental health. "You make of it what you want to," Rosalynn told me. "I just knew when Jimmy was Governor there were a limited number of things I could do, and therefore I worried about my priorities. I feel the same way about the Presidency. There's no end to what I can do in the White House."

"She'll be more like Eleanor Roosevelt," Jimmy told me. "She'll be active in both her domestic and foreign programs, and she'll help me to carry out mine, both in this country and abroad. She will do what she did as First Lady of Georgia. She probed to see how she could be of service to the people. She involved herself in programs to combat alcoholism and drug abuse as well as in the arts. She took the initiative in mental retardation. She'd come to me and say, 'This is what we need to do.' She'd come back to me and write a description of what was necessary and that's what we implemented. It was innovative and workable."

Would he object if she were to be as outspoken as Betty Ford? "No, I wouldn't object," Jimmy laughed. "If I did, it wouldn't do any good!"

PART

III

JIMMY
CARTER

CHAPTER 8

THE BOY

JAMES EARL CARTER, JR., was born number one son to the number one family in Plains on October 1, 1924. He was raised in Archery, a black section of the area. Even in the bad times the Carter family represented money, power, prestige, social standing, aristocracy. Rural Kennedys, if you will.

Earl Carter was a plantation owner. His simple clapboard house may not have had white pillars but he owned a thriving farm industry and thirty-two hundred acres of farmland. Two hundred blacks manned his plantation. He ran a store next to his house, which supplied the locals with overalls, work shoes, sugar, salt, flour, meal, Octagon soap, tobacco, snuff, and rattraps as well as products off the Carter farm: syrup, side meat, lard, cured hams, loops of stuffed sausage and wool blankets. He bought peanuts from other farmers to process and eventually began to sell fertilizer, seed, and other supplies to neighboring farmers. He owned an insurance business and a dry-cleaning store. He served on every important community board—the Moose Club, the Elks, the Sumter County School Board, and became one of the first directors of the Rural Electrification Program in the area. In 1953 Earl Carter was elected to the Georgia state legislature.

In spite of what Jimmy writes about their simple family farm life—"For years we used an outdoor privy in the back yard for sanitation and a hand pump for water supply," *—they lived well com-

---

* Until Jimmy was nine years old, the family pump was in the back yard. Water had to be hand pumped both for household use as well as for all the livestock. With rural electrification in 1933 also came electric lights to replace the kerosene lamps the family had used until that time.

pared to their neighbors. His sister Gloria giggles about Jimmy's log-cabin version. "Everybody else in town had to go to the well. At least we had a deluxe pump on the back porch and a windmill so we had running water. Jimmy never had to get up at four-thirty and neither did I." Miz Lillian says the Carter family farm house "had electricity as soon as everyone else in the countryside." And while Jimmy was growing up they had plenty of household help, a cook for a dollar a week, and a black girl named Annie Mae who worked for the family from the time she was thirteen for fifty cents a week, baby-sitting and rolling the children in their carriages. Gloria recalls, "Mostly she played with us and told us fascinating stories."

"We were an average family," says Miz Lillian. "We weren't poor. We had plenty of food and clothes." Earl Carter used to brag that he had one of the first cars in the county—a Model-T Ford. After Earl Carter died, leaving an estate valued at approximately a quarter of a million dollars according to some, a million dollars according to others, Miz Lillian graduated to a string of three or four Cadillacs ("Mah one luxury is a cah") and also a Lincoln Continental.

Mr. Earl also had a piano (Miz Lillian played), a large record collection, ("Every record that ever came out," says Gloria), and an old pool table which they kept on their front porch. "When Daddy's friends would come out," Gloria remembers, "sometimes he'd casually say to me, 'Go-Go, come out here.' Their faces would absolutely drop to see some little kid come out and start playing pool, but I beat the slop out of 'em."

The Carters also owned tennis courts as well, although it probably cost less than one hundred dollars to haul in clay by mule and wheeler and to flatten it with a slip-scoop. "The only expense was chicken wire at three dollars a roll and it took six rolls to fence in the tennis court," says a friend. And the family owned a spacious pond house made out of pine with a thirty-five-foot rumpus room that Earl loaned out to anyone who wanted to use it for wedding receptions and junior and senior proms. "The community nearly tore it down from overuse." It burned down mysteriously. The Pond House is where Jimmy learned to dance to the music of the old Carter jukebox. "Usually he'd fill out one girl's prom card and dance with her all night," his mother recalls. "He just liked girls. But when he got older he liked the wild ones."

Earl Carter was Prince of Plains. A jolly, stout man, slight of stature but generous of heart, he was well liked by the community. In spite of his traditional Southern attitude toward blacks, he believed in noblesse oblige, often caring for families in need without telling anybody about it. Although he paid them a pittance, black workers knew they could go to him for loans and handouts and he was always forthcoming. One black in Plains told me that when his wife was sick in the hospital Earl Carter came to his door almost every day to inquire after her health. "He'd always say, 'If there's ever anything I can do to help, let me know.' " When he died, two hundred blacks came to his funeral and wept.

Jimmy's father helped whites as well. Mrs. Eleanor Forrest, who taught Jimmy when he was eight years old, recalls needing sixty dollars to get the school piano tuned. She had collected most of it, but lacked twelve dollars. "I told Earl and he just reached in his pocket and gave it to me."

His children followed his example. Mrs. Forrest remembers Jimmy coming to her one day and saying, "I'm going to give you my mother's diamond ring. My daddy can get her another one." And Ruth came to her once and presented her with a pair of her mother's shoes.

Earl Carter's magnanimity toward the blacks who worked for him did not signify any acceptance of them as social beings. In a segregated society he was just as prejudiced as his peers. Like his brother Alton, he called them "niggers." He neither went to school or church with them, nor was he buried with them. Even Bishop William Johnson of the African Methodist Episcopal Church in Archery, who had spent many an evening singing Baptist hymns in Lillian Gordy's home when she was a child, was barred entry at Earl Carter's front door. If Johnson wished to see Jimmy's father, he would park in front of the Carter store and send one of his drivers to the back door to tell him that he would like to speak with him. The only black face that ever saw the inside of Earl Carter's parlor was Bishop Johnson's son, a college-educated youth whom Miz Lillian once received in her living room. When she did, Earl Carter left.

Living for thirty years with a man who, according to Jimmy Carter, walked out the back door if a black man came in the front, was not always easy. And yet Miz Lillian becomes fiercely defensive if someone suggests that Earl was an incorrigible segregationist. When *New York* Magazine Writer Orde Coombs said to Miz Lillian during an interview, "Your son says that your husband was a segregationist and all the black people around here who knew him say he was a terrible man," Miz Lillian rose in her chair, jaws set tightly. "Earl was of his time. He was not like me, certainly, but he did not stop me from doing what I wanted to do. You are too young to know, but I am talking about the Twenties when we had nearly two hundred black people working for us on our farms. It shames me now to talk about it, but they made practically no money. So they couldn't pay for any medical expenses. Well, I would go to their homes and nurse them and deliver their babies. And Earl, yes, Earl, would pay for their expenses. He never interfered with me, and in spite of everything, he was compassionate. Oh, he said things. He believed in the black man's inferiority, but he was no different from all those people around here and all over the country who are now trying to pretend they were never prejudiced. Earl would have changed like everybody else who has changed. It annoys me to hear people denounce him when he was simply a Southern man who lived at a certain time."

Carter told me in an interview that "There was nowhere in the South that black people habitually went to the front door, or went to the same bathroom or sat on the same seat in a bus. That didn't come till later after my father died. He would have been just as eager to change. He was a segregationist. There was never any doubt about that. But there wasn't any animosity against blacks. He bent over backward to treat them fairly and openly. And if you talk to the blacks in Plains you would never hear a critical word.

"He was very much loved and respected by black people. There was no challenge, even back in those days in the Thirties and Forties among any of the even more militant blacks against the segregation of our two societies, but it would be a travesty for a white person to try to cheat or take advantage of a black. That would have been a terrible thing to have done. The division between the races in schools and public places was very rigid, and it wasn't challenged by anyone."

Growing up in the predominantly black community of Archery, most of Jimmy's early friends were black. "There were seven or eight of them living on the same farm with us. Sometimes they were employees and sometimes they weren't." If they worked for his father, they all worked together in the fields, sometimes sixteen hours a day. And when work was done, they played. They rolled steel barrel hoops with a heavy wire pusher, slid down pine straw hills on the old disc plow blades, hunted with sling shots and flips, flew homemade kites and Junebugs on a string and threw spinning projectiles made of corn cobs and chicken feathers. Jimmy Carter recalled, "We dug honey out of bee trees and harvested wild plums, blackberries, persimmons, chufa, and sassafras roots. We built dams on small streams and tree houses where we lived overnight or for weekends. We hunted arrowheads in the fields."

But just as they called his father, "Mr. Earl," the black farmhands and their children called him, "Mr. Jimmy." They opened doors and gates for him. He was "mass-uh." It was not until Carter left for the navy following college that he realized the racial attitudes of Plains were abysmal and archaic. Yet he only once discussed race with his father, and when he realized that centuries of tradition were too firmly ingrained, he never broached the subject again.

When he was not playing with black children, he often visited his cousin Hugh Carter, four years older than he, whose family was as wealthy as Jimmy's. They played football, basketball and baseball together. "Jimmy was no star," says Hugh. "He was a medium player, but he was O.K." They rode horses. "One time we were riding an old yellow horse out at Jimmy's house and the horse bucked Jimmy off and broke his arm in two places." They built a swimming pool fifteen feet long by six feet wide in the creek or "branch" that ran through Jimmy Carter's back yard. "We'd go swimming in our underpants. Sometimes we'd run our hands in the corner of the pool and catch crayfish and sell them to folks who were going fishing." And they played in a sawdust pile about a mile behind the Carter house. "Jimmy would come and spend the night with me and we'd sleep out by the sawdust pile and cook a side of bacon and swim in the Rabbit Branch and hunt sweetshrub and honeysuckle for our mothers, and look for arrowheads. That's still Jimmy's main hobby." Sometimes they'd hitchhike to Americus to see a Tom Mix movie. They'd watch traveling medicine shows, log cutting contests and circuses when they came through town.

Hugh and Jimmy never received an allowance; in spite of their prosperity, their fathers wished to impress upon them a respect for hard work and the value of a dollar well earned.

To raise money, Hugh and Jimmy started a variety of joint business ventures. They ran a mini-McDonald's—a hamburger/hotdog stand on Main Street, hawking five-cent weenies purchased from Alton Carter's grocery store. "We made the hamburgers ourselves with onion and chopped-up bread and cooked them over an oil stove," says Hugh. When Jimmy was nine and Hugh thirteen they opened an ice cream concession outside the old bank, and sold three dips for a nickel. "Our mothers, of course, would make the ice cream for us. We colored it red to give it color, but we had other flavors as well, like chocolate and vanilla. Saturday afternoon and Saturday night we'd sell as much as six to ten gallons."

They also dragged little red wagons around town collecting old newspapers from whoever wished to give them away. "Then we'd sell to two blacks who had a fish market and sold mullet fish." And they scavenged scrap iron which they peddled for twenty cents per hundred pounds.

Earl Carter put his firstborn son to work in the fields and around the house. Carter's chores as a small boy began at dawn. Before school, he carried water to field hands, toted wood to the fireplace and coal stove, and stacked peanuts. Carter would walk two miles home after school, and finish his list of tasks for the day. Since most of his classmates lived in town, he could not enjoy their comradeship. He had to work. "I remember when he was older, his friends used to drive up to the house and ask him to go with them, but he used to just smile and wave and go on doing his work," says Miz Lillian.

Jimmy led a sheltered, isolated farm life with few friends. His role model was an authoritarian father whose love he had to earn by dint of top-flight performance in all things.

"Earl Carter was a fun-loving man," says an old Carter school chum, "but he was a disciplinarian. When he gave an order, it had to be done. And Jimmy adhered to that."

Carter told me one day in an interview, "Daddy never assumed that I would fail at anything. If Daddy told me to go to the field to bring back something or carry out a task, he never doubted I would do it. I don't have any doubt about my children either. If I tell Chip or Jeffrey or Jack to go five miles out in the country and bring back two six-ton loads of peanuts, I don't have to worry about it. I know they're going to bring in those loads of peanuts. If the tractor bogs down in the field or if the wheel comes off the wagon and spills all the peanuts out in the middle of the road, they'll never call me. They'll correct the problem and it may be four o'clock the next morning, but they'll come in with those peanuts. I think my daddy had the same expectation from me.

"Daddy was extremely intelligent, hard working and sure of himself, and a very close friend to me, but always . . ." Carter paused and looked out the window, "always very much in charge. I never disagreed with anything my father told me to do. I sometimes thought he was telling me to do the wrong thing, but I'd never let him know it. He never told me to do anything. He called me 'Hot,' and he would say, 'Hot, would you like to turn the sweet potato vine this afternoon?' or 'Hot, would you like to go and fix the windmill?' He never said, 'Go fix the windmill." And I always said, 'Yes sir, Daddy. I would like to.' "

Earl Carter was Jimmy's only real companion for many years, and he tagged along with his father on his rounds. "Daddy worked a lot, but I participated as much as I could." Carter continued. "See, I was the only boy. Billy's thirteen years younger than I am. So I was Daddy's only boy and we were very close. When my daddy would go fishing when I was little, ten or twelve years old, with a group of other adults, he would take me along and we would wade in the creek. I was an excellent swimmer by the time I was three or four years old. And when he went hunting, went to a dove shoot, he'd take me along to pick up the doves for him. When we rode around to the different farms when I was too young to work, I would go with him and when it got real hot in summer, I would lie under a tree and sleep until Daddy got through in the field and came back. We were very close. I slept in the back room where there wasn't any heat, all my life, in the northeast corner of the house, and during the times when I was very young, when my mother was out nursing, I would come in and get into bed with my father and sleep with him."

But for every fond memory, there was a harsher one. Although Miz Lillian never laid a hand on her offspring, Earl Carter brooked no impertinence, "sassing back," or dishonesty from his children. Transgressions were met with swift and painful justice in the form of a peach-tree switch. Jimmy recalls each of his six whippings vividly. Once he was beaten when his father discovered that he had not only kept the coin he was supposed to put in the offering plate at church, but had pilfered one as well.

Another time he was paddled for running away from home. Says Miz Lillian, "I had told him not to do something he wanted to do and he got very mad and ran away. But he didn't go very far. He went to the gate and hid behind the garage door. He stayed there all day and when his father came home he asked where Jimmy was. I told him, 'I think he's down behind the garage door.' And when it got dark, Jimmy came back. And his daddy took him into the bathroom and gave him a lil' talkin' to and then he gave him a little switchin' with a lil' ole peach-tree switch. No, not a whippin'. You Yankees don't know the difference between a whippin' and a switchin'."

Earl Carter was not a man to be teased. Jimmy tells the story of his father's first tailor-made suit arriving. The tailor had made it much too large for him, but no one in the family dared to laugh or even smile.

Earl Carter's formal schooling was cut short in the eighth grade when his father died and he and his brother, Alton, had to go to work to support the family. Earl wanted to make sure none of his children would have to suffer the same deprivation. He not only stressed the importance of education, he demanded that his children stretch their minds to the maximum. He demanded only the best. His motto was, "You're not better than anyone and no one else is better than you."

Gloria recalls, "He thought he had the most beautiful daughters in the world and the smartest children in the world." And he never let them fall short of his expectations. "No mark was ever good enough," she adds. "If we got ninety-seven Daddy would say, 'Why didn't you make a hundred?' " Gloria recalls. "If we got a B we were sentenced to dig ditches. He was never happy with our grades." This later caused strong resentment among the Carter children.

While Earl emphasized education, Miz Lillian stressed the importance of the children saturating themselves in good literature. Reading was of paramount importance in the Carter household, often to the exclusion of conversation. The entire family read constantly. "We always took a book to the table," Gloria says. "At least everyone except Daddy, and we never talked at the table. In fact, we never talked very much at all."

"I'm an avid reader," says Miz Lillian. "I made them read. I allowed them to read books at the table, especially if they had a few minutes before the school bus." Earl Carter brought nothing to the table. But Miz Lillian excuses his disinterest. "My husband had bad eyes." Earl was more inclined to read the Bible than Balzac. He read the Book of Ruth every night. "That was his favorite. That's how Ruth got her name," said Miz Lillian.

Like his mother, Jimmy read day and night. He liked to lie on his stomach on an ottoman and read. Whenever he was asked what he wanted for Christmas or a birthday, Jimmy would reply, "Books." At the age of four his godmother gave him a set of the complete works of Guy de Maupassant. When he was twelve his teacher told him he was ready to read *War and Peace,* a title Jimmy associated with cowboys and Indians. He was disappointed when he discovered that it was not. Nevertheless it became one of his favorites.

Reading at the table is a habit Carter has maintained all his life. Jimmy's friend John Pope recalls that when he and Carter were building a community swimming pool, they went to the Carters' home for lunch every day. Carter would read a magazine or a book throughout the meal while Pope and Rosalynn conversed. "And when he had finished eating, without losing his place or taking his eyes off his magazine or book he would move over to the couch, stretch out and read until it was time to go back to work." Carter told me, "There's hardly a meal ever gone by that we were in the privacy of our own home that we didn't take something to the table to read. At Rosalynn's family's house they read three or four things simultaneously, newspapers, magazines. There's an adequate chance to talk. No constraint there. It's pretty impossible to avoid Amy telling us what she's reading about. We have a good, easy-going relationship."

Learning was a pleasure for Carter because of a unique teacher named Miss Julia Coleman. Besides his father and Admiral Rickover, Miss Julia was one of the three most important influences on Jimmy Carter's life.

Carter has written of her: "As a school boy who lived in an isolated farm community, my exposure to classical literature, art and music was insured by this superlative teacher. She prescribed my reading list and gave me a silver star for every five books and a gold star for ten book reports.

"Miss Julia remains alive in my memory. She was short and somewhat crippled, yet she was quite graceful as she moved along. Her face was expressive, particularly when she was reading one of the poems she loved or presenting to a class the paintings of Millet, Gainsborough, Whistler or Sir Joshua Reynolds."

Miss Julia was a special fan of Franklin Roosevelt's. She served with Eleanor Roosevelt in a special group that selected textbooks for high schools. She also was a polio victim and, like the President, overcame her handicap to lead a productive life of service to others. Miss Julia was once invited to spend a night at the White House, and her tales about Washington and the White House and her descriptive stories about the President sitting with his little dog, Falla, on his lap, made vivid the White House and the Presidency to all her students, and to one in particular, Jimmy Carter.

Although Carter was a first-rate student, who surpassed the others in his class without much effort, he was more of a scholar than an athlete or leader. His classmates remember him as brilliant but timid, and slightly uncoordinated. He was the kind of boy who did not like to play in the yard and get dirty like the other little children; whose jeans were too short for him and often reached just to the tops of his brogans; who was fast on the basketball court as a forward, but never a star player; who never became president of his class, or vice president, or treasurer or secretary, or anything. He studied debate with Miss Julia, but it was painful for him to get on his feet and talk. No matter how many times Miss Julia yelled "Projection!" at him from the back of the room, little Jimmy never could feel quite comfortable. Jimmy says, "We had debate on Friday, but it was hard for us who were timid or backward. I used to get very nervous ahead of time." Classmate Richard Salter adds, "He was on the debate team and his facts and material were always tops, and he could give you quick references, but his delivery wasn't tops."

"He wasn't shy," his sister Gloria remembers. "He was little. He was only five foot three when he went away to college. He was always wondering if he'd ever grow. Of course he did, but he was never really aggressive either until recently. He was never a leader except in the family because he was the oldest."

In an interview one day Carter told me he does not recall having an inferiority complex because of his height. "I don't think it bothered me any. I was very small but I was on the first team in basketball. I grew about three inches my first year in college. Yes, I was shy, but a better word would be isolated. I grew up away from civilization to a great degree. I would go to Plains, which was two and a half or three miles away, and walk back home along the railroad tracks in the afternoon. My life was centered on the farm. I may have had some feelings of insecurity. I had such a different world to live in. I liked to read and study and learn, or to be in the woods and the swamps. And my daddy was very strict with me. When I got home from school there was always a list of things for me to do, some chore like bringing in the firewood, milking the cows and keeping the yard swept. I was expected to do those things. It was a full-time job from six o'clock till dark. We went to bed early when it got dark because we didn't have electricity, like nine o'clock. That's when Glenn Miller used to be on. And they would let me stay up and I'd lie on the floor in front of the fireplace and listen to Daddy's battery-operated radio for fifteen minutes and go to bed.

"The family was so close knit. It's hard to imagine in this modern technological world how small our world was. It was built around the house and the field, and the classroom, and on Sunday the church, and that was it. There wasn't any opportunity for me to go away from my father and do different things. I was with my daddy and my mother almost all the time."

CHAPTER 9

THE MAN

GETTING TO KNOW JIMMY CARTER was one of the most baffling experiences of my life. Even intimate staff members have been known to say the process of understanding Jimmy Carter is mystifying. One of them said, "To know Jimmy Carter for six days is to love him; to work for him for six months is to detest him and after six months you begin to respect him."

Reporters who followed him during the campaign were continually befuddled. "I've been down here for six weeks," one Associated Press correspondent in Plains told me, "and I just can't get a handle on him." One radio correspondent told me in late October, "I've covered him for months. I don't understand him and I detest him, but I'm going to vote for him with my eyes shut because I think he's more intelligent and better than what we have now."

Few liked him or found camaraderie with him as they did with Robert Kennedy, although they respected him and stood in awe of his brilliant, facile mind. Most had an uncertain and inexplicable distrust of him. The comment I heard again and again was, "There's something about this man I just don't like. And I don't know what it is." And yet countless reporters called him "the most interesting politician I've ever covered." As verbal scientists they found their subject fascinating to dissect.

More words and air time have been devoted to Jimmy Carter than probably any other Presidential candidate in memory, and yet after all the punditry, analyses and appraisals, very few claim to know what kind of person Carter really is. Only days before the election

I found both newsmen and people across the country who still did not feel they knew what Carter was about or who they would vote for.

After following Carter on and off for ten months on the campaign, and having interviewed him six or seven times over a two-year period, I still find Jimmy Carter an enigma. The public image he creates and the image that lurks beneath the surface do not always square.

The motto of André Gide could best be applied to the Georgia peanut farmer. "Do not understand me too quickly." Carter is not just complex, he is contradictory. His paradoxes are multiple. He is at once vain and humble, sensitive and ruthless, soft-hearted and tough, conservative and liberal, country boy with city wisdom, spiritual and pragmatic, loving and cold. He can be fascinating and dull. His sister Gloria once told me, "He's the most boring person I ever listened to." His speeches could sparkle or flop. He is not open to others. His innermost thoughts and desires seem known only to a few. Looking back over the thousands of words I have recorded, few reveal the inner man. He does not take easily to new associations. His friends are few, and his enemies legion, particularly in his own state of Georgia, where it is said he could not return to run for anything, so he chose instead to run for President.

My perceptions of him over a two-year period were as complex and contradictory as he was himself. At one moment, he seemed unimpressive, small, average, pleasant enough, but hardly Presidential. At another moment he could be the statesman, grappling with the most complex issues of our day. He could put an audience of labor leaders to sleep, stir an audience of blacks to tears.

When I first began to write this book, all I could do was draw up a list of adjectives most often used to describe him: cold, strange, intelligent, complex, tough, vindictive, ambitious, moral, fair, interesting, fascinating, driven, single-minded and honest.

Personally, I find when I am in Carter's presence I am mesmerized, overcome by his charm. He can be hypnotic as a snake, tantalizing as a spider, and he is as disciplined, spiritual and brilliant a man as I have ever met. And yet, five minutes after I've left him I find myself questioning the favorable impression.

It was difficult to have a simple conversation with him. Carter disdained small talk, always wanted to get to the heart of the matter. No interview was ever preceded with small talk. "So what do you want to know?" Carter would say. And he revealed little of himself.

Most questions he answered the same way to reporters, over and over, as if by rote.

He is silent and withdrawn, serious and solitary, often totally introverted. The stewardess who served Carter exclusively during the last two months of the campaign on Peanut One complained to other flight attendants that she was "miserable." He sat looking down with his left hand shielding his eyes throughout the flights, reading or thinking. Carter never acknowledged her presence or spoke to her. And ex-speechwriter, Robert Shrum, recalls how Carter would often just stare out the plane window or at the bulkhead. "I think I'm isolated or withdrawn sometimes," Carter said by way of explanation, "but I don't have timidity to meet people." Staff members explained his airborne introversion as normal. It was, after an eighteen-hour day, or in the midst of a hectic schedule, his only time to think and get himself together.

I have never heard him say anything genuinely funny. Sarcasm is his sword. He would often take a swipe at others. Once when Curtis Wilkie of the Boston *Globe,* a paper that attacked Carter in the beginning and later endorsed him, asked him during an impromptu plane conference if he had any self-deprecating humor, Carter replied coldly, "I'd have to check my character analysis in the Boston *Globe* to find out."

Late in the fall, when Carter's physical exhaustion was manifesting itself in Fordian fluffs, Mississippi-born Wilkie asked Carter if he were tired. "No," Carter answered, never willing to admit a weakness. "Well, why the scrambled syntax?" asked Wilkie. Snapped Carter, "It's just a Mississippian's inability to understand English."

At a September breakfast for Carter in Des Moines, Iowa, Tom Whitney, an early Carter supporter, told the audience how he had shown up an embarrassing twenty minutes late for Carter's first appearance in the state. He didn't know in those days, he said, that Jimmy not only came on time but that he came early. When it was Carter's turn to speak, he wasted no time in castigating Whitney with a grin. "As I recall Tom, it wasn't twenty minutes. You were forty-five minutes late!" With that, Carter belly-laughed for what seemed an eternity. It was one of few times I heard Carter genuinely amused. Tom Whitney's face turned scarlet.

Carter also embarrassed Jim Wooten of *The New York Times* at a Seattle press conference. Wooten, one of the *Times'* prize political writers, was asking Carter to explain his semantical distinction between pardon and amnesty. "I always get confused about this,"

Wooten began. He spoke slowly, thoughtfully, trying to make sure he had Carter's tricky self-made definition right. "You say that amnesty means you were wrong, pardon means you're forgiven right or wrong . . . now . . ." Just as Wooten was coming to his point, Carter cut him off. "Do you have a question?" he asked.

Just before the New Jersey primary, Carter speechwriter Pat Anderson and I were talking to Carter near the front of the plane when he mentioned something about the latest joke being passed around. "They're saying 'Jimmy has a peanut,' " said Carter. When I began to laugh at the double entendre, Carter looked at me and said, "What kind of a sense of humor do you have, Kandy?" and stalked back to his seat. End of conversation.

Robert Scheer mentions in his article in *Playboy*, "Jimmy, We Hardly Know Y'all," that after interviewing Carter for hours on end, Carter invited him to a fish fry at the Pond House, telling Scheer it would be mostly family, and a good time to see the Carters at ease. (In the meantime Jody Powell opened the event to the press.) The afternoon of the fry, Scheer was on the porch, chatting with Gloria and Walter Spann when Carter walked over, kissed his sister on the cheek and shook Walter's hand. He totally ignored Scheer. "What made it even more awkward was that he began to speak about the press in unflattering terms to Gloria and Walter, as if I were not present," Scheer writes.

"The press people are afraid I'm going to eat a fish bone and choke on it," Carter told Spann. "They're afraid they won't have a picture when it happens." According to Scheer: "The tone wasn't bantering; it was more on the bitter side."

I had a similar experience with Carter in Iowa. After many hours of taped interviews with him, and weeks of travel, I dropped off to do some other writing. When I returned for a campaign trip through the West Coast and Midwest, Carter seemed aware of my presence, but never acknowledged it. Not that one expects formal salutations or personal greetings from a candidate, but normally they were forthcoming from Carter. This time, silence. One morning in Des Moines, after about five days of silence, I tailed Carter around a dozen or so breakfast tables while he greeted supporters. I was within three or four inches of him, taking notes, but each time Carter turned in my direction to move on to another table, it was as though I were invisible. I attributed it to his single-mindedness, and yet it made me feel awkward.

This contrasts with earlier treatment I received from Carter. For example, one April morning in Detroit as Carter was leaving a press conference, I was standing near the front of the room leaning against a wall taking notes when he suddenly stopped his Secret Service, reached out, placed both hands on my shoulders, and stared soulfully into my eyes without saying a word. After five or six seconds, he released me and walked on. It was not a lustful leer, rather more of a blessing-greeting. He did it another day when I went to his house in Plains for an interview. Carter walked out of his study in to the formal living room, followed by Rosalynn, took me gently by the shoulders, looked into my eyes and said nothing.

Carter gave me his special blessing a third time, in April at a dinner for black business leaders in Philadelphia. Again, I was following Carter around the tables, listening to him banter, when he saw me, walked over and greeted me with his soul stare. That was the last time, mainly I think, because I had looked so perplexed each time that I must have made him feel uncomfortable as he did me. At any rate, that was the end of it.

Ethel Allen, a black surgeon in Philadelphia who received similar greetings from Carter, called it "his Jesus bit." "He comes up to me, puts his hands on my shoulders like he's giving me his blessing or something. Another time, he'd cup my face with his hand, ever so gently, like he was the Messiah. It drives me crazy. I got real itchy when he did that. The thing is, it works. Most black people think it's fantastic."

I have since heard that the laying on of hands is Carter's very special way of saying hello or telegraphing an unspoken message. For example on election night, just after the news came that Jimmy Carter had been pronounced the winner, there were hugs and kisses all around, but only Jody Powell, Carter's long-time sidekick and press secretary, received Carter's blessing of the eyes and then a hug.

Some worried about Carter's Messiah complex. An aide once told me Carter said he left the military because "the Lord didn't want him making weapons of war anymore." And his friend Lehman Franklin told me he had tried to dissuade Carter from running for President, but Carter indicated that it was meant to be.

I asked him once if he felt he was fulfilling his "mission" by running for President, but Carter denied it. "I don't feel like I've been anointed to be elected or there's some destiny I have to be President, but I have derived my own sense of confidence from the meticulous planning and the assessment of my opponents and the correlation with issues I think are key concerns of the people of this country. The first two years we planned my campaign, the presumption was that I would be running against Kennedy and Wallace and I still felt that I would win. I saw some strengths that I had and some potential I had, and full-time campaigning outside of Washington, a superb, harmonious campaign staff, detailed organizational structure, freshness, and some political handicaps that Kennedy and Wallace may have had that made me confident even then, but I never have had the feeling that I had to win, or that I was destined to win."

And yet from the very beginning of his campaign, Carter said over and over again, "I will be President," or "When I'm President," or "I don't intend to lose." And friends like Mrs. Eugene Wyman recalled Carter telling her back in 1975 he felt certain he would not only be nominated, but would be elected.

Carter's friends were often amazed at the almost inevitable course Carter's campaign took. "Why, it's just like a master plan. It just had to be," said Betty Pope. And Carter himself was bemused at the way his life had seemed to fall into place. Just before the third debate he called his friend John Pope and asked him to come over to the house to talk for a few hours. Carter reminisced about old times. He had started out as a young man with no political plans, he said, but after his father's death he had become president of the Lion's Club and the Georgia Peanut Growers Association and a member of the school board and had then run for the state senate, and if the results of the senate race had not been reversed, he would still be a peanut farmer. He was glad too that the bank he, Pope, and John Deriso tried to start back in the Sixties had fallen through at that time, "or today, I would just be president of a bank."

Webster's defines megalomania as: 1) a mental disorder characterized by delusions of grandeur, wealth, power, etc. 2) a passion for, or for doing, big things; hence, 3) a tendency to exaggerate. Carter fits the second two categories.

"Arrogance? I can't deny it," Carter told me. "I would prefer not to use the word arrogance, it has some domineering connotations. But it certainly is true that any person who hopes to be a member of Congress representing five hundred thousand people, or a Governor representing five million, or a President representing two hundred million people has a lot of ego. You have to think you could not only beat your opponents, but also that you could serve adequately. There is some substantial aspect of ambition and a search for recognition and power. There's no doubt about it."

From childhood, Carter was a shy, retiring boy, who as Allie Smith, Rosalynn's mother says, "Just sat around with a book in his hand," and was never particularly aggressive or outgoing, until he grew older. But he always had dreams—not medium-sized dreams, that any normal child has, but giant-sized dreams. Jimmy was not content just to go to the Naval Academy and become a midshipman. For Jimmy it was admiral, and CNO, the highest position in the navy. "From the time Jimmy was five there was no doubt that he would be an admiral," his sister Gloria told me. Why an admiral? "Why go to all the trouble to go to the Naval Academy if you were not going to go to the top? It was just always assumed he would be CNO."

When he changed his course and abandoned the military for politics, his eyes were again on the summit. Gloria says her brother was thinking about the White House even before he ran for Governor the first time. "I'll never forget it because when he decided to run for Governor, I asked him if he were going to run for President. He said he thought he had waited too late. Jack had been President at forty-two and Jimmy was thirty-eight when he got started in politics."

Carter responds by saying, "I don't have any doubts that the conversation took place, but I think my ultimate aspiration was to be a United States Senator. When you're the junior member of the Sumter County School Board, the U. S. Senate is a very exalted position. And that was just a distant dream. When I was Governor, it wasn't long before I started thinking about running for President. I'd only been Governor eighteen months when I decided to run for President, so that was a fast evolution." That was one of Carter's few understatements.

Exaggeration is one of Carter's most noticeable traits. "We've had possibly the best-organized campaign the country's ever seen," Carter told me one day. He told voters over and over, "My strength lies in an intimate relationship with the people of this country. I don't think there's a single race-car driver that hasn't been in my house," Carter told tobacco growers and beer distributors in South Carolina. "No powerful politicians endorsed me," he often repeated, forgetting about Mayor Daley and George Wallace. In New York City, after a Garment Center rally in October, he told volunteers that the crowd that welcomed him was the biggest since the return of Douglas MacArthur. He had forgotten about Pope Pius XII, the Beatles and John Glenn.

Often exaggeration bordered on absolute untruth. Carter is fond of saying that when he was Governor he cut the number of agencies in Georgia from three hundred to twenty-two, when in actual fact there were only sixty-five budgeted agencies when he started out. He also claimed to have eliminated 2,100 unnecessary jobs, but State Auditor Ernest Davis points out that these jobs existed only on paper. No jobs were eliminated, and the number of state employees increased from 34,322 to 42,000 during Carter's term in office.

And Carter's claim to the American voter during the primaries, "I'll never lie to you. I'll never mislead you," was not necessarily so. Carter was fond of telling crowds about how he used to get up at 4:30 A.M. to hitch up a mule, that he grew up poor without electricity and running water. But both his mother and Gloria deflate those statements. "We had electricity as soon as anybody in this region had it, soon as rural electrification went through," counters Miz Lillian. His campaign pledge to appoint "new faces" to his Cabinet also seemed to be forgotten once he was elected. The Georgian not only chose a predictably conformist Cabinet, but one that included two Washington lawyers as well as men who were involved with the architects of the Vietnam War and the Bay of Pigs invasion; and in spite of his ostensible rapport with blacks, he picked as his Attorney-General Griffin Bell, a man insufficiently committed to civil rights and liberties.

Carter has told other tales about members of his family that were at best, dubious. Sally Quinn of the *Washington Post* wrote that Carter had told her in an interview, "When he and his wife, Rosalynn, have arguments, he will take her by the hand, lead her into the bedroom and they will kneel by the bed and pray aloud to God, each one telling his or her side of the story, then they will embrace each other," but when confronted with the story Rosalynn replied, "That's Greek to me." Rosalynn told me, "We don't pray over disagreements. I might pray myself, but I don't kneel down with Jimmy and pray when we have an argument. I've never done that. We've prayed together once or twice in our married life over very difficult situations. For instance, when Jack dropped out of school to join the war to go to Vietnam, but not just to settle arguments."

Carter told me that Rosalynn knew about his lusting in his heart after other women, but when I asked her about it, she said they had never discussed it, "never had any reason to."

Carter has little tolerance for the faults of others. Lateness particularly galls him. Once when Carter was Governor, a Georgia commissioner came huffing and puffing onto the runway at Atlanta Airport at seven A.M. for a departure at that hour. Carter was on board the plane that had already begun to taxi down the runway. When Carter spotted the man, he instructed his pilot to take off. "If he can't be here on time, it's too bad," Carter said.

During the early primaries, Carter once left the press behind at Keene Airport when his chartered plane was late arriving. Refusing to wait, Carter sped off in a staff car, leaving reporters assigned to him to fend for themselves. They didn't catch up with Carter until some three hours later.

At four o'clock the morning of his election, an impatient Carter stalked back to the press section of Peanut One, looked at his watch and told Jody Powell it was time to take off, although the second press bus had not yet arrived at the airport. Bus Two had followed a police squad car that took a wrong turn but Carter neither knew nor cared. All he knew was the schedule called for take-off forty minutes after the Carter traveling party had departed Atlanta, and the forty minutes were up.

Carter's temper usually manifests itself in icy stares and snide remarks. Aide Tim Kraft tells the story of scheduling Carter for a press conference in New Mexico early in the campaign, causing him to be late. En route in a private plane, Carter ordered the pilot to fly low and ignore the bumps. "Remember," he glowered at Kraft, "I'd rather be fifteen minutes early than fifteen minutes late."

But often his pique would slip out unexpectedly, like the time he was approached by a small boy outside a subway station in Boston where Carter was passing out leaflets on a bitter February afternoon. The child, who had been enlisted to help with the leaflets, was so enraptured by the presence of a celebrity that he could not resist dashing up to Carter and squeaking at him, "What's your position on welfare?" The first time the boy trundled up Carter ignored him. But the second time he pushed him away with his hand. "Get out of my way, will you?" Carter steamed. The boy skulked away dejected.

And at a press conference outside his home in Plains in the spring, Carter demonstrated his imperious streak. All cameras were in place except CBS, which was still setting up. "Wait a minute, can you?" the producer called to Carter. But Carter was not to be directed. "Are you running this press conference or am I?" Carter tongue-lashed the producer.

Carter's temper is not always limited to icy eyes or stinging remarks. After the first debate he is reported to have hollered in rather high decibels at members of his staff about the failure in ABC's sound system, which left Carter and Ford standing on stage with nothing to do except stare at the audience for twenty minutes. Late that night one staff member told an acquaintance over a drink that Carter bellowed words to the effect: "How could you let me stand there and make a fool of myself for twenty minutes? Why didn't you do something!" as though it were their fault.

And yet, for all his arrogance, his sarcasm, temper, Napoleonic tendencies and his isolation, Carter can be tender, immensely human and compassionate. Maxine Wiggins, a clerk at the Best Western Motel in Americus, whose son Devane grew up with Chip Carter, recalls the time in 1966 when her husband, Charlie, fell from a ladder and broke his back. Recuperation involved four months in the hospital and almost one year out of work. The Wigginses could no longer keep up the payments on their home. One evening, just when they were worrying where the next nickel would come, "Mr. Jimmy" knocked at the door.

"I had my apron on and was cooking dinner," says Maxine. "Mr. Jimmy and Charlie spent quite a time talking in the living room. When he left, he gave us a brown envelope and said, 'This is just a token of our appreciation.' When I opened it there was eight hundred and fifty dollars in cash that he and his friends had collected from everyone in town. Then because Charlie couldn't get to Bible class Jimmy brought the class to our house. For eight or nine Sundays they conducted the class right in our bedroom with Charlie propped up on pillows." Ten years later when President-elect Carter heard Charlie Wiggins had been stricken with a massive heart attack, he sent eighteen roses and invited Maxine, her daughter, Cindy, and infant granddaughter, Charity, to come to the house for a visit. "He even sent a car to pick us up at church," said Maxine, "and he spent an hour with us and let us have our pictures taken with him and the baby."

Unlike other candidates, Carter seemed to be genuinely fond of children. Although I noticed in particular Ronald Reagan's painful awkwardness with little people, in comparison, Carter was the great Earth Father. And compassionate. When he discovered, for example, that a prominent Washington newsman's daughter had leukemia, he wept. Then he went out into the fields searching for arrowheads to send to her as a gift. He felt no hesitation about picking up babies and kissing them gently or having extended conversations with preschoolers. I was unprepared for the kindness he showed my six-year-old daughter, Brooke. When I covered the Illinois primary, I took Brooke with me to Chicago to visit her grandparents, Mr. and Mrs. Louis Meyer. After the primary, we rendezvoused at O'Hare Airport for the return trip to Washington. As it turned out, Carter would be on the same plane. Before boarding, Carter, who came sweeping through the airport at twenty miles an hour, stopped to meet my mother-in-law and her sister. Then he noticed Brooke. As is his wont with small children, he bent down to ask her name and her age and to tell her about Amy. He did this as he often does with children by whispering into her ear, as though they were intimate friends. "I have a little girl just like you. Her name is Amy—and she's eight."

Brooke, who normally exhibits a cautious reserve with strangers, fell head over heels in love. She pleaded with me to let her sit with him so she could talk to him again. I explained he was a very busy and important man running for President and did not have time to sit with little girls. In the tourist section Carter had the window seat in the first row. The seat between him and his aide, Greg Schneiders, was unoccupied. As we passed, Brook paused and looked longingly at the vacancy. "She says she wants to sit with you," I teasingly told Carter as we passed.

"I can't think of anything I'd rather do. Come here, Brooke." Brooke's eyes widened to full aperture as the Presidential candidate lifted her over Schneiders and placed her gently in the middle seat she had so coveted. After we were airborne for fifteen minutes I came to collect her. Brooke and Carter were engrossed in conversation and Carter again insisted that she stay. The conversation, to the best of Brooke's recollection, went something like this:

BROOKE: "How many hours a day do you work? Do you work as hard as my mommy?"

CARTER: "I work about fourteen or fifteen, sometimes eighteen."

BROOKE: "Why do you read so many newspapers?"

CARTER: "Because I want to know what people are saying about me."

BROOKE: "Are you going to be President and live in the White House?"

CARTER: "Yes, and when I am, you must come and play with my little girl, Amy. She's eight years old and she would love to have you come over."

Forty minutes passed. I was concerned Brooke would be pestering

Carter with too many questions. Just then Greg Schneiders appeared. "The Governor wanted me to tell you that Brooke has eaten all her dinner and is being a very good girl."

Ten minutes later after the trays were cleared I gave Carter one more opportunity to have a free moment to study his issue papers. This time when I approached to take Brooke back to her own seat, he was leaning over her, drawing a cartoon on the spiral sketchbook she carries for plane trips. Ironically, it was a Model-T Ford going down a steep hill.

As the plane landed, Carter had to deplane quickly to be interviewed by television newsmen who were waiting for him, and left Brooke to wait for me at his seat. But as we left the airplane he was standing in the hall waiting to make sure Brooke had gotten to me all right. "Just wanted to make sure everything was O.K. Thank you, Brooke." He smiled. "I enjoyed it."

If journalists are meant to be objective, are not their daughters? However, from that moment on, Brooke was smitten. She watched every news program that had anything to do with Carter, lobbied for him at her second-grade mock election, came to the convention and even stayed awake through his acceptance speech (although my five-year-old son slept soundly) and watched much of the election-night coverage November 3. When I called from Plains to say I was on my way home, Brooke squealed into the phone excitedly, "Mommy! Guess who won?!"

Until press relations became terribly strained during the general election, whenever he saw me, Carter never forgot to inquire about Brooke. "How's my sweetheart?" he would say.

A particular baby I recall Carter kissing with greater affection than usual one gnatty August Sunday morning outside the Plains Baptist Church, turned out to be his godson, seven-month-old Sean Mahoney Robbins. And Sean's parents, Anne and David Robbins of Rockville, Maryland, told me an interesting story about Carter.

Anne Robbins, a portly woman in her thirties with a cherubic Irish face, dancing blue eyes and a gold donkey pin from JFK in her lapel, has been active in Presidential campaigns since the age of seventeen when she was John Kennedy's youth coordinator in Pennsylvania. Today, a middle-class housewife, she is also the sort who became so incensed by Richard Nixon's wrongdoings, that in 1974 she wrote hundreds of letters to Congressmen, labor leaders, Governors and influential members of the press urging that he be impeached. Having read in *People* Magazine that Carter branded

Nixon the first person to occupy the White House who was person-ally dishonest, she fired off a letter to Carter as well, and received a speedy reply. She was deeply impressed with the eloquence of the letter, so much so in fact that she showed it to a friend, former Kennedy associate Dave Powers, exclaiming that Carter sounded like another Kennedy. Powers laughed at her.

That was the beginning of a lengthy personal correspondence be-tween Anne Robbins and Jimmy Carter. They wrote about politics, but they also wrote about literature, such as *Pilgrim's Progress* and the books by Baron Tweedsmuir that President Kennedy loved, and about Dylan Thomas. Anne's husband, David Robbins, an adminis-trator with the Department of HEW, had occasion to hear Carter speak several times and was also impressed. Both wanted to meet him. Carter had become interested in meeting Anne. She had ap-prised him in her letters of her long background in politics and her many contacts in Boston and Pennsylvania, and told him if he needed file cards on political people, it would be good to keep in touch. One morning in October 1974, Anne received a call from Madeleine MacBean, saying, "Y'all got to come down." Carter sug-gested a meeting at his office in the state capitol.

The next time her husband had a business trip to Atlanta, Anne went along. Her audience was a fifteen-minute session in the Gov-ernor's office at the state capitol. "I was ushered into his office at eight o'clock one morning when he was on his way to the airport," Ms. Robbins recalled. "And I'll never forget it, because he had the same charismatic impact on me as John Kennedy did."

Carter told her he was going to run for President and could use her help. "I thought to myself, 'He doesn't understand, it's im-possible. He'll be viewed as a kook.'" She changed the subject and they turned to a discussion of Lord Melbourne and John Buchan and *Pilgrim's Way*. Carter talked about how more people in public life should read. He also invited the Robbinses to come down and spend a weekend in the Governor's mansion with him and Rosalynn. "When I left there, my head was spinning," says Anne Robbins. "I found his presence so powerful. It was almost a religious experi-ence."

In December the Robbinses accepted Jimmy Carter's invitation and drove to Atlanta in their Chevy Vega for their night at the Gov-ernor's mansion.

Carter came bounding out the front door in his "peanut clothes" Anne remembers, and showed them to the Presidential suite.

That evening they ate with Rosalynn and Jimmy and Amy upstairs in the family dining room and talked politics. Anne peppered him with strategic political advice, emphasizing that no matter what he did in the grass roots, he should not neglect powerful political leaders like Mayor Daley. Who should be included in the Democratic Convention, if Carter ever got that far. "What amazed me was that he really listened. He didn't seem to care that I was a woman, he didn't seem to care about our station in life. He treated us as equals." One thing she noticed about Carter was that he was "very blunt and brusk." "I was amazed when I saw him hugging and kissing in public during the primaries. I said, 'That's not him.'" At one point during their conversation she asked Carter what he thought of Spiro Agnew. Carter told her, "I always found him very approachable." Thinking of Agnew's alleged acceptance of cash under the table, Anne teased, "Yeah, especially with a brown envelope." Carter did not find that funny. "He just glared at me."

That evening Carter invited the Robbinses to accompany him to a speaking engagement he had before a group of environmentalists at a supporter's house, and she recalls that en route Carter freely discussed political strategy with his aide Hamilton Jordan. Carter did not seem inhibited by the presence of two strangers in the car. "He just seemed very open about everything."

Later, back at the mansion, they repaired to the upstairs den where Rosalynn wrote notes at a card table, Amy took a bath, and Anne and Carter pursued a lengthy discussion of Bob Dylan's music and the poetry of Dylan Thomas. Anne recited some Gaelic poems she knew, and in return, Carter not only marked his favorites in her book of Thomas' *Collected Poems*, but he began to recite a number of them by heart. At two o'clock Carter was still going strong. He vanished to the kitchen for a minute and reappeared with a large tray of Scotch and sodas.

One Dylan Thomas poem he knew from memory and recited with enthusiasm was reminiscent of his life on both sea and farm, of his Huckleberry Finn-existence as a child. It was the story of a boy, born as he was in October, entitled appropriately, "Poem in October."

After that he recited yet another poem by memory in his soft Georgia accent, a poem about death which had fascinated him for many years called "A Refusal to Mourn the Death, By Fire, of a Child in London":

Never until the mankind making
Bird beast and flower
Fathering and all humbling darkness
Tells with silence the last light breaking
And the still hour
Is come of the sea tumbling in harness

And I must enter again the round
Zion of the water bead
And the synagogue of the ear of corn
Shall I let pray the shadow of a sound
Or sow my salt seed
In the least valley of sackcloth to mourn

The majesty and burning of the child's death.
I shall not murder
The mankind of her going with a grave truth
Nor blaspheme down the stations of the breath
With any further
Elegy of innocence and youth.

Deep with the first dead lies London's daughter,
Robed in the long friends,
The grains beyond age, the dark veins of her mother,
Secret by the unmourning water
Of the riding Thames.
After the first death, there is no other.

"I didn't understand the poem," recalls Anne. "I kept questioning him about it. So he would recite it again and again. I thought how morbid. Perhaps he had had a child that died. Finally I understood from the last line that he was talking about his father. And I understood that he had felt about his father the way I did about mine." Anne's father, a manager of a Social Security office in Pennsylvania, had been interested in politics like James Earl Carter, and often took her along to various political gatherings. "My mother and my brother never wanted to go. They never cared about it, but I loved it, so my father groomed me to do the things he could not do publicly because of the Hatch Act. But he pushed me to get A's in school. He drove me, and it was not until after his death that I realized how much I really loved him. I realized we had had a similar experience."

The death of his father in fact was probably responsible for Jimmy's entrance into the world of politics and the transformation of his life. Before that he had never given consideration to any career but a naval one. As a small child, Carter was tantalized by the seas and the lure of far-off ports of call that he learned about from his first hero, Uncle Tom Gordy. Tom Gordy, his mother's youngest brother, served as a radioman in the Pacific during World War II. He often sent young Jimmy letters and photographs from exotic places and before he even entered the first grade, Carter has said he set his sights on the Naval Academy at Annapolis.

To a rural Southerner, selection by a military academy was the highest honor a young lad could attain. It had to do with Southern ideals of chivalry and gallantry, and the Southern tradition of hunting. It had to do with macho and leadership and the fact that because the South was eliminated from the ruling political caste, it could therefore monopolize the military hierarchy. Carter pursued the goal with every ounce of mental and physical energy he possessed. He read books about the navy and Annapolis, wrote away to ask about the entrance requirements, almost memorized the Academy's catalogue, enthusiastically planned and studied.

His lifetime commitment made the years of homesickness at the Academy and the rigors of military discipline tolerable, and his career provided him the opportunity to finally visit such faraway places as Jamaica, Trinidad, Puerto Rico, the Virgin Islands, the Far East and for him and Rosalynn to live in Hawaii, New London, Connecticut, and Schenectady, New York.

He rose through the ranks swiftly, qualified to command submarines, and was accepted into the navy's prestigious nuclear submarine program where he went to work for Admiral Hyman Rickover, who had a profound effect on Carter's life, "perhaps more than anyone except my own parents," Carter writes.

To Carter, Rickover, like his own father, was an example of hard work, competence and authority, a man who demanded total dedication from his subordinates, as Carter was later to do with his own staff. He inspired fear and awe and exacted only the best from his staff, rarely complimenting his men, but was swift to criticize. These were all traits Carter assumed himself.

More significantly, Rickover also caused Carter severe misgivings about his failure to exert maximum effort in his endeavors, a failure he would never tolerate in himself again.

During an interview with Rickover, the fierce admiral queried Carter on a variety of subjects ranging from electronics and gunnery to music and literature.

Finally Rickover asked him, "How did you stand in your class at the Naval Academy?" Carter swelled with pride at having finished fifty-ninth in a class of eight hundred and twenty. But Rickover was unimpressed. "Did you do your best?" he asked. Carter gulped hard. "No, sir, I didn't always do my best."

That admission of failure haunted Carter for years, and finally surfaced as the title of his own personal biography, timed to appear before the election. (By that time, of course, *Why Not the Best?* was a double entendre, meaning, why not the best man? Jimmy Carter.) Carter, so naturally intelligent that he never had to study diligently at Annapolis even to get the highest grades, was determined never to be lackadaisical again. From that meeting with Rickover, it was his best performance only. And the morning of his election, as we walked from the polling place to Billy's office, I asked Carter how he felt now that the campaign was over. "Satisfied," he smiled. "I did the best I could."

Carter's job, he recalled in his biography, was "the best and the most promising in the navy," and his contact with Rickover was stimulating and challenging. He had no intention of leaving the navy.

But the death of his father was a trauma that erupted into the classic identity crisis most youngsters go through in adolescence. For the first time he began to examine his life's purpose and what his roots meant to him. Carter left home at sixteen with contempt for a father who issued impossible demands, who offered love then withdrew it in punishment. His last memories of him were as an unschooled, extremely authoritarian figure. He stayed away for eleven years and rarely returned until he received the news his father was dying of cancer. The day Earl Carter died, James Earl Carter, Jr., discovered that his father had been much more of a man than he believed him to be.

Rosalynn told me that when Carter and his sister Ruth went out to tell the farmers of his father's death "Jimmy heard things about his father that day he had never known. It made a great impact on him when he learned the things his father did to help other people. They went to see the customers, out in the field on the tractors, and Jimmy came home just really shaken. He said no matter who he talked to, black or white, they'd just fall across the tractor and weep, and say, 'He was the best friend I ever had.' 'If my child didn't have shoes, he got shoes for him, to go to school.' 'If I had a child sick and couldn't afford a doctor, Jimmy's father would get his mother to come.' " Rosalynn continued:

"One woman said her husband had gotten sick and died back in the early Thirties when nobody had any money, and Jimmy's father brought her twenty-five dollars a month for over two years. That was a lot of money back then, and she said if he hadn't done that, they couldn't have lived. They were destitute. His father was really a great man. And Jimmy came and said to me that he could spend the rest of his life in the navy and never mean to anybody what his father meant to these people in Plains. That's when we decided to come home. And I know, if he hadn't gone out and visited those farmer customers that day, I don't think he would have gotten out of the navy, because he liked what he was doing, but he felt that his life would mean more if he came home." From that day forward he vowed to relinquish his selfish ways and carry on his work, to be to the community the pillar his father was, to do for others as his father had.

Carter seemed to experience what Professor Robert Jay Lifton describes in his book, *Death in Life,* "an immersion in death." Lifton wrote:

"The embrace of the identity of the dead—may, paradoxically enough, serve as the means of maintaining life. For in the face of the burden of guilt, the survivor carries with him, particularly the guilt of survival priority, his obeisance before the dead is his best means of justifying and maintaining his own existence. But it remains an existence with a large shadow cast across it, a life which, in a powerful symbolic sense, the survivor does not feel to be his own."

When Jimmy Carter returned from the navy to assume his father's role in running the family peanut business, he began to will himself into an avatar of his dead father. He became involved in the community. He joined the Sumter County School Board and the hospital board which his father had belonged to. He ran for the Georgia legislature as his father had. In fact, he even kept certain articles of clothing that had belonged to his father. His friend John Pope recalls going on a quail-hunting trip with Carter once with a group of influential friends. Jimmy showed up in his father's World War I cavalry leggings and lace-up boots to wear on the shoot. "I was almost embarrassed for him, but he didn't care," says Pope. Pope finally persuaded Carter to borrow some of his more conventional hunting clothes.

Rosalynn remembers she never knew Jimmy was interested in running for election "until he got up on his thirty-seventh birthday on October first in 1961 and put on slacks instead of the khakis which he always wore to the warehouse and I said, 'Where are you going?' and he said, 'I'm going to Americus to see who's going to run for the state senate.' He came back home and said no one from Sumter County was going to run for the senate and asked me what I thought about it, and I thought it was great. I was all for it. But that was the first time I ever knew he was thinking about it."

Carter inherited two characteristics that are at the core of his personality. They are competition and religion. His central values are toughness and morality, determination and discipline.

Carter's father instilled in him an almost obsessive compulsion for educational growth and self-improvement, competition and victory. "Winning was always important to mah daddy. He was very competitive and I think I got that from him." Carter told me, "We used to have a tennis court alongside the house and I was a good tennis player as a child of say, twelve, fourteen or fifteen. But I never beat mah daddy. He was an excellent tennis player. He was too good for me." And since as a boy Carter was small, shy and poorly coordinated, it made him try even harder to keep up with the pressure of competition.

Carter was never a particularly good basketball player in high school either, according to his schoolmates, but although he was never "a star," he made up for his lack of height and coordination by being the fastest on the team and the smartest in his class.

When Carter was a teenager trying to enter the Naval Academy, he knew he could never pass the physical entrance requirements because of flat feet, but he rolled his arches on Coke bottles every day until they measured exactly the right space off the ground.

I once asked Carter if he thought of himself as a finished man. "No," he said, "I like to think I'm still growing." When he was in his thirties he took a Developmental Reading and Study Skills course at Georgia Southwestern with Rosalynn and their best friends, John Pope and his first wife Marjorie. Mrs. Llewellyn Finkle, his teacher, remembers Carter had "more determination in the course than anyone. He set out to see how far he could go with it. He was reading up to five hundred words per minute with ninety to a hundred percent comprehension when he came in. Halfway through the course the machine checked him up to a thousand words per minute with a hundred percent comprehension and if you gave him a book he could read more than two thousand words per minute."

Already excellent dancers, the Popes and the Carters also took lessons in square dancing at the Americus Country Club once a week, "just for fun," to become proficient in more of the intricate swirls and turns. "I remember once we went to a rally on Labor Day, 1975, in Blue Ridge, Georgia, in Fannin County," says Pope, "and they had a square-dance band in the high school gym. Well, Jimmy and Rosalynn were the first ones on the floor. They just started to do-si-do country style and the people couldn't believe their eyes. They were like professionals. That entire county voted for him in the general election."

Today, Carter reads constantly to enrich his mind. The minute he was elected President he said he was going home to study and "learn how to be a good President."

Jimmy Carter makes a concerted attempt to keep up with the times. When he was Governor, already knowledgeable about classical music, he turned to rock in order to familiarize himself with modern music. He told me during an interview, "I used to be obsessed with classical music when I was a midshipman and when I was in the navy. Then I started to listen to Bob Dylan's music primarily because of my sons, but I got to like it and I used to spend three or four hours a day listening to Paul Simon, Bob Dylan and the Allman Brothers. At home I'd study government reorganization or budgeting techniques while I listened to rock."

During his own Presidential campaign he punished his body beyond endurance, working longer and harder than anyone else. While other candidates started often as late as nine o'clock, Carter started at 4:30 or 5:00 A.M. pumping hands at a plant gate factory shift change. Said Carter, "I can get up at nine and be rested or I can get up at six and be President." While other candidates napped, Carter turned off for a while by staring out the window of the plane before emerging rejuvenated for the next leg of the trip. While other candidates finished their campaign days at midnight, Carter often pushed on until one or two in the morning.

While those of us in the press corps moaned and groaned at the five o'clock baggage calls and the days that sometimes required a morning of rallies on the West Coast, an evening of rallies back East, and a Midwest rally in between, Carter did not see the grueling campaign as hard work. "I've always worked this hard," he told me one day as I collapsed into the green-and-yellow swivel chair facing him across a conference table on Peanut One.

"I didn't work any harder than I did ten or fifteen years ago. I enjoy the working, the planning, the striving, the analysis, the study, the interrelationships and I began to know that I enjoyed the achievements and I think the same thing would be extant in my life if I were still a scientist or an engineer or naval officer or if I had gone into business in a major corporation, which I almost did once. I think if I had gone to work for Electric Boat Company, which later became General Dynamics, I would have worked just as hard. I never have seen my navy records, but some people did and they were telling me the other night they couldn't believe all the good things my superior officer said about me, which is gratifying. When I undertake a project, it's almost like an enjoyable game for me. When I get ready to reorganize a state government or put into effect a new mental health program, or reorganize the Georgia court system, all of which I did with a lot of help, study, analysis, planning it's not a chore that I'm driven to, something that's distasteful. It's something very pleasant for me, almost like a solitary chess game."

He is a most disciplined man. His years at the Naval Academy taught him that. Every morning to keep his body in shape, he arose to do one hundred situps. And every night, to keep his soul in shape, he read a chapter of the Bible in Spanish. That way he killed two birds with one stone. He fed his spirit, at the same time he managed to keep his Spanish sharpened for political rallies and brief conversations in the Latin communities. I remember the first morning of the fall election campaign he told me, "I've already read through the New Testament once and now I'm on the twelfth Chapter of Luke, reading through the New Testament a second time. I haven't missed a single night. Well, actually, I missed two nights in Spanish. Once I spent the night with Rosalynn in Atlanta and I left the Bible in the hotel room, so the next night I had to read it in English. And another trip we lost my luggage. It didn't get to the hotel until two or three A.M., so I read a chapter in English that night." Some aides who traveled with him don't remember him reading the Bible at all.

Carter suffers from a bad knee, which is one reason he avoids cocktail parties. If he has to stand on his feet for long, it aches. Yet I saw him stand for over two hours in a receiving line without flinching. He stood with his feet eight inches apart, firmly planted on the ground, only rocking back and forth for temporary relief. And he never walked down the steps of a stage. Instead he springs cowboy-style into an audience to shake hands.

Carter prides himself on moderation in all things. He is a simple dresser. He wore the same three-button navy blue polyester suit, alternating with a gray plaid suit for over ten months, and not only managed to look impeccable, but made the Best Dressed List. I thought if I saw the same red tie one more time I would scream ("His lucky tie," says sister Gloria). He likes only light starch in his shirts. He spurns pajamas to sleep in his underwear (jockey shorts) and lives in the same pair of black wing-tipped shoes day in and day out until they begin to curl at the tips like bananas. His eating habits are far from gourmet. His breakfast is black coffee and orange juice except for an occasional batch of eggs and grits on Sunday. He eats hamburgers for lunch with buttermilk or tea. His favorite foods are collard greens, squash, butter beans, eggplant, and peach ice cream. He's a cheese lover—especially "rat" cheese, the kind that comes in a wheel. And he munches crackers and butter as a snack. He cuts the butter with a cracker instead of a knife. He also loves sirloin steak rare.

He is not a wine drinker, enjoys a Scotch or two, but gave up drinking and even Coke to stay at tip-top energy levels during the campaign, never smokes (except an occasional cigar. "His father made him promise he wouldn't smoke till he was twenty-one," says Rosalynn) and takes no medication except vitamins, not even an occasional sleeping pill. I found it hard to believe Carter had no problem sleeping before the debates, but Rosalynn insists, "He never had a sleepless night in the campaign. He goes right to sleep. And he wakes up wide awake. That really bothers me!"

Carter's Calvinistic fixation with determination and self-improvement has its side effects on the rest of his personality. He tends to be intolerant of anyone he feels wastes time, seems lazy or does not make maximum use of his ability. One reason he did not like a particular former Presidential candidate was because he appeared to be indolent and drank too much. And of course, it affected his political judgments. Jimmy Carter preached the work ethic, and espoused a conservative welfare position. He would offer job training to all welfare recipients able to work. Those who did not take a job would have their welfare payments cut off.

One of the most crucially important aspects of Jimmy Carter's character, life and political thinking is his devotion to Christ and the Baptist church. It predates his politics and has weathered the test of time. Carter says his Bible-reading and Sunday-School-going began when he was four.

"I remember the first memory lesson I heard from my mother was 'God is love,' " says Carter. The love theme seemed to become the leitmotif of his political speeches, his Sunday-school teaching and his personal life.

Mrs. Ethel Harris, the widow of former Plains Baptist Church pastor James Robert Harris (better known as "Brother Bob"), has known Carter since 1955 when Carter would accompany her husband in his "witnessing." Mrs. Harris recalls, "Jimmy had a real Christian love and concern about people who might go to hell. My husband often called Jimmy to go with him to visit non-Christians in the community. Jimmy was always willing to work, to witness. Witnessing means talking to someone about their relationship with God, and about God's plan for a person. It's giving that person the opportunity to do something about their life and to make a choice about God. Jimmy was very helpful in winning people to God. He would tell them how much Jesus meant to him. And many of the people whom he witnessed to accepted Christ and came into the church. I remember one man he visited was a hopeless drunk. Jimmy went to see him over and over. I remember when he joined the church and was baptized, we all felt like singing. Another man, named Dickerson, had a family of ten children. Jimmy and my husband went out in the fields and visited with him and went to see him in his home. One night in his yard that man made the decision for Christ."

A close friend recalls the time Carter visited another family that had never even been to church. "The most country people I ever met. They had nothing. Not even decent food. Jimmy visited them often and one Sunday invited them to his home for Sunday dinner. They all went to church first, and they went for quite a while after that. I remember Jimmy and Rosalynn were just thrilled to have them in their home."

After he returned home from the navy in 1953, Carter was also active in leading "cottage prayers." "We would divide the community up into areas and try to get a volunteer from each area to open their home for a prayer meeting. Then we would meet in the homes. Someone would lead the meeting, someone would lead the hymns, someone would read the scripture passages and pray for people by name. Jimmy would always come and lead off the discussion of Bible passages," says Mrs. Harris.

Carter taught Sunday school to young girls when he was a student at Annapolis, and to elementary-school boys when he lived in Plains. He taught in Atlanta throughout his term as Governor and continued to teach throughout his Presidential campaign.

According to Mrs. Clarence (Anne) Dodson who has known Carter for thirty-nine years, Carter used to go out of his way to get to Sunday school. "Little Jimmy lived in the country and I remember when he was ten, eleven and twelve years old and just a little thing, he would drive his mother's old black Plymouth and round up all the little boys whose families didn't have a car to bring them to Sunday school. He could barely see over the steering wheel. I'll never forget the sight of all those little boys piling out of that car at the church on Sunday morning."

The Presidential race interrupted his regular church-going and Sunday-school teaching, but friends say Carter would always attend if he came home to Plains. "He and Rosalynn would get to church Sunday mornings even if they got in at three in the morning," says Sandra Edwards, wife of Plains Baptist Church pastor Bruce Edwards.

Carter's religion has been both solace and psychiatrist to him in moments of deepest depression and self-doubt.

After Carter's bruising defeat in the Governor's race in 1966, he had become painfully thin and emotionally distraught. While many politicians suffer deep and long lasting depressions, Carter channeled his grief into an abiding faith. In a walk in the woods, he told his sister Ruth he wanted "what you have," total dedication to Christ, and went off to Pennsylvania to become a Baptist missionary.

Carter's Baptist morality reinforces other parts of his personality. He has a strong sense of service, sacrifice and responsibility, a strong sense of Good and Evil. Of his Presidency, his mother, among others says, "He'll always do what he thinks is right." The fear, of course, is that what he thinks is right may not be what others think is right.

Dedication to his wife and family stems in part from his strong Baptist morality, but also from deep abiding love. In spite of his admission of lusting in his heart for other women, Carter has never succumbed. He told me, "Yes, I've been tempted, but I've never chosen to give in to temptation. Why? Because I love Rosalynn. I've never loved any other woman except Rosalynn."

A tremendous depth of feeling exists between them. "Marriage is the easiest thing I've ever done in my life," he told me. "I know it sounds corny, but I still get a thrill if I walk into a hotel lobby or see her across the room someplace."

Carter called Rosalynn "an equal part of the campaign." His "secret weapon." "When we began planning the campaign more than three and a half years ago, Rosalynn and I were the ones that discussed every facet of the prospective campaign; the basic strategy, the political connotations of my background, my strengths and weaknesses and how to overcome the weaknesses. She sat in when we began to have larger group meetings with immediate staff advisors. Since the campaign began, she's been on the trail for voters and for money full time. She operates independently from me. She's just as much an attraction almost as I am. She gives a superb speech. She can appeal for organizational support, recruit volunteers. On a couple of occasions last year we had to quit campaigning and come home and get on the phone just to raise money to pay our debts. Rosalynn spent just as much time on the phone calling people. She can do everything as well as I can. We have long discussions at home about the campaign, the problems ahead, the potential pitfalls, the financing and my basic stands on issues. She helps to form my position on issues because she has a sensitive way of understanding what other people feel. Also, she is able to get a much more frank and unbiased and unembarrassed expression of criticism from voters than I am. They can approach Rosalynn and say, 'I think Jimmy ought to do this' or 'He's hurting himself when he fails to do this.' She is also an avenue between me and voters, that really is of tremendous benefit in the campaign. So in every possible way she's a full partner or better and is a superb campaigner on her own."

Carter takes his role in an equal partnership in marriage seriously. Too seriously, in fact, for his mother sometimes. She would often complain that Jimmy was spending too much time with Rosalynn and neglecting her. His mother could never understand why Jimmy bothered with housework. One time she told me she dropped in on Jimmy during the campaign to find him peeling peaches. "I said, 'Jimmy, why are you peeling all those peaches?' and he said, 'Mother, somebody's got to peel them. If they don't get peeled and put in the freezer they'll spoil.' "

"He helps me with everything," Rosalynn boasts, "he doesn't wash and iron his shirts, but he takes Amy for walks, he goes to the grocery story for me, he helps with the cooking and opening the mail. We're both gone all the time, so when we're home, we share."

Which is not to say theirs is a perfect marriage. Like any other couple they have had difficult times, major arguments, and minor squabbles. Carter admits their biggest blowup involved leaving the navy and moving back to Plains because Rosalynn did not want to have his mother and her own controlling their lives. And Rosalynn admits that Jimmy Carter's morning exuberance "really bothers me," and his penchant for blasting music as loud as it will go throughout the house drives her up a wall.

Rosalynn said, "His roommate at the Naval Academy was a pianist, a classical pianist, and had all kinds of records—mostly piano concertos. When they left the Naval Academy they flipped a coin. One got the record player, the other got the records. Jimmy got the records. So the first years that we were married, that's what we listened to . . . tuned up as loud as it would go. The house just shakes. When I come in he turns it down because he knows I don't like it. He can listen to it and it closes off everything for him, but it doesn't shut things out for me . . . it just grates. On the other hand, I know he gets upset with me because I want everything to be clean and neat. The other day for instance we were home and the carpet was getting red from the mud that people track in. I said, 'That carpet's getting red.' He said, 'Rosalynn, that's because people live here.' And that's the way he feels about it. He just wants to be comfortable . . . I'm not organized like he is. I stretch out the things I have to do and work all the time. And he fusses at me because I don't take enough time to play."

But their devotion to each other and the physical warmth between them is real. Once after they had been separated for a week Carter did not hesitate to kiss her, three times in fact, in front of a crowd of three thousand. Many times I have caught a glimpse of them holding hands in church or sitting with their knees touching. Separation was always difficult. Although Rosalynn once told me she preferred to campaign alone to cover territory where Carter could not be, their reunions were always "ecstatic" and their partings painful.

The depth of feeling was never more noticeable than Rosalynn Carter's impressive appearance on *Meet the Press* in October when she defended her husband's positions on the issues, his ethnic purity gaffe and his statements in the *Playboy* article, fending off criticisms like a marine disguised as Scarlett O'Hara. "I'm so proud of him.

I think he's doing a great job. I know he'll make a great President."

Nor was his feeling for her more evident than the morning after the third debate when Rosalynn and Jimmy made a joint appearance at Schuetzen Park in Trenton, New Jersey. Rosalynn had been traveling all over the United States for six weeks lionizing Jimmy Carter. She would make the same speech every time, telling her audiences about how they both came from Plains, how they "scrimped and saved" to make the peanut business a success, and how the country needed someone like Jimmy Carter who knew what it meant "to work for a living." On the stump Rosalynn always gave the speech her all, but that morning there was even more soul. She was showing her stuff for Jimmy. Carter had never heard the speech before but he was paying no attention. He was busy going over notes with a man sitting next to him.

"I've known him all my life," she said. Suddenly Jimmy looked up and smiled broadly.

"I think his background is so important, the fact that he's a fah-muh, he's worked for a living. The fact that he's a businessman is SO impoh-tant. I worked. The children worked. I kept the books. We worked hard. We scrimped and saved to make the business a success." Jimmy was listening intently.

"When he was Governor he abolished two hundred seventy-eight out of three hundred agencies. He got the telephone company to check how much waste there was and he saved eight hundred thousand dollars just on the phone bills . . . Jimmy Carter knows human beings in this country. Jimmy has never had any hint of scandal in his business or his personal life."

I looked at Carter. Tears were beginning to trickle down his face. He brushed them away with the index finger of his right hand, and as she finished her speech, he sprinted to the lectern to thank his wife, kissing her and squeezing her so hard he lifted her right off the ground. "That's beautiful," he whispered. "Beautiful . . ." Carter stepped up to the microphone with his arm around Rosalynn. "How many of you would like to have Rosalynn as First Lady?" he asked. A roar of approval went up from the crowd. Carter's face radiated contentment. "So would I."

PART

IV

GOD
AND MAN

CHAPTER 10

BORN AGAIN

THE CARTER HOUSE is a one-level ranch-style home constructed of brick and timber. It sits on a wooded side street four blocks away from Main Street. Charlie Wiggins, who built it, says it's worth about $75,000 today; though handsome and unlike any other in Plains, it is far from ostentatious. It could be anybody's house.

The living room is small and formal with grass-cloth wallpaper, turquoise and white French provincial store-bought furniture, a gold rug and very few objets d'art except one Grecian bust, a pair of landscapes from a political friend, and a gilt-on-wood prayer of St. Francis Assisi on the end table next to the couch. The room is nevertheless dominated by a massive portrait of Amy that hangs over the couch.

The dining room looks like an advertisement for Karastan Carpets, with straight-backed chairs around an average medium-light wood table, silver and crystal on the sideboard and a small gold Chinese screen on the wall at the far end of the room.

Carter spends no time in either of these rooms. He relaxes in the high-ceilinged family room just behind the living room—a spacious paneled area cluttered with thousands of books, family photos, a long couch Carter is reported to have made himself, and more paintings of Amy. It opens onto a large patio and a back lawn with Amy's trampoline.

Carter was sitting on that couch calling dozens of uncommitted delegates when we arrived at two o'clock sharp to do a TV interview for NBC. A Secret Serviceman answered the door unsmilingly and checked through all the equipment. Carter remained on the phone until he knew the cameras were entirely set up. He wanted to make maximum use of his time.

At 2:20 P.M., when every piece of equipment was in place and the camera ready to roll, Carter emerged through a set of double doors, followed by Rosalynn. He was wearing a blue work shirt, straight-legged jeans and brogans dusty with red Georgia clay, a stark contrast against the formality of that room. He walked right over to me, placed his hands on my shoulders and looked into my eyes for a long moment, but said nothing. Then he brushed his cheek against mine and turned to greet the crew.

We talked for a while about the importance of Plains in his life, and why he made a point to return home every weekend. Then the cameras began to roll. "Sometimes we campaign seven days or fourteen days without stopping or without coming home and it's a constant frantic sixteen-hour-a-day schedule. I don't feel the physical fatigue very much but I need to get off by myself. I need to think and I need to read. I need to exercise, see my farm, and I still have a substantial business to take care of. I would say mostly it's the change of pace and the opportunity to refresh my whole attitude. When I start out on the next week, I always feel like I've been on vacation if I've been in Plains for a day or two."

In Plains he could read and walk, and hunt arrowheads with Rosalynn, visit his and Rosalynn's mothers, read the mail and play with Amy.

"Amy's a special thing in our lives. Rosalynn and I had three boys in the navy. Jack is twenty-eight, he was born in Virginia, Chip's twenty-five, he was born in Hawaii. Jeffrey's twenty-three, he was born in Connecticut. Then Rosalynn and I had an argument for fourteen years, which I won. And we had Amy after we had been married twenty-one years. She's just eight years old and like a separate family for us because all of our boys are married. I figured out the other day that I'll still be going to PTA meetings when I'm sixty-one years old." Rosalynn laughed for the cameras, even though she'd heard the same line a thousand times, and would hear it another thousand times before the November election.

The campaign had affected his family life in a beneficial way. "Strangely enough," Carter said. "Since the boys have become adult and have married, a family of that age tends to fragment, but this campaign has brought us all back together. All three of my sons and their wives campaign full time, so we're kind of like a basketball team playing on five or six or sometimes eleven courts at one time."

He would maintain the spirit of Plains in the White House he told us. "I will maintain, as we did in the Governor's mansion, a close intimate relationship with the people of this nation.

"I didn't change when we went into the Governor's office. We didn't become enmeshed in the Atlanta social life. We maintained an intimate relationship as Governor that had been built up during the campaign itself. I think one of the major reasons for my success in the campaigns and the primaries to date is that we form a close personal contact, an intimate relationship between myself, Rosalynn, our family and the voters themselves. And if I fail to maintain that intimacy between myself as President and the people of this country when I am in the White House it would be a very drastic departure from my commitments. I'll do everything I can within the constraints of the Presidency and the requirements of the job to let the people of this country know that I have that attitude which will be a very beneficial thing."

I asked him why he smiled so much and he laughed. "I have a good life, and I feel in tune with my surroundings. I like all kinds of people. I'm not fearful about the future. I have a feeling of inner peace and assurance. And I genuinely like almost everyone I meet. When I shake hands with a thousand people in a factory shift line before daybreak in the snow, every time a person comes by, for that fleeting moment I genuinely care for them. That's the kind of attitude which quite often causes my smile."

We talked about his prayer life. He prayed ten or twenty times a day, he said. "It's a natural habit of mine. Some of my prayers are quite short. Some are pertinent for the moment, some are prayers I've memorized. I guess one of my favorites is 'Let the words of my mouth and the meditations of my heart be acceptable in thy sight, O Lord, my strength and my redeemer,' which is kind of an orientation of my thoughts and my words to be acceptable in every way. And I don't ever pray that I'll win the election or that God will do me a favor. I just pray that what I do will be acceptable. Sometimes when I go into a room and I don't know what to expect, I ask for assurance and God's presence so I can know what the right decisions or answer the questions properly. And if I meet someone who has a special problem sometimes I say a silent prayer for that person."

The room was hushed and Carter's eyes were so flooded with light, I felt an overwhelming sense of his prayerfulness. I shall never forget that moment as long as I live. I chastised myself after the interview for allowing myself to consider a politician godly and worked myself back into my usual cynicism.

Carter had said during the primaries that he went to church every Sunday, but I did not believe that after a grueling week such as he had just spent he would actually get up and attend services.

Sunday morning at ten o'clock, I drove to the Plains Baptist Church suspecting Carter would be home sleeping. Coincidentally, as I walked in the side door of the white clapboard building, Carter walked in behind me. He had been up since six, and was going to teach Sunday school he said, bounding up the old wooden stairs with his Bible tucked under his arm to a room on the second floor. Twelve men waited to hear him talk to them of God. It seemed a rather Pentacostal setting for a Presidential candidate.

The men included his first cousin, state senator Hugh Carter, his chief peanut competitor, Frank Williams, Dale Gay, a contractor with Americus Home Construction Company, Ralph Speegle, a dairyman, Cody Timmerman, a retired railroad engineer, Albert Williams, a rural mail carrier, Frank Whitley, a Plains businessman, Clyde Chavers, a farmer, P. J. Wise, an engineer from a local hospital, Theron Hobgood, a federal worker, William Cochran, a farmer, and Clarence Dodson, business manager for South Georgia Technical and Vocational School.

When Hugh Carter saw me he invited me to come inside. I slipped into the tiny wooden room with one overhead lightbulb and took a seat. Carter introduced me to his class, adding, "This is the first time we have ever had a reporter or a woman in this class. We've never even had a black." The men laughed. I cringed.

Then he began to teach, and the room fell silent. It was a side of Carter that seemed more genuine and expository than any I had seen so far. It also struck me as extraordinary that a Presidential candidate would take time out from the political world to steep himself in the supernatural. Ten years ago, such a venture would have put an abrupt end to any Presidential ambitions.

Standing behind a round table in the stark white room, the sandy-haired Carter pressed his ten fingers together as if to form a small church and told the Men's Bible Class, "The main point I want to leave with you today is that we should lead our lives with the Holy Spirit within us and be ready to face Our Saviour. We should leave here today and live our lives as though Christ were coming this afternoon."

Wearing a blue seersucker suit, blue shirt, red tie and black wing-tipped shoes, Carter spoke for an hour about the section of St. Matthew's Gospel that deals with the Second Coming of Christ and the Destruction of the temple of Jerusalem. (Matthew 24: 36–51) He spoke of the mysteries of God with as much familiarity and ease as he brings to his discussions of political issues. It was a riveting performance.

Carter began teasingly. He had been introduced to the congregation of a black church in Buffalo, New York, last week, he said, and had shaken hands with hundreds of people. One parishioner who did not meet him, later asked the preacher who the visitor had been. "Why, that was Brother Jimmy, that's who," the preacher replied. Jimmy was proud of that.

"So many wonder why black people like me and vote for me and I think the answer is because we share the same faith and we feel the same kinship which is more important than race."

Carter discussed what he called the "eschatological and apocalyptical" meaning of Matthew's Gospel. "Eschatology means prophecies that concern the close of an age, when something is going to come to its termination or end. Apocalypse means an uncovering, an explanation, an unveiling. And there are two ages discussed here—one in Jerusalem, the other is the coming of Christ.

"Last Sunday we saw that the Pharisees were asking Christ questions, trying to trip Him up. He challenged them and told them they were a generation of vipers who ignored the general teachings of God. This was the week before He died and after that encounter with the Pharisees there was no doubt in the minds of His disciples that He was going to be crucified. The last Tuesday of His life He went into the Temple. Rosalynn and I have been in the old Jerusalem. We were there for three or four days and we would get up at daybreak and walk in the old city with maps and try and figure out where different places were that Christ had gone. And we saw the Temple. In Christ's time it had been the third temple built. The second one was built about 516 B.C. The third temple was built by Herod. It was sturdy and some of the stones were eighteen feet thick. Some of them were as big as a house.

"As Christ and His disciples were leaving the Temple, they went up in the hills to spend a night and the disciples were saying that the Temple would last till eternity. But Jesus replied, 'Not a stone will be left standing.' When they got to the Mount of Olives, the disciples asked Him what He meant. They were all sure about this time that His life was going to be over. They had a premonition about it. There was a building hatred against Him. Christ told them the Temple was going to be destroyed and He went on to tell them that the other Jerusalem to be destroyed would be the coming of the Judgment. And that is the purpose of the lesson this morning.

"Jesus discussed with His twelve disciples 'the terrible days coming ahead.' He told them 'I'm going to be dead. I'm going to be gone and you must carry on my work.' He told them they would suffer, that they would be accused of being fakes, even devils, betrayers of God, that they would be hated and killed and betrayed, even by some of the members of their own families . . . But Christ did not say, 'Aha, when I'm gone, you're going to have to suffer.' He said, 'You will suffer, but you'll have my protection and my love. I love you.' And the disciples knew that whatever happened to them, Christ would be with them every minute in the Holy Spirit. He loves us too and He told us as well that we all have the opportunity to be with Him every minute of our lives if we want to. Jesus stands at the door and knocks, but He can't break down the door. He doesn't want to. It must be opened by our understanding. It must be self-willed. And His work has to be carried on by those of us who love Christ. If we don't carry it on, it won't be carried on at all. We are the Johns and Peters and Matthews and Pauls."

Then Carter asked his class: "Suppose you were informed this afternoon that Jesus was going to come tonight and you had just five more hours to live. What would we do to get ready for Christ's presence?" He paused. "You might think of all the people you had hurt, or of those for whom you had some hatred in your heart, and you might get on the phone and call them and say, 'Look, I'm sorry.' You might talk to your wife about something you had said to her, you might think of something you had never admitted you had done, or of something you hadn't been able to carry out, or someone you had intended to witness to about Christ who had not known Him. And you might say to him, 'Let me tell you about Christ dying on the cross.' " The room was hushed. The men were at rapt attention. Carter spoke ever so softly and movingly.

"But those things we would do in those five hours are the things we should be doing this afternoon. We should live our lives as though Christ were going to come this afternoon, so we would be prepared when Christ put out his hand and said, Frank, or Clarence, or Hugh, 'Here we are together now.' Jesus hasn't told us when

He's coming, but we should change before Christ comes. Let's do it!"

Carter finished his lesson just as the bell rang for the eleven o'clock "preaching service." He closed his Bible and joined Rosalynn and Amy, both of whom had been at other Sunday-school classes downstairs. Sitting in the third pew on the right of the church, Carter shared his hymnal with Rosalynn and sat with his arm around her throughout most of the hour-long service. He joined in the singing and prayed intently with his head in his hands when the Reverend Bruce Edwards suggested that men had a tendency to "trust ourselves, to lean on our own ability, and intellect instead of trusting God."

After the service Carter chatted with members of the congregation on the steps of the seventy-year-old white church where he has attended services and Bible class for forty-seven years. I asked him how much time he had spent on the lesson. "Only a few minutes this morning," he said. "I spent an equal amount of time reading the Sunday papers. After all, I've been coming to this church and studying the Bible since I was four. Everyone here has a great familiarity with the Bible."

According to Clarence Dodson, the regular Men's Bible Class teacher for whom Carter substituted, not "everyone" has a fund of Biblical knowledge equal to Carter's. "The Bible teachers here are specially selected by a committee. They have to be active members of the church and members of a Bible class. They are trained at special courses and know the Bible extremely well. Jimmy is a Biblical scholar and a very fine preacher. He comes to class every Sunday he's home, but he only teaches if he has time to study. Then he'll call and ask me if he can fill in for me. He teaches about every six weeks. He called me last night at eleven o'clock and said, 'Clarence, would you mind if I taught your class tomorrow?' I'm always delighted."

I asked Carter teasingly if he were prepared for the Second Coming himself, but got a serious reply. "I'm ready. I have no fear. I'm not afraid of dying."

The next time I heard Jimmy Carter preach Sunday school it was the Sunday after the New York Convention and he was the Democratic nominee for the President of the United States. The class had quadrupled in size and spilled out of the tiny room into

the central hall. Reporters, women and out-of-towners now represented at least half the class. As Carter himself said surveying the
scene, "It's really integrated this morning."

While the class was settling down, making a racket with folding
chairs, Carter waited patiently and silently, Bible in hand, sitting
on a small round piano stool in the corner of the room. It seemed
incredible that a Presidential nominee would take the time to teach
Sunday school at that juncture, but he seemed so comfortable in
the role.

Again, never looking at a note, Carter preached about St. John's
Gospel, which he called the gospel of Love, and the simplicity of
faith. The sermon seemed to capsulize the Carter philosophy and
to echo the themes of his acceptance speech in New York's Madison
Square Garden. He also seemed to be speaking of his own struggle
with vanity, pride, and success, of his community's disharmonies
and prejudices, and of his own father.

He spoke of the need for a solid foundation in faith, for without
it, "We might have the most incredible intellects in the world, we
might study under the greatest philosopher or theologian, we might
have a Ph.D. or understanding of the interrelation between people,
but without a solid base under our lives, all of this learning is super-
ficial, and there's no foundation there for a meaningful existence."

Faith, Carter pointed out, is very uncomplicated, and often provides simple answers to complex problems. "When we reach a point
in our lives where problems occur, several times a day sometimes,
when we want to know how to deal with an unforeseen circumstance
or how to orient our lives toward a proper decision, when these difficulties present themselves to us and we know Christ, if we ask
ourselves a simple question, 'What would Christ do?' then we have
a very simple answer to a very difficult question."

"John of all the teachers personified the word love. John was
almost obsessed with the word love. He starts off his admonition
saying 'Beloved' and beloved means you who are loved, by me. He
calls the people of Ephesus, grown men and women, 'Little children.'
He wasn't looking down on them, but he was their teacher, their instructor. He loved them as though they were his own children.

"The tendency of people is to be attracted by success, by a popular
exposition of a thought and a popular teacher attracts people to
them, even if they're not telling the truth. But the test of the doc-
trine is over a long period of time.

"You'll hear all kinds of theologies, that's the studies of the different kinds of gods, but out of theology, which is very complicated, comes a simple message of love. God wants us to have the expression through Christ of a simple message you can understand, even children four years old can understand.

"What's the first memory verse you ever learned? I learned from my mother when I was four years old that God is love. We're going to get to that in a minute. And out of love, and I put this in my acceptance speech the other night, has to come one more step . . . simple justice. You can't just encapsulate yourself in isolation or be a hermit and have love for people unless it's put into practice. Christ didn't get into an ivory tower and preach about love. John didn't go off by himself in Jerusalem and preach about love. Paul was persecuted. He suffered in many ways in order to put into practical application the principles of the word love. We have that responsibility in our own modern-day lives. Too often the Christian church has formed a kind of mutual admiration society. We kind of check off the folks who walk into church on Sunday and say, 'Well, that person came to church, therefore that person might be almost as good as I am.' You know that's not what Christ did. Christ was with prostitutes, cheaters, tax collectors, common people, dark-skinned people. The average person with whom Christ lived wouldn't speak to dark-skinned people. Christ did. Do we do the same thing?

"Quite often if you go into a Baptist church in an average town, certainly in the South, you find a social and economic elite. We're the ones who are kind of the prominent people in town, and we have a tendency—all of us, certainly I have myself—to think because I have been accepted by God, because I have eternal life, because I have the peace of the presence of the Holy Spirit, because I have eternal salvation through Christ, I have a tendency to think I'm better than other people, that surely God must have recognized my worth and my goodness and therefore wanted me because I'm better than others."

Then he raised a series of rhetorical questions which he answered himself. "But we're saved through what? Grace.

"Grace means a gift, a gift of God. Through what? Through faith. In whom? Christ. We're saved by grace through faith in Christ. And when we have that faith, along with it should come humility. Christ more than anything else talked about pride and deplored pride. Because He saw that when we think we're better than anyone else we almost automatically are separated from others. When his disciples struggled over who's going to sit at your right hand, who's going to sit at your left hand, who's going to be highest when we all go to heaven? Christ said the greatest among you are what? Servants.

"There's one thing that I wished the Southern Baptist Church did, that the Primitive Baptist Church does—the washing of feet. That's one of the most moving Christian experiences. Because you can imagine in a little tight-knit community like ours, there are always disharmonies. It's human nature. You get jealousies between people. One farmer gets good rain and makes a good profit. The farmer right next to him might have worked just as hard, misses the rain and doesn't make as much of a profit. Tensions build up. And in the Primitive Baptist Church, I think once every quarter, or maybe once every year, they have the foot-washing ceremony, because Christ said to do that. They try to figure out the person with whom they feel most estranged and they get on their knees and wash each other's feet. Christ did this.

"One time when His disciples were arguing among themselves about who was the greatest, Christ got on his knees and said, 'I'm just a servant,' and He washed the disciple's feet. Peter said, 'No, don't do that,' and Christ said, 'If you love me you'll let me do it.' " (Carter often told his campaign audiences, "I want to be your servant.")

"Love in isolation doesn't mean anything. But if it is applied to other people, it changes their lives for the better through what I described to you as simple justice, fairness, equality, concern, compassion, redressing of grievances, elimination of inequalities. The poor are the ones that suffer the most. Even in our society which is supposed to be fair. There's a great responsibility for those of us who believe in Christ. For us to sit in isolation and say 'I love everybody' means nothing. What is God? God is love. That's a very, very simple thing and it gives us unbounded opportunity to study, to learn, to challenge ourselves, to express our own lives in a meaningful way.

"So if you're looking for something complicated, or wish to expand your tremendous mental capacity, the simple concept, 'God is love,' is a very challenging expression. Simplicity doesn't mean that there's not a challenge there. One of the things that Christ points out is that all of us sin. Christ says you're supposed to be perfect, but all of us sin and come short of the glory of God. How to translate an understanding of Christ, the simple thing 'God is love' into a meaningful Christian life, a closeness with God, a compatibility with what Christ did, is an unbelievably complicated and inspiring challenge.

"One of the favorite expressions that I like to point out is by a theologian named Paul Tillich who said, 'Religion is a search.' It's a search for the truth about man's existence and man's relationship to God and man's relationship to other people. When we quit searching we lose our religion, we become proud, self-satisfied, sure of ourselves. We anoint ourselves with a benediction and we lose that struggling to get back down where we ought to be in the spirit of a servant. The more powerful a person is, the less one has to prove his strength.

"You've all seen I'm sure very small people, like a man who's five-foot-three . . . quite often they'll be cocky and have to prove that they're real men. But a great strong, sure person need not prove it always. That's the way it is with Christ. And that's the way it is with Christians. When you're sure of your strength, you can exhibit compassion, emotion, love, concern, equality, and even better than equality, the attitude of a servant. You can say, I'm not only not better than you, you're better than I am. And I want to work with you. So, love, simple justice, theology."

Later that morning, at the end of the church service, Carter was asked to stand up and give a benediction. He prayed with closed eyes and clasped hands: "Our Father, we come to the conclusion of another opportunity to learn about Thee. Let our minds be kept open to the message that's been given to us. Let us realize that Christ stands ready, knocking on our hearts to become a part of our eternal life, and although we might have very difficult decisions to struggle with or burdens that seem sometimes too hard to bear, although we might have sins that have been a constant oppression on our consciousness for years, all this can be wiped away in just a moment if we accept Christ as our Saviour and open our hearts to Him. He is the eternal yes to our lives. This is the message we've had presented to us. Let our hearts be constantly searching for a close relationship with Thee through Christ our Saviour, Amen."

It was hard for me to believe that what Carter said in Sunday school and in prayer—unlike many of his campaign positions—did not come from the very core of his being.

CHAPTER 11

CARTER AND THE BLACKS

CARTER WAS OFTEN ACCUSED of using his religion for political gain, a charge he vehemently denied. But if there was a political advantage to Carter's Baptist religion, it was a major one—instant communication with blacks. Had it not been for the overwhelming black vote Carter received both in the primaries and the general election, Carter would be back in Plains peddling peanuts.

His faith gave him a pulpit, literally, from which to address black audiences. Carter often spoke in black churches during the primaries and was usually addressed as "Brother," by both minister and parishioner.

More importantly, his religion gave him a link with powerful black leaders such as the Reverend Andrew Young, Reverend "Daddy" King, and Coretta King, widow of the slain civil rights leader, Reverend Martin Luther King, Jr., all of whom telegraphed the word like a drumbeat through black churches that Carter was a born-again Baptist just like them. Young's and Daddy King's endorsements contributed greatly to the substantial and often crucial number of black votes Carter received during the primaries. Carter's enemy, State Senator Julian Bond, said, "Reverend King's and Young's endorsements have been the key. They made Carter legitimate in the eyes of blacks all over the country."

It was through Young and the Kings that blacks learned of Carter's solid, albeit short civil rights record. And even if he never fought for integration as a member of the Sumter County School Board during the divisive Sixties, even if he had never taken a liberal public position before he decided to run for Governor, even if his family's lonely stand in 1965 against a resolution banning "Negroes and other civil rights agitators" from membership in the Plains Baptist church occurred just before he ran for governor, and even if he ran a racist campaign in 1970, blacks believed Jimmy Carter was on their side. He had, after all, grown up with them, worked side by side in the fields with them. And if they did not worship in the same church, they at least sang the same hymns, and shared the same religion. As Sam Evans, a black leader said, "We will be proud to have a Baptist teacher as President of the United States." And as Daddy King said in a telegram to a black audience one night: "I know a man I can trust, blacks can trust, and that man is Jimmy Carter . . . Jimmy Carter was for equal justice when it wasn't a good thing to be for, and Jimmy Carter spoke out in favor of integrating his rural Southern church many years ago . . . he appointed blacks to judgeships when he was Governor, desegregated the Georgia State Committee, passed Georgia's first fair housing law and gave my son, Martin Luther King, Jr., an honored place in the state capitol. These are the things that tell me what is in Jimmy Carter's mind and heart." King defended Carter's ethnic purity remarks as well. "He was with black people when it wasn't easy and we will be with him on the road to the Presidency even though it is bumpy . . . It is wrong to judge a man on a slip of the tongue."

When I was in Philadelphia covering the primary I had lunch at the Bellevue Stratford with Ethel Allen, a black surgeon who chaired the Ford for President campaign in the city. Allen, who has been active in the civil rights movement and knows important black leaders throughout the country, admired Carter's clever use of his religion. " 'Born again' is the secret of his success with blacks. Whites do not understand this, but it's essentially a black saying and it carries with it the connotation of exceptional worth beyond the norm. 'Born again' is keyed to the fundamentalist Baptist who goes through a rebirth, having no religion and finding it. Carter exploits that and his sister Ruth exploits the other black codeword, 'evangelist.' There are more evangelists in the black church than any other. And the Carters know how to use both words to their advantage."

Dr. Allen called Carter's "ethnic purity" statement a "brilliant" political move. "He calculated the timing of that statement to get the Wallace vote in Texas, Missouri and Georgia, and it's paying off handsomely. It made him an instant household word, and it didn't antagonize the Ku Klux Klan, the White Citizens Council or the American Nazi Party. He didn't lose points with them by apologizing because he had already said it.

"He didn't lose points with blacks because blacks can forgive a man who's religious sooner than they can forgive a man who's not close to God. That's why they didn't turn off when they saw the pictures of Daddy King embracing him [a photo that made the centerfolds of many local black newspapers] like they did when they saw Sammy Davis, Jr., hugging Nixon. He's astutely assayed the mood of the country. People are looking for God and honesty in the post-Watergate era. They voted for Nixon and they need to be exorcised of this devil. The exorcist appears to be Jimmy Carter."

I went to see Andrew Young at his red brick Atlanta home one day last spring. He told me he had once had real misgivings about Carter. "I was a victim of prejudice. I was prejudiced against anything that came out of southwest Georgia." But after meeting Miz Lillian he was more favorably inclined toward Carter. "Black people have a radar about white folk. She's so warm and loving to everyone." And when he observed Carter as Governor he grew to appreciate him. Carter first impressed Young with his political astuteness and his concern for "little people." When he visited a black restaurant called Paschals, where black pols would usually gather for breakfast around seven or eight o'clock, he would not only greet the black political establishment, he would go out into the kitchen and shake hands with the cooks and the waitresses. "That single incident set him apart from most of the other politicians in my mind."

He also remembered the time Carter quelled racial tensions in Hancock County, about 120 miles east of Atlanta. "There was a little race war brewing and the whites were buying guns and one of the black leaders went out and bought a carload of machine guns. And it looked like they were really going to get it on. Jimmy went on up there by plane and sat down and went from one side to the other talking to people and finally gave everyone the kinds of assurances that they needed to survive, picked up all the guns and brought 'em back to Atlanta."

But more importantly, as a black Baptist minister who was shot at and jailed during the days of the civil rights struggles when he marched in the Mississippi mud with Martin Luther King, Jr., Young learned that it is better to preach from the winning political pulpit than to be a voice crying in the wilderness. As Sammy Davis, Jr., said during the 1972 convention when I asked how an ardent

Robert Kennedy supporter like he had been- could ever embrace Richard Nixon, Sammy said, "Listen babe, it's better to be standin' in the Oval Office than bangin' at the gates."

Young felt the same way which is why he decided to convert his ministry to elected political activism. "Religion is about life. When you pray the Lord's Prayer, you say, 'Thy kingdom come on earth.' And in a Democratic society if the kingdom is going to come on earth, it's going to come by voting and by legislative action that appropriates taxes humanely and spends money on life and development rather than on death and destruction.

"In the Old Testament, the prophets helped name Kings," Young said, "but they were also responsible to see that the Kings did right." And Young not only planned to be a Carter Kingmaker, but to make sure that Carter did right by his people.

Daddy King joined the Carter bandwagon for the same reason. When I went to see King at the Ebenezer Baptist Church in Atlanta, King, sitting in a small room surrounded by his son's awards and pictures, told me point-blank his candidate was really Nelson Rockefeller. "I told Jimmy that when he came to see me. I told him, if Nelson ever decided to run I would have to support him because he's my favorite." But he had given Carter his blessing because Carter was not only for black people, he was a winner.

But if Carter was able to capture the black vote, through the clever use of King and Young, blacks also brought out the best in Jimmy Carter.

Black audiences seemed to turn Jimmy Carter on. There was rapport between them. A soul thing. And unspoken magnetism.

On April 22, for example, Carter was guest of honor at the Family of Leaders Dinner at the Holiday Inn at 1880 Market Street in Philadelphia. One hundred or more outstanding black community leaders from the fields of health, education, law, religion and politics had assembled to dine around three oblong tables. The main table must have been fifty feet long covered with lace and silver candelabra.

Carter worked his way slowly around all three tables, casually, warmly, fatherly, shaking hand by hand. There were no quick hellos, with eyes focused on the next face. This was more like a pastor greeting his flock. There was eye-contact and a personal word for everybody.

When Carter rose to speak, there was communion. Speaking to that black audience is one of the few times I saw Carter moved to eloquence. Carter does not play as well in print as he plays in person. With Carter it is necessary to savor the emphasis, the voice modulations, the facial expressions, the sincerity, the churchly quiet that prevails as he delivers his low-key diatribe against social injustice.

". . . We have circumstances in this country that evolved over a period of years . . . thirty-six members signed the Declaration of Independence and nine of them were from Pennsylvania. They pointed out the right to life, liberty and the pursuit of happiness. We've come a long way in the pursuit of life and liberty, but we have a long way to go in the pursuit of happiness . . . I've seen hunger and diseases that should not be with us . . . I've seen persons deprived of jobs. That deprives a person of peace and pride in himself. The first responsibility of the next administration has got to be jobs. Fifty percent of young blacks today are unemployed . . . There is nothing worse than an atrophied shrunken-up mind . . . I have gone to schools late in the afternoon and seen kids who had never known books, who didn't even know their last name, but with education they'll blossom forth. As a child I didn't have indoor plumbing, but I had good health care. How can a person find happiness in a jammed-up ghetto, paint peeling off the ceiling . . . threatened by crime. Our people need the chance to have good homes."

They do not interrupt him with applause, only "Yes, suh," and "Amen, Brother." Listening to Carter is like listening to their preacher. "He gave me the chills," said one black woman. "He looks like John Kennedy, it's eerie," said another. "He doesn't sound like a politician," says Orville Steadwell. "When I first heard the statement about ethnic purity my reaction was outrage," said Leo Winson, a research analyst, "but after hearing him tonight, I was really impressed." "Ethnic purity's nothing. If that's his only sin, I'm not worried. You've got to look at the record and his is impeccable," said George Garfield, administrator of a community health center.

Shortly after midnight the following night, Carter was aboard his United Charter, en route from Memphis, Tennessee, to Johnstown, Pennsylvania. He had just gulped down a dinner of veal parmigiana, skipped the wine, and was slumped in the first seat of first class, left foot propped against the bulkhead, jacket off, shirt sleeves rolled up, his face collapsed with fatigue.

His first event had been a 7:30 breakfast with supporters. But even after sixteen and a half hours without rest, Carter still seemed totally in control of his mental energy. There was no letting down. His guard was up. "I thought you had exhausted the entire Carter family," he quipped, somewhat piqued at having to be grilled at midnight. He made almost no small talk, strictly a perfunctory "How are you?" There was no Carter smile. I told him my suitcase was lost by the Carter baggage department and had been missing for two days but he seemed unconcerned. "Rosalynn just bought a wraparound skirt," he said. "That's all she's got. Someone broke into her car in Boston last week and stole everything. She didn't even have a lipstick or her wig or a pair of shoes . . . Now, what did you want to ask me?" he said softly. We talked about his harmony with blacks.

He didn't know what had formed his rapport with black audiences, except he'd always felt closer to people who were "disadvantaged" in some way. Besides, he grew up with blacks and felt completely at ease with them. A few white families moved out to Archery, but those that did only stayed a year or two and left, so basically all his playmates on the farm were the children of blacks who worked for his father. Many times they all worked together in the field, sometimes as long as sixteen hours a day. "On rainy days we'd go down to the creek and spend all day catchin' catfish and eels and cooking 'em. And we made tree houses together and played baseball and talked with each other and my parents would go off and I would stay with the black families. We ate together and played cards together. The mother in the black family was my boss while my parents were gone, and I was under strict orders to obey. There were seven or eight living on the same farm with us, sometimes they were employees and sometimes they weren't. But livin' right next to us was a family who worked on the railroad, a section foreman and an independent farmer who owned his own farm. But they were my playmates and I just grew up that way."

Carter disagreed with Ethel Allen that he used the black codewords "born again," and "evangelism" to appeal to black Baptists. "It's just a common language we speak. It's the thrust of the ease of communication I have with black people." But he acknowledged the vital importance of having Young and Daddy King on his side. "There's a complicated infrastructure among black people. They have leaders whom they trust. Whites have no equivalent. Blacks were persecuted for so long that there were only a certain few spokesmen for them that communicated with the white world and were emissaries to the white political structure. The spokesmen, often their preachers, would come back and tell their congregation what was best. The bonds between the congregation and the pastor far transcend the religious world, as well as the political, economic and social worlds. It is a very precious relationship. There is a slow reluctance on the part of black leaders to commit themselves to a candidate or to an idea or issue. They're very cautious about it and their commitment is a very valuable thing. If they go back to their congregation and say 'This is a good man, you can trust him,' they put their reputation on the line. And if they should ever betray their congregation and support the wrong person, they would be damaged severely. These would include people like Andrew Young and Vernon Jordan and Daddy King, and their friendship and support is one of the major factors of my political campaign. I recognize the responsibility that has been put on me by their unequivocal commitment. Their commitment is not a tentative thing. It gives me entry to a group like last night that I could not derive from just a common religion or a great compatibility or basic philosophy or a compassionate attitude toward the people they represent. The Daddy King letter was a crucial element in their acceptance of me. There's an almost constant communication and exchange of ideas and information among black leaders of this country about changing times and political leaders that has no parallel among whites."

Does he purposefully try and sound like a Baptist preacher in order to woo black audiences? "No, I can't help the way I sound. I don't contrive or put on airs, I just speak as clearly as I can to each group. Sometimes, as you know, my relationship with a group is very transient, like the one night I walked into a group of three hundred people and I didn't have a chance to shake hands with them or get to know them. I had barely twenty minutes. I made an eighteen-minute speech and left. When I make eight to twelve speeches a day, as I have on occasion, I don't have an ability for an instant rapport with each group. Half the time I don't know until five minutes ahead the nature of the group I'm going to visit. The campaign moves too fast for me to prepare myself for every speech or study of a group's character, but I get a fairly good briefing."

Carter did not feel his best relationship was with a black audience. "Quite often I have just as intense a relationship with young people. If I have time to prepare for it and speak with them and know what their motivations and needs are, I can relate myself to them very vividly and very succinctly, and very sincerely, but I don't think that relationship is as easily attained as it is with black groups."

PART

V

THE
GEORGIA
MAFIA

The Dons: Then and Now

Hamilton Jordan: Campaign Manager. Assistant to the President.

Patrick H. Caddell: Campaign Pollster. Unpaid Advisor.

Charlie Kirbo: Campaign Éminence Grise. White House Éminence Grise.

Jerry Rafshoon: Campaign Media Expert. Unpaid Advisor.

Robert Lipshutz: Campaign Treasurer. White House General Counsel.

Stuart Eizenstat: Campaign Issues and Policy Director. Assistant to the President for Domestic Affairs and Policy.

Jody Powell: Campaign Press Secretary. White House Press Secretary.

Greg Schneiders: Campaign Coat-Toter and Advisor. White House Director of Special Projects.

THE GLORY BOYS

The Georgia mafia was composed of two schools. One was mostly liberal, gentlemanly, soft-spoken, nonaggressive, pinstriped and polished.

The other school was hardly what one expected to find surrounding the Christo-centric candidate. It was composed in large part of men who embodied qualities almost entirely opposite to their leader's. One member of the inner sanctum described them as a "morally degenerate corrupt staff." They placed less of an emphasis on candor than Carter. ("Jimmy won't lie to you, but I will," said one.) They lusted after other women with more than their heart ("What's a campaign about but screwing and drinking, anyway?" another told me.) They were irreligious, undisciplined, arrogant, disorganized, rowdy and nonideological. Their loyalty was reputed to be founded on ambition and personal trust rather than on dedication to a noble cause. What ideology they had tended to be conservative, in the George Wallace vein. They didn't answer phone calls sometimes even from their fellow staffers. They lost their briefcases, told dirty jokes, uttered profanities and four-letter words with regularity, smoked too much ("There's plenty of dope around. You just have to ask the right people," one of them told me), drank too much and wenched too much.

They disdained the intellectual, harbored a grudge against the Eastern Establishment, preferred open shirts, blue jeans and cowboy boots to suit and tie.

They were chauvinists as well. They tended to disregard the most competent women reporters traveling on the press plane. Even White House veteran correspondent Helen Thomas complained that most Carter aides would not give her the time of day. *People* and NBC correspondent Clare Crawford called them arrogant and unhelpful. *Newsweek*'s Eleanor Clift and *Washington Post* Correspondent Helen Dewar complained of shabby chauvinistic treatment from the Carter staff. The few reporters they allowed an inside glimpse of the campaign were men. Some however, offered information in return for sexual favors. "Come to my room and watch the debates and I'll help you write a good book," one of them said to me in Williamsburg. The offer was made earlier during the primary campaign as well. "Your last chance to have some fun," I was told when I walked away from a seductive situation. Some women reporters who acquiesced were given special entrée. When I complained that one woman I know had been given a lengthy interview with Carter the same week I was squeezed out of the schedule I was told by a member of the Carter inner sanctum, "The trouble with you is you don't sleep with the right people like she did."

But they were shrewd politically, intellectually bright, extroverted and fun. Life-of-the-party-types. Unlike their candidate they were capable of soaring wit and great camaraderie. They were the kind many journalists sought out as friends, or wanted to spend time with.

CHAPTER 12

HAMILTON JORDAN, CAMPAIGN MANAGER

HAMILTON JORDAN (pronounced Jurdan) is sprinting down the hall like a boxer in his yellow Alligator shirt, khaki pants and short, square-toed boots carrying a battered plastic briefcase, when a reporter informs him Senator James Buckley of New York may enter the Republican Presidential race. Jordan screeches to a halt and stops chewing gum for an instant. "Jesus God! That'll screw old Reagan. No. It'll take votes away from Ford in the New York delegation. Hell. I don't know. I haven't thought it through. Well, who cares. I don't care what they do." As far as Hamilton Jordon is concerned, his man Jimmy Carter is going to the White House come hell, high water, Ford or Reagan, and he's going with him.

The thirty-two-year-old campaign manager has never been to the White House in his life. And he's not sure he'll know how to act when he gets there. "Maybe I'll have to change," he says, pausing to sit on the corner of the receptionist's desk. "I never wore a tie when Jimmy was Governor, and I swore I never would, but maybe I'll have to in the White House." Then his gray eyes dance mischievously. "Maybe I'll dress like the *touristas,* in Bermuda shorts, a red-white-and-blue hat and a Brownie camera around my neck."

Jordan spots his pollster Pat Caddell with a woman friend. "You with Caddell tonight?" he yells, stepping into the elevator on the twenty-fourth floor of the 100 Colony Square building. "Be careful!"

The same thing has been said to women about Jordan. He has an eye for a svelte body and a pretty face. And he is sometimes known to be indiscreet. In Philadelphia, after Carter won his smashing Pennsylvania primary victory, Jordan finished a press briefing and stood in a corner of the room eye to eye with a voluptuous brunette.

A minute later in the elevator Jordan kissed her good-bye in front of several staff members and a reporter. "See you in Palm Beach next weekend." As the young woman stepped off the elevator Jordan grinned and puffed out his chest. "She was one of the best volunteers we've had. Invaluable services!" Jordan is about the only sexy man in the upper echelons of the Carter staff. The others are either aggressively lecherous, patently homely, cold, old or solid family men. But the thirty-two-year-old campaign manager exudes flirtatiousness, boyish good looks, a rather swashbuckling air and a certain machismo, albeit a chunky one.

With his polished-apple cheeks, immaculate nails and shiny boots, Jordan always appears squeaky clean. "He always looks fresh out of the shower," says Jim King, the Carter advance man. "He always looks like there's an enormous mother who wraps him in his suit, either that or he's put together by an automatic dressing machine. He always looks so unrumpled and refreshing."

Those who work for or around Jordan like his courtesy and his genial good nature. Volunteers and staff members say Jordan goes out of his way to introduce himself if he spots a new face in the hall. He's not self-important like other campaign managers who treated their drones like unworthy creatures.

"He's always happy and cheerful," says Edie Poe, his scheduling assistant, a beautiful black woman with an afro like a helmet. "He's a very polite man, and so easy to work for you wouldn't believe." If there's a fault, it's his inability to say no to anyone. "The problem is he's so considerate, he tries like hell to see everyone, so handling his scheduling is the most difficult thing in the world."

The phone rings outside Jordan's twenty-fourth-floor corner office. Jody Powell calling from Plains. Jordan picks up the receiver. "O.K. I'll do that. Yeah, I'll see him. Sure." Another name is squeezed into an already-filled time slot.

His assistant, Caroline Wellons, calls Jordan "a riot." "He's a big kidder, he loves to laugh. He's more fun than funny. He puts people at ease. We work long hours here so it's easy to get down and out. If you get low, he uses his ability to joke and be cheerful. You can't help but laugh at him and feel better."

Jordan was being interviewed by Australian TV at one point during the campaign. The spot was being beamed back live via satellite. The reporter was asking Jordan what was said in a meeting he had just had with the Australian prime minister. "Well," said Jordan, with a cocky grin, "It was a private meeting, but your prime minister said he would vote for Jimmy Carter."

If there was one man primarily responsible for strategizing Carter's cataclysmic success, it was Hamilton Jordan. Charlie Kirbo calls him "a brilliant planner." Stu Eizenstat says Jordan "is one of the most intelligent young men I have ever dealt with, and he didn't go to Harvard." Although almost everyone is fond of Hamilton Jordan, he is not without his enemies. Some in the campaign felt Jordan was too insecure to stand competition and quickly edged out anyone who encroached on his territory.

Yet if some of his critics admit Jordan would "stab you in the back, at least he'd do it because he had to, not because he didn't like you."

"He's a real classy guy," says Pat Caddell, Carter's poll taker. "I'll never forget when Bob Shrum, a speech writer, resigned, because he felt Carter's character was flawed. Jordan didn't turn on me for bringing him on board, in fact he said, 'I have to admire someone who had the guts to leave on principle.'"

The driving force in his life was getting Carter elected. "I'd just like to see him President." At thirty-two he still has no idea what he wants out of life. His is an existential philosophy. "I don't have any long-range goals. I don't have any for myself anyway. Things just take care of themselves."

Ham Jordan rolls back and forth on a battered typing chair in his bare office, drinking black coffee and chewing gum at the same time. Dozens of pink slips line his army-issue desk. Today he is wearing jeans, boots and a white tennis shirt with crossed blue racquets at the breast. Unlike Carter, Jordan is not a religious man. "Very few of us are." Raised a Baptist, he no longer attends church, reads the Bible or prays. The church to Jordan is an obstacle to change. "Although," he said, smiling, "I think I have the potential emotionally for being very religious." Carter has talked to him a "couple of times" about his worldliness. "He said, 'You should think more about the religious aspects of life,' but he hasn't brought it up in a couple of years. I think he's given up on Jody and me being born again.

"Jody and I are the complete opposites of Jimmy. Neither of us are very disciplined or organized. Drink too much, smoke too much and everything else. Well, I don't smoke, that's about it."

"Want to see my magic briefcase?" he says, rolling his chair to his army-green portfolio and opening it for examination. A batch of letters lies loosely inside, but not thrown in helter-skelter or mashed. He does not really look disorganized. "You wouldn't say that if you had written me a letter four months ago." Jordan laughs. "Files? I carry everything around in my head."

If he's disorganized and undisciplined, how does Carter put up with him? "Our styles are complementary." Jordan, like Carter, and two other top advisors, Kirbo and Powell, was born in deep southwest Georgia of a "middle-class average family." His father is the general manager of the Life Insurance Company of Virginia. Jordan considers himself "generally liberal."

Jordan's strength as a campaign manager was long-range planning. "Knowing how little money we have to work with and making the most of it . . . but what I do best is trying to stay one step ahead, being able to look six to seven months down the road. I've learned that from Jimmy. He's a planner . . . a person who sits down and looks ahead and says this is what has to be done."

Jordan first met Carter back in 1966 the night after his announcement to run for Governor. He was struck by the man's sincerity and his moderate approach to the race issue. Jordan was of a new generation of Southerner who claims he saw the folly of his parents' racist attitudes. Unfortunately, he says with regret, growing up in deep southwest Georgia he had shared their outlook for most of his early life. "You always had black friendships, but there were always these artificial barriers that stood between you in terms of going to school together and socializing. When I was a sophomore or junior in high school I viewed the people who were demonstrating and marching with Martin Luther King and Andy Young as my enemies. They were a threat to my life and my life-style. They were challenging things about the South that I thought were very precious."

But like his peers, he was influenced by the voice of the Sixties, by John F. Kennedy and the liberating experience of college. "There was a very dramatic change in my attitude over a five-year period from 1960 to 1965. My generation in particular now has a tendency to want to go back and compensate for earlier feelings. I compensated, not by taking to the streets, but by working for a man running for Governor who had a different attitude toward race and race issues. I felt like that was one of the strong attractions Carter held. He represented a new moderate voice."

He was twenty-two and a junior in the Political Science Department of the University of Georgia when he signed up to help Carter with his first gubernatorial race. Each day he drove thirty-five miles from his home in Albany to Plains to file or write letters for Carter at the peanut warehouse. In those days Carter farmed by day and campaigned by night. "He'd get into his car and drive to Augusta or Tifton, to women's clubs, or Lions or whatever. Then he'd come back with a batch of business cards and the next morning Rosalynn and I would write to the people he had met."

Jordan laughs. "When I started working for him there were so few people willing to work for him I ended up being his campaign manager."

He ended up as Carter's Executive Secretary too during Carter's term as Governor and was the mastermind behind Carter's extraordinary climb to the White House. It was Jordan's 72-page memo written November 4, 1972, that Carter used as a blueprint for his campaign.

The Jordan memo was treated like the Magna Charta. The original was kept under lock and key and copies were not available to the press. Anyone wishing to read the memo was required to make a special appointment in Jordan's office and any excerpts were to be approved by Jordan himself. The day I went, although I had an appointment, I was asked to wait until Jordan returned before I was allowed to begin reading. Jordan wheeled in a typewriter next to his secretary and insisted that I sit there to excerpt it while she watched. My eight pages of typed notes had to be O.K.'d by Jordan. Only three pages were returned to me, and those had been retyped and edited by his secretary. No exact quotes were to be used.

The following is a paraphrased sample of the memo:

1/ Get to know someone with "good Washington contacts."

2/ Realize your liabilities: a poor record on women's rights and a poor speaking ability.

3/ Get to know someone who "has guts and knows how to put the squeeze on fat cats."

4/ Cultivate a rich man like McGovern's Henry Kimelman. (Carter chose Morris Dees.)

5/ Cultivate and get to know the Eastern Establishment press, Wicker, Reston, Graham, Broder. "They have undeniable power. If they take your candidacy seriously, they can influence others."

6/ Read the *Times,* the *Post* and the *Wall Street Journal* every day. The *Atlanta Constitution* does not have everything you need on international affairs, etc.

7/ Use Don Carter's contacts. [Don Carter is Hugh Carter's brother.] Have him invite someone like Tom Wicker or Reston for the weekend. Go fishing at Cumberland Island.

8/ Establish a personal relationship with members of the press.

9/ It is an asset to be an ex-Governor. Governors and Senators have to spend time in their states and in Washington tending to official duties. You would be free to campaign full time.

10/ Hire a speechwriter immediately. You need to say things of substance.

11/ Get to see Senator Kennedy. He may tell you inexorably he is not going to run. This will help you know where he stands. [Carter did not go to see Kennedy until the day he announced, December 12, 1974.]

12/ Get Dean Rusk to fill you in on international affairs.

13/ Scoop Jackson: I notice you've been using his name with regularity. Be careful not to sound like you're promoting him. I think he has a fine reputation in the Senate as a leader, but think he's a man of the 50's and 60's who has lost touch with what's really happening in the country and world today. Although you're compatible on most issues, don't promote him or you will sound like you're touting him for 1976.

14/ Askew and Bumpers: Concern about both having the same ambitions you have. Don't think Bumpers has the guts or the drive to run for national office. "A lightweight." Askew has respect and could run. But afraid he may lose Senate seat.

15/ Talmadge and Nunn: Get to know both Senators. Assure them you are not going to run for the Senate, so they're not afraid of you. They can be of invaluable help and will be delighted to have someone from Georgia running for President.

16/ Pretend you're running for the Senate so you can have access to the papers on government and domestic issues. By pretending you are seeking a Senate seat you won't frighten off people who might think you were crazy to try this or try to beat you to it.

17/ The Primaries. It's important to have a strategy. Muskie acted like the front runner and tried to run in all of them.

McGovern picked and chose wisely so as not to squander time and resources.

18/ We need to have an early showing in New Hampshire and win Florida so as to dispel the notion of Southerner.

19/ Need some position from chairman of the Democratic National Committee that will allow you to go around speaking.

20/ Cultivate Kennedy smile.

The adjectives Jordan uses to describe Carter are "stubborn," "shy," "tough," "an overachiever," "well disciplined," "a man who doesn't like to lose," a "complex man" with "apparent contradictions," a peanut farmer who likes square dancing, but also classical music and art. "He's not easy to understand. The key to understanding Jimmy and Rosalynn is that they're both from the same little town, and both are basically very reserved kind of people. Neither was extroverted fifteen to twenty years ago. It took a special effort for him to go into politics, to go in and shake hands with people and to meet people. He had to overcome a basic shyness. What happened at one point in their lives was that Jimmy got into public office and realized that to compensate for that he had to become more extroverted. The same thing happened with Rosalynn. They're both able to do things now, but they're still basically reserved persons whose privacy means a lot to them. That's part of the mystique of understanding them."

Jordan believes Carter's dictatorial manner is a virtue. "Compromise is a desirable part of the political process, but in Jimmy's mind, compromise as an attitude is not good. He doesn't think, and I don't either, that the President of the United States stands up in front of Congress and says, 'I'll meet you more than half way on any bill or legislation.' You know, I saw Jimmy in numerous political situations with the Georgia legislature where there would be a bill and there would be ten key elements of that bill, and the members of the legislature would say, 'O.K. Governor, this is a fine piece of legislation but we disagree with these four or five points. If you give in on those four or five points, we'll let the other four or five go.' Jimmy would say, 'Hell no! All ten aspects of this legislation are important to me and I'm for 'em.' The legislature leaves and Jimmy holds a press conference, talks about the bill, maybe blasts the legislators. Then the next day they run back down and say, 'O.K. Governor, we're willing to give you six or seven of the ten points.' And then, finally, with Jimmy's persistence in his commitment to all ten things, maybe he has to compromise on one. Maybe he wins nine of the ten points. Generally it's been a beneficial political trait in terms of getting things done. But most people who deal with him in a political situation are not accustomed to that. They're used to sitting down at a table and just trading back and forth. But he's a tough person to trade with. I've never seen him outtraded."

The success of the campaign was simple, says Jordan—organization, hard work by the entire Carter family and staff, and common sense, coupled with the elements of good luck and timing.

"It was good for Jimmy to lose in 'sixty-six. He was not ready to be Governor of Georgia. And we could not have done in 'seventy-two what we did in 'seventy-six.

"The consolation I had in the early days when it all looked so big and impossible was I knew it was as big for any other candidate as it was for us. It was as big for Ted Kennedy as it was for us. But I knew none would work harder than Jimmy and I knew Jimmy was smarter and more capable."

Jordan says he's always been interested in politics, from the time he was a class officer in school, but he didn't like holding office and would never run for anything himself. "I could never personally tolerate all the things a politician has to do." His parents say Jordan has been a political animal since eighth grade. "If he didn't win himself he'd run his cousin for office," says his mother. His life will never be politics, Jordan claims. He might stay one term in the White House, but not two. "The key is being able to walk away." Besides, there are things he wants to do with his life while he is still young—return to an academic situation perhaps, or possibly write. Ham Jordan vows he will never "run another campaign. Unless of course in ten years Jimmy runs for President of the World. I would run his campaign."

One afternoon toward the end of the election campaign on the landing strip at Albany, Georgia, Jimmy Carter paused to single out from a crowd of welcomers a pink-cheeked but frail man with wispy hair. He hugged the man, kissed his cheek and said, "I couldn't have done it without Ham." Then he turned to me and said, "I want you to meet Hamilton Jordan's father."

The tears were streaming down the man's face, and for a brief moment, although we had only met with our eyes, he wept on my shoulder. "I'm so proud of my son. And I'm so thrilled that Jimmy took the time to tell me that."

* * *

One afternoon I stopped in Atlanta and saw Ham Jordan outside his office. I told him how Jimmy Carter had paused in the midst of a hectic afternoon to tell his father what a fine job he had done as campaign manager, and that his father had wept. I told him too that his father had asked me to come over to the airport fence to meet his mother, a stately woman with a cane, who was unable to walk onto the tarmac to greet Carter. "Yeah," said Jordan. "My mother has multiple sclerosis and my dad's dying of cancer. So this is a pretty emotional time for them. They're pretty proud."

CHAPTER 13

PATRICK H. CADDELL, POLLSTER

PAT CADDELL is going bananas. "What's the matter? I'm three hours behind schedule! First I had a meeting with the issues people, then another with the political people. Sure I just do polls! The trouble is everyone wants a piece of the poll."

Before he tears off down the carpeted hall of the Carter Campaign headquarters in Atlanta, Eleanor Clift of *Newsweek* asks if she can nail Pat down for an interview the next morning. "Yeah." Does he promise? "Sure! I'll never tell a lie. I'll never deceive you."

Patrick H. Caddell jots the time in his black appointment book, and heads for the bar to meet his next appointment. "I'll just never get it all done. There are only eleven weeks left. I just wish he'd hurry up and drop in the polls. I'm getting nervous. He can't stay up there forever."

Pat Caddell is lovable in a funny way. He looks as if he had been put through a wrinkle machine. He wears expensive suits, French cuffs and cuff links, but he is forever disheveled. Swarthy and slightly oafish, he looks like Eeyore from *Winnie the Pooh*. His mouth is small and sits somewhere down on his chin. It's hard to tell where the chin ends and his neck begins. And yet women are attracted to him because of his sweetness, his boyish and disarming personality and his extraordinary intelligence. Caddell's mind works so fast his thoughts spill out in an avalanche of words. He is the most gregarious of the Carter staff, its best raconteur and salesman.

"He also is one of the few around Carter who has strong convictions and concerns," says a staffer. "Caddell cares about the country and about Jimmy Carter." "I really think this country has one last chance. A country that doesn't believe in itself can't survive," Caddell said, talking nonstop over dinner in the Fairmont Hotel in Atlanta. "If we can't get the country to believe in itself again, it's curtains. That's why we need what I call a 'finished man,' someone with a great sense of himself, like Jimmy. Someone both tough and shrewd and compassionate, and not ideological. Those are the ingredients we need to move, but the first thing is to heal the country."

Caddell thinks Carter can do that. Not that he knows what Carter would do in office. But then FDR, whom he calls "the greatest President in this century, didn't know what he was going to have to deal with in office, but he was elected because people knew he would at least try something." He believes in Carter not because Carter has any specific programs but because "I have a sense of his value system and his passion to do what is right."

Caddell thinks Carter's meteoric rise was due in large part to timing and fate. "He was the right man at the right time at the right place. I don't think he would have been successful in 1972. He'd have gotten eaten up in the Vietnam War issue. He was a product of Watergate in a way."

The strange thing, says Caddell, is the ironic twist of Presidential politics in 1972. Carter might have been Vice President if he hadn't spoiled his chances by nominating Scoop Jackson at the convention. But Jordan, Powell, Bourne and Rafshoon were novices in the big leagues and were naïve in nominating Jackson. "They thought they could get national attention, get on TV, but they really got into hot water." Caddell, McGovern's pollster at the time, was pushing for a Southerner on the ticket and submitted Carter's name along with Reubin Askew's of Florida for consideration to McGovern. He laughs. "If I had gotten him on the ticket, he would have gone down to an ignominious defeat with McGovern and that would have been the end of Jimmy Carter. In a way I saved Jimmy's political career," Caddell says with a satisfied grin, and takes another sip of wine.

The second coincidence was the way the Eagleton fiasco developed. The day McGovern picked Eagleton, a friend of Pat Caddell's tried unsuccessfully to reach a member of the McGovern staff to divulge the story about Eagleton's history of psychotherapy and electric shock. His message never got through. "The irony is that he called Anne Wexler, told her about Eagleton's psychiatric history and asked her to get the message to McGovern quickly. Anne went to look for someone immediately. She ran into Rick Stearns, a Mc-

Govern aide, and told him, 'Eagleton has a problem.' Stearns said, 'We already know about it.' But Sterns was talking about another personal Eagleton problem. It was just a lack of communication . . . she went off thinking McGovern had been told about Eagleton's emotional problem. The funny thing is he had tried to reach all the other people on the staff, who were busy, but he never asked for me. I was in the situation room taking a nap. If he had asked for me, I would have been right there and conveyed the message. He says to this day he can't figure out why he didn't ask for me. It was just fate.''

In Caddell's *Weltanshauung*, fate brought us Nixon and Watergate, and consequently the fertile ground for the flowering of Jimmy Carter. Caddell first met Carter in June 1972, when he was serving as George McGovern's pollster and the Presidential candidate came to Atlanta to campaign. McGovern stayed overnight at the Governor's mansion and Caddell, who had spent four years at Harvard studying Southern Baptists, the South, and its changing mores (the subject of his unfinished thesis), spent twenty minutes at the Governor's mansion briefing Carter and McGovern on the same subject. "Carter really liked it," says Caddell, lighting his next Winston, "and we really hit it off. After McGovern went to bed, Morris Dees, who became Carter's finance chairman, Jack Carter, Hamilton, Jimmy and I sat in the kitchen drinking beer until three A.M. It was a great time. I really liked him. We had a long esoteric discussion about politics. I found him very intelligent, bright and stimulating. He really understood what was going on in the country. He had the best antenna of anyone I had ever met in national politics. I think that's partly because he lives in Plains where he's in touch with 'people.' "

Caddell liked Carter so much at that first meeting, he spent a lot of time at the Democratic Convention with the Georgia delegation talking to Carter, in spite of the fact that Carter's cronies were still trying to stop McGovern.

By the same token, Caddell admits that "early on" Carter "scared him." "He was so cautious and reserved until you got to know him." He calls Carter an extremely serious and tough person, who wears "brass knuckles" under his velvet gloves. "He tends to hit too hard, he doesn't just tap people."

He has seen Carter depressed only once—in Massachusetts when he lost the primary. "When I told him the polls showed Jackson closing fast he said it defied everything he knew about politics. He was shocked. He doesn't like to lose. He was tense, off balance, groping, perturbed. It put his back against the wall.''

He saw Carter excited only once—in Wisconsin, when Carter's defeat by Morris Udall became a last-minute victory for Carter. Carter was in a sour mood by the time of the Wisconsin primary. "He had just been through 'ethnic purity,' which he could never understand anyhow, just couldn't see what the flap was all about. He was tired too and I didn't help any when I walked into his hotel room in Wisconsin and told him he was not going to win big. He got very depressed." That night around eight ABC called a Udall victory. NBC followed. Caddell refused to believe it. "I had lost my source, I couldn't get him on the phone, so I asked a reporter from U.P.I. what [districts] were out and what were in. The minute I saw the figures I knew Green Bay and the rural areas, our territory, were still going to come in. I knew we'd win by a few thousand votes. I raced upstairs and told Carter. He really got excited. He smiled a lot. He really wanted to win. When the TV coverage went off the air, we all sat around the radio listening intensely. We were trailing by two hundred votes, then we went ahead by one hundred, then six hundred and seven hundred. It was one of the most dramatic moments of the campaign. It was Jimmy's idea to go downstairs and hold the newspaper over his head like Truman had when Dewey lost."

One thing that impressed Caddell was Carter's attitude when his friend Bob Shrum quit after eight days as Carter's speechwriter, citing problems with Carter's character as the reason. Caddell had brought Shrum on board and was almost apoplectic over his resignation. "I saw Jimmy the Tuesday night of the Georgia primary. I walked into his room and he was lying on the couch. When he saw me he started laughing. He said, 'Did you bring me another speechwriter?' I said, 'No, but Ham's going to make me head of personnel.' He knew how badly I felt and he went out of his way to talk to me and to say good-bye when I left the suite. He never said another word about it."

Carter was also supportive when Caddell's professional ethics were questioned by the national media. Caddell's firm, Cambridge Survey Research, was providing survey information for an environmental group as well as a nuclear power lobby. He was taken to task by the press for blatant conflict of interest. Columnist William Safire of *The New York Times* blasted Caddell on July 22, saying, "Patrick Caddell—Carter pollster, strategist and apologist—was not only on the payroll of the Saudi Arabian Royal Embassy for $80,000 per year, but provides poll answers to questions submitted by them and 'personal consultations' to help them 'employ the information' he gathers in their behalf." Says Caddell: "Jimmy wrote a very kind letter for me to the *Times*." The letter said in part: "I don't have anything to conceal about it, and I don't think that because we have a contract with Mr. Caddell to do political polling that he should have to give up all his other subscribers where most of his income is derived."

Although Caddell says one of his major areas of interest is foreign policy, an area he would want to work in during a Carter administration, he bristles when the subject of conflict of interest arises. "Look, I merely sell the Saudis a book of research. It's available to anyone who wants to buy it, like a syndicated column. They don't hire me to lobby for them. You could raise the same questions about Clark Clifford if you wanted, or about Charlie Kirbo for representing Coke. Just because Edward Bennett Williams represented John Connally doesn't mean he agrees with him."

Caddell is sitting in an expensive French restaurant in the Fairmont Hotel, but he swings one foot up on his wing-back chair as though he were in his own living room. None of those fancy French dinners in Washington for him or the Carter staff, he says. He is more comfortable at a hamburger joint like Clyde's in Washington than the snooty Georgetown circuit. "That's the most obnoxious thing I've ever seen. It's so incestuous. It's not who you are, it's what you are and who you know. Boy, you can get old fast on that merry-go-round. And if you need it for your amusement, you've really got problems." Caddell predicts the Georgians will probably be cliquish and "avoid the Washington dinner-party set." "No, they won't be like Ehrlichman and Haldeman and the Nixon set. Those people were really sick."

He describes the Carter staff as "well balanced," "unpretentious," "unaffected," "self-confident." "They don't take themselves all that seriously." What impresses Caddell, who has worked for numerous candidates, including Senator Edmund Muskie in 1971 and George McGovern in 1972, thirty Senate campaigns and dozens of gubernatorial, Congressional and municipal elections, "is that there's no jockeying for power like I've seen in all other campaigns. No one seems that hungry for it. By this time in 1972 everyone was already measuring their White House offices." The lack of clawing for power is partially due to the easy access to the candidate. "No one depends on anyone else for access. All of the top staff can call him. I called the house in Plains last week to talk to Jody. Jimmy answered and we talked for twenty-five minutes."

And yet he draws a picture of a tightly knit staff that allows few if any outsiders to penetrate, a mafia extremely protective of Jimmy and of each other. "They've been friends for a long time," Pat Caddell says. "They're like brothers. They really care about each other. There's never any friction between them. If anyone makes a mistake, their instinctive reaction is to protect."

The organizational chart is eternally fixed too. "Each one has his area without crossing over." But if the lines are overstepped, retaliation is swift and not always just. When Dr. Peter Bourne stepped into Hamilton Jordan's domain, trying to steal the spotlight, getting more national media play, and some said, attempting to edge Jordan out of his job, Jordan came down hard. Bourne was shunned by the inner sanctum, uninvited to Carter victory celebrations at the Democratic Convention, sniped at by the other members of the staff. Where were Peter and Mary Bourne? I inquired of Jerry Rafshoon the night of Carter's nomination, when the couple was conspicuously absent from the victory celebration in the Carter trailers at Madison Square Garden. "Probably in Georgetown," Rafshoon snapped sarcastically.

Caddell simply dismisses the Jordan-Bourne feud as a matter of "style" and "distance." Then, damning with faint praise the doctor who helped Carter become known in Washington and toiled for him for over six years, he adds, "Peter has many talents, but politics is not one of them."

Caddell also describes the staff as somewhat vindictive. He recalls the 1974 Democratic mini-convention when Carter had already made plans to run for President, but no one was taking him seriously. In fact, there were jokes about the Carter candidacy floating around the convention floor. "I'll never forget how upset Jerry, Ham and Jody were about it. I remember Ham saying to Jerry Rafshoon, 'We'll show them. You just wait and see.'" Until then, even Caddell had considered the idea of a Carter candidacy somewhat preposterous. "But when I heard that, I realized they were deadly serious."

Caddell, the son of a retired Irish Catholic Coast Guard officer, Newton Caddell, grew up first around various Coast Guard stations, but mainly in Jacksonville, Florida, and Falmouth, Massachusetts. He was first in his class and a baseball fanatic. He took up polling as a math project in his junior year in high school, fashioned a voter election model of the Jacksonville area, predicting elections based on early returns. "I set up at the courthouse and called all the elections early with great abandon, I had no idea what I was doing, but they all turned out right." In 1968 he polled and predicted election returns for Fred Shultz, the speaker of the Florida legislature and for the *Post-Newsweek* television station in Jacksonville. After Harvard, where he was not what his professors would describe as "an outstanding student," Caddell worked in an Ohio gubernatorial campaign, then set up an association called Cambridge Survey Research, Inc. near Harvard Square.

The firm, which rapidly became one of the nation's most influential and highly respected public opinion research organizations, conducts in-depth interviews four times a year with two thousand men and women on such topics as credit cards, abortion, Henry Kissinger, school busing, détente, and the Warren Commission report. The take is over one million dollars annually.

The polls are computer-tabulated and analyzed, then compiled in a massive loose-leaf binder—a three-hundred page report about the nation's political, economic, social and cultural attitudes.

After one year of polling, Caddell concluded that the United States was in the midst of one of the most profound changes in history. Basic values had almost been destroyed. Vietnam destroyed the belief that America always won. Assassinations destroyed morale and faith. "Perhaps most important was the overriding belief that we were a nation of special people, that we could always bend events to our will, that things in America always got better. Today, most people no longer accept that cherished notion."

Since Caddell started Cambridge Research Survey, his life has not been his own. In 1971 back in Florida when he was introduced to Gary Hart, then campaign manager for McGovern, Caddell signed up to do McGovern's polling. Overnight fame struck at the tender age of twenty-one and brought him an impressive roster of clients. In his first year, some of the major corporations that signed up for Caddell's services included Sears Roebuck, Westinghouse, Federated Department Stores, and Aetna Life and Casualty, all of whom pay handsomely to find out what Americans are thinking. His other clients read like a Political *Who's Who:* Senator Edward Kennedy of Massachusetts, Alan Cranston of California, George McGovern of South Dakota, Birch Bayh of Indiana, Governors Hugh Carey of New York, Michael Dukakis of Massachusetts, and Milton J. Shapp of Pennsylvania.

Although the reports are confidential, *Parade* magazine obtained copies of documents. Here is a sample of some 1976 polling, some of which found its way into Carter's campaign rhetoric.

• Fifty-two percent of the men and women polled this past summer said they think the worst economic times are "still ahead of us," compared with 36 percent who believe they are "behind us."

• Fifty-six percent said the nation's energy problems were "primarily the result of greed on the part of oil companies and will be solved as long as they get their price. While another 28 percent said the problems are the result of scarce natural resources and will require massive efforts to resolve them.

• Forty-one percent said that "the best way to deal with crime is to impose stiff penalties and punish the criminal severely," while 51 percent said the best way to deal with crime is to clean up the social and economic problems that cause it. Nine percent were not sure.

• Cadell found the American public overwhelmingly believes that the entire federal budget is bloated and in need of substantial trimming. But in one category, health care, people are willing to pay higher taxes for expanded government services.

• On cutting the federal budget, the largest group of 34 percent identified military and defense spending as the place to begin.

• On politicians, 68 percent of the public believes that in the last ten years "America's leaders have consistently lied to the American people."

To Carter, Caddell became more than just a pollster. He was friend and political advisor to Carter and an indispensable catalyst for all the campaign.

But Caddell does not plan to hang around now that Carter has been elected. He is not interested, he claims, in a White House job or even in coming to Washington other than to open a branch office of his firm.

"Oh, I enjoy the power. I'm fascinated with it. It enables you to do things. And I'm intrigued about seeing things done. But I'm not interested in going to D. C. and heading up the Census Bureau. I'm not ready to give up everything I've built.

"First of all, I don't want to work that hard. I'm a dilettante. I'm spoiled by my own independence. The nice thing about my job now is I'm into everything. I'd rather be in a position where I didn't need the White House job. It's important some people hang back. I can have more of an impact on Jimmy from the outside anyway.

I'd rather be able to call up and say, 'God damn it . . . let's do something about such and such.' Eight years is a long time. I'd rather be able to come and work for a year sometime."

In the meantime Caddell wants to complete his education. He never finished his thesis at Harvard. Never really studied that hard. Now he wants to make recompense. "My life has been screwed up backwards since I was an undergraduate. I'd like to straighten it out."

CHAPTER 14

CHARLES KIRBO,
ÉMINENCE GRISE

MOST TIMES Charlie Kirbo does not laugh, does not smile, does not shake hands, does not trust anyone, especially a reporter. On a first meeting he neither cracks a joke nor takes one. He can be a joyless, humorless man. And yet there are moments when he relaxes that his dry wit crackles through and hits home. Says Kirbo, "Jimmy and I both have the same sense of humor." However, his ice-blue eyes rarely focus on an interrogator's unless the question is extremely penetrating. Then they narrow suspiciously. Reporters like Ken Auletta of the *Village Voice* say the vibrations they get from Kirbo are "very strange." "He's one of the coldest men I ever met." I thought that until I had interviewed him four times.

Charlie Kirbo is Jimmy Carter's "father figure," and the "wise man" of the Carter campaign, "the man who slows things down." And like Carter, a man of many facets. John Pope, one of Carter's oldest friends, ran into Kirbo at the Atlanta Airport the day before the Democratic Convention started. Pope asked Kirbo why he was not on his way to New York like the rest of the Georgians. "Cuz I gotta go home and pick muh beans," Kirbo replied. "I got thirty rows to pick. I already picked half of 'em but I gotta finish."

Says Pope, "He's real country, one of the most country people I've ever met. He really likes being on his farm, likes animals. Someone gave him a goat once. Now he's got twenty-seven." But this country gentleman with sleek white hair and red nose and the world's slowest speech also has two hundred head of Black Angus cattle, over three thousand acres of farm- and timberland in the deep south of Georgia, a twenty-five-acre farm on a lake just outside of

Atlanta where he lives in a spacious antique-filled brick home with his wife and four children, and a chain of building-supply stores in North Florida and South Georgia known as "Stones, Inc.," that grosses two to three million in sales annually. He also has Coca-Cola as a client and Attorney-General Griffin Bell as a partner.

Kirbo's law firm of King and Spalding occupies extremely plush offices on the twenty-fifth floor of the Trust Company Tower overlooking Equitable Life, the National Bank of Georgia and most of downtown Atlanta. The highly polished parquet floors, strewn with oriental carpets, massive paneled walls bearing the portraits of stern-looking founders, brass urns filled with sprays of eucalyptus and large leather chairs, all indicate the enormous affluence this country lawyer has accumulated over the years.

Kirbo says his friendship with Carter developed because they have much in common. Like Jordan and Powell, Kirbo was born in a small town in deep south Georgia. One of eight children, he was brought up in Bainbridge, one hundred miles south of Plains, population of 10,000, where his father, like Carter's, was a big fish in a small pond. Kirbo's father not only founded the "Christian Church" in Bainbridge, which Kirbo's family still attends, he became a businessman, court reporter, lawyer and later an elected official—clerk of the court. But in spite of his family's prestige and social standing, Kirbo learned the value of a dollar. He worked as a hired farm hand at thirty cents a day, and later on road construction for seventy-five cents a day.

Kirbo enjoys hunting quail and turkey, and fishing for bass and bream on his property in south Georgia. And like Carter, he claims to have a sensitivity to the plight of blacks which he learned, he says, from his father. "When I was a little boy a good many of the people we knew were in the Ku Klux Klan, and they were constantly putting pressure on Papa to join. He didn't, and I didn't understand it at the time. He was only one I'd ever seen that shook hands with black people. The things he told me when I was a boy about this racial thing have come to be the way he thought they should be."

Unlike Carter, who fared poorly in high-school physical education, Kirbo excelled in sports. He played guard on the high-school varsity football team. Yet Kirbo was a poor student. "I never did make real good grades. I only went to two years of college so I had a great deal of difficulty in law school."

But Kirbo had a deep religious commitment and adheres to a puritanical life-style. He taught Sunday school until three years ago, served on the board of his church, still attends services every Sunday, and reads the Bible, though "not as much as I used to." He neither drinks (occasionally a glass of white wine) nor smokes. "I quit after smoking three packs a day for twenty-five years." One thing he has in common with his friend of fourteen years is that "We both enjoy a certain type of humor. He has a good sense of humor and I think I do too."

If Carter has hidden his sense of humor on the campaign, says Kirbo, it is because "He was in the fight of his life and he just disciplined himself in every area, including his sense of humor. You have to control it. You can be so humorous that you're not taken seriously. And it's easy to get misquoted. That's where I get into trouble a lot. But Carter was getting attacked from the very beginning by certain writers and he just had to play it close. He's also been under a financial strain. It's easy to get a million dollars in the hole right quick. He was worried about that too. There just didn't seem to be a time for the guy's sense of humor to flourish, but they're seeing it now. When he's relaxed he has a fine sense of humor.

"I always thought of him as a very fine campaigner, the best I'd ever seen, but wondered about his executive ability until I saw him operate as Governor." Yet Carter was only in office for six or eight months when Kirbo, Rafshoon, Powell and Jordan decided he was a "gifted" man who could be President. "He was certainly far more qualified than anyone running at the time. He had a tremendous capacity to govern, good judgment and could make strong, bold decisions. I also knew he could get elected. We discussed it back in 1971 when I was state chairman and I'd see these other candidates and knew Jimmy was in their league. He was more capable politically. I knew it was an open ball game that anyone capable could get in there and run. I wasn't the only one who talked to him. Bert Lance (president of the National Bank of Georgia and Carter-appointed highway director as well as Carter's unsuccessful choice as his successor and his selection as Director of OMB—Office of Management and Budget) talked to him, as did Dean Rusk back in 1971. It was a slow process, we talked about it for a long time."

Kirbo never had a second thought about a Southerner coping with the problems Carter might encounter as a Presidential candidate because of his south Georgia background. "That's a lot of bunk!"

The Atlanta lawyer suggested to Carter that if he were going to run he should begin to attract national attention. "He was receptive, so we started planning."

I saw Kirbo four times. At no meeting did he ever smile or laugh. The first time was on the twenty-first floor of the Americana Hotel in New York during the Democratic Convention. Kirbo had just come down from Carter's suite, where he was advising the future nominee on his Vice-Presidential choice. A dedicated family man, he refused a breakfast interview because he wanted to eat with his wife and children, but preferred to meet instead after breakfast in the blue-and-white lobby coffee bar. He had a glass of milk. Speaking in a slow, barely audible Southern drawl, Kirbo said he first met Carter back in 1962 when he was retained to press his claim against ballot fraud in his first race for the state senate. The two men became good friends and he's been coaching Carter ever since. He helped him run for Governor, and was part of the original clique that put together Carter's Presidential strategy. "I told him after I watched McGovern on TV," said Kirbo, in his painfully slow drawl, "that McGovern would get nominated but would get wiped out because I didn't believe he had the political capacity for getting elected. I thought Jackson or Humphrey would do a better job." Soon after that, Carter launched a "stop-McGovern" movement. "I told him to do that. It was a mistake."

"I see him maybe twice a month, talk to him once a week. I write him memorandums whenever I have something on my mind, or I send a message or suggestions sometimes through Hamilton Jordan or Jody Powell. I try not to bother him. If he knows I have something I want to talk to him about, he calls me."

Kirbo's suggestions have ranged from advising Carter on his Vice-Presidential choice to keeping Bob Strauss as Democratic National Committee chairman to the campaign strategy. In the beginning of the race Kirbo suggested that Carter not run his campaign on issues. "I told him people were not so concerned about issues as they were about finding someone they could have confidence in and who they thought would treat 'em fair. I told him not to run his campaign on an intellectual approach to issues, but on a restoration of confidence in government. I thought people would buy that. They were wore out on issues."

When Carter asked Kirbo to interview Vice-Presidential candidates, Kirbo flew to Washington and questioned dozens of Senators, businessmen, twenty-eight to thirty people in all. "I was sort of confused. I was so impressed with all of them, they were all clean. They all had strength. But I told him Mondale was the least complicated. He and Jackson; they hadn't run on a ticket and been defeated. They hadn't been involved in a lot of controversy. Well, Jackson was a little more complicated and most of the others had something that was not bad, but complicated. Muskie had run for Vice President and gone down to defeat. Then he had a losing run for President. Glenn was an astronaut, but he and Jimmy were both military men, which wasn't good. And Glenn had considerable business holdings that would be scrutinized. I also told him one thing McGovern did wrong in 1972 was he resented anyone who opposed him. Carter should reconcile people who opposed him. Mondale had supported Humphrey, for example, but he had the same views."

Kirbo's advice has not always been good. When Carter made his catastrophic ethnic purity remark in April, Kirbo cautioned him not to apologize. "I told him I thought most people knew what he meant, and my advice was that it wasn't necessary to do anything." According to sources, Rosalynn Carter, Andy Young and Vernon Jordan finally persuaded Carter to admit his mistake, a gesture that helped save his political neck.

Kirbo also admits he got Carter into difficulty in 1972 when Carter was seeking the Vice Presidency. "I wrote him a memo saying if he had aspirations to be on the ticket, he should take a strong position for or against somebody. I told him if he supported Hubert Humphrey or Jackson, even if he failed, it wouldn't hurt his chances. It would get him some attention. If McGovern was going to select him, he'd select him in spite of his stand." Kirbo was wrong. The rest of the Carter staff admits that the national attention Carter received in Miami as a result of nominating Jackson amounted to a bowl of grits. The action soured relations with George Wallace, because Carter had promised to nominate him, and with George McGovern. Says pollster Pat Caddell, "McGovern had just stayed at the Mansion the week before and they had gotten along so well. McGovern took it as an act of betrayal."

My second meeting with Charles Kirbo took place in his paneled law office. Again there was no attempt to shake hands, no greetings, no small talk exchanged. And his gray eminence spoke so softly I had to strain forward to listen.

Kirbo sat stone-faced on the couch in a gray glen plaid suit, blue shirt and scuffed black shoes, surrounded by pictures of his children, Susan, Kathy, Betsy and Charles—on the walls and on the credenza behind his cluttered desk are more pictures of his children. Nowhere was there a photo of Jimmy Carter or for that matter one of Kirbo's wife of twenty-five years. "I guess I should have one of her," he said, "she's a very pretty girl. She's twelve years younger than I am. I don't know why I don't." His eighteen-year-old daughter Susan is a student at West Georgia College. Betsy, sixteen, and Kathy, thirteen, are students at a public high school. Charles Kirbo, Jr., is a college dropout turned rock musician.

"He didn't want to go to college so I made him quit," says Kirbo. All four children live at home, and that is where Kirbo prefers to be. "I go home most evenings. It's tough to go out. We don't go out much, maybe one or two nights a week. I like to spend more time on my farm. Two people work for me. One black and one white. The black man has been one of my best friends for seventeen or eighteen years. I like to work by myself with my flowers and vegetables. It's a good way to reflect." It is late afternoon and Charlie Kirbo rubs his eyes with his hands. He seems tired and he scowls like a man with a headache.

Charlie Kirbo did not always plan to be a trial lawyer. He had political aspirations from the time he was a young man. "There was a time I wanted to be a judge. Then I thought I'd like to be Governor." What happened? "Oh, I don't know," says Kirbo. "I just got further into trial practice. This gives you plenty to do too." So Charlie Kirbo takes vicarious political pleasure in his friend Jimmy's political success.

Eight o'clock the next morning Kirbo arrives at his office and heads for the coffee machine. His blue blazer and gray slacks both need pressing. His black shoes still need polishing. "Excuse me, I have to make a phone call."

Kirbo is back in five minutes. "I talked to Jimmy. I had to give him some advice on the speech he's making today." Carter was going to address the American Bar Association in Atlanta and was livid. Kirbo reported that his research staff had not given him enough input on the speech. "He had to write it himself. We just talked about the shortcomings of the judicial system, his desire to help the bar restructure the delivery system so they can get a workable one. We talked about the cost of litigation, the delay in litigation, the sheer volume of it and the inability of the courts to deal with it. There need to be some substantial changes. We used the speech he made on Law Day as the basis. I just gave him some ideas on the subject matter."

What does Charlie Kirbo want out of his political association with a President? He does not plan to open a Washington branch of his law firm or to expand his Atlanta law firm past the eighty-five lawyers there are now. "We have all the business we can handle." Nor does he want to join the White House staff. "I'm just interested in the moral factor in decision-making, having a voice in what is the right thing to do, the proper thing to do."

(And it helps to be able to suggest one's law partner as Attorney-General.)

CHAPTER 15

JERRY RAFSHOON,
MEDIA EXPERT

JERRY RAFSHOON calls himself the Carter "Media Masturbator."

On a cabinet behind him sits a wooden sculpture of a fist with the third finger raised.

Rafshoon is the advertising genius behind Carter's campaign. He is the father of the five-minute and the two-minute television ads that played a crucial role in electing Carter.

He is also the divorced father of four children—one nineteen-year-old girl studying premed at the University of North Carolina, two teenage girls at a private high school in Atlanta and one eleven-year-old son. "You know, I get to see more of my kids now than I ever did when I was married, because I have them all day Sunday and we do fun things together. The time is all theirs."

Rafshoon never had a particularly happy childhood either. Born in Brooklyn, the son of an air force policeman, he says, "I didn't like my father. He was a mean man. We had a lot of arguments and he left us. That's how I developed my rapier wit," Rafshoon says, half-teasingly. "Sarcasm keeps people at arm's length. That's what went wrong with my marriage. At least that was part of it." As a boy, Rafshoon lived in a variety of air force bases—California, Texas, South Carolina, Hawaii, Colorado Springs. Bouncing around like that made him "very abnormal and shy. I was always the new kid. I was small and not very athletic and the other kids beat the hell out of me. So, I read a lot and played with girls instead."

Rafshoon went to the University of Texas and graduated in 1955 with a degree in journalism. He had worked on his campus newspaper, but decided on advertising rather than news. "I wanted to make money." He wrote advertising copy at Lyndon Johnson's station KTBC Radio for fifty dollars a week at the same time Bill Moyers was there writing news. Rafshoon lasted for a year and then joined the navy. From 1956 to 1959 he served as a communications officer on a tanker in the Mediterranean. He never saw combat. "There was no war, but we got lost one time and almost sank the *Forrestal*. We missed."

After a stint at an Atlanta department store writing copy and three years with Twentieth Century-Fox in New York as national advertising manager, he founded Gerald Rafshoon Advertising, Inc. in Atlanta.

Now, twenty-seven awards grace the wall of his eighth-floor chocolate-brown offices at 1422 West Peachtree, just three blocks from the Carter campaign offices. It is Rafshoon's world which he does not plan to relinquish for a job on the White House staff. "I'm more interested in the journey than the destination."

Like others on the Carter staff Rafshoon calls himself an atheist. A genial man of forty with a quick sense of humor, he's been a friend and advisor to Carter for ten years. Rafshoon stretches his feet on his desk and talks about Carter. He was introduced by Hal Gulliver, now the editor of the Atlanta *Constitution,* who has covered Carter since he ran for the state senate. In 1966 Gulliver was working in the state capitol when Carter was running for Governor. Says Rafshoon, "I had just opened the agency. And I was impressed by how bad Carter's advertising was. I'll never forget hearing a jingle on the radio . . . 'Jimmy Carter is his name. Jimmy Carter is his name.' No one knew who the hell Jimmy Carter was anyway, so what good was it singing 'Jimmy Carter is his name?' I called Gulliver and said, 'Your friend Carter needs help.' "

Carter asked Rafshoon to make a presentation. Jack Kaplan, then his creative director, and Rafshoon "threw together one hundred and twenty pages of bullshit" and met Carter and a group of his friends at the Dinkler Belvedere Motel. "He liked what we wanted to do. It had not been done in Georgia advertising, it was like *cinema verité*. Our idea was to follow him around the state, show him in action and have the announcer say, 'Jimmy Carter. They say he can't win. You're the only person who can decide. Meet him. Talk to him. If you like what you see, vote for him.' "

Most of the people in the room did not like Rafshoon's presentation. "They were used to seeing politicians speaking from behind a desk. But while they were arguing I felt myself being kicked under the table. It was Jimmy and he was smiling. He told me after the meeting broke up . . . 'Don't listen to those people. I'm the only one. Go ahead and do it!' That was so refreshing. It started me liking him. I went to Plains that weekend and stayed at Miz Lillian's Pond House and got to know him. He was one of the few politicians who seemed to give a damn about what I had to say. So many of them lose their humanity, but this was a real person.

"I remember he changed into jeans and we went out to a bar, drank beer and threw darts. I was impressed by his intelligence and I liked his instincts about the state, race and what was good for people."

After he lost in the 1966 race for Governor, Carter called Rafshoon and said, "Let's start next week. I'm running again."

Rafshoon, who had worked for Bob Kennedy in 1968, finds many similarities between Bobby Kennedy and Jimmy. "He has the same toughness combined with compassion and sensitivity. And they're both superachievers.

"From 1970 on I figured he had as good a chance as anyone to be President. I knew he was capable of competing in the big leagues. Then I saw the stuff the big media wizards were putting out and I said, why not me and why not us? I started talking to people in 1970. I was always cognizant of his national image. I knew he wouldn't just finish four years and go back to Plains. It would be a waste."

By 1972 they were ready to move. Carter would push Henry Jackson for Vice President. "He never would have supported Wallace, so Jackson was a good out, acceptable in Georgia and a good compromise choice," Rafshoon said. "We had dinner Sunday night before the convention at the Playboy Plaza Hotel and he said he would agree to let us put him up for veep. It would be good exposure for the future if he should decide to run for President."

Both plans backfired. "I remember walking back from the convention hall at three A.M. the night McGovern was nominated and saying, 'If those schmucks can do it, Jimmy can do it.' We all decided to get together to start planning, but Peter Bourne jumped the gun on us and wrote him a memo."

CHAPTER 16

ROBERT LIPSHUTZ, TREASURER

ROBERT LIPSHUTZ, fifty-five, the campaign's chief fundraiser and national treasurer, is one of the rare members of Carter's team to mention ideals and principles as the reason for affiliation with Carter.

Lipshutz says, "We have a number of similar ideas about what's important in life, what's the purpose of existence, a similar sense of value about what's significant and worthwhile, a desire to make the most of our talents and maybe leave a little bit of a trail that has some meaning.

"Jimmy's also the most self-disciplined person I've ever seen. I've believed in the purposeful control of one's time since college, and if someone thinks the way you do, it's reassuring."

Lipshutz, one of the friendliest men on the campaign staff, is all work and no play. To him relaxation is going home after work, working some more, and getting a "decent night's sleep." "I relax when I work, relaxation is an emotional thing, not physical. It's a state of mind. To me relaxation is working twelve hours a day and being able to take things in an orderly fashion so I'm composed and not feeling pressed." Lipshutz smiles easily, oozes Southern charm.

His manicured hands are folded placidly on the desk in front of him. Yellow sheets, budgets and checks bearing his signature in blue felt tip are laid out in perfectly straight rows.

Robert Lipshutz used to ride a lot, in fact he was in the United States Cavalry before it went out of existence, but he no longer rides, or plays tennis. "You know we belong to the country club, but we never go," he smiles. "One part of my life I've neglected, is scheduling some exercise."

There are no long vacations and no frills in Bob Lipshutz' life either. "No siree, I haven't had a long vacation in thirty years." Two weeks a year does nicely.

One or two nights a week he and his second wife, the former Betty Beck Rosenberg (he has four children by his first wife), go out to dinner, but he would avoid the social set in Washington. He may be a partner and founding member of the prestigious law firm of Lipshutz Zusmann & Sikes, but he does not flaunt his fortune. He does not drive a sports car or opt for a limousine. He wears a drugstore wrist watch, polyester suits, and carries a badly beaten leather briefcase. He ordered army surplus furniture for the Carter offices.

And yet Robert Lipshutz was not raised frugally. Although his great-grandparents and grandparents had been serfs in that part of czarist Russia known as Latvia, he was the "spoiled only child" of an Atlanta garment manufacturer. Lipshutz never had to work summers to help the family make ends meet during the Depression, like other boys did; "I was never deprived." He went to a YMCA camp, where, although Jewish, he attended morning and evening Christian services. Consequently he is not uncomfortable with Jimmy Carter's born-again Christianity. "I don't believe in Christ, but I have a great respect for Him."

There was plenty of money for college too, and he attended the University of Georgia. It was only in his twenty-first year that his father's garment business floundered and Bob Lipshutz had to think about money for the first time, and his current specialty, budgeting.

He had to borrow money to open his law practice and to live on "close funds."

Lipshutz says he admired his father greatly as a person "even though he failed in business, because he treated everyone, no matter how low or high, the same. He was always decent to people. He was as equally at home at the filling station and at the country club."

A black woman reared Bob Lipshutz, and although there was a "master-servant" relationship in those days, he claims they treated each other with "respect." And through his synagogue, Lipshutz says he learned respect for all minorities.

His congregation was active in the civil rights movement, and Rabbi Rothschild in fact worked with Martin Luther King. But although Lipshutz calls himself "liberal" on social issues, "I didn't have enough confidence to be out in front in those days."

Robert Lipshutz considers himself a good Jew. He attended Sunday school since kindergarten. He is a past president of the Jewish

Reform Temple in Atlanta, a past president of the Atlanta Lodge of B'nai B'rith and believes in applying religious concepts to daily life. He is also a member of the Commerce Club in Atlanta, which Carter has asserted admits neither blacks nor Jews.

He says the driving force in his life is helping people who need help . . . the old, the mentally retarded, the less fortunate. "This country provided a unique opportunity for my family and I have a tremendous sense of obligation to it."

He had never worked on a Presidential campaign before, but was interested in helping Carter because "Jimmy can set the tone of morality in government that can spread and help turn it around. He might get more people to look up instead of down."

CHAPTER 17

STUART E. EIZENSTAT, ISSUES AND POLICY DIRECTOR

UPSTAIRS AMID THE CHEERFUL CHAOS on a top floor of an Atlanta office building, Stuart E. Eizenstat is pasty white from too many days behind a desk. The expression on his face is perpetually troubled. The permanent frown on his brow looks ironed in place. At thirty-three, he looks fifty.

"His sense of humor doesn't show on the outside," says Orin Kramer, his deputy assistant. "But he has a good one. He's very controlled, disciplined and he concentrates carefully."

Eizenstat is Carter's calm, purposeful, horn-rimmed-spectacled is-sues-and-policy director in charge of packaging the positions the candidate should take during the Presidential campaign on issues ranging from abortion to zero-based budgeting. The Chicago-born lawyer has helped Carter since 1968 with the formulation of opinions, and was responsible for smoothing away most of the rough edges for Carter during the drafting of the Democratic party platform, one of his proudest accomplishments. Under him works a youthful staff of a dozen issues coordinators, highly respected by all for their intelligence and selfless dedication.

"We are responsible for helping formulate the Governor's stands on all issues," says Eizenstat. Some two hundred fifty experts from all over the country have been enlisted and grouped into task forces to help "plug Carter in to the best thinking available."

The issues "coordinators" do not generate scholarly tomes on their own. They produce quick studies that incorporate the candidate's policies with material gathered from outside advisors on specific topics. "We assign a speech to a particular substantive person who acts as the coordinator for that speech," says Eizenstat. The coordinator contacts several outside advisors, sends them a rough draft, redrafts the speech and gives it to Eizenstat, who then sends the draft to Carter for comment. "His input is substantial. He writes massives remarks in the margins."

"One of the unique things about Jimmy is his insistence he get the widest range of opinion and be aware of the full range of views. He wants a clash of viewpoints. He's not an idealogue. He's tough-minded. It's what has to be done and what's the best way to do it."

Carter rarely compliments him, says Eizenstat who puts in eighteen-hour days and sacrificed a law partnership for his candidate. "You know Jimmy's satisfied when he doesn't compliment you, although he did compliment me on drafting the 1976 Democratic platform."

He is angered if someone doesn't perform up to snuff. Eizenstat was out of town before Carter gave his speech to the American Bar Association in Atlanta and was not able to get him all the material he needed. "He had to write most of it himself and he told Jody the night before the speech, 'Tell the boys I appreciate all the help they gave me.' He can cut right through you."

What about the fuzziness? "This is the year people are tired of ten-point programs. They are dubious about the cost of programs. But our position papers have been as detailed as any." What about lunching at the exclusive "21" in New York and consoling corporate executives that business will not suffer under a Carter administration, and yet telling the "little man" that his day has come? "Well, he said he'd end the deferral on taxes too. One guy just called me and said, 'Get him off that goddam issue.' Look, no politician tries to rub something into their face they don't like. You can't do that in a political campaign anymore."

There were three themes Eizenstat and Carter worked out for the campaign:

1) *Open and responsible government:* Sunshine laws; merit appointments of judges.

2) *The need to restore competent government:* Government must have a role; 1600 categorical grant programs, but the money is not getting to the people. The problem is to get the programs working well.

3) *Efficiency:* Streamlined efficient government. Over thirty-two agencies administer health programs. The need to organize.

"He'll be talking basically about the same issues as he did during the primaries, but he'll elaborate on them."

Eizenstat was not heavily involved in issues from the outset of the Carter campaign, simply because there were few issues Carter addressed himself to except a small number of key themes of his own choosing. His early pitch called for welfare and tax reform, government reorganization, love, trust, compassion. There was no need for spelling out any complex programs. "He gave a fairly standard speech six and one half days a week fifteen or sixteen hours a day," Eizenstat says. It was not until February 1976 that Carter called Eizenstat and said, "I need you full time." It was March before any major organization took place. "Frankly, before that it was difficult to get people to work for him; he was so unknown."

Eizenstat, who considers himself a "JFK Progressive," first met Carter in 1968 when a friend insisted they get together. "I didn't know him from Adam and I was dubious about a guy who was a peanut farmer. But he was so bright and attractive. He was obviously dynamite, and he seemed capable of bridging the rural-urban gap which the rural farmers had usually won. He seemed to want to bring the state into the twentieth century. But I wasn't sure so I made no commitment to help him in that first campaign. He was such an underdog, it seemed like a waste of my time. But he called me twice and asked me to help him, so I did. My job was to see he was briefed on all the issues and help frame his position on the issues."

What intrigued Eizenstat was Carter's assimilative abilities, and his attention span. "I remember the beginning when he would send me position papers and every one of them would be thoroughly read with interlineations and comments. Howard Samuels from New York tells the story about sending Carter a very detailed survey on New York City's debt problem. He fully expected Jimmy would never read it. Four months later Jimmy was in New York for meetings and launched into a discussion of New York's debt. Samuels said it was the most incredible performance he had ever seen. He had obviously read and assimilated everything."

Al Stern, Eizenstat's long-haired deputy, a professor of philosophy at Wayne State University who teaches "the history of ideas," and has worked in every Presidential campaign since 1948, went to Plains for a foreign-policy briefing. Says Stern, "Jimmy has an unbelievable attention span. He sat through the entire thing for almost five hours. No one even got up to go to the bathroom. You could never get Hubert Humphrey to do that." "It was hard enough to get him to concentrate for five minutes, no less five hours," says Eizenstat, who was research director for Humphrey's 1968 Presidential campaign.

"This candidate is more deeply involved in the issues process than any candidate I've worked for."

Eizenstat practiced law while Carter was Governor, but late in 1974 Carter called to say he was going to be chairman of the Democratic Campaign Committee and asked him to put together a briefing paper to advise the various candidates on the issues, on Nixon policies, and recommended alternatives. In their discussions Eizenstat found Carter had developed a sizable grasp of national issues, "He had gone well beyond the parameters of the Governorship."

"I called him up one day in mid-1974 and told him I'd like to have lunch," Eizenstat recalls. "We went to Crowley's in the Underground. I said, 'You know, it's obvious you have a tremendous grasp of the issues, and considering the people on the horizon I think you should run for President!' He just smiled and said he'd been giving it some thought. He didn't tell me then he already had a plan, he just said to keep in touch, that he was considering doing it. A few months later, I said, 'Look, if you really want to, if you're really going to go through with this, we really need to sit down and examine the issues.' So, I went to Plains and we talked over a two-day period with a little dictaphone. We started with A for abortion and went through Z for Zaïre. I'd try to shape his perspective. I'd suggest the political ramifications of different bills and positions."

Stu Eizenstat is a rare breed in the upper reaches of the Carter stratosphere. He is religious. He neither drinks nor smokes, and he is one of the few long-standing inner-circle members with both Washington and White House experience. A graduate of the University of North Carolina and Harvard Law School, he served as speech writer on the White House staff of Lyndon B. Johnson in 1967–68.

Born in Chicago, the son of a shoe wholesaler, Eizenstat was an only child who remembers that "I didn't see my father a hell of a lot because he traveled all week."

The father of two children, Eizenstat is determined his family will be closer than his own was. Although politically he is a "JFK Progressive," he calls himself "a Social Conservative." "I believe in marriage and the family. I don't believe in extramarital affairs. It's just not for me. I'm not a devotee of the new single way of life either. I believe in commitment. I spend as much time home with my wife and kids as I can."

Eizenstat is what Carter most admires in his co-workers, a no-

nonsense workaholic. From childhood, Eizenstat has always been a superachiever. He was both an honor student and All-American basketball player in high school. In four years at the University of North Carolina he scored almost a perfect average, 3.8. "I had only eight B's in four years. Everything else was all A's," he says proudly. "Out of eighteen hundred to two thousand students at the university, I was in the top ten or twelve."

He was also vice president of his fraternity, a member of the student attorney general's staff and a writer for *The Daily Tarheel*. But he didn't date much. "I thought it was a waste of time. It took time away from my work and I wanted to do well in school."

He married a Jewish girl from Brandeis University when he was in law school.

Their life together is not exactly jet set. Most of his nights are spent at home working. Eizenstat set himself a goal after law school of writing one law article a year. So far he's published five. He is active in community affairs as well, serving on the executive board of the Atlanta Jewish Community Center. He is vice president of the Atlanta Board of Jewish Education for Youthful Leadership.

What motivates him? Eizenstat removes his horn rims, rubs his tired brown eyes, runs a hand back over his straight brown hair and stretches one foot across his paper-strewn desk. "I don't know. Certainly not greed or ambition. I guess it's the desire for excellence. I'm Jewish for one thing. And I care deeply about people, especially people who are not able to help themselves like other people can. I think everybody needs a shot at life. And I think the government has the responsibility to play a role and be an active instrument for change."

Like Robert Lipshutz, he says his Jewish training developed his sensitivity toward the less fortunate. "If you don't assimilate the the lessons of your religious talks and teachings, you're not a good Jew. The only definition of a good Jew is one who made those lessons part of his life. Anyone who has a sense of the holocaust and of history will be sensitive to others. That's how I came to it. I also feel very strongly about the Democratic party. I think it's the instrument to accomplish some of the ideals concerned with people, whereas the Republican party has always been concerned with vested interests.

"I strongly believe in tax equity, that the tax burden should be equally shared. I believe in civil rights and civil justice and I believe in a compassionate government that ought to concern itself with the problems of the average person."

CHAPTER 18

JODY POWELL,
PRESS SECRETARY

A TEEMING CROWD madly waved and thrust Right-to-Life banners, pictures of grotesque infant corpses and placards bearing the word "Murderer" at Jimmy Carter in front of a Scranton, Pennsylvania, hotel. Jody Powell, inching his way through the mob, spotted one man with a gaunt face and a floppy hat pulled down over his eyes, jumping up and down hollering, "Bully, Bully, Jimmy Carter!" With a slightly bemused expression, Powell yanked the ever-present cigarette from his mouth and muttered, "Now there's one they should have gotten in the third trimester."

It was past midnight in the opening weeks of the campaign when the Carter staff found out there were no rooms left in the Detroit Holiday Inn. At the end of an eighteen-hour day that had begun at 5:30 A.M. there was nothing to do but laugh and make the best of it. While the hotel tried to make accommodations available nearby, the Carter mafia gathered in the staff room. It happened to be next door to Jimmy Carter's suite. Between the comical Jim King and Jody Powell the laughter became uproarious. Suddenly it was interrupted by a phone call—Carter's Secret Serviceman calling to say "the Governor thinks it is inappropriate for the staff to be making so much noise." A pregnant pause. Then Powell blurted out with a grin, "Tell him to go fuck himself. At least he has a room."

The bus rumbled along the potholed roads between the airport in Albany, Georgia, and the Best Western Motel in Americus, thirty-five miles away. Powell dragged on another True Blue, jammed his foot against the armrest of another seat and told his joke for the fourth time since the primaries. "There was a revival meeting going on somewhere in southwest Georgia and this derelict rolled up the aisle and said to the preacher, 'Brother, I've sinned.'

"The preacher answered back, 'Tell it all, Brother.'

" 'Well, I've given in to the demon drink,' the derelict said.

"And the preacher replied, 'Tell it all, Brother.'

" 'I've gone through every scarlet woman in town,' said the derelict.

"Said the preacher, 'Tell it all, Brother.'

" 'I can't go on,' said the derelict. 'I just can't go on any further.'

" 'Tell it ALL, Brother,' the preacher replied.

" 'Well, when I was twelve I screwed a goat.'

"Said the preacher, 'I wouldn't have told that one, Brother.' "

One afternoon on the Carter charter, Joel Weisman, a reporter, was looking for the bathroom. Jody Powell, Carter's press secretary, turned to him and said, "I should have made maps for the *Washington Post*. Do you have trouble finding your ass too?"

Jody Powell is a "good ole boy," easy to be around and to banter with, witty, unflappable, relaxed. And he shares the media's propensity for hefty doses of alcohol, nicotine, coffee, profanity, humor and sex. He is also reasonably tolerant of their problems. And he translates Carter well. To most press people Jody Powell is Mr. Popularity.

The problem is, the news people just don't trust him. "Basically it's just that we're the enemy," says one reporter. "The name of Jody's game is win. At any cost." One television correspondent says he trusted Jody until the time Billy Carter's gas station caught on fire and Billy went bananas in public. "Jody demanded our film. He tried to take it away from us. These people don't want to see anything on the air or in print that's going to lessen the possibility of a Carter victory."

I'm convinced, if Jody were not as well liked as he is, he would have been lynched a long time ago, because Jody does not return phone calls. Anyone's. Ever. "He's just not very organized," says Carter's secretary, Maxi Wells. "He's totally disorganized," says Carter campaign manager Hamilton Jordan. Others ascribe Powell's inability to make a decision to an overinvolvement with Carter, trying to do too many jobs at once and having no time for such a press secretary's basic responsibility.

Over a ten-month period, I placed literally dozens of phone calls to Powell and never had one returned. *Playboy* author Bob Scheer told me he called Powell thirty-six times and never got a callback. John Osborne of *New Republic* tells the same tale, as do dozens of the most powerful members of the media. Attempting to set up an interview with Carter was tantamount to all-out war. Since Jody travels with Carter it was necessary to first track him down. In February that was a great game. By March it became a perseverance builder. By April it was a major frustration, a horror by May, heart-attack material by June, and just cause for murder by September. Most reporters found the only way to beat the system was literally to fly to where Jody was (sometimes less expensive than the sum total of the long-distance calls it took to get one question answered) or to hold onto the phone regardless of the time, distance and cost. One time I was put on hold for forty-five minutes before Powell came to the phone, another time, thirty-five minutes. Neither time was there an apology for the delay. "Yep," says Powell, by way of greeting.

Getting through to Powell was no guarantee of an interview, and an interview, once arranged, often turned out to be only ten minutes on a plane. It was also likely to be mysteriously canceled at the last minute. I remember Robert Scheer grousing in June that he had had to fly all the way across the country to get a twenty-minute interview with Carter. Says Scheer, "From there on, I had to beg for ten minutes here and five minutes there to finally get the time I needed. When I finally completed the article, I could never get Jody or anyone else on the staff to look at it." With a little vigilance, Powell could have spared his boss a precipitous drop in popularity and a major disaster at a most crucial time in the campaign.

I first met Powell in the ante-chamber of Mayor Kevin White's office one blustery February Boston afternoon while Carter was in the inner sanctum pleading for help. Powell seemed younger and more amenable than any press secretary I had met in eight years in Washington. And unlike some other Presidential press secretaries I have known, he did not seem self-impressed, egocentric, haughty or unapproachable. He seemed like one of us. I thought. We chatted about the nature of a television interview I wanted to do with Carter. It was to be part of a series I was filming for WRC-TV on the Presidential candidates. We would like to film Carter at his home in Plains one weekend in March. It would take an hour, possibly two, of his time. Jody foresaw no problem. Just talk to him a week or so before we planned to set it up. Powell never indicated that usurping part of a Carter weekend was anathema to the candidate.

I talked to Jody again in Orlando, Florida, the morning after the Carter primary victory about the interview. We checked Carter's schedule for the following weekend, March 17. It was clear. He and Rosalynn would be in Plains. The interview was agreed to for the following Saturday. It was my son Lindsay's fifth birthday that weekend and my husband and I had planned to go to a nearby ski resort with a group of Lindsay's friends and their parents. Because of the interview we agreed to celebrate the birthday early with a party at home instead. We scrapped our ski plans.

Midweek I saw Jody on a flight from Chicago to Washington after the Illinois primary. "It looks like we might have a problem next weekend," Powell said. "I thought Carter was going to have Monday free which would have meant he had two days at home. Now it looks like we have to schedule him for Monday, so I don't want to use up his only time to himself with an interview." We agreed to reschedule the interview for the next weekend. "Sure, there should be no problem," he smiled reassuringly.

I notified NBC of the change, packed my bags and left for Plains to begin some preliminary research. Powell had never specified a time, so I called him from Plains on Wednesday to check. "He's on long distance, he'll call you right back," his secretary said. I waited in my hotel room. One hour became two. I called again. Powell was still on long distance they claimed. I asked to be put on hold. It was forty-five minutes before Powell finally came on the wire . . . with a familiar refrain. "It looks like we may have a problem next weekend, the campaign is really heating up."

I could barely believe my ears. I was already in Plains, the film crew was ordered, NBC had planned to air the piece the following week. Powell promised to talk to Carter and call me that night in my hotel room. The call never came then or the next day. I phoned an aide to Carter and asked for his intercession. There was no way, he replied. Powell was the keeper of the gates. The lines were firmly drawn. His suggestion was to appear with my film crew at Carter's house as planned. "Jimmy will never turn you down."

Reluctant to appear out of the blue, I called the Carter house Friday night. Rosalynn answered the phone. "Jody never said anything to us. I'm sure Jimmy doesn't know a thing about this." I explained the predicament. Sympathetic, she said she would talk to Jimmy but not until the morning. He was expected after midnight and she would be asleep, but "Call at nine A.M. and I'll see what I can do."

It was teeming rain the next morning, hardly a day conducive to filming Jimmy in the peanut fields. I met the film crew at 6:30 A.M. outside of the Carter warehouse and went to the home of Carter's sister, Gloria Spann, who had agreed to ride her motorcycle for us and did so good-naturedly even in the downpour. At exactly nine A.M. I called Rosalynn. Carter answered the phone himself. "I don't know anything about any television interview," he said coldly. "No. Jody never talked to me. And if he had set up an interview on my one day off, I'd fire his ass." I went over the dilemma—how the interview had been agreed to first one weekend, then the next, how the film was scheduled to air next week, how Peter Bourne, who is as close to Carter as any of his aides, suggested we simply arrive at the house. "If Peter Bourne suggested that, I'll fire his ass too," Carter sputtered.

I was losing ground fast. I looked out at the deluge; I thought of the vast expense of bringing a crew from Atlanta for the day and of returning with no film. Somebody would fire me too, I told him. Carter stuck to his guns. My daughter, Brooke, was standing beside me. She had been smitten with Carter after he invited her to sit with him for a two-hour plane trip from Chicago to Washington the week before, drawn cartoons for her and talked to her about his Presidential race. She had pleaded to come along to Plains, to see Carter, and since it was spring vacation, I had consented to bring her to the interview. It was the first time she had ever asked, and the first time I had ever allowed her to sit in on an assignment. I was just as disappointed for her as I was for myself. I told him so. He was moved. "You know I love Brookie," he said. But he still refused to give in. I felt my voice crack. In all my life I had never shed a tear over an interview, but somehow I felt I was dealing with the military. I began to say thank you and hang up before I sounded like a complete idiot, when Carter sensed he had brought me to tears. "Don't cry," he said softly. "You know I love you. Can you be here by two o'clock?"

When we arrived at two sharp, Carter greeted me with one of his blessings, hands on my shoulders, a soulful stare, and a brush of his cheek. We filmed for an hour and twenty-seven minutes until the vein on his temple began to throb with impatience and Carter said in his controlled way, "I've got to get inside and call all those uncommitted delegates." But he was gracious to the end.

I saw Jody Powell the next week. He said nothing more about the NBC interview than "I heard about it." The difficulties I met in the first campaign interview proved to be no exception. From there on, like so many other reporters, every interview request was met with considerable opposition. During the Pennsylvania primary, I traveled with Carter for several days asking for some time to interview the candidate. Provided I fly all the way to Memphis, where Carter was going to attend an event, I could have fifteen minutes on the return flight to Johnstown, Powell said. The Memphis log was a trip most reporters skipped because it was so needlessly expensive. A twelve-minute interview with Carter well past midnight cost me close to two hundred dollars.

"The trouble with you," explained a close Carter aide the following week, "is you don't sleep with the right people. If you did you'd have no trouble getting an interview." The aide told me one woman writer had taken up bed and board with a Carter staffer and ended up with two hour-long interviews with Carter at his home in Plains.

Evidently Hunter Thompson of *Rolling Stone* wasn't sleeping with the right people either. Thompson flew all the way to Orlando, Florida, from Aspen, Colorado, during the Florida primary to interview Carter. When Thompson arrived and found the interview was off, he went in search of Hamilton Jordan, who had arranged the interview. Jordan was in his room, but refused to open the door. Thompson merely poured lighter fluid on the door and set it afire.

Jody Powell looks like an anemic Robert Redford. At least he did at the beginning of the campaign, before he smoked so much his face lost its healthy glow and his pale blond hair began to thin appreciably from the daily tension. He is still very macho movie-starish.

Many people think Jody looks like Jimmy Carter's son. And, in fact, it is often said there is a father-son relationship between the two. Powell denies it of course, although he admits, "I feel a certain affection for him." And from the way Jody looks at Jimmy, often standing three steps above him at an impromptu airport press conference, smiling, even beaming, hanging on every word with rapt attention, it is obvious their relationship transcends the purely professional.

Powell has become over the past seven years, since he began

chauffeuring Carter around the state of Georgia, his closest confidante. Carter told me one day, "Outside of Rosalynn, Jody understands me best." Some think it unusual that Carter, who prizes moral standards and Christian values above all, would choose as his mouthpiece a man who was bounced out of the United States Air Force Academy for cheating, and whose favorite word is "shit."

The attraction it would seem is that the two are opposites when it comes to personality, soul brothers when it comes to background.

They share, as Powell puts it, "a great commonality."

Both were born under the sign of Libra in deep south Georgia, to farming families that enjoyed considerable social prestige in their communities. Both were Baptists and firstborn sons. Both had poorly read fathers, and domineering, liberal, highly educated mothers. Both attended service academies and both ended up, after their fathers' deaths, in politics.

Powell was born September 30, 1943, in a town called Vienna (pronounced Vi-anna). His father raised peanuts, corn, cotton, canteloupes, pecans, watermelons and some beef cattle and hogs on a four-hundred-acre tract of land ("the land actually under cultivation" says Powell). His maternal grandfather, Grady Williamson, was the town banker and a deacon in the local Baptist church, as prestigious a combination of positions as one could come by in a small town. Grady's daughter, Jody's mother, was a public-school teacher, a status position by Southern standards. His father had worked for the United States Post Office in Miami for a while, but decided there was more to be gained from tilling the soil. Like Earl Carter, he was a "strict disciplinarian." Jody added, "I never disagreed with what he said or was whipped sometimes with a belt."

Growing up on a farm provided Jody, as it had Jimmy Carter, with a "uniformly happy, pleasant, very secure existence, a very untraumatic childhood." He felt loved and accepted in his family and his home. Like most farm boys, he had his share of chores, some pleasant, some not so pleasant.

"One of the most distasteful things I ever did was to walk behind the peanut pickers that went through the field with a pitchfork. Fairly regularly the picker would throw back with the chaff, and whole clumps of peanuts would still be on the vine, leaves, stems and dirt and dust. In fifteen minutes you were absolutely covered with red dust. You couldn't tell the black workers from the white workers. We were all a mutual shade of red."

When he was ten or twelve he milked a cow every morning and

night, that he not so affectionately referred to as "that damn cow." "When I was ten or so, it was clear the cow and I both discovered who was boss. Up until that point it was clear the cow was boss," says Jody.

His only crisis as a boy were troubles with his legs and feet. He remembers his family building a house and burning the stumps of trees leaving small smoldering pits here and there. Jody, six or seven at the time, gamboled barefoot about the yard until, by accident, he found he was tramping through a sizzling bed of ashes and fried his feet but good. He spent the next several weeks in bed. He suffered too from an unusual blood infection, which resulted in large oozing sores on his legs that kept him bedridden for long stretches of time over a three-year period. His mother read to him constantly. "There was nothing else to do." The result of these years of physical disability and confinement was a deep love for reading. He read as much, maybe more, than Jimmy, he thinks. By the time he was in high school he had even read all his mother's course books. He had no trouble maintaining a straight-A average in school.

Jody was a God-fearing boy too, who attended Baptist Sunday school and church and, like Jimmy, taught Bible classes, at least in high school. In fact, it was his mother's dream that Jody would choose the clergy for his profession. Powell snickers at the suggestion, "not being exactly what you would call a born-again Christian." Today Jody only attends church for his daughter, Emily's, sake. He believes Bible-training ("It's part of our literary heritage if nothing else") and church-going are vital to a child's upbringing, "An integral part of your whole experience, something that goes into making you what you are." But he does not see the value of church-going forever. "Whatever view she takes of religion in general is her own affair, but she just ought to know about it." Powell, like Jordan, believes the church as an institution neglected its Christian duty to help bring about social change in the South.

Powell opted for a more martial career than the clergy. One of Vienna's more outstanding young men (class president, A-average, baseball, football and debate teams) Powell was a prime candidate for one of the service academies, almost a mark of nobility in backwater towns in the Deep South.

He was selected by the Air Force Academy. But although Powell left Vienna a hero, he returned four years later with the tarnish of disgrace. Powell was expelled for cheating on a final exam. "It was a four-hour final in the history of military thought. After several hours I took a break. Someone had left a copy of the course reader in the lounge. I just sat down and there it was. I was having trouble with revolutions, like the revolution of 1848 and so forth, so I figured if I could just get the right facts with the right revolution I'd be O.K., so I opened it up and looked at it. I don't know if someone saw me or not, but they came to me the same day. After some deliberation, and consternation, I finally admitted that I did it. Then I drove home. It was three-thirty Christmas Eve. I remember that was not my best Christmas."

He looks on that upheaval in his life as a learning experience now. He had never failed before, he had always been top dog, big man on campus, teacher's pet, Mamma's boy. "It was probably a good lesson in learning to accept the consequences for your own actions. I guess at one point or another, most of us run up against something that brings us down to earth. We realize by our actions we can do a considerable amount of harm." Another trauma in Jody's life was the death of his father by a self-inflicted gunshot in 1975. He had been suffering from a lingering illness. Like the death of Carter's father, it made him seriously ponder the meaning of his own life and roots. "Jimmy and I talked a long time about that."

Powell had no long-term aspirations, no idea of what he wanted to do with his life, so he finished up his political science major at Georgia State, in Jody Powell's words "a receptacle for rejects." "After getting kicked out for cheating, politics seemed like the next best thing," he said jokingly.

Toward the end of 1969, Powell, at Emory University in Atlanta, was working on a Master's degree paper dealing with the American Independent Party and third parties in general, and the Southern populist movement in the last quarter of the 1960's. He spent hours talking to sheriffs and county chairmen and mayors. "I knew that there wasn't going to be a lot of support forthcoming from them anymore, that essentially the back of the old courthouse-style politics had been broken by Maddox. Whoever ran had to have grass-roots support." He knew Jimmy Carter was planning to run for Governor again, and wrote to him. "I told him that I had voted for him in 1966. That I understood him a bit and that I had a good feeling for the populist movement and was eager to help him.

"He seemed like a decent progressive sort of fellow from my part of the state, which had always been considered by the folks from Atlanta and other points of sophistication, just a breeding ground for demagogues and less respectable political candidates. I told him that I didn't think he was going to get much of the establishment support, that most of it would go to Sanders but that he shouldn't worry. I also felt that we had gnashed and suffered and struggled with the race problem for a decade and a half, that there was a whole lot of unrest. A good part of the nation was caught up in the war, but Georgia wasn't. We had gone through a social change that was more real, personal and traumatic than the Vietnam war. It was a very fluid situation and just right for an upset."

And Carter understood. He wrote to Powell and invited him to come for the weekend with some other students. Powell went. "I was taken with him. He seemed so down to earth. What appealed to me about him was we had just come through a long hard struggle for a decade and a half and the last thing we needed was another Lester Maddox. We needed someone who understood Georgia, and I felt like he understood that we had made a major decision in the South and now it was time to move on and be done with it. If you were going to help the folks in rural Georgia with one of the most dramatic social changes ever in a society, you needed someone who understood people, not made them mad. I remember the first really long conversation we had. The gist of it was that if you want people to move, you've basically got to lead rather than drive. You can't expect a person to start treating a black as a neighbor if you tell him what an ignorant bastard he is and start beating him over the head, or his first inclination will be to tell you to kiss his ass. Instead you reach for the part of that person that's been telling him all along there was something wrong with the way things have been. You get there faster by showing them how to do it."

In spite of Powell's reputation as a Wallace conservative who reportedly discouraged Carter from hanging Martin Luther King, Jr.'s portrait in the state house and encouraged Carter to nominate Wallace in 1972, Powell felt that the way to bring justice to the South was by getting blacks enthusiastic enough about a candidate to vote.

He was away in college when the major civil rights marches took place, but says he and Carter have a common attitude toward blacks. "My mother, like his, was a moderate-liberal influence in the family. My mother's racial attitudes were based on the Golden Rule rather than the Bill of Rights. She always taught me, you ought not to treat people that way." During the days of the civil rights marches Powell never felt like his colleague Hamilton Jordan, that Martin Luther King and his colleagues were the "enemy."

"I felt ambivalent, but I think you developed a siege mentality in the South in those days that everyone was against you. That there was a bunch of folks sitting away in Washington correcting you. I never resented the blacks, because you knew who they were. It was the Northern white politicians who were the outsiders. I remember on more than one occasion when white politicians from the North would come down and march arm-in-arm in Albany and Jacksonville. Justly or unjustly you resented them. I remember one in particular, who came down to march with King, and I thought to myself, who does he think he is and what is he trying to do except get his name in the paper?"

Powell became Carter's inseparable sidekick and chauffeur in the 1970 gubernatorial race. Together they drove all over the state of Georgia, often sleeping in the same hotel room to save money. Powell learned the ropes from Carter quickly and, according to Kirbo, turned into a brilliant political strategist with a thick skin and a flair for speechwriting. At the end of the campaign Carter reportedly told Powell, "You've written a couple of speeches for me. Why don't you try press secretary?"

Those few speeches, a chauffeur's license and a crack political mind were to put Jody Powell in the White House.

CHAPTER 19

GREG SCHNEIDERS, COAT-TOTER AND ADVISOR

THE FIRST TIME I laid eyes on Greg Schneiders, he was a stranger, crouched on his haunches at my feet. My six-year-old daughter, Brooke, was Carter's seatmate on a flight from Chicago to Washington and Carter had sent Schneiders as an emissary to the rear of the plane to tell me she had eaten all her dinner. Schneiders had been traveling with Carter for weeks at that point but made himself so inconspicuous almost no one had noticed him.

The twenty-nine-year-old ex-restaurateur spent much of his time during the 1976 campaign quietly performing menial tasks for Carter. He served as porter, coat-toter, and all-around step-and-fetch-it.

One Carter associate recalls early in the campaign Schneiders, suffering from a miserable cold, arrived in Plains with the candidate at two in the morning after a grueling day in Iowa. When a crisis arose unexpectedly, Carter needed Schneiders en route to Atlanta by four o'clock. Schneiders' head was buried under his pillow when a friend of Carter's came banging at the door at the Best Western Motel in Americus to rouse him and drive him to Atlanta. Uncomplaining, Schneiders went.

Schneiders' quiet subservience paid off handsomely. This last man on the campaign totem pole rapidly rose to first on Carter's list of close advisors. "The day I heard Jimmy say to him, 'I want you to stay close to me,' I knew he was in," says a friend.

Schneiders was obviously "in" during the transition when I called the Sheraton Park Hotel where the rest of the top Carter staff, including Jody Powell and Hamilton Jordan, were staying. Schneiders, however, was staying at Blair House with the President-elect. "Nice little cottage," Schneiders said facetiously of the Presidential guest-house when I finally reached him.

Within a few short months, this Georgetown University dropout and former Capitol Hill bar owner had become a political consultant, no-man, confidant. "He's one of the few people who understands me," Carter said.

In January Schneiders was almost invisible. By December he was the keeper of the keys to Carter's kingdom. "If you need to speak to Jimmy, need to send him something, want something done, you go through Greg," said a staffer. "He's it."

Then, just as swiftly as he rose to prominence, he fell. In January, Carter canceled his plans to name Schneiders to the top-level White House post of Appointments Secretary after receiving an FBI report on Schneiders, documenting a history of bad debts and bounced checks. Schneiders incurred large debts when his restaurant business was failing. He had trouble paying his rent, owed money to his lawyer, was taken to Small Claims Court three times, was sued by his accounting firm and had one bank close his account. Schneiders said he had done nothing illegal and some members of Carter's staff suspected he was the victim of a purge. And yet, in spite of it all, he emerged like the phoenix and ended up in a prominent White House position as Director of Special Projects. It was Charles Kirbo who looked into the charges against Schneiders and found that he had done nothing illegal or injurious.

Detroit-born, New York- and Boston-bred, Schneiders was raised in a Catholic household. Three of his seven siblings are nuns and Schneiders himself once considered entering the priesthood. "That is, until the seventh grade when I started going to mixed parties." He laughs. His father, Alexander Schneiders, a psychology professor, taught at Jesuit colleges, such as Detroit University, Loyola University in Chicago, Fordham University in New York, and Boston College in Massachusetts. A Jesuit product himself, Schneiders attended Georgetown University in Washington, where he majored in philosophy and minored in psychology. He dropped out one course short of graduation. Classmates recall Schneiders as "different," "a nonconformist," "eccentric," "the kind of a guy who stuck to himself and nobody got to know very well. He was fat, always wore a beard and blue jeans, and well, he was kind of a blob." "Nobody paid very much attention to him," says one girl who knew him.

Schneiders did not abandon his college career for politics or some noble cause. He left to run a couple of bars. When his father died, Schneiders used part of his inheritance to buy Whitby's, a Capitol Hill restaurant. Then he bought the Georgetown Beef Company, a mediocre steak-and-burger eatery in fashionable Georgetown, directly across the street from its highly touted competitor, Clyde's. Both businesses went deeply into arrears, and businessman Schneiders sold out.

Schneiders had never worked in politics before he heard Jimmy Carter speak. His brother, Paul Schneiders, who had been "peripherally involved" with the campaign, gave Greg an extra ticket to a fund raiser at Pier Four in Boston in July 1975—a luncheon peppered with old Kennedy supporters in search of a new Camelot. Schneiders considered himself a Kennedyphile. Although he was only sixteen when Kennedy died, he remembers that his own disillusionment dates back to the assassination. "I thought the single most important thing about the 1976 election was that we recapture what we had lost in 1963."

To Schneiders, Carter came closest to Kennedy of all the other candidates. "I was an instant convert. I was very impressed. He seemed to have an overriding concern with trust in government and truth." Truth is tantamount to Schneiders. "One thing that came out of a very quiet and reflective period I had in high school, when I was doing a lot of reading, Salinger and things like that, was the realization that nothing mattered if you didn't tell the truth. Any pretense at all is just a waste of time."

Schneiders decided to learn more about Carter. "I read everything I could, I went to hear him again. I heard him at a ten-dollar fund raiser in D.C. And although I had never worked in a campaign before, I decided to offer my services."

Neither Southern nor small-town, city slicker Schneiders seemed out of sync with the rest of the staff. While many seemed like hail-fellows-well-met, indulged in bawdy humor, and extensive beer-drinking, serious, courteous Schneiders was always the perfect gentleman. While they spurned ties and most sartorial distinction, Schneiders was always well groomed. He wore horn-rimmed glasses, often a three-piece suit and seemed more like an Ivy League sophisticate than a good ole boy.

It was Peter Bourne who first brought Greg Schneider on board. Independently wealthy, Schneiders had volunteered to help Peter Bourne set up the Washington Carter headquarters. He did advance work in upstate New York and managed to impress everyone he worked with, with his quiet competence. Bourne is very high on Schneiders. "He's a spectacular guy. Fantastic worker. He's quiet and approachable. He has mature judgment and he's discreet. And in spite of the fact he has had no previous experience, he has political savvy. He's always been aware of the staff problems. He knows what a morally degenerate bunch we all are, but he bends over backward not to be judgmental."

At a meeting in Hilton Head, Bourne introduced Schneiders to Hamilton Jordan, who took a liking to the tranquil, but occasionally zany city boy. And since Jody Powell was looking for someone to help him handle the press, Schneiders was dispatched.

During the course of the campaign, Schneiders became as indispensable to the press as he did to Carter. In fact, many considered Schneiders, along with advance man Jim King, one saving grace of the campaign. When Powell was incommunicado, abrupt or unavailable, Schneiders answered phone calls, was approachable, polite and always helpful. More and more people turned to Schneiders as a funnel of information and an avenue to Carter.

Schneiders never seemed too busy to answer questions—any question, from queries to why speechwriter Bob Shrum quit to what Carter ate. Schneiders would listen quietly, nod his head before the question was finished. "Yes," he'd say in his soft deep voice, his small blue eyes peering out from behind his heavy glasses, before expounding at length. Even close Carter friends were crushed when Schneiders was eliminated from his exalted positions. "He was the best of the lot," said one.

Above all, Schneiders was always frank about Carter and himself. I asked him once if Carter slept in the nude, expecting him to bolt out of his seat. "No, jockey shorts," Schneiders replied, matter of factly. About Carter's sense of humor he'd say, "It's good, but he doesn't display it publicly and he's not much good at it when he does." Asked what Carter eats, he'd run through the menu—"He eats whatever they're serving on the plane, but he prefers hot sandwiches like hamburgers. He likes buttermilk and hot or iced tea. He used to drink Cokes, but he's given them up. He's allergic to Swiss cheese." Why did Carter carry his own suitbag? "He never wanted to come out here on the campaign trail carrying one hundred pounds of stuff."

Schneiders called Carter "ambitious, singleminded, disciplined and driven." He described his philosophical commitment as "somewhere between the polar extremes of Dewey and the existentialist Sartre." He has the pragmatism of Dewey, but the Myth of Sisyphus characterizes his view of life. In Camus, the basic option is suicide or an active life. He puts the meaninglessness behind him, involves himself in doing and acting and tries to lead a meaningful life.

He agreed Carter is shy. "I'm not sure I ever fully understand what has made him overcome that shyness. It's absurd he's so shy. There may be a bit of Dale Carnegie in all of us, but to overcome shyness by becoming President is a little much."

Schneiders disagreed with the characterization of Carter as a loner who preferred the plane seat next to him vacant and liked to stare out the window or at the bulkhead. "I always take personal offense at that," he says, "because the seat next to his is my seat. On a two-hour plane trip I'd be next to him for probably an hour to an hour and a half. Some flights I'm not there because he would sleep or do interviews, but at least half the time, if not three-quarters of the time I'm there. I think one of the reasons he likes me there is he doesn't have to entertain me."

Many feel Schneiders' low-key approach to life, and what some describe as a nonpersonality, is what attracted Carter to him. "I'm very even-tempered and I think that's attractive to Carter. He found me the same every day. I stay pretty stable."

Schneiders' role expanded gradually throughout the campaign. He gradually accumulated more and more power and access, until eventually he superseded even Jody and Hamilton. It was hardly a coup. It was more of a quiet evolution. And some say it's what did him in, more than bad checks.

"My role probably changed more than anyone else's in the campaign," he told Sally Quinn of the *Washington Post*. "But I never expected to be only a bag carrier. At first I was supposed to be someone who traveled with Carter, who did whatever job needed to be done, the way Jody had done before. But as Carter got to know me better and began to feel more comfortable with me, I became freer with offering my thoughts and he became more open. My role just expanded. I still carry the bags, but as the entourage grew we got to the point where I had someone working for me and there were fewer technical jobs for me. I was almost without a job except being available to see that the decisions he made were executed, to give him feedback on what he was saying and offering my opinion."

Schneiders graduated from porter to pundit. He proffered his opinion on everything from politics to humor. Some say Greg Schneiders is even the man behind "ethnic purity." One day on the plane Schneiders was teasing Powell about his meek behavior when

Carter's statement that Ted Kennedy "can kiss my ass," hit the papers. In front of reporters Schneiders mimicked Powell's kowtowing—"Shall I call him for you, sir?" "O.K. Schneiders," Powell shot back, "we'll see who gets the buddy-fucker award. Next time they do a staff piece I'll tell them who thought up ethnic purity."

Schneiders learned Carter's ways. "He often tends to work alone in the early hours. In the White House I'd say he'd be in his office by seven o'clock or seven-thirty at the latest. Then he'd work until ten on his own. Have a midday appointment period from ten until two-thirty. He'd use his afternoons for staff work and appointments.

"He'll probably use Camp David more than Nixon did, not go back to Plains except on Thanksgiving and at Christmas. But he likes to get away weekends. He likes quiet evenings at home with one or two other couples close to him and Rosalynn and he appreciates getting away from everybody once in a while."

I asked Schneiders once what he and Jimmy talked about on the airplane or when they traveled. He said, "We've talked a lot about Catholicism, believe it or not. He's asked me a lot about the Catholic religion, holy communion and mass and things and I've asked him about his Baptist religion. He calls me his 'Catholic advisor.' "

Schneiders has not painted the best picture of the Catholic church. He's called it "a farce." "I used to be fairly religious, but I think the Catholic church did a better job of screwing people up than any other institution." Schneiders has totally abandoned the precepts of the church. He has been what the Catholic church would refer to as "living in sin" for the past five years, with a pretty woman in her thirties with long salt-and-pepper hair named Marie. They married in December. Carter had been aware of Schneiders' entaglement, but said nothing, even when they took an apartment together near Plains. "He's like a father in that respect."

The young man who once wanted to be a priest today has more wordly ambitions. "I think if I could pick a job, any job, I'd probably pick the Senate. I think that would be a nice reflective place to be."

If he pays his bills, that is.

PART

VI

THE
PRIMARIES

CHAPTER 20

BEGINNINGS: IOWA AND NEW HAMPSHIRE

THE IOWA CAUCUSES held on January 19, 1976, were the first political event of the year, and the number one target on the Carter strategy map. Iowa, with the heavy media coverage it would attract, would provide a natural springboard into the national consciousness if Carter won.

As it turned out, Carter swept the caucuses with 27 percent of the vote. Although fewer than 14,000 voted for Carter, not enough to elect a city councilman in most average-sized cities, it was nevertheless a stunning victory over nationally prominent candidates. Birch Bayh had limped into second place with a weak 13 percent. Fred Harris came in third with 10 percent, Mo Udall won a mere 5 percent, Sargent Shriver 3 percent and Scoop Jackson 1 percent. Jimmy Carter's face was suddenly seen on NBC's *Today* show, the CBS *Morning News,* ABC's *A.M.* The man no one knew on *What's My Line* a few months earlier was an instant celebrity.

Iowa may have taken most Democrats by surprise, but it was really a sample of the simple Carter technique that was to be used in every primary state after that—grass-roots organization, and hard work combined with the Carter personal touch.

"Iowa was no phenomenon," said Richard Meyers, a Carter supporter, over coffee and rolls at the Des Moines Hilton one morning in August 1976. "There was nothing but hard work, organization and leadership. Jimmy Carter outworked everyone. He's tireless."

Jimmy Carter recalls the early campaign in Iowa. "Those were lonely days. Often just Jody and I would fly into the state in a small private plane. When I began my campaign I didn't have a built-in organization. There were no television cameras, no tape recorders, no radio reporters. I was a lonely unknown candidate. I came here looking for a TV camera, I never found it. I never saw a tape recorder or a radio reporter. But I found a lot of people who were interested in me. And we began going from one living room to another, from one labor hall to another, from one livestock feed hall to another. I would make a ten-minute speech and then answer questions for forty-five minutes and that personal give-and-take was the decisive factor in getting me known."

Elaine and Harry Baxter are one of the many couples who opened their living room to Jimmy Carter. Elaine Baxter serves on the Burlington, Iowa, city council and once ran an unsuccessful race for mayor. Harry, a stockbroker and the Democratic County Chairman for Burlington, was among the first to begin working for Carter in Iowa. Baxter saw Carter on *Meet the Press* in December of 1974. "I remember I leapt out of the chair and said, 'This is the guy who's going to win.' I liked his overall personality and his charisma. I felt just like he was talking to me. It was a coincidence that within the next two days the editor of our local newspaper wrote an editorial endorsing him." Baxter mailed a note and the editorial to Carter, called Hamilton Jordan, and volunteered his services to help organize the state. He received a swift handwritten reply from Carter asking Baxter to help identify and recruit campaign workers.

"We had worked for a lot of local races, and I managed a Congressional campaign in our county," says Elaine Baxter. "We were thinking it would be an interesting experience to work in a big city mayor's campaign or a governor's campaign, but then Jimmy Carter looked so interesting, Harry contacted the Carter people and they gave him the go-ahead."

In March 1975, the Baxters hosted a breakfast for Carter in Des Moines. Only four people showed up. "We were very apologetic," says Baxter. "But he said not to worry, that he'd come back again and he would win. He knew next time there would be more people. Well, everything he said came true. The next time four hundred people showed up to see him."

In March 1975, Carter's bushy-haired political gypsy, and state coordinator, the irrepressible, immensely likable Tim Kraft, who was to become White House Appointments Secretary in the Carter Administration, showed up at Harry Baxter's home. "He took names and names and names" from an assortment of Democratic lists Baxter had. "About three hundred names in all." From there Kraft went to work asking for assistance all over the state, setting up steering committees, opening storefronts, raising money.

Carter kept returning to Iowa. While other candidates targeted major primary states and wrote Iowa off as unimportant, Carter blitzed the state 110 times. The Carter staff saw the media value of the publicity of a Carter victory on January 19. It would vault him into first position for the crucial New Hampshire primary, due on February 24, about five weeks hence. Iowa was domino number one.

"I remember the first meeting we had in Iowa City, in June of '75," says Baxter. "One hundred and fifty people came. I made sure Carter gave the steering committee some private time before the meeting began. When they talked the vibrations were excellent. The big thing was the guy's personality."

Another asset was Carter's availability. "Every time we needed him, felt something was important for him to do, he'd come. He was never too busy."

But the most important aspect of the Iowa organization was follow-through. Although large crowds often appeared at Udall, Harris and Birch Bayh meetings, and dozens of Iowans would volunteer their names to help no one ever heard from the candidates again. It was a hit-and-run approach.

Carter, on the other hand, often wrote personal handwritten letters to those who were interested. No name was ever allowed to slip unnoticed through the system.

Henry Cutler, a Waterloo lawyer, heard Carter speak at a New Frontier dinner in Des Moines in June 1975. Morris Udall was speaking at another meeting in the same hotel, so Cutler went to hear both men. "I noted that Tim Kraft was following behind Carter, taking names of volunteers by the dozen. And I remember thinking, here's a guy who can't possibly win, but he's a good liberal, and I'll take part in the pleasurable indulgence of working for him. He's a hell of a nice guy. He had very direct responses, a very firm pro-Israel stand and he was very concise in his thinking. So I signed up and gave Carter ten dollars. I got a thank-you call within days and they asked if I wanted to work in northeast Iowa. There was immediate follow-through."

"Anyone could have done it," says Hazel Hammer, whose husband, Charles, is professor of physics at the nearby University of Iowa. "The trouble is, no one else worked as hard. I remember I met Fred Harris and he asked me to be on a steering committee, but no one on his staff ever let me know who signed up to work, or who gave

money. He could have won if he had done what Carter did."

Iowa farmers recall Carter or his wife Rosalynn sitting in their living rooms answering questions about farming by the hour. Carter had been perceived as a liberal, and yet the farmers found they would sit and nod their heads in agreement with him whether he talked about welfare or amnesty. Farmers also recall the ease with which Rosalynn Carter discussed farm parity, the price of seed and fertilizer with them. "I really enjoyed talking to them," said Rosalynn. "It was like being back in Plains." And they sensed it.

United Auto Workers, who played a major role in Carter's Iowa victory, perceived him as conservative. Chuck Gifford, chairman of the Iowa Community Action Program, remembers hearing Carter at a Democratic issues convention in Louisville in October 1975, and at first thinking of him as another Harry Truman liberal. Then they talked. He liked Carter's ideas on social action, National Health Insurance, job training and tightening up welfare. "It was not the usual 'We'll take care of you' speech. He told us, 'You've got to do your part.'" Gifford returned to Iowa and began organizing for Carter in December, sending rank-and-file members around the state to precinct caucus meetings. "I told them he was the best thing since JFK. I wasn't railroading them, the natural support was there. People liked the guy. He can commonly relate to workers. There's nothing complicated in what he says."

Soapy Owens, a former UAW Community Action Program (CAP) chairman, laughs about his early support for Carter. Owens met Carter in early 1975 at a meeting in the Iowa legislature, liked what he saw and wrote for some information. In October 1975 he invited Carter to be a speaker at a UAW state convention in Marshalltown, Iowa. "When the members found out I had invited a Southerner they never stopped harassing me, but after they heard him speak, there were quite a few converts in the room." They went back to their locals and talked to the leadership and the local unions responded. Each UAW chapter has a CAP committee and they talked Carter up in their neighborhoods. "We turned people out at the precinct caucuses and packed the Presidential groups with union delegates." Out of the forty-seven delegates Iowa sent to the New York Democratic Convention, eleven were UAW union members. "They could have gone with Jackson, but to the UAW Jackson was a heavy-handed military guy. Udall had our respect, but we had gone through the trauma of nominating one liberal, and we thought the mood was more center of the road. Birch Bayh had been a favorite, but he started too late and he was short of money. We knew he was not going anywhere. Carter seemed like the best bet."

Owens admits Carter had him fooled. "He's turned out to be much more liberal than I thought, but he's a winner. He reached a nerve with the people. He acted as though he was their next-door neighbor. They liked his very low-key approach. They were tired of table-bangers."

David Garst, an Iowa businessman and farmer, had never supported anyone in a Presidential race before, but went to work for Carter in Iowa after he read his book *Why Not the Best?* Garst raised $50,000 for Carter without batting an eyelash. "Most Iowans had been waiting for Hubert, but Carter just seemed to be the right man. He could appeal to both liberals and conservatives. He could talk to my farm workers as though he were one of them. And he reflected confidence. He told people he was going to win. I knew he was a winner."

On Saturday, February 7, twelve months behind Jimmy Carter, eleven members of the Carter family and "The Peanut Brigade," President Ford made his first campaign trip to New Hampshire. For all the support he mustered, he might just as well have stayed home and played golf.

A planeload of media preceded his departure from Andrews Air Force Base and bitter cold numbed our feet as we awaited his arrival in ten below zero weather on the tarmac at Manchester. An airport crowd of less than three hundred had gathered, unlike the thousands who had eagerly welcomed candidates like Nixon and Johnson in campaigns past. This was not a well-advanced crowd of GOP workers and well-wishers peppered with "We love you Gerry" posters and placards. Most were parents who came out of "curiosity" and brought their children hoisted on their shoulders to "see a President." And most were unimpressed by Ford. As Joe Quinn, who called himself a conservative Republican, said, "I've lost faith in Ford. If he gets the nomination, I'll vote Democratic this time. As much as I wouldn't want to, I'd even vote for Kennedy. I don't like the way Ford shifted from the little man to big business." Many in the crowd predicted Reagan would show tremendous strength in New Hampshire and possibly even win.

When Ford emerged from Air Force One with Mrs. Ford and

his daughter, Susan, I counted only three people clapping. Ford worked the fence for seconds before launching into an important press conference and family photo session. "Mrs. Ford and Betty should be along in a minute," he shouted unaware that he had meant to say "Mrs. Ford and Susan."

That morning a busload of press followed Betty Ford to two brief stops. The First Lady, unlike her predecessor, Pat Nixon, had abandoned the traditional Republican cloth coat for a full-length fur and rode in a dark-blue Lincoln Continental. While Rosalynn Carter plodded tirelessly through drugstores, barber shops, restaurants, art galleries, and city halls, pumping hands, pleading for support for "Mah husband, Jimmy Carter," and taking her campaign directly to the people of New Hampshire, Betty Ford's limited campaign schedule called for two short media events. The first was a visit to Lancaster Elementary School where a program for the mentally retarded was in session. There the press was herded behind ropes in one corner of the gymnasium by strong-armed Secret Servicemen who barked, "Up against the wall. Up against the wall." One cameraman and a smart-alecky White House advanceman broke into fisticuffs over where to stand.

Mrs. Ford seemed very low key and tired, which immediately led to speculation that her cancer had recurred and rekindled talk of Ford's quitting. While a group of students attempted to play basketball, the usually game First Lady sat demurely on a folding chair. And when a group of Senior Citizens performed the "Hully Gully" and the "Snoopy" for her, she refused their invitation to join in. "That looks too tricky for me," said the former Martha Graham dancer.

Her next stop was the Nashua Phone Bank, a small, hastily thrown-together operation in Nashua, New Hampshire, and one of ten phone banks throughout the state making about a thousand calls a day, targeting "undecided" voters and trying to entice them into Ford's corner with a second or third call.

Again the press was pushed "against the wall," this time by Peter Solen, a White House staffer with a sour disposition. An eighteen-year-old campaign worker named Larry was dragged away from a conversation with columnist Mary McGrory and forbidden to speak with the press. Mrs. Ford sat with her back to the cameras and placed a dozen barely audible calls. "Hello, this is Betty Ford. I'm calling to ask your support for my husband on February twenty-fourth," she said to disbelieving voters. "No visuals!" cried the cameramen. "No audio," the radio correspondents complained. "No story," huffed columnist Mary McGrory. I telephoned several of the people Mrs. Ford had contacted. Few had been swayed by her call to vote for Ford. As Mrs. Lorraine Drouin of Nashua said, "I knew I didn't want Ford. But I tried to be polite. I told her, 'I'm listening to all the candidates,' but I'm really leaning towards Udall."

Back at the Nashua Holiday Inn, where we were staying overnight, White House Press Secretary Ron Nessen said over drinks, the President would not campaign much. The campaign strategy was simply to present Ford as a "working President." "He is so well known he doesn't have to campaign in person. Look. Everyone is after his job. But he's got the job and he's doing it. They have to prove why he shouldn't have the job again."

Ford attended the Nashua Chamber of Commerce dinner as Nixon had in 1968. But Ford's audience was not only largely Democratic, it was also peppered with Reagan fans and workers, like New Hampshire chairman Hugh Gregg. Mary Sullivan, whom the Chamber had voted Woman of the Year, received a greater ovation than the President, and Sam Tampose, who introduced Ford, turned out to be a Democrat supporting Reagan and seized the opportunity to insult Ford in front of the large audience. "We all know you're a proficient skier, but of course, skiing is a sport that's all downhill." Ford was nonplussed by the introduction and his cool reception, and bumbled his way through a dreary speech on revenue-sharing that put what few ardent supporters he had in the audience into a comatose state.

Ford referred to "this month of January . . . I mean February." "Resilient" came out "resolent." And he told his audience, "All Americans in all forty-eight, I mean forty-nine states can learn from your example." Ford was halfway through his next paragraph before he corrected his state count to fifty. His one funny line failed to hit its mark. He said, "I don't think the U.S. Government could make beer for less than fifty dollars a six-pack." Several observers commented, "If he thinks government is so bad, why doesn't he get out?"

A Ford delegate named David Nixon stood in the rear of the hall shaking his head. "I told the White House not to have Ford campaign in New Hampshire. If Ford wins next week by one vote he'll be lucky."

Washington had been talking about the ineptitude of the Ford campaign for months. White House staffers were appalled at the lack of imagination and organization of the President Ford Committee. One White House lawyer told me in January that the White House had been sending heavy position papers to campaign headquarters around the country when what "they really wanted was buttons, banners and bumpers stickers. How can you turn on volunteers with position papers."

"The problem is," said a former Agnew aide and then Ford assistant, "that they're totally disorganized. No one knows what they're doing. All the pros who ran the 1968 and 1972 campaigns are in jail or on the way. There's no one left after Watergate. So to find someone without taint, they had to dig way down to the bottom of the barrel. They came up with Bo Callaway, who is a fake. And then they picked Rog Morton who's a hell of a nice guy, but a lazy bastard. So nothing's getting done. There's no long-range planning. No one has given any thought to the fall. It's all minute by minute. The other problem is that the President is just no good on the stump."

Ford did recognize his deficiencies in the art of public speaking and later took on a speech coach, Don Penny, who improved his delivery immensely. Penny even accompanied Ford on his successful whistle-stop train trip before the Michigan primary at the end of May and primed Ford before every speech from the back of the train platform. But somehow the proper elocutionary chemistry was always missing. Throughout the campaign and in spite of economic gains, he was perceived as lacking in leadership and inspiration, a colorless, interim President. The one common thread uniting Republicans in the Bicentennial Year seemed to be a desire to expiate the sin of having supported Richard Nixon. Nixon and Watergate drove many Republicans into the Democratic fold—one-quarter of all Republicans defected according to a Gallup poll taken in May.

On March first I had drinks at the Last Hurrah in Boston with Kenny O'Donnell, President Kennedy's Appointments Secretary and one of the former New Frontiersmen, now in his fifties. Ford had barely beaten Reagan in the New Hampshire primary and had squeaked by in Florida. O'Donnell said, "No one, not even an incumbent President, wins Hampshire with only fifty-one percent of the vote against a guy who isn't even an elected official, and stays alive. Besides, when people laugh at you, you're dead. People laugh at Ford. You can't fall off airplanes and be President. You have to play the role all the time. Jack Kennedy never forgot it for a minute. When we went to Berlin I remember Kennedy standing in front of a mirror on the airplane, combing his hair for almost fifteen minutes. I was impatient and so was the crowd and I told him, 'Mr. President, we have to go.' But he kept on grooming himself. Finally he turned to me and said, 'It isn't John Kennedy walking off this plane. It's the United States. And I want to look like the President when I walk down those stairs!'"

The difference in the stump styles of Ronald Reagan and Gerald Ford and the reaction to them was oceanic. If Ford aroused apathy, Reagan instilled dedication and interest. Ex-New Hampshire Governor, Hugh Gregg, a moderate Republican and former Rockefeller supporter had been asked to manage Ford's New Hampshire campaign but turned him down to manage Reagan's. Gregg believed Reagan more electable. Gregg was less concerned about philosophical differences between Ford and Reagan than with political reality —namely the dim future of the dwindling GOP. "We're in trouble up here. We've lost two Congressmen and two Senators. Now there's only the Governor and one Congressman. We don't want to lose everything. The only thing Ford's got going for him is the incumbency, but he's killing himself with a negative campaign. You can't win with a deadpan approach. Reagan mixes it up a little, tells a few jokes. So does Carter. That's why he's done so well."

Gregg did not predict a Reagan victory in New Hampshire. He believed a 40 percent showing would establish Reagan as a major vote-getter and after a few victories down the line, like Texas, Florida, and California, the screen actor would prove his worth. "Delegates are like sheep. They're going to go with a winner." Even Democrats had to admit to Gregg that they would have a harder time beating Reagan than Ford. "The New Hampshire Democratic chairman, Larry Rodway, told me he was concerned. He said, 'We might end up running against Reagan. Ford's a patsy.'"

Reagan turned out enthusiastic crowds even in the tiniest of New Hampshire towns. In Somersworth, a Democratic stronghold, fifty-three turned out to see Reagan. "What do you mean, small!" said Johnny Fisher, an unemployed carpenter and father of nine children. "It's a fantastic crowd for this apathetic town. They don't turn out for anybody. Mo Udall only had twenty people at his rally."

Reagan himself was the pluperfect candidate for 1976. At six-foot-two, with great broad shoulders, a firm build and polished-apple face he still looked enough like a movie star to make women swoon. Nevertheless, he was painfully shy and withdrawn.

On the plane, Reagan sat in first class, napped or held interviews. He did not come back to chat with reporters, or make small talk with them. I was amazed one night on a flight from Santa Barbara to Los Angeles to look up and see Reagan coming down the aisle into the press area. He returned my look of surprise by pretending he was riding a horse. He grabbed hold of make-believe reins and posted a little, like a kid playing cowboys and Indians. It turned out he was only going back to use our bathroom because his was occupied. When Reagan passed by again I asked him if he was going to visit with reporters. "Nope," he said. "I just went for a little walk, and now I'm going back," He seemed afraid of his own shadow. When somebody called him Mr. President that day he shot back, "That's scary."

It was obvious too that he despised campaigning for a variety of other reasons. At the airport in Santa Barbara under azure skies, he began, "Sometimes I think those who plan campaigns have a streak of sadism. Nancy is always on one campaign trail and I'm on the other. They say politics makes good bedfellows, but this campaign is breaking up a couple of good bedfellows. It's sadistic."

So while the press was filing at Howard Johnson's in Goleta, Reagan snuck off to his ranch up in the hills twenty-five miles north of Santa Barbara, with a few pool reporters. Reagan was like a new man there. He heaved a sigh of relief as he walked into his rustic living room with the rattan furniture and the huge stone fireplace. "Do you relax here?" one newsman asked. "Oh boy, yes," said Reagan, suddenly a cowboy. He and Nancy see no one here except family, he explained. Neighbors are uninvited. "That's the nice thing. It's kind of in a saucer. We've got six hundred and forty acres and we go riding on the trails. On a clear day you can see the whole Santa Ynez Valley and the Channel Islands." Reagan quietly turned and stared for a long moment out the dining-room window. Then he patted the top of his large round dining-room table and said almost to himself, "But this. Just to sit here in the evening and watch the sun get low is my idea of heaven." When his aide, Mike Deaver, announced it was time to go, Reagan responded like a man being led to the electric chair. "Do we have to?"

And yet the minute he appeared on stage Ronald Reagan was in his element. There, where lesser mortals are reduced to quivering paranoia, he became strong, vibrant, alive, confident and very funny. He was so very much better on the stump than Jerry Ford. Even Carter staffers worried about the possibility of a Carter-Reagan race. Had the election been based on charisma alone, Reagan would have had the upper hand. Nolo Contendere.

New Hampshire was the Big Casino. It was more than the opening of the campaign. It was traditionally the bellwether state. No one who has ever transferred his residence to 1600 Pennsylvania Avenue ever lost in New Hampshire. The eyes of the nation were watching to see whether nonofficeholder Reagan would outdistance the nation's first nonelected President, Gerald Ford, and whether an upstart Southerner could make inroads in Yankee snows.

The day of the primary, the Sheraton Wayfarer teemed with newsmen and activity. David Brinkley swaggered by to do his radio cuts. Tom Brokaw dashed about. Tom Pettit strolled back and forth waiting for something to happen. Joe Kraft appeared. Word had it that Walter Cronkite was downtown standing in line for election night credentials just like everyone else. NBC public relations officials circled a twenty-five-foot table pasting names on twenty typewriters that would be manned by reporters whose news operations had purchased NBC's computer election services. Besides typewriters, there were headphones and a bank of Xerox and teletype machines that would become engorged with political analyses of Carter's victory in a few short hours. The security was as tight, if not tighter, than the White House. Police guarded every corridor. The hallways were glutted with hordes of Secret Service guarding candidates who came to predict their victory. Bags were checked.

At five o'clock I drove over to Pineconia Grange, a small white clapboard polling place in a low- to middle-income two to one Republican district on the edge of Concord. The muddy parking lot was jammed with cars. Voters of all ages stood in line waiting to fill out their ballots. It was a large turnout for Pineconia. Over a thousand had already been through to vote, and Ford was the overwhelming choice among those I interviewed. Why? "Reagan hasn't come up with any better programs," said one housewife. "The economy is improving pretty good and I don't like Reagan's ninety-billion-dollar tax cut proposal," said a carpenter named Vieger. "Reagan? He's still an actor," said another. Three Democrats came through the line. They were all voting for Udall but would vote for Ford in the general election because "none of the Democrats are strong enough." Eight other voters said they were casting their votes for Carter because, "I like his way of speaking" . . . "He's going to change some of the policies as far as jobs go" . . . "He's honest." The last voter I spoke to, standing in the mud, said he would vote for "Birch Bear," but would write in Hubert Humphrey's name in November.

At Reagan headquarters in the New Hampshire Highway Motel the mood was grim. Secret Service guarded the entrance to the ball-room, funneling fans, freaks and press through an aperture between two tables. All were scrutinized, frisked and appropriately scowled at. Every purse, tote bag and camera pouch was emptied of its contents and inspected with a pocket flashlight. Just behind me a pudgy blonde, about five-foot-six, and perhaps thirty-five, had her pocketbook opened. There, nestled comfortably between her green wallet and a pack of Kleenex sat a gray-black snub-nosed revolver. "It's just plastic," she giggled. "I brought it as a joke." The blonde was whisked away to some torture chamber.

Newsmen and Reagan-supporters thumped up and down the cor-ridors at breakneck speed as the results began to come in from around the state. Ford was leading. "It was pretty bad in Manchester, really bad. And there's a light turnout in Nashua," said Lucy Cutty, a portly Reagan volunteer in a gray dress and jacket. The Reagan staff was more optimistic. One Reagan staffer bet twenty dollars Reagan would win with 55 percent of the vote.

Reagan was upstairs on the second floor relaxing in a batik shirt and slacks dining on veal cutlet and wine with Senator and Mrs. Paul Laxalt, and listening to the results on the radio.

At 11:30 the results were final. Reagan with 49 percent of the vote. Ford, 51 percent. A narrow victory for an incumbent President, but nevertheless a critical blow to Reagan.

Reagan came down at midnight to concede. He looked craggy and beaten, his smile pasted on like a felt-board cutout. "We came here believing that if we could achieve forty percent of the vote, it would be a viable candidacy . . . now we'll go home and change the laundry and go on." Hardly his loftiest speech to date. "I can start growing my fingernails again now." He chuckled, placing four fingertips between his lips. "I may even take up skiing." "Give 'em hell," someone shouted. The applause was courteous.

At 1:45, a group of Reagan staff gathered in Bob Tuttle's room to listen to the final returns on a small portable green plastic radio. Reagan taped a *Today* show piece with Barbara Walters across the hall. Two champagne bottles were carefully wrapped in white linen, wilted now from melted ice. No one uncorked them.

In contrast, the Carter people were exuberant. Jimmy Carter was the unmistakable winner of the New Hampshire primary with nearly 30 percent of the vote, followed by Udall with almost 24 percent, followed by Bayh, Harris, and Shriver. The scene that evening of February 24 at Carter headquarters was like New Year's Eve on Times Square for the hugging, kissing, dancing, and hollering. "The Green Beret of the Campaign," as Mary McGrory called him was on his way to the nomination. "I remember when we couldn't even find a microphone," Carter said jokingly to his campaign workers.

At the Boston airport, waiting to board a flight to Washington the next morning, there was suddenly a great flurry of whispers as Senator Ted Kennedy joined the queue with his nephew Joe Kennedy, Jr. Kennedy was not effusive in his praise for Carter, but was nevertheless courteous. "I congratulate him. He's got a lot of friends here," he told me. He seemed unconcerned about his brother-in-law Sargent Shriver, who had come in fifth in New Hampshire with only 9 percent of the vote and would undoubtedly fare worse in the upcoming Massachusetts primary. "Don't know, I haven't been in Massachusetts," he said, though his press secretary, Dick Drayne, said he had been spending practically every weekend there.

Shriver forces were furious that Kennedy had not given the signal for his troops to come to the aid of his relative. But Kenny O'Donnell, a close ally of Teddy's, told me that Kennedy was taking his revenge because Shriver had not helped Bobby Kennedy in 1968. "Who is Shriver?" O'Donnell had asked. "Head of the Peace Corps? How'd he get the job? He was Eunice Kennedy's husband. Head of the Merchandise Mart? How'd he get the job? He was Eunice Kennedy's husband. Ambassador to France? How'd he get the job? And why didn't he help Bobby? Because of Johnson! Sure Shriver has asked for our help, but I'll do what the Senior Senator of the State of Massachusetts tells me to. Maybe!"

On the plane, Kennedy rode in the coach section with Senator Claiborne Pell of Rhode Island. I could hear only snatches of conversation, but Pell was making comparisons to the Kennedy-Nixon campaign. "It's just like 1960 . . . He's the New South . . . we need a Southern mainliner . . . he'll never get to Washington." Kennedy, in shirt sleeves, did not respond. He stared out the window for a long time. He gobbled a lunch of soggy fried chicken, beet salad, cake and two 7-Ups and said almost nothing to Pell. He seemed to be contemplating the drastically new complexion of the campaign and his own dashed hopes.

At a Washington dinner party the next week I found myself seated between Senator Ed Brooke (Republican, Massachusetts) and author Susan Mary Alsop, both unimpressed with Carter's unexpected victory in New Hampshire. Both predicted Ford would be elected anyway because the country does not like to change Presidents and because people feel "he deserves a chance." Brooke said the Hill scuttlebutt was that "Kennedy will take second spot on a ticket with Humphrey" and that Hubert is "so excited about his new popularity he sails through the halls with a smile on his face."

CHAPTER 21

DERAILED: MASSACHUSETTS

ON THE BITTER COLD afternoon of February 23, a yellow cab lurched into the driveway of the Saltonstall Senior Citizen's Center in Medford, Massachusetts, a modern glass-and-brick nursing home, obviously for the affluent elderly.

"Move ahead," a maintenance man shouted to the cabbie, flagging him on with his arm. "The next President of the United States is about to arrive."

"Oh, yeah? Who's zat?" asked the cabbie.

"Jimmy Carter," the man replied.

"Nah," said the cabbie. "He ain't the next President of the United States. Scoop Jackson is."

Waiting for Carter in the warm, saffron-colored lobby, a film crew discussed a meeting between Ted Kennedy and Hubert Humphrey which they had filmed a week earlier in Fall River, Massachusetts. The two Senators had come to a Congressional hearing on jobs and the economy and at the end of the meeting, the inevitable question was posed by a reporter, "What happens if the convention deadlocks?" Humphrey, ebullient as ever (Eugene McCarthy calls him the "crocus without a spring"), was all smiles. "I'm sure," he said, wrapping an arm around Kennedy's shoulders, "that either Senator Kennedy or myself would take a lead from the people." That night Humphrey had attended a fund raiser for Kennedy and Kennedy promised to be at Humphrey's Minneapolis fund raiser in May. The consensus in the lobby that afternoon was that something might be boiling between the two.

There was. Washington was buzzing that the Massachusetts Senator was open to running on a ticket with Humphrey this year. Kennedy intimates confided that, if elected, Hubert's health would cause him eventually to step aside, giving Kennedy the reins of the White House. Some said Kennedy had not dismissed running the race himself of course (although Kennedy friends denied this emphatically) and contingency plans had been made. At one time, Kennedy forces even considered having Ted enter several of the primaries. California was mentioned at a private round-table meeting in a Washington restaurant with Kennedy in attendance. The family seemed to be shaping up for a campaign too. Teddy lost weight, Joan went to Alcoholics Anonymous, and Teddy Junior was considered to be back in good health. But sources said Kennedy was enough of a realist to understand that the party wanted Hubert. There was a sense of indebtedness to the Happy Warrior. He had come so close in the past. He deserved another try.

Carter arrived an uncharacteristic twenty minutes late and stalked into the "ballroom" where some 250 retired citizens were whooping it up with Canada Dry and cheap wine. They were irritated that a candidate was going to interrupt their afternoon merrymaking. But in minutes, Carter dissipated their ire and wooed them, as he would millions, with a whopping dose of Southern charm.

He swept seventy-year-old Agnes Conway into his arms, fox-trotting cheek to cheek with her to the strains of "Georgia on My Mind." Agnes was swayed, she confessed. However she was not taken in completely. "I want to know why his mother never had to spank him. I haven't decided yet. I'm still weighing whom I'll vote for."

Carter waited for Art Smith's electric organ and orchestra to finish playing. One hand in his pocket, he perched on the edge of a table, next to a stack of green-and-white leaflets featuring a picture of his mother, Miz Lillian, and the saga of her Peace Corps experience. Then he sprang to the stage, balancing on the edge of it with the front of his wing-tips pointing down, as though he were about to pounce into the audience like a cat. He spoke with his pale blond eyebrows and his pale blue eyes imploring them to listen, and they had to because he spoke so softly many had to crane their necks to hear. He told them he'd rather spend the rest of his day dancing with "all the pretty women in the room." He told them about his seventy-eight-year-old mother ("She's just my age," shrieked one woman in a pink suit) and how hard she had worked. When he was growing up during the Depression, he rarely saw her because she worked twenty hours a week for a salary of four dollars a day. She went to India at sixty-eight and worked as a nurse until she was "past seventy," and today she still "has determination every morning to learn more about God's world and to see how many people she can love that day." He told them not to worry about Social Security, that no one would ever let the system default. And he told them to vote for him. "When I'm in the White House my heart will be with you." It was schmaltz for the geriatric—so heartfelt and personal that in spite of the fact he had said nothing substantive, many made up their minds then and there to vote for him. "I like his tone of voice," said one woman. "I made up my mind because he's honest and not political," said a man named John Lennon. "I like his eyes," said another. No one mentioned anything except his personality.

The press bus moved on to Quincy. In a huge skylit inner courtyard of the Kemper Insurance building, Carter delivered his standard speech about love and trust in his quiet way to an audience of some three hundred, clustered like birds on a wire around the balconies overlooking ficus trees and rubber tree plants.

Scoop Jackson, who also spoke, had blown it. "He was just plain rude," sniffed one secretary. "He ran down the other candidates. The folks don't like that. They're looking for a nice guy with plenty of charisma like Carter. He seems to have a magic quality." Carter's charisma was hardly the kind of animal magnetism Bobby Kennedy exuded or the puppy dog exuberance that belonged to Hubert Humphrey or the aesthetic quality that was Eugene McCarthy's, but a rather sexless, priestly purity.

They would kiss him and touch him, but never claw and paw at him or tear at his clothes. And yet when he looked at someone it was as though he created a magnetic field around them. There was no escape, no chance to look away. One was transfixed.

In the Kemper cafeteria a local reporter stopped to ask Carter about his health regimen. In spite of the simplicity of the question, Carter gave the reporter his total attention, as though he had just been asked to analyze the solar system for a symposium on interterrestrial bodies. Taking the reporter aside, Carter, standing straight as a tree, held him with his penetrating eyes. "I'm very conscious about staying healthy. I walk a lot every day. I eat fairly well. I weigh one hundred and fifty-three, the same that I did twenty-five years ago. A week ago I went down to about one hundred and forty-eight but I went back up the next week. I get about six hours of sleep a night. I go to bed around eleven or eleven-thirty, sometimes midnight. I'm up around six or six thirty. I've lived my life for almost fifty years that way. I was a farmer you know. And I was a cross-country runner in college. That helps."

In the gray frost of late afternoon the Carter entourage drove to Boston to the Government Center subway stop at the corner of Tremont and Cambridge streets so Carter could shake hands with rush hour commuters on their way home from work. Wearing just a light topcoat, collar turned up, wind tossing his layered, blow-dried hair, Carter looked uncannily like Robert Kennedy, a look he obviously capitalized on. "Hi, I'm Jimmy Carter." "Hi, let me shake your hand" . . . "Let me give you a pamphlet personally." One woman wanted to know if he was as charming in person as he was on TV. "I don't know about that," he said, and kissed her.

"What makes you think you should be President?" asked one passerby. "Because I love my country," he told her. "I'm concerned about the nation. I've got a good background. I have sensitivity about what I think the people would like our government to be. I'm a farmer, a scientist, and a deeply religious person. I think we ought to expend our talents for God's service and I think as President I could do that, and my base of political strength is not in Washington." He had said nothing about why he was qualified, but the man was snowed by the intense eyes. "You're going to get my vote," he said and disappeared into the subway.

Carter was peeved at being encircled by the press. "Can you move over?" he growled at the cameramen. "Let the people come up!" They moved. He still wasn't satisfied. Carter called for his press secretary. "Jody! Can you see if you can get the producers up against the wall." Powell cleared a space of about ten feet around Carter. "Now you've got it. That's great." Jimmy smiled again.

He bristled when a stranger asked him about Steven Brill's article in *Harper*'s, which had been severely critical of Carter's years as Governor. "Was that an accurate article?" the man inquired. Carter's eyes blazed. "You talk to Jody Powell," he snapped and turned away to shake another hand.

Later at a $250 per person cocktail fund raiser at the Copley Plaza, he was telling guests how much he disliked the growing legions of the press around him. "You lose that intimacy with the people. I can't get to them. It's almost impossible to maintain an intimacy with them," he complained, glimpsing a reporter at his elbow.

The press did not fare as well during the primaries traveling with the Carter contingent as with some of the other candidates. While it was the policy of the Reagan camp to keep the fourth estate well watered and stoked with food ("the easier to evoke good coverage if dispositions are kept pleasant," said Reagan press secretary Lyn Nofziger), the Carter policy was not-so-benign neglect.

Every morning on the Reagan press bus, giant vats of coffee, fresh Danish and pastry were provided free of charge. In the afternoon, roast beef, ham and turkey sandwiches were laid on. No matter how remote the location, a press room was always provided to work in, well stocked with coffee and snacks. Arriving with Carter at the Copley Plaza that afternoon, there was not even a glass of water, not to mention a press room, a typewriter or a phone to file on.

Some of us wrote at a small round table in the lobby bar. After midnight that same night, most reporters had not had time to eat dinner, but in spite of the long ride to Manchester, New Hampshire, ahead, the Carter staff had not thought to lay anything on board to munch on. The bus driver was more considerate. "I thought you might be hungry," he said, producing a large bag of apples as twenty bone-weary, starving journalists pounced on him. At midnight Jody Powell finally had the bus stop at a liquor store. Everyone chipped in for several six-packs of Budweiser and a bag of potato chips which Jody passed. My dinner that night consisted of three cold hors d'oeuvres, one apple, half a beer and a handful of potato chips.

In the early days of the campaign, covering Carter was often catch as catch can. Tuesday, the day of the New Hampshire primary, for example, the networks had planned to accompany Carter to New York for some event. So did Eleanor Clift of *Newsweek*. But Jody Powell forgot to tell the reporters assigned to Carter that Carter's charter had only six seats. Three were allocated for the press and two were already filled. "You'll have to flip a coin to see who gets the third seat," Powell announced. Sam Donaldson of ABC called heads and won the seat. Everyone else was told to find their own way to New York. Powell explained that Carter could rent a jet for an exorbitant amount of money, but preferred to spend the money on TV spots. In this campaign, the sole priority was winning.

Earlier that evening the press had been mysteriously banned from the 6:45 reception at the Copley Plaza. Possibly because the crowd that had gathered in a first-floor room were more interested in consuming hors d'oeuvres from a round center table and swilling Scotch than they were in Jimmy Carter. They were mostly cronies of former Governor Endicott "Chub" Peabody who was there to endorse Carter that night. Most had been hastily rounded up at the last minute and agreed to come strictly as "a favor to Chub." At the last minute the edict was revoked and the press were granted entree.

Watching Carter at a distance, Dace Moore, an attorney and former Peabody campaign manager and Eric Powell, a black contractor, sipped their drinks and compared notes. "You've got to admit, it's a superb public relations campaign to date. For a conservative, he's been able to project himself as middle of the road. I don't know what he's running for. Probably vice president. Who knows?" said Moore. Moore and Powell agreed that Ted Kennedy would be nominated by a "well-organized draft. That's what's in the works."

Jim Hennegan, a tall, burly Irishman who had drunk one too many martinis that evening, disagreed vehemently. So did Dan Murphy and Dick Horan, former Robert Kennedy supporters and neighbors of Senator Edward Kennedy in Hyannisport. "We're with Carter. We've had it. We can't stand around waiting for bridesmaids," said Murphy. Hennegan, Registrar Probate of Suffolk County, said he had worked for RFK and JFK's Presidential campaigns and predicted, "Ted will not come in. Carter will be nominated on the first or second ballot." Hennegan's Irish prescience was right on target.

Mo Udall was the liberal's liberal. Which explains, aside from his lack of name recognition, and the bizarre, mannequin quality his glass eye gave his appearance on television, why his campaign was nipped in the bud. Even eighteen months of campaigning in New Hampshire failed to give his campaign the necessary lift to topple Jimmy Carter.

The country had moved too far right to swallow the thought of another "Great Society." "Mo" never had much of a prayer.

But Udall had been a fun candidate, the one the press liked to travel with. Udall was human, real, good-natured and witty. He possessed the self-deprecating humor Jimmy Carter lacked. He would laugh when he lost and call himself, "Second Hand Mo." He also told the best jokes and the most amusing stories and he liked to ride the press bus with reporters. On the "Mo-bile" inevitably some crazy antic would help relieve the tension of an eighteen-hour day.

One day reporters bought Udall a set of wind-up teeth which they said he could use to look more like Jimmy Carter. Another time they threw a rubber chicken at him. Once traveling through the Ohio suburbs, Mo and his wife "Tiger," as he called her, stalked up the aisle of the press bus brandishing water pistols. "O.K. you guys," said Mo as he and Ella fired away. They took their own eventual dousing with good humor.

Mo was accommodating too. When I filmed the Udalls at home for NBC, no one on his staff had bothered to tell him the news story was supposed to be a "Life-style." Besides an interview we wanted to film Udall doing something around the house, perhaps gardening, because that is what he liked to do best. Although Mo was all dressed for a committee meeting on the Hill, he never hesitated to run upstairs, change into a pair of white shorts, mow the lawn, putter at his workbench, climb a ladder and trim the Pyracantha for us without grumbling.

I first interviewed Udall during the Massachusetts primary at the Parker House Hotel in Boston. When I opened the door to the Longfellow Room I found him sitting on the edge of a table, a phone pressed to one ear, a finger plugged in the other. He was taping radio shows. He was comfortable on the table, he said, because no chair in the room was high enough to accommodate his lanky body and long legs.

We talked as we drove out to WBZ Radio where he was to tape an hour-long program. The comfort level with him was high. He seemed totally at ease in anyone's presence. Udall had just been solidly trounced in New Hampshire. Carter had collected fifteen delegates to his two, but in 1976 defeat was given a new twist. All the losers turned their losses into victories. With thirty primaries to play with, every candidate looked forward to a victory somewhere down the line. Udall was no exception.

He said of his New Hampshire defeat, "To get twenty-five percent of the vote and nearly a full quarter of the votes when I was competing with three liberals and one conservative in a conservative state, I felt it was a really solid victory. In these early primaries you can have more than one winner. The job is not to pick the winner, but to sort out the losers and narrow the field. I was delighted. Jimmy Carter had the whole right side of the road to himself. He didn't have a job to attend to, so he just literally moved in there with his wife and family and spent just endless weeks in all these little towns shaking hands. But I would have had the Harris votes nearly all over him and most of the Shriver and Bayh votes if they had been out of the picture. I would have beat Jimmy Carter in a one-on-one race."

Then he laughed at his own foolishness. "Hell, you've invested all this time and money, so you can't get up and say, Well, I was a turkey and I lost, good-bye." Everybody, including Harris, Shriver and Bayh who were also-rans in New Hampshire "had to put on the best face." "But I told a press conference the other day, I said, you can make a pretty good speech about victory if you're second, and if you strain a little you can make one with the third, but someone is gonna come in sixth and seventh next Tuesday and I would pay an admission price to listen to one of those speeches claiming that's a victory."

Udall was surprised that Jimmy Carter had suddenly come on so strong. "I really didn't believe that just sheer will power and determination to be President could do it, that you could handshake and smile your way into serious contention for the nomination. But his strategy has been brilliant. His tenacity has been too. It's quite a phenomenon. I no longer discount the possibility of the nomination. I keep thinking that he's peaked, but he keeps making progress. There was a long period when all kinds of liberals liked him, felt it was nice to have a fresh voice, and wasn't it great that you had a reasonable, sensible, Southern Governor in the contest. But they weren't really looking at him closely and saying, 'Do I want this man to be President,' because they didn't think seriously that he was going to be. And on that basis he got all kinds of money, got Leonard Woodcock to agree to campaign for him and turn out labor in Florida. He got blacks like Andrew Young to endorse him, got all sorts of people, and now they're all saying, Who is he and what does he stand for? *The New York Times* told the liberals he was liberal, the conservatives thought he was conservative and the moderates thought he was moderate. In Iowa he had both the abortion vote and the antiabortion vote, he had labor and antilabor. He had opposites on all sides. In politics, you can't do that, but he's done it."

Udall did not think his close friend Humphrey would emerge from the convention. "Hubert doesn't think so either. We agree the winner will emerge from the primaries." He kept using a Vicks inhaler as he spoke. He had caught a cold again and he had to be careful, he said. At one point earlier in the campaign he had to be hospitalized from sheer exhaustion that turned into viral pneumonia, so he'd had to learn to pace himself with afternoon naps and rest.

Udall didn't seem to really have his heart in the campaign or the stomach for it. While Jimmy Carter seemed to thrive on the masochistic demands of a campaign, he talked about the endless travel, the pressures of trying to be both Congressman and candidate, not to mention husband and father for a year and a half. "It's just a feeling that you never have a break where you could sit down and rest or have a day off to sleep late." Staff problems plagued him too. "It's just endemic to the whole campaign way of life."

As he spoke, Mo Udall looked at you with his good eye, looked away, looked back quickly. If a person were on his bad side, he would rotate his head ninety degrees to see them. In private conversation Udall's glass eye is barely noticeable but on television it did not work to his advantage. He looked slightly peculiar on the air. Unreal. And it hurt him in this age of media campaigning. Unfortunate that sometimes the best men are lost to prettier images.

At WBZ before the show began, the host told Udall his bitter feelings about Carter, that the Carter people are "vicious. I can't pinpoint it, but they're like the Sun Myung Moon people. They're dangerous. They smile a lot, but behind that facade, they're mean."

Udall responded. "Yeah. All the Southern Governors detest him."

The very first call Udall received on the air sounded vaguely familiar. That afternoon a group of us had been having drinks with Carter's press secretary, Jody Powell, in the Parker House bar and Powell had said, "Wait until we get Udall on the fact he didn't come out for impeachment until three days before Nixon resigned." It seemed coincidental that the first caller said, "I have the *Congressional Record* here in front of me and I want to know why you waited until three days before Nixon resigned to ask for his impeachment." The show's host mouthed "Carter people" at Udall.

Udall answered drolly. "Do you always just happen to have a copy of the *Congressional Record* with you? Doesn't everybody? I must say, you don't sound like a Udall supporter. The reason I waited was because I knew if Nixon was going to be impeached, I was going to have to be a member of the jury and I wanted to wait until he had time to defend himself. I thought it was important we get Nixon out, but to do this the right way. I was trying to be a responsible member of the jury."

The host was apoplectic. "See what I mean about the Carter types? There's that vicious streak."

The next call was apparently another Carter plant; a girl with a thick New York accent who told Udall she resented him for slinging mud at other candidates "like Carter."

Udall replied he had never attacked any candidate's character or integrity, only differed on the issues: In between questions, Mo read the *Wall Street Journal* and glanced at the *National Enquirer*. He seemed unflappable, but so gray, like Jackson—gray suit, gray tie, gray hair.

In the car on the way back to the city, Udall waxed melancholy. "It's all such a blur. I don't know. If I just hang on, I think they'll begin to pay attention."

Massachusetts momentarily derailed the Carter campaign. Jackson won with 22.7 percent of the vote. Udall finished second with 18 percent, Wallace was third with 17.1 percent and Carter finished fourth with 14.2 percent. Carter had not campaigned extensively in Massachusetts because the original primary date was much later in the year and the Carter people expected to be able to concentrate on Florida at that point. Consequently, Massachusetts was largely a political void for the peanut farmer. Nevertheless, Carter expected that his momentum from Iowa and New Hampshire would carry him through Massachusetts easily. What he had not anticipated was Jackson's heavy get-out-the-vote organization which turned out Jackson voters at the polls despite a heavy blizzard that dumped fourteen inches of snow on election day.

Returning from the Massachusetts primary I ran into Vince Clephas, a top assistant to DNC Chairman Robert Strauss, walking through National Airport. He said Strauss was "delighted" with Jackson's victory. "We finally got rid of Carter. He can't roll 'em up now. The bloom's off the rose. Now, four candidates will come to the convention with an equally divided vote and the convention will nominate a regular. Not Carter. He's not a regular."

CHAPTER 22

CRUSHING WALLACE: THE NEW SOUTH VS. THE OLD SOUTH

A MAJOR FACTOR in the 1976 Presidential race was George Wallace. In 1972 Wallace had racked up an impressive number of delegates —381.7—and an overwhelming amount of nationwide support before he was cut down by a bullet in Laurel, Maryland. For the next three years, Wallace plotted and schemed and collected close to eight million dollars to run again. The challenge loomed formidable, wheelchair or no. The Democrats, determined to recapture the White House, saw Wallace as a threat to that goal. Another Southern sweep by George Wallace would mean the Democratic nominee would have to bargain with the racist Southern Governor at the convention. Worse still, it was not inconceivable Wallace could win. He had to be stopped and Jimmy Carter was chosen as the dragon slayer. Carter's task of unhorsing Wallace was simplified by Wallace's health.

On March 1, I went to see Wallace at the Orpheum Theatre in Boston. I had forgotten what a Wallace rally was like—a deluxe tour of Dante. If Hell ever had sound, this was it—deafening, shrill, ear-splitting, *Grand Ol' Opry*, bleating out through giant speakers; the air was thick and bitter with the smell of perspiration. "Y'all, is this Wallace country?" asks Billy Grammer of *Grand Ol' Opry* fame, whipping the crowd into a frenzy. Whistles, stomps, shrieks. A hundred members of the audience break into a march, trooping up and down the aisles, brandishing Wallace banners past the press section, glaring at reporters like they were the Vietcong.

And then it happens. The crowd is ready for its first orgasm. "And now . . ." says Grammer, "Alabama's fightin' Govnuh . . . George! C! Wallace!" Yahoos, whoops, hands clapping in rhythm to the electric guitar music. Just like the good ole days . . . but this time, it is different. The feisty populist hero—now a diminished, crumpled mass of humanity—is wheeled into his bulletproof plexiglass box like an animal returned to its cage. Wallace no longer is able to raise himself out of his wheelchair and speak to the audience while sitting on a high stool behind the lectern. One leg is still broken. Sitting there, he resorts now to a series of hand gestures—the old Nixon double-V signs, Winston Churchill Vs, Castro salutes, Ike waves, blown kisses, Lawrence Welk wrist twists.

But when he begins to speak, he assumes the proportions of a Goliath. The wheelchair suddenly seems to vanish. His voice creates the illusion of physical strength, trumpeting a message that sounded at times like a translation of vintage Jimmy Carter into the vulgar.

"Yes, you are the working people of this country. Yes, you have been forgotten, but you are going to be remembered. Don't you forget that. Yes, the great mass of people in this country have awakened to the point that those in government have not paid sufficient attention to unemployment and inflation and the recession that affects the lives of most of our people . . .

"The hi-arky of the Democratic party and the culture merchants who look down their nose at you and me. They're not supporting me. But if you go out and vote we can s'prise 'em 'cause there are more of us than there are of them . . .

"Yes, the issue in this country is getting people back to work . . . You're ground down by high regressive taxes. The income tax is the most regressive tax this country knows. It hits the little man while it exempts those who are super high . . . the Mellons and the Carnegies. They ought to pay taxes just like the working people of Massachusetts pay taxes . . . Take the welfare rolls, we have spent billions more than we should spend for those who are not entitled to it . . . It's going to take an uprising of the American people to get some of these parasites off your back and get them into private industry where they can make a living on their own."

The theme was the same as always, but the perception of Wallace had changed drastically. The health issue had hurt Wallace in the state. No one wanted to elect a paralyzed man President, or a deaf one either. And Wallace had grown quite deaf.

Two weeks later, after he had lost badly in Florida Wallace held a press conference the morning before the Illinois primary to say all was not lost, even though it was.

He brandished a copy of the Chicago *Tribune* that had recently misquoted him. Wallace had been talking about foreign aid, but his Southern accent got in the way and the headline came out "Wallace Wants to Cut Farm Aid," the wrong kind of publicity to receive in the heart of the corn belt, two days before the primary. "Well, Governor," asked a reporter, "What DO you want to do about farm aid?"

"Fahn (foreign) aid?" said Wallace. "Mah fahn policy would be . . ."

"No Governor. Farm. F-A-R-M."

"That's what ah said," Wallace thundered. He beckoned an aide over. " 'Nterpret for me. I cain't hear 'em good."

After the press conference Wallace stayed around to talk a bit. He seemed to have lost his fight. He appeared a beaten, lonely figure. He wanted to linger although his aides were telling him he had to leave. I asked him whether he agreed with his wife, Cornelia, who said in her book that any man running for the Presidency must suffer from some inadequacy.

"Yes, I think I have inadequacies. Lots of 'em," said Wallace, pensively. "You know Cornelia's Uncle Jim Folsom used to say you had to be half crazy to run for Governor. I agree. But if you had wanted to do something like run for Congress and didn't you would always think, 'If I had just gotten that seat, I could have helped so many people!' Y'know, so many people are miserable. I didn't realize before what they were going through, so many people lyin' in the house all day with nobody to care for 'em. One quadriplegic called and told me the other day, 'Mah life isn't worth living now.' Ah got a program to train people to help these poor souls now.

"I agree that sometimes when you've already been Governor a long time you sometimes look back and say, 'Well, I wonder if I have really missed something?' I should have spent more time with my children and family. But there's no way to turn back. If I could turn back, I wouldn't have gone to Laurel, Maryland."

As I watched him rolled away I knew that the wheelchair campaign was coming to an end.

Wallace stuck it out through Michigan and I saw him once again during the primaries at what was billed as a rally at the Ramada Inn near the Detroit airport. Only fifty people had gathered in a small ballroom, and they sat quietly in one row of straight-backed chairs against the wall like children at a dance class. Many of them called it "Wallace's Last Hurrah." But the feisty Southern Governor went down hurling insults at Jimmy Carter.

"There are those with their grins and their smiles . . ." he said that night. "The leading candidate has never made a definitive statement on any issue in his life. At least Mo Udall says what he thinks. He said he would never support me and I doubt I'll support him, but at least he says so. Carter said he never supported me and never intended to, but when he ran for the Governorship of Georgia in 1966 my name was on his tongue in every speech he ever made. In 1970 he used my mailing list. He got my organization together and we worked for him. He was going to be a Wallace man. And yet, a few weeks before the Democratic convention in 1972 he said, 'I've never been for Wallace.' But he recommended me for Vice President in 1972 at the Governor's conference on a ticket with Hubert Humphrey after I was shot. He went to Alabama and made a speech about it too.

"What does that mean when you say 'I am for him for Vice President?' Does that mean you are for someone or not? But when asked questions by the news media, do you know what he said? He said, 'I never have voted for George Wallace.' I didn't say he voted for me. I was not nominated, but he asked that I be nominated. I did not seek the Vice-Presidential nomination. But we agreed in Georgia in the state capitol that I would not run any caucus precinct delegates against his in 1972. And that if I went to the convention in 1972 with three hundred or more delegates, he would vote for me and ask all the Georgia delegation he had any influence over to support me. Since I had four hundred delegates, I called him and asked him to nominate me for Vice President, but he said, 'I'm sorry, I'm going to vote for my old friend Scoop.' And yet Scoop said, 'I never knew him until he was Governor of Georgia,' and we said, 'Well, Governor, you promised to vote for George Wallace. What about that handshake we made in the little office behind your main office?' "

Yet in spite of his bitter diatribe George Wallace was the first politician to call and endorse Jimmy Carter after he won the Ohio primary. I was there at 2:15 A.M. when the message was handed to Carter outside the depot where he was greeting well wishers.

Carter had taken the political world by storm when he ran in Iowa, New Hampshire, and now, to the utter disbelief of the Democratic establishment, Carter was going to win in Florida. Using the argument that he alone could eliminate Wallace, Carter had persuaded some of the major candidates to stay out of the state and had enlisted the help of powerful pols like Leonard Woodcock, president of the United Auto Workers, and Max Palevsky, a major Democratic fund raiser, arguing that his winning would smooth the path for a more clear-cut victory by one of the acceptable Democratic candidates. Politicians like Congressman Andrew Young, who at the time did not particularly like Carter, fell for the theory and campaigned vigorously for Carter among Florida's blacks.

Mo Udall avoided the state entirely, as did Sargent Shriver, thinking that Florida would be nothing more than a "stop Wallace" state. Jackson agreed to curtail his campaigning there too.

As I traveled through the state with Rosalynn Carter, who had visited Florida 27 times, it was quite obvious Carter would win. One asset was the large percentage of retired Georgians living in the Sunshine State. Those Georgians not only would vote for the hometown boy but also had relatives all across the country and would spread the word. The ripple effect after Florida was crucial to Carter's success.

At the time the other candidates ceded the state to Carter it seemed the most promising way to dispose of the Wallace problem once and for all, but Carter succeeded beyond all their wildest expectations and the party regulars were now faced with an entirely different problem. Jimmy Carter himself. The one candidate who did recognize the trap was Jackson, who reversed his strategy at the last minute and decided to make a major effort in Florida. But it was too little too late.

I went to Miami with Scoop Jackson the day Birch Bayh "suspended" his Presidential campaign after a disappointing seventh-place showing in Massachusetts. The *Miami Herald* suggested Bayh dropped out because of his association with Gulf Oil contributions.

"Super Scoop," as he is known to reporters, ran his campaign like a sophomore's tour of Europe. It was lackadaisical, lackluster and late. The morning of March 5, Jackson was an hour late getting started, an hour late returning that evening and late in between. While Carter would desert reporters on the runway in order to be on time for an appointment, Jackson would lollygag around waiting for journalists to make phone calls, even when he was way behind schedule. "That's all right, we'll wait." Forty-five minutes passed.

Jackson may have had more money and labor support than other candidates, but he traveled as though he were penny poor. The Senator from Boeing flew around Florida in a decrepit Naples Airline Martin 404 so battered around the fuselage that it looked like they must have beaten it with a hammer to get it started. At one stop, Carter's sleek white United Boeing jet sat on the ground next to Jackson's yellow banana, causing some consternation. "We've got to get a jet next week," Jackson muttered.

If the Jackson campaign short-circuited, it was because Jackson was not what the voters had in mind for a President this year. They wanted honesty, but they also wanted style, looks, charm. Jackson had the charisma of a pet rock. He waddled. He looked like an overgrown baby—a Gerber's ad—with a bright-pink cherubic face, short, pink baby fingers and wispy baby hair. He wore baggy gray trousers and carried so many things in his pockets that they bulged.

If anything, he was too accessible. Unlike Carter, Jackson rode in the center of the plane with reporters. He loved to banter with them and talked incessantly. One day he must have talked eighteen hours nonstop. When I interviewed him late one evening his voice had become raspy with fatigue. But in spite of the fact he had a radio show and a Latin American fiesta ahead at the next stop, Jackson did not wish to terminate the conversation. He launched into a monologue, leapfrogging from campaign strategy to defense spending to his ill-defined National Health Insurance plan to his childhood. Jackson was convinced that hoards of uncommitted delegates would move to him after his victory in the New York primary. Then with the momentum gathered from Massachusetts and New York and "hopefully" Florida, he would roll up delegate support in the Iowa, Missouri and Kansas caucuses from April 9 to 20. "If they don't get on board, the train will pull out of the station." He was not surprised that other Democrats had fallen by the wayside so soon. "The name of the game is money. You can't count on future contributions based on how well you do in this state or that state. You have to have the money collected." Jackson had it.

"Where's my tea bag?" Jackson hooted at an aide. His subluxury liner did not even carry tea on board. Jackson had to bring his own.

"My faults? My staff gives me hell because I don't smile enough. My wife gives me hell a lot of the time on that too. But I have terrible inhibitions. If I'm trying to respond to a serious question, I feel like I'm smirking. My worst vice is working too much. I'm too righteous to be interesting. And if I get onto an issue that I care about, I have a little bit of the tiger in me. I won't let go . . . I need more breaks too, but if I see the target down the road, I don't stop. My wife says I never know where to stop. I do better with a little rest. But the Good Lord has given me something I should be thankful for. I don't have the problem of flying off the handle."

But Jackson was not fighting hard enough in Florida. The next day, for instance, although Daniel Patrick Moynihan and others were flown in to prop up his faltering campaign, Jackson was an hour late getting to the Fort Lauderdale armory for a labor rally with Moynihan. More than 150 people had left by the time he arrived and volunteers had to fold away the empty chairs so it wouldn't look as though they hadn't been able to fill the place. The union members who remained formed an enthusiastic cheering section, hollering "Scoop, Scoop, Scoop." It was a strange guttural chant that came out "Hoop, Hoop, Hoop." That kind of cheer alone would win the election for the Republicans.

One Jackson worker told me, "The Florida operation is lousy. Beyond repair. They brought a group of us in from Boston, but it's too late."

At eight o'clock, March 9, the night of the Florida primary, Rosalynn and Jimmy Carter nestled together on a couch in front of three television sets, in their room, in the Carlton House Hotel in Orlando, hurriedly devouring hamburgers and chocolate milk shakes. Rosalynn was rapidly hemming the skirt of a khaki-colored dress she had bought that afternoon for the occasion—another Carter victory.

Amy Carter cavorted outside, skipping barefooted along the flagstones leading to the pool and bouncing a ball, oblivious to the hoards of reporters now converging near her parents' room.

By 8:20 P.M. it was clear Carter had swept the Sunshine State and Carter Campaign Manager Hamilton Jordan appeared beneath the overhang by the Carter suite. A hundred questions were hurled at him. "God! I'm not used to this," Jordan tried to explain. "We said we had to win in the North as well as have a victory in the South. We've had a one-two punch now. We've elected a quarter of the delegates but we've got a long way to go."

Was he dismayed by Governor Reubin Askew's lack of participation? "Not at all." What about George Wallace? "We have five more confrontations. We'll beat him in Illinois and North Carolina." Jackson? "He's got a good chance in New York." How did Carter win Florida? "We spent more time. No other organization spent as much time here. We had good media and the best voter contact program." The nomination? "We have a good chance now, at least a better chance. In terms of the South, the Democratic party can't capture the nomination if they write off the South. The South has one hundred twenty-eight electoral votes . . . We can't skip any states . . ."

Carter's suite was packed with well-wishers. Carter, in shirt sleeves, seemed impervious to the mayhem around him, a calm in the midst of a storm. "Jimmy Carter has eluded prognosticators," a commentator was saying. "He has beaten George Wallace."

Carter looked pleased. When he turned to talk to me I was stunned by the powerful concentration of spirit in his eyes. Carter is possessed of the same kind of hypnotic presence that Lyndon Johnson had. Only Johnson's eyes were dark, narrow, impenetrable slits, cold, brown and suspicious. The first time I spoke to LBJ in January 1968 at a White House dinner, I was captivated by the man, but frightened by his eyes. Nixon's eyes were similar, but less intense, their energy scattered by a weak, insecure personality. I recall my first interview with Nixon in a car in 1968. In 30 minutes, he never once looked directly at me. His eyes darted back and forth observing the scenery outside the window. Carter's eyes on the other hand were deep, clear, calm, wide-open pools. I understood now why he used them to such advantage, and why his staff found it so important for Carter to meet people, one-on-one.

In spite of the cheerful chaos erupting in the room, and the cacophony of news pouring out of three television sets, Carter concentrated on what he was saying and on his interviewer. He didn't seem to mind being interrupted. "This was the state we had to win. There would be no excuse to lose here," he said. "We made thirty-five campaign trips here. We had a good media effort, enthusiastic volunteers, and my family helped a great deal. My family won for me." He pulled Rosalynn to his side and kissed her. "When I couldn't be here, Rosalynn was here. She made a similar effort in Iowa. She is an almost equal extension of myself in this campaign. She can answer questions on any conceivable issue. She magnified my presence here greatly. She's not only helpful by her presence—she helps in all the basic strategy decisions. She has a very sensitive relationship with the voters and quite often if people criticize me, she can tell me where to correct my errors."

A television commentator on the news said, "It looks like thirty-six percent for Carter." For an instant he turned to look but finished his statement. "Our strategy depends on one week at a time. The next major confrontation is Illinois, and North Carolina, Wisconsin and New York. We're in all of them, and we're picking up in the competition. There's been a slow increase in the national polls that gives me the image of a potential winner."

Minutes later across the courtyard, Carter and Rosalynn sat on a radiator, their knees touching as he explained his victory to the press.

The nation was looking for "fresh leadership," he said. It was not a "sectional" thing. The stop-Carter movement "was supposed to start the day after Iowa, then the day after New Hampshire, now it will be one day after Florida, but it hasn't started yet." He was very angry about the New York situation where Jackson operatives had managed to have Carter delegate slates thrown out in several districts. The laws there were "contrived" by party bosses to prevent "New Yorkers from casting their vote in a free and open manner."

At 9:00 o'clock pandemonium reigned in the ballroom where over a thousand volunteers and fans pressed in on Carter and his family. Carter was caught in the ebb and flow of the mob as it surged forward through the lobby, sweeping him with it in a swirl of Secret Service until he reached the stage. "We're Number One!" they chanted over and over. It was the most enthusiasim I was to see for Carter in the entire primary season.

Lehman Franklin, a friend of Carter's from Georgia and a schoolmate of Hamilton Jordan's from Georgia State, was back at the Carter suite drinking with the staff and watching the news reporting Carter's delegate lead: 71 delegates to Wallace's 58, Jackson's 50, Udall's 23, Shriver's 11, Harris's 6 and Bentsen's 1.

Carter came on the air being interviewed. "Governor Carter, you said if you won here in Florida, you couldn't be stopped," said the reporter.

Carter smiled, "I don't say that."

Lehman Franklin laughed. "That's what he says on TV, but in private he says he can't be beat. No way. It's like a messiah, manifest destiny thing. It's been decreed. I've said to him, 'Jimmy, let's talk practical politics,' but he says, 'No way.' He's gonna win. Besides, honey, he's from Plains. And there ain't nothin' in Plains. He couldn't succeed himself when he left office as Governor, and he sure didn't want to go back to Plains, so he ran for President. There was nothin' else to run for."

Carter had now won three of the first four primaries along the road to the Democratic nominating convention in New York in July

—New Hampshire, Vermont and Florida. (He had finished fourth behind Jackson, Udall and Wallace in Massachusetts.)

Carter also held an edge in the caucus states. He won the early first level of competition in Iowa, Maine and Oklahoma and finished second to Wallace in Mississippi and South Carolina, the latter by an extremely fine margin. And he was favored to lead in caucuses in Virginia and Kansas within the next few weeks. What was obvious was that Carter had regained the head of steam that seemed to have evaporated in Massachusetts just a week previously.

CHAPTER 23

ETHNIC PURITY

GERALD FORD MAY HAVE bumbled his way through the snows of New Hampshire, but he won; and his small margin of victory there was enough of an aphrodisiac to spur him on. He also proved the incumbency a powerful asset. The administration flooded Florida with pork-barrel projects just weeks before the primary and Ford benefited from statistics showing inflation had been arrested and unemployment was falling. He won with 53 percent of the vote to Reagan's 47 percent.

Ford began to develop as a skillful campaigner. His appearances in Florida and a swing he made through Illinois the following week proved that a few speech lessons could make a major difference.

The day Ford arrived, a tornado hit Chicago's suburbs, just missing the President by eight minutes and a thousand feet. The entire roof of the Howard Johnson's across the street from the Marriott Motel where Ford was staying lay in shreds on the ground. Reporters who still referred to Ford as "Bozo" quipped that the headlines the next day should read, "Ford Rips Through Illinois," or better yet, "Ford's Tornado Strategy Woos Voters."

In fact the former Michigan Congressman was taking the state by storm. His speech to the Foreign Policy Council at the Palmer House on March 12 in Chicago was *nouveau* Ford. The Reagan challenge had definitely shaped and honed his style to a razor sharpness. His manner was crisper, his delivery more forceful and his fluffs, fewer. His only fumble that day was the name Karamanlis, which he pronounced, Ka-ra-man-lee-sees, but it passed unnoticed. Even Democrats in the audience were impressed. Fred Bernheim, a short man wearing a Mike-Howlett-for-Governor button found Ford's sincerity attractive. "There were no fumbles. His whole pattern has improved immensely." Democrat Stan Babash thought Ford projected the image of a "winner." "He exudes confidence. If he continues as he is and continues to straighten out the economy, even as a Democrat I'd say he'd be tough to beat."

That night at Buffalo Grove High School, in a brand new gymnasium where thousands of multicolored balloons tumbled from a net onto a cheering, whistling audience that popped them with gusto, the President proved himself to be Super Candidate. Ford gave his "peace with strength/the economy is improving" pitch. He rarely glanced at his notes. "I intend to keep the pressure on the budget busters . . . anything that has excess in it, I'll veto one after another so we have a balanced budget by 1979," he said in his foggy voice.

He seemed equally at ease with questions ranging from abortion to national defense. When one nine-year-old boy stood on a chair and hollered in his soprano voice, "I think we should take more power in more countries or the communists will take over the world," Ford charmed the parents in the auditorium. "I think that's a very legitimate question. Yes, we will have an adequate defense budget and we will make it a safe country for you, young man." From the decibel level and the overwhelming response to Ford even here in the heart of Reagan territory, it seemed Ford's support was congealing. Marjorie Balzer, who coordinated Ford's campaign in the 12th District, confirmed that the momentum had picked up dramatically since his Florida victory. "The enthusiasm is tremendous all of a sudden. In three days the support has jumped from one third for Ford to a half for Ford and a half for Reagan. The President's son Jack was here last week too and went over big. He could answer all the kids directly on the question of marijuana and all the other things they were interested in."

Upstairs in the press room after Carter's boring speech before the Foreign Council, Jody Powell waited for the press to file. Sitting on the floor in the rear of the room, knees folded to his chin, Powell talked to the Atlanta office. "Well, crap. Oh shit. Well, tell that guy he's full of bullshit. Tell him that the Wallace people have been trying to peddle that story for months now and they finally found a buyer. Shit, Carter doesn't remember. And he never was in Lakeland until 1975."

(An Atlanta reporter had been checking out a story that Carter autographed a Wallace poster at a Wallace rally in Lakeland, Florida, back in 1972.)

Two reporters, waiting to talk to Powell, were sitting on the floor near him. "Well, shit, I can't talk about that now. I'm surrounded by little pitchers. Look. Sam Donaldson [ABC correspondent] has to have an answer. Can you check the schedule? He wants to come down and film Miz Lillian watching the returns, but she just canceled out on a local station because she got burned the last time, so she's a little touchy. Some girl from the Atlanta *Constitution* came over to watch her watching the returns and wrote about how she swang her drink around over her head three times." Donaldson groaned. "We just don't do that sort of thing."

Powell continued. "Listen, that Gallup Poll was the front page of the Chicago *Sun-Times* [the poll showed Carter beating Ford in November by an astronomical margin]. I think we should be able to get some money off that. Tell Dees [Morris Dees, Carter's chief fund raiser] to get busy with it."

En route to the airport, Jody is draped over the back of a seat on the press bus talking to a reporter. The reporter had talked to Max Palevsky, a Democratic fat cat who threw a five hundred dollar per plate fund raiser for Carter in Los Angeles the previous week. "Palevsky's still not sold on Carter," said the reporter. "He still has reservations." "What kind of reservations?" asked Jody, dragging on his cigarette. "Just reservations," said the reporter. "Well, if he keeps giving us five hundred dollar parties he can have all the reservations he likes." Powell laughed. "He can have any ambassadorship he likes, too."

If traveling with Carter was difficult, traveling with Fred Harris was impossible. By the time I linked up with Harris in Chicago, before the Illinois primary, the populist candidate had no press buses, no transportation, no money, no staff and no crowds. His staff that day—one surly woman with a red Richard Nixon nose—had forgotten to put up signs at the Jewel Supermarket on the outskirts of the city announcing that he was supposed to speak at 10:30 A.M. His audience consisted of five reporters, one lady with a baby, one old man with a basket of groceries and one gas station attendant. Harris drove up in a blue Cutlass, zipped into the market, filled a shopping cart to use as a prop to underscore the soaring cost of food, and rolled out to discover his microphone did not work. He talked without a microphone. Bread used to be 37 cents a loaf in 1968, he said, it's now 63 cents. Milk was once 49 cents a gallon, it's now 81 cents. As President he would try and pass the McFarland Bill to break up regulation of prices through competition. But Harris refused to tour the market. "I think I've gone far enough. I don't want to interfere with their shopping."

Harris admitted his campaign effort was "idling" in Illinois, that there was no money left for advertising, but he would nevertheless press on to Pennsylvania's primary. Why? "Because I feel strongly about the issues. That's what this campaign is about. I really thought my stands on the issues were so distinctive that I'd do well. But everybody else outspent me. Sure I'm discouraged, when virtually every day things are going badly. But that's the story of my life since I was born."

It was a runaway victory for Carter in Illinois. Carter received 48 percent of the vote, and fifty-five delegates. Wallace was second with 28 percent, Shriver was third with 16 percent and Harris fourth with 8 percent. Favorite son Adlai Stevenson received only 161 votes, but garnered eighty-five delegates. Ford won 59 percent of the vote to Reagan's 40 percent. Two hundred thousand fewer voted in the Illinois primary in 1976 than voted in 1972.

Howard "Bo" Callaway, Gerald Ford's campaign manager, resigned because newspaper accounts accused him of intervening with a federal agency to benefit his Colorado ski resort. The uproar did not appear to have injured Ford's chances because it was handled swiftly. As it later turned out, Callaway was cleared of all charges.

Carter was still campaigning full tilt in Wisconsin. On Monday, April 5, wake-up call was at 5:15 A.M., baggage call at 5:55. I bolted out of bed ready to meet the day and ran out of steam in about fifteen minutes with the flu. What was I doing here?

I also got left behind by the press bus when I walked around the corner to buy a Dunkin Donut, the first morsel of food I had put in my mouth in twenty-four hours besides penicillin. The Carter bus waits for no man . . . or woman. Not even for Jody Powell who got left the next day.

Carter had already pumped five hundred hands and flashed his smile twice as many times by the time I got to the Allen Bradley Corporation in Milwaukee. He always noticed who was late. "Oversleep?" He grinned. Carter thinks all reporters are depraved, degenerate and lazy.

He had evidently read an article I wrote about his Bible-school teaching that appeared in the Washington *Star* on the previous Sunday. Carter had spoken about visiting the temple in Jerusalem with Rosalynn, and I quoted him as saying "in Christ's time it had been the third temple built. The second one was built about 516 B.C. The third temple was built by Herod. It was small compared to what Herod wanted, but it was sturdy."

"You had it wrong about Herod." Carter smiled. "He built a big temple. He had the second one torn down because it was too small. The one he built was twenty acres."

Jody Powell said Carter rarely misses anything. He reads two or three papers a day, and "anything else he can get his hands on."

Carter had a cold that day, and yet in spite of his sniffles and hoarse voice he was not even wearing a topcoat. What's he doing for his cold? "Nothing. I just let it degenerate."

By 7:20 A.M. Carter was campaigning at the Allis-Chalmers plant, a farm machinery and tool factory. The morning shift was arriving, the night shift departing, and Carter was grabbing hands like a machine on his right while conversing with reporters on his left. Most of the workers were too busy trying to get to work on time to even look at Carter. But Carter churned out his plant-gate spiel. "How you gettin' along" . . . "Have a nice day" . . . "Jimmy Carter" . . . "Nice to meet you" . . . "Pleasure" . . . "Mornin' to you" . . . "Mornin', sir" . . . "Came here 'cuz I want you to vote for me." "You will? Good deal, man."

I asked Carter in between handshakes how he thought his bornagain Christianity was going over with the Jewish voters. "I don't object to their religion," Carter replied. "Anyway, I've only got twenty-one percent of the Jewish vote. Jackson's got sixty-five percent." It sounded reminiscent of what he told speechwriter Bob Shrum: "Jackson gets the Jews. We get the Christians."

Carter was learning how to adjust to gaggles of reporters pressing around him, but still always on guard, either sermonizing or chastising. That morning he was doing both. He had closed the gap in Wisconsin against Udall only within the past week, he said. "Up until a week ago, Udall was moving. Our TV made a difference. TV has a major impact in a nonissues campaign. We're running polls every day and our strength has not declined." And he was not worried about Hubert Humphrey being drafted at the convention. "I would be disappointed and amazed."

He goaded *Washington Post* reporter Joe Weisman with the

fact that the *Post*'s political reporter, Jules Witcover, had followed him through the snows of New Hampshire, dogging him on the issue of reorganization. Witcover had interviewed him for an hour in a car, and then come to his home, asking over and over, "What agencies would survive at the end of your administration?" Carter told us that he let Katherine Graham know he didn't approve at a little luncheon she had for him in Washington, after he had emerged as the front runner and was suddenly everybody's darling. "I said that the *Post* was the only major newspaper so far that had not recognized the substance of my campaign."

Later that day he growled and flogged the *Post* again, as well as *The New York Times*. At an airport press conference in Green Bay, Carter sniped at the *Post*'s Joel Weisman and Christopher Lydon of the *Times* for probing too deeply into his tax reform program. Carter had been campaigning on the promise of "total tax reform." He would revise the tax code during his first term as President. But he insisted it would take at least a year of study before he could actually make recommendations to Congress. That day he added he would "treat all income the same." What did that mean? Weisman asked. "Some people don't understand how it will affect them." Carter dodged the question. Weisman asked again. Carter clenched his teeth, evaded the question with some verbal antics, but Weisman asked again . . . and again. "All right. I'll give you the same answer three times . . ." The vein in Carter's temple throbbed and his eyes blazed with anger, but he kept his hands folded placidly in front of him. Chris Lydon pursued Weisman's point. "I'm not qualified to give you specifics now," Carter steamed, practically green at the gills, "but when I'm President this is going to be done . . . I'm not trying to be evasive."

Weisman tagged after Carter when the press conference ended. "Look, I'm a taxpayer. I own a house. I have capital gains too. And I want to know if I'm going to have to pay." In his softest Southern accent and with a sinister smile Carter said, "You will," and walked away.

On the bus, many railed at the injustice of a candidate being able to get away without addressing the issues specifically. "The people are entitled to know what he is going to do as President."

But George McGovern learned in 1972 that spelling out programs can be disastrous. And even Rosalynn Carter had called her husband, telling him specifics "only confused" people. In 1976 issues were no more important than the price of hoopskirts.

On the morning of April 6, on the day of the voting in the New York and Wisconsin primaries, Carter embroiled himself in another brouhaha with the press, this time the biggest one of his campaign to date.

The Southern Governor came downstairs to the lower level of the Indianapolis Hilton for an early press conference. There was the usual gamut of questions. How did he feel about Mo Udall being ruled off the ballot with delegate slate problems? Carter understood; he had had similar problems in New York. Shirley Chisholm had been talking about a Humphrey-Carter ticket. Impossible! Carter said he would go into the post-primary season with less than a thousand delegates and would be difficult to stop.

Out of the blue Ed Rabel, a CBS-TV correspondent, brought up the fact that in an interview the previous week with the New York *Daily News* Carter had used the phrase "ethnic purity" when discussing the stability of established neighborhoods. Carter had said in the interview that he was opposed to "arbitrarily using federal force" to change a neighborhood's ethnic character.

"Explain," said Rabel. Carter replied, "I have nothing against a community that's made up of people who are Polish or Czechoslovakian or French-Canadian, or blacks who are trying to maintain the ethnic purity of their neighborhoods.

"This is a natural inclination on the part of people, and I made this statement in Milwaukee where there has been over a period of one hundred or one hundred and fifty years a compatibility among neighborhoods, for the churches, the private clubs, the newspapers, restaurants, all designed to accommodate members of a particular ethnic group. I see nothing wrong with that as long as it's done freely.

"I would never, though, condone any sort of discrimination against, say, a black family, or any other family, from moving into that neighborhood. But I don't think government ought deliberately to try to break down an ethnically oriented community—deliberately by injecting into it a member of another race. This is contrary to the best interest of the community. It creates disharmony. It creates hatred."

"Ethnic purity." It was a tiny cloud, no bigger than a man's hand, but it began to develop. After the press conference a group of reporters formed at the rear of the bus hovering over Joel Weisman's tape recorder. Whrrrr. Buzzzzz. Whrrrr. "What the hell does he mean by that? Sounds like some goddam Hitler," someone said. One hundred pens began scribbling down the quotes. Whrrrr. Buzzzzz. They played it back. Again and again.

Chris Lydon of the *Times* rushed off to call his New York desk. Ethnic purity. It had a peculiar sound. Betty Rainwater, a Carter press aide, wandered to the back of the bus to overhear the fuss, then quickly left to warn Carter he should expect further questioning at the next stop.

The next stop was a UAW plant which Wallace had won in 1972. Carter was sullen and pensive. "This used to be a big Wallace plant, but not anymore," Carter told Don Lee of the American Independent Party. "Yeah," said Lee. It went 30 percent for Wallace in '72. Now he'd be lucky to get 15 percent. John Messer, a UAW vice president, disagreed. He mentioned that Wallace and Carter were going to run very close in this plant. Carter seemed to have Wallace on his mind.

When we landed at South Bend airport at 2:20 P.M. Carter stepped into a hornet's nest. It was a press conference for local reporters, but national reporters monopolized the time. Ed Bradley of CBS, a handsome bearded black man, sat on his haunches. Chris Lydon in gray slacks and bow tie sat in a lotus position on the floor just two yards from Carter's feet. Joel Weisman of the *Washington Post* stood with tape recorder poised behind the roped-off corner. What did he mean by ethnic purity? Ed Bradley began. Carter wedged himself deeper and deeper into the mess. Instead of softening the phraseology, he intensified it, using unusually blunt language about social differences. He spoke of "black intrusions" into white neighborhoods, of "alien groups" in communities, and of the bad effects of "injecting" a "diametrically opposite kind of family" or "a different kind of person" into a neighborhood.

Carter's pique was beginning to show as the peppering persisted. One from Lydon. Two from Bradley. An uppercut from Weisman. Carter, for the first time, was perspiring heavily and appeared nervous and angry. "If you're trying to make something out of nothing," Carter told Lydon, "I resent that effort. I'm not trying to say I want to maintain with any kind of government interference the ethnic purity of neighborhood. I didn't say that at all. What I say is the government ought not to take as a major purpose the intrusion of alien groups into a neighborhood, simply to establish that intrusion."

He said no one had paid much attention to his comment in the morning, or during the past week. "There was nothing notable about it. Now in retrospect, you're trying to make something out of it, and there's nothing to be made of it."

Carter went on to say that as Governor of Georgia he had sponsored the state's first open-housing law and enforced it vigorously, although in Atlanta "there was adamant opposition to the intrusion of blacks into those all-white neighborhoods."

Betty Rainwater was hopping around as if she had been attacked by fleas. "The buses are leaving. The buses are leaving."

"Why won't you let us get to the bottom of this?" Lydon insisted.

"We're already behind schedule," said Rainwater.

Lydon was apoplectic. "For a man who chooses every word with such precision, is such a master of language, I cannot believe he chose such racist vocabulary."

Carter knew he had squeezed himself into a tight bind and it was pinching. But he was hell-bent to convince Lydon that he was right on ethnic purity, or retrospectively, says Lydon, he was determined that his message get out to the right people. "He wanted ethnic purity known."

After a successful visit to Notre Dame University in South Bend, Indiana, Carter seemed buoyed enough to confront reporters again. On the airplane, he stalked to the fifth row of tourist class where Lydon was sitting. Carter fixed his eyes on the *Times* reporter, and perched one black wing-tip shoe on the armrest of Lydon's chair. A dozen other reporters gathered around. For a while they beat around the bush, talking about Kennedy. Carter told Lydon he went to Teddy the day he announced to tell him he was going to run and Teddy assured him that under no circumstances would he be on the ticket. He told Lydon he thought his own candidacy would end the Kennedy era, but by the same token he did not feel Kennedy was spent as a Presidential hopeful. "Chappaquiddick could be dead in eight years." He said he would not consider Kennedy as a running mate.

Lydon, who had been making an occasional note on a yellow pad on his lap, stopped writing, looked up and searched Carter's eyes. "For a person who chooses language with a surgeon's precision, you have chosen some very strange words to use today. I never heard you talk that way—black intrusions, alien groups, a different kind of person—what were you trying to say?" Carter's laser eyes seared through Lydon. He responded slowly, purposefully, softly. "I don't know how to use the English language if you don't know what I'm saying." He neither softened his phraseology, nor retracted a single word.

The next day ethnic purity hit the front page of every newspaper. Representative Andrew Young of Georgia, Carter's foremost advocate in black communities North and South, called the blunder "A disaster for the campaign." "Either he'll repent of it, or it will cost him the nomination." However it was forty-eight hours later when at Rosalynn's insistence, Carter, at his first press conference of the day in Philadelphia, issued an apology. "The word purity bothers me too," he conceded. Then he restated the position he took on Tuesday, that he would not arbitrarily use federal force to move people of a different ethnic background into a neighborhood just to change its character. Many wondered why Carter waited so long to apologize.

Only Mo Udall seemed to catch the drift of what Carter was really trying to say. Udall thought the timing of Carter's words was "remarkable" coming "When Wallace is leaving the race and Pennsylvania and Michigan [both ethnically populated states] are coming up."

During an interview I once asked Carter if he had given any forethought to the political effect ethnic purity might have on the Wallace vote. Carter, who had been looking out the plane window, spun around and cut me off in midsentence. "No," he said firmly, looking straight into my eyes.

"You rarely deviate from your prepared speech," I told Carter. "You even say the same things over and over in interviews. That's why new phraseology, particularly jarring words such as *ethnic purity, black intrusions, alien groups,* seem out of step with your regular speech pattern. Was there any—"

Carter interrupted again. "No! It was said in an interview with a *Daily News* reporter and I never thought about it again and nobody else did either." He made several phone calls right away to Vernon Jordan, Andy and Coleman Young. "I just told them what I said, described the circumstances."

Did he tell them, as he reportedly told black leaders of Georgia back in the 1970 gubernatorial race, that they might not like his campaign, but they would approve of his actions once elected Governor?

Carter burned with quiet fury. Without raising his voice he replied, "I never said that. I believe that comment originated with Julian Bond. It never has been attributed to anyone. When first reported it said, 'a prominent black leader in Georgia said,' but Julian, as you know, is a Udall delegate, and he's been going around the country accusing me of all kinds of weird things. But I never made any such ridiculous statement as that."

Seven months later Carter told reporters in an off-the-cuff statement, "I never do anything unintentionally, even if it looks unintentional."

Although it was reported that ethnic purity was a concept conceived in Atlanta and propagated by memorandum, Carter firmly denied it.

CHAPTER 24

ALL THE DRAGONS ARE DEAD

CARTER HAD BEEN in a foul mood the day of the Wisconsin primary. His back was against the wall. He was incensed by the flap caused by ethnic purity and convinced that what he had said was perfectly innocent. He was further irritated by reports from his pollster, Pat Caddell, that Mo Udall might defeat him in Wisconsin. He lashed out at press and staff all day.

That night he closeted himself in his room at the Pfister Hotel in Milwaukee to watch the returns. At 8:30 ABC's Sam Donaldson marched down the mezzanine level outside the Carter victory ballroom flashing election figures over his head on a note pad. 37% Udall. 36% Carter. ABC was projecting Udall the winner. NBC followed suit. Reporters raced to write of the Carter upset. Carter staffers and supporters moped and brooded in the ballroom. Suddenly Jody Powell appeared in the hall and took Carter's brother Billy aside. "Jesus, I'm so nervous I feel like I've got a green plum up my ass. Listen, it's going to be close as hell, but we're going to do it. The rural areas haven't come in yet. Spread the word down here so everybody doesn't leave."

Peanut Billy swilled some more bourbon and whispered through the silent ballroom, distributing kisses as he went, "We gonna win."

Over at Udall headquarters pandemonium was breaking loose. It sounded like the fourth quarter of the Army-Navy game with a tie score. "Go-go-go-go-go-go-go!" they were bellowing until Udall stalked victoriously into the ballroom at 10:30 and paused while the crowd finished screaming and the band finished playing "On Wisconsin." "Oh, how sweet it is!" said Mo.

Fred Harding, who organized media support in Wisconsin's black wards for Udall, was gloating. "Carter can never get the nomination now. The blacks have finally seen that he's been talking out of both sides of his mouth."

The gold-braceleted, polished, Diane von Fürstenberg, liberal set that gathered to lionize Udall were hugging each other and dancing on table tops, singing of Carter's downfall. It was Udall euphoria.

Ella Udall was bursting with pride as she sashayed around the ballroom, swinging her hips like a sexy teenager in a clinging ivory knit, jangling gold bracelets, downing Scotch and smoking one ciga- rette after another. We sat down in a corner of the room surrounded by overflowing ashtrays. "I predicted a victory tonight," said Ella. "This is Mo's bailiwick. I had a gut feeling."

Out of nowhere Billy Carter appeared and kissed Ella. Bourbon Billy was having a ball for himself in Wisconsin, celebrating his freedom from Plains twenty-four hours a day. He had even helped Udall workers hang up posters one day. (It was one of his last cam- paign trips.)

She was really getting into the campaign now, especially now that he'd won a primary, she said. And she went off to bed.

Udall was lounging upstairs in a suite celebrating with his staff and preparing to tape the *Today* show, "Wisconsin is the key state traditionally," he told me. "It made John Kennedy. They saw some- thing special in him."

I began to suspect something had gone amok when a *Today* show producer ambled down the corridor and informed Udall that there were some new developments. He would have to wait a while before they taped the segment.

It was almost one in the morning. The network crews in both the Udall and Carter ballrooms had packed up their gear and gone home. Charlie Fay, the NBC cameraman, was turning in after an eighteen- hour-day. Don Oliver, the Carter correspondent for NBC, was sound asleep.

But in the Bombay Bicycle Club, the bar of the Marc Plaza Hotel, Billy Carter was still downing bourbon with a table of friends and regaling visitors with tales of how he wooed voters upstate in Pulaski and Gillett (which he pronounced Gillit as in skillet) mostly by drinking a lot of good Wisconsin beer with them.

Members of the Udall staff straggled in one after another and sat at the next table as the tide began to turn in Carter's favor. Two clean-cut business-suit types wearing Udall buttons walked in and gloomily announced to a group seated at the Udall table, "We're behind by twelve hundred votes."

Billy reached around and plucked one of them by the sleeve. "Bee-hahnd who?" he asked in his honeysuckle drawl, flashing the Carter family grin until his eyes almost crinkled shut. The Udall worker, a dark moustachioed young man, glared at Billy with contempt and stormed off.

Two more Udall workers slunk into the dark bar. "How much y'all losin' by?" Billy grinned, then turned to chuckle mischievously with his visitors.

Two Georgia matrons, members of the famous Peanut Brigade that flew into the state during the week to help Carter in the closing days of the Wisconsin campaign, swept up to Billy's table to announce jubilantly: "Thirty-seven hundred votes!"

"Whose favor?" Billy inquired loudly, his face crinkling again as he looked at the Udall table to make sure everyone heard him.

It was an unfortunate and fatal blow to the Udall campaign—and a fluke for Carter. Enormous publicity resulted from Carter's Trumanesque 1:30 A.M. reappearance in the ballroom holding "UDALL WINS" headlines over his head. The victory out of defeat reaped enormous benefits that carried over to the Pennsylvania primary the following week.

It was Udall's Waterloo. But he was philosophic about it. He would continue to campaign out of loyalty to fellow liberals who were still opposed to the Southerner.

Phil Berg, a candidate for Democratic committeeman in Philadelphia, decided to come out of the closet. He was wearing his huge orange "Hubie Baby" button right on his lapel. "Well, he's the man, isn't he?" Berg grinned. "What I see is a Humphrey-Carter ticket. Hubert's the elder statesman and Carter's the man who can pull the South. That's the way it's going to be, honey."

Berg was one of 2700 Democrats, at the annual Jefferson-Jackson Day dinner in the cavernous Philadelphia Civic Center, who had already turned a deaf ear to a bellowing Scoop Jackson. Jackson was on the podium in his wire-rimmed glasses looking like the spirit of Christmas Past, flailing his arms and ranting about how a Democratic Presidency would save the economy, which according to the *Washington Post* was booming again under Ford.

In a state supposedly gung-ho for Jackson nobody was listening. Most of these Dems were clustered around the ends of their tables kibitzing about the kids and the bad fishing weather and price of coffee. Two women who looked like former madams sat elbow to elbow buzzing about what a great man Philadelphia Mayor Frank Rizzo was.

On the dais, AFL-CIO Leaders Ed Toohey and Jim Mahoney yawned. "Jeeezus, it's been a long day. As soon as this guy finishes . . . schvisssssssst," said Mahoney with a broad sweep of his hand toward the exit. Only three hours earlier Mahoney and Toohey and twenty-five other labor chieftains had stood like toy soldiers at attention in the Poor Richard Room of the Bellevue-Stratford Hotel to declare before a battalion of the media their love and devotion and determination to turn out the vote for good ole Scoop.

Now it was a different love song. Steve Wojak chomped on a cigar. "Look honey, everyone here's for Humphrey. It's an undercurrent, a conspiracy." State senator Paul McKinney, a black pol from the 8th Senatorial District, flicked his Jackson button. "It's just for show, honey. I'm holdin' for the Hump. The Hump's mah man. When did I know he was running? The minute Nixon resigned. That's when." With that he slapped his thigh, thumped his six-studded diamond ring against the table, whomped the solid gold Ram suspended on a solid gold chain around his neck and guffawed. "I used to be committed to Shapp. Now I'm uncommitted for Humphrey." Freeman Hawkins, a black senator from the 7th District, agreed with his dinner partner. "I'm committed to support Jackson right now, but what happens at the convention is a different story. I want a Humphrey-Carter ticket."

Pennsylvania party chairman Dennis (Harvey) Thiemann was trying to blame the media for Carter's success. While Jackson was imploring the distracted crowd to join him in Washington at his victory party in November, Thiemann was grousing. "Trouble is when Carter stops in front of the same church Ford went to, he gets four and a half minutes of national TV time. Nobody else gets anything. That has to influence the vote. Now I have no animosity toward him for that, but I think it's time we get back to a little Harry Truman plain talk on the issues and away from Madison Avenue. If the campaign continues the way it's going and the candidates are allowed this evasiveness on the issues, Carter is going to be the benficiary just because he has more charisma."

Wendell Young made no bones about supporting the Hump. Young, a five-foot-seven-inch thirty-seven-year-old version of Jack

Nicholson in a tan suit and brown-and-white polka dot open collar shirt, is the head of the Retail Clerk's Union, Local 1357, and one of the gutsier union leaders to support a recall Rizzo petition. Young met me for dinner at the not-yet-Legionnaire's Disease-ridden Bellevue Stratford Hotel and told me how he had tried to bring the Humphrey movement out from under the rocks.

"I'm running openly as a Humphrey delegate. I'm not going to get pressured into supporting Jackson. When Mahoney [Jim Mahoney, vice president of AFL-CIO] called me about Jackson I said, 'Make like you didn't talk to me. I won't do it.' I told him we should start an open Humphrey movement. We shouldn't try and do this with mirrors. I told him labor lost one already when they tried to pull Jackson out of the closet to stop McGovern. The guy just doesn't have it. He doesn't relate to the masses."

Young had recently taken a poll at his local. Humphrey had won six to one. Out of a thousand questionnaires that asked who they would like to see win the nomination, 46 percent voted Humphrey, 12 percent Carter, 8 percent Jackson and 4 percent Udall. "I told Mahoney, 'Look, labor can only pull out the vote when we have a winner,' but he wouldn't listen and neither would the Humphrey people. They're the ones running the Jackson campaign here. They say this is the way Humphrey wants to do it. They're sorry now too. They know Humphrey should be in the race. And they're frustrated. But they said he'll get into the race around May 8. They're just trying to decide about the New Jersey primary."

After dinner we drove to a combined meeting of wards 66 A, 66 B and 57 in northeast Philadelphia where Young was campaigning for his delegate seat. I got a taste of how Rizzo runs things, this time to benefit Jackson/Humphrey.

The wards, which had gone for Wallace in '72, are Rizzo puppets. And, as they had been directed, had just finished voting unanimously, albeit unenthusiastically, for Jackson when we arrived. The air inside the pale blue dance hall over a dingy bar was putrid with smoke and the stench of stale beer. Young stood in the back of that room, shoulders squared, hands folded in front of him, waiting to be recognized. His greeting from the thirty or forty people in the room was disdainful glares and sneers. Suddenly, Steve Wojak, who was in the middle of a speech, spotted Young and paused to introduce him. "A fine young man, a union leader running for delegate, I want you all to meet . . ." As if on cue, half the room stood up, knocking chairs over, shoving their way into the aisles, thumbing their noses as they passed Young, and marched downstairs to the bar. "We're holding our meeting downstairs, buddy," they snarled at him. "We ain't comin' back until you leave neither," said one. "Why don't you get your car out of the driveway," said another. "It's blocking mine."

The mob waited in the bar until Young left. "He's not for Rizzo and we are. It's as simple as that,' their leader, Bob McGlone, told me. "Our party supports Rizzo and whatever he does. And we're supporting Jackson because Rizzo says so, even though deep down we're supporting Humphrey. Young has no business being here if he's not for Rizzo and not for Jackson."

A few offered apologies to Young as we walked to the car. "Listen Wendy, there would be reprisals if we supported you. We just don't know what Rizzo would do to us."

Young was clearly shaken as we drove away. "Some of those people who walked out on me were my shop stewards. This is fascism, sweetheart, right here in the Bicentennial City, the City of Brotherly Love."

Rank and file certainly weren't backing Jackson. Outside the Western Electric plant in Allentown on April 26, although spring had suddenly snapped back into bitter winter dampness and the sky had sealed over with gray, Jimmy Carter was positively joyous. He could sniff victory. Labor chieftains had obviously not made a dent in the Carter support among their minions. One out of every three workers who passed Carter on their way to the morning shift was wishing him luck, wanting "to shake the hand of the next President" or shouting, "Go get 'im, rebel." Carter practically burst with enthusiasm, reaching for hands like a swimmer breaststroking his way from shipwreck to shore.

It was the same at the Boeing Vertol plant on Industrial Highway, a strange place for Mr. Peanut to overwhelm the Senator from Boeing, but Jimmy had made his mark. Out of the fifteen laborers I spoke to, fifteen had decided to go for Carter. Jackson was anathema to them. Like Bernie Bowman, a tooling inspector and Joe Hickey, Shop Steward for Local 575, said, "When we were on strike in Christmas of '75, the UAW appealed to Jackson to help and he told us to go scratch. So we're tellin' him to go scratch now. The day of the ignorant factory worker is long gone. We don't just do like the bosses say."

The enthusiasm was deceiving however. For every one that wanted Carter there were more that didn't. Didn't want anyone for that matter.

The morning of the primary apathy was running high. It might have been that the steel-gray skies kept voters away from the polls, but only about 30 percent pulled the lever that day in Pennsylvania. By one o'clock only one hundred had shown up to cast their ballots at Dr. D. A. Santarsiero's garage in a middle-class area of Scranton, a ridiculously low turnout by past standards according to the local Republican committeeman who said three times that number normally voted. Of the ten I polled there, six were voting for Carter however. "Honest" and "open" were the words they used to describe him. Some said friends had convinced them to vote for Carter as late as the day before.

Rizzo was suspected of playing his usual election day stunts in Philadelphia. Voting machines went out all over the city—primarily in the pro-Carter black wards, and Information stopped giving out the number for Carter's headquarters. Telephones were mysteriously disconnected at Carter storefronts. Paul Kalill, a Springfield, Massachusetts, city councilman, on loan to Carter, who had inspected the situation, said it was something out of *The Last Hurrah*. Kalill had made the rounds of the 13th and 16th wards and the 20th and 23rd divisions to find that voting machines had been delivered broken, and the local committeemen in each area who promised to produce a mechanic, never did. Even after the Carter special task force finally located a mechanic who would handle the job, by late afternoon only one out of four machines was back in commission. The others still had missing levers, next to Carter's name, of course. Fewer machines meant long waiting lines, fewer voters and the likelihood that the Rizzo organization would work its will. But the voters were not listening to Rizzo any more than rank and file were heeding the voice of their labor leaders.

And, strangely enough, reporters had been digging up labor henchmen handing out sample ballots at polling places that showed no name at the top of the ticket. If labor was so turned on by Jackson, why didn't they print his name at the top of the handout? "Because we want a winner this year," said Bob McHugh, President of UAW Local 1069 in Eddystone, Pennsylvania. "It was only a verbal commitment to Jackson, a courtesy. We just couldn't get out and work for him."

Carter was swamping the state, thanks to the help of a young denim-and-turquoise-covered political gypsy with long curly hair named Tim Kraft. Kraft was hardly the type one would expect to swing major political states in Presidential campaigns or for that matter to end up as White House Appointments Secretary.

Kraft, who was born April 10, 1941, in Noblesville, Indiana, received a B.A. in government from Dartmouth in 1963 and dropped out of graduate studies in Latin American Affairs at Georgetown University to join the Peace Corps, is more at home recruiting volunteers for Vista, working on rural development for the Peace Corps in Guatemala, riding horses around haciendas in Colombia, South America, or playing in the Caribbean. But this thirty-five-year-old maverick, who had been broke most of his life after wild flings of sunning on exotic beaches or floating up the Amazon with georgeous girls or trying to develop Caribbean islands for investment purposes, finally found his niche in politics. New Mexico politics. A Congressional campaign, a gubernatorial campaign, an executive position in the party. But Kraft had never involved himself in any Presidential effort until he met Carter in 1975. Nevertheless he had earned his stripes. He organized the critical Iowa caucuses for Carter and now, thanks to Kraft, Pennsylvania was falling from Hubert Humphrey's hidden hands.

How? I asked Kraft over coffee in a greasy spoon in downtown Philadelphia. He had started as he had in Iowa, well in advance of the others. In Iowa, he began organizing a year in advance. In Pennsylvania, however, he had worked for only a little over a month. When he arrived he found only one Carter storefront at 22nd Street and another in Pittsburgh. Kraft blitzed the state in his cowboy boots, opening twenty Carter headquarters. He imported his guerrillas from Wisconsin, Georgia and Florida, hundreds of them, platoons of them to ring doorbells, distribute literature and call voters. Kraft's volunteers placed over 300,000 calls. "You can't get local county chairmen to do that." Kraft winked. "That's what Jackson relied on and it didn't work." Scheduling the candidate in the state for ten days instead of the original five was key too. "Once you meet Jimmy, you don't forget him."

That's how Kraft got the bug. Governor Jerry Apodaca's campaign manager, Chris Brown, introduced Kraft to Carter in January 1975. He was taken with the man, with his low-key approach and lucid way of expressing himself. He liked the fact that he was arrogant enough to predict he was going to be President and win. He liked his disdain for "big-shot treatment." Carter didn't demand to be driven straight onto the runway like other pols. He carried his own suitcase through the terminal.

By September of the general election Kraft had switched to three-piece suits and cut his hair. "Got to look the part if you're working for the President."

The night of the Pennsylvania victory the big-shot treatment suddenly began. In the early days when Carter was hungry for media coverage it was easy to get "five minutes" in the candidate's suite, even the night of the primary. Now even the regular Carter traveling press was banished from his door. The Carter rooms 2154, 2156 and 2158 of the Sheraton Hotel were located at the end of a long corridor guarded by a covey of beady-eyed Secret Service, men of two words, Yes and No. Mostly No.

Only photographers were permitted a short session in the inner sanctum where Carter, Rosalynn, sons Chip and Jeff and their wives, Caron and Annette, munched hamburgers. Jody Powell occasionally appeared to parcel out promises. "I'll try and get you five minutes." Five minutes never materialized.

Bob Shogan of the Los Angeles *Times,* Sanford Ungar of the *Atlantic Monthly,* Eleanor Clift of *Newsweek,* a reporter from the *Philadelphia Inquirer* and myself found ourselves tailing Carter down the carpet like puppy dogs hoping for a crumb, before he gave the big bones to the networks. "How does it feel to be a shave away from the nomination?" asked one reporter. Carter's back was against the wall of the elevator. His eyes on the door. He was stonefaced, authoritarian, an instant Admiral Rickover. "I feel fairly confident. Very good." "Were there moments of doubt?" "Yesterday our polls were very strong. I never got worried. Every week I get more optimistic." "Did you ever doubt this would come to pass?" "No." Toothy smile. Elevator door opened. Carter marched forty paces down the hall and vanished.

Sam Donaldson had been delighted to open his interview to any press who wished to sit in. Now the door was bolted and the corridor blocked by SS men. The Presidential thing was happening. Fifteen minutes later Carter reappeared. He walked like a midshipman passing in review toward the elevators. No comment. Another TV interview, another closed door. No questions asked. Forget it.

As usual a very low-key atmosphere prevailed in the Carter ballroom and upstairs in the staff rooms as well. The aura of *fait accompli,* "Reserved emotionalism," the staff branded it.

No one got carried away at 8:01 when NBC predicted "a substantial victory" or at 8:15 when the networks projected Carter the winner with 36 percent, Jackson with 26 percent, and Udall with

18 percent. Aside from a few whoops and hollers, all was still. Bill Vanden Heuvel, a former RFK friend and New York campaign coordinator for Carter, stood in the hall chatting with volunteers. "I figured if he won by more than 5 percent, Jackson would be finished." Just then ABC's Barrie Dunsmore announced from Jackson headquarters, "The race for Jackson is essentially over. There is no more money and after tonight, no more can be expected." Vanden Heuvel smiled again, and stated flatly, "Carter has the nomination now." It would be impossible for the Democratic convention to thwart the will of the people and draft a Humphrey or a Kennedy, he said. Carter had proved himself. Pat Caddell popped his head into the suite. "They didn't steal a vote from us." Caddell had been confident of a 12-point victory. Although his polls had been soft in the beginning, they firmed up in the past ten days. The day of the primary he was so confident he just took off and went to the races.

Senator Joe Biden of Delaware appeared on the twenty-first floor. Biden had met Carter three and a half years ago and was invited to spend a weekend with him. Carter had wanted to pump him on how he ran his Delaware senate race. "He questioned me for hours about my campaign against Caleb Boggs." (Then a twenty-nine-year-old lawyer Biden had upset the election by winning 50.3 percent of the vote against an established Goliath, using guerrilla campaign tactics.) I told him I felt people were more interested in believability and whether a candidate cared for them than programs and problem-solving. I said constantly that 'I don't know the answer.' People want to know how you sound really. They don't think any of us politicians are worth a damn. It's faith and love they're yearning for. That's how I ran my campaign against Caleb Boggs. Brown does the same thing, except Brown has an acid personality and he's a pain in the ass. But Carter comes across as a common-sense guy and he says 'I'm not sure' a lot. Carter's the only guy who understands what's happening out there. And that's one thing the press doesn't understand. People are not using issues to determine where a candidate stands."

Minutes later, Carter bounded down the winding staircase into the ballroom, waving and smiling. This was the turning point . . . The war was over. Not only the dragon Wallace lay in his wake, but Humphrey too.

Despite his dazzling Pennsylvania victory which essentially clinched the nomination for Jimmy Carter, part of the glow was dimmed by internal upheaval. In a staff that had been free of internecine warfare, a political bomb exploded. Robert Shrum, a brilliant young liberal speechwriter who had penned many of John V. Lindsay's, Edmund Muskie's and George McGovern's orations had joined Carter's team at the behest of pollster Patrick Caddell.

Shrum lasted only eight days from April 19 to April 26, when he quit in disillusionment and disgust.

In Shrum's view, Carter was "a dangerous man." He did not like Carter's public smiles and private scowls, "The smile goes on and off like a lightbulb." He was disturbed by Carter's stubbornness, by the fact that he was a loner "so withdrawn" he preferred to sit by himself in the first-class compartment of his campaign plane staring at the wall rather than share the camaraderie that was available to him. "On the plane, when he isn't reviewing a memo or meeting with someone he often just stares at the bulkhead. I never saw a book in his hands while traveling or on the nightstand in his hotel room," Shrum wrote in an article in *New Times.*

Shrum told me over a Coke at the Hyatt Regency bar on Capitol Hill, "that Carter would try and leave a double impression with the people. He has the laborers believing he's with them and the business moguls at '21' believing he's going to do everything for them. When he's President, someone's going to be disappointed. It's bad for the country. People will become even more disillusioned."

But Carter's mortal sins in Shrum's eyes were his failure to pass the liberal litmus test, and his unwillingness to use specifics in important areas such as defense, tax reform, child care, mine safety. Shrum was shocked when Carter would describe tax reform as "a disgrace to the human race," in his speeches, and yet appeared not to have any basis for the statement, or when Carter said he would veto the child-care bill, just as Ford had done. He was appalled when he asked Jody Powell how much reorganization in Georgia had saved and the press secretary replied cavalierly, "We say $30 million, but no one really knows how much it saved or cost. It depends on how you calculate it."

But Carter's worst offense, said Shrum, was striking from a statement he had prepared a provision to extend automatic black-lung benefits to all miners with thirty years' service.

Carter read Shrum's prepared text in a car in Pittsburgh en route to a steel plant, approved it, and then after Shrum had rushed off to Xerox it, abandoned the statement altogether. To compound the offense, when Carter later apologized for scrapping the proposal, he explained, "I don't think the benefits should be automatic. They chose to be miners."

"He just does not have many deeply held convictions," Shrum said. "He has convictions about lunch-counter civil rights, but no convictions about fundamental economic change. His preferences are largely conservative."

Shrum quit in a huff, leaving a note for Jody Powell which Jody never gave to Carter.

And yet Shrum admits Carter "has an unbelievably retentive memory. One day I told him my grandfather, Matt Welsh, had been in the Pennsylvania state legislature. And several days later at a breakfast in Johnstown, he told the county chairman, 'You know Bob's grandfather, Matt Welsh, was in the state legislature.' He remembered his name and the area he came from." Shrum also admits, "Carter possesses a tremendous capacity to move people," that "He's very smart, has great strength of intellect and could be an inspirational and successful President."

Carter staffers countered Shrum's charges saying the speechwriter's problem was basically that he was too much of an "ideologue," who didn't understand Carter's pragmatism. "He was 15 percent to the left; Jimmy was only 5 percent," said Kevin Gorman, a media aide. "He was used to working for Senators," said Jerry Rafshoon. "They don't have to worry about what they say."

"He didn't know how Carter operates," added Carter's traveling aide, Greg Schneiders. "Shrum had never worked for someone not willing to take his ideology intact. But Carter would question his statements and say, 'I'm not sure I want to go this far.' "

"Carter is his own speechwriter when you get right down to it," Schneiders said. "That's the way he and Pat [Anderson] work. First Pat collects ideas from other people and puts them into a first draft. Jimmy pulls it apart and rewrites it and then they sit down and go over it together. But Shrum would write his stuff with an ideological approach, and then expect the candidate to read it. When he wrote the black-lung disease statement we talked about it over dinner the night before and I've never had a more intense meeting than that one with Shrum. It went well after midnight. He was saying, 'We've got to have more time with Carter. We've got to go over it with him. We've got to have time to rewrite it, and Xerox it and then give it to him to read.'

"I tried to work with him and told him, 'Look, Jimmy will probably just read it, assimilate it, get the gist of it and then speak impromptu at the mine.' But I told him I'd get him in the car to go over it with Jimmy that morning." And he did. "The main thing

Shrum didn't like was that Jimmy struck out a provision that would have provided mine workers with automatic benefits after thirty years. Carter's point was, what if there's no evidence that a man has black-lung disease after thirty years, why should you assume he has it? And if he hasn't, he shouldn't receive benefits. The bill never made it out of committee anyway. Besides the United Mine Workers' representative Carter rode with in the car that morning told him he was right. He said, 'Look, you don't have to endorse all these bills, these are positions the union has to take, but you don't.' And Carter was very well received at that mine. Chip Yablonski of the UMW gave him a ringing endorsement."

Greg Schneiders saw nothing wrong with the way Shrum referred to Carter's statement "Jackson gets the Jews, we get the Christians." He went on, "Carter had expressed frustrations during the primaries from time to time because he felt his positions and attitudes relevant to the Jewish community were better than the other candidates, yet he still only got fifteen to seventeen percent of the vote. So he said it would not be effective to continue to seek their votes. Every politician has a limited amount of time and we have to spend it on things that are politically productive.

"Look," said Schneiders, "sure Carter is ambitious, driven, disciplined and singleminded, but he's not some demonic, cynical machine."

Three days after Shrum quit Carter's staff and two days following the Pennsylvania landslide for Carter, I was interviewing Mo and Ella Udall for WRC-TV in the den of their McLean, Virginia, home around eleven o'clock in the morning. The cameras were rolling and Udall was trying to sound confident. Jackson's campaign had collapsed. Frank Church's effort was too little too late, which meant if Carter faltered, Udall was number one. In the middle of his reply, his press secretary, Bob Neuman, appeared on the stairs and announced a phone call. Udall raised his hand as a gesture he did not wish to be disturbed, but Newman persisted. "It's Senator Humphrey." With that, the Congressman bolted for his former laundry room, now a den that he had paneled himself and cluttered with photos, including one of former Arizona Senator Carl Hayden drooling over a buxom blonde with a chain of hibiscus around her neck captioned, "Hayden's last lei." Udall sat down at his desk just beneath the largest and most prominent photo in his office, a portrait of Hubert Humphrey inscribed, "To my very dear friend Mo, with deepest affection and respect," and listened to Hubert's last minute indecision. To run or not to run.

"He was really anguished and torn," Udall said after the call. "He really just wanted a sounding board. He's still trying to weigh the pros and cons. He said that no one knows enough about Carter, that he has been told by so many people that he is the only one who can put the party together, and he still wants to be President. He still has a lot left to give. But on the other hand, he realizes it's awfully late. If he enters now, he'll be viewed as a spoiler, and he'd be breaking his word about standing back as the Grand Old Man. He said, 'The last thing I need is to jump in and be a spoiler again.' And he doesn't relish looking foolish if he loses. We've talked a lot about this recently," said Udall. "Two days after Pennsylvania he knew he could only run in the New Jersey primary. We talked about the fact if he came in, there would be no way he could get it on the first ballot, and no way I could get it on the first ballot. But he was still undecided. He was groping for help. I said, 'Hubert, it's a personal judgment. It may be that you can put it together in a fast way, but you have to weigh the embarrassment of losing. I told him I was in it till the end myself, that I wasn't going to drop out with only a month to go, that I was the last surviving liberal and I felt an obligation to continue, but I said, 'You're a great guy and you're my friend and either way you decide, it's all right with me.' Before he hung up Hubert said, 'It's a tough personal decision, isn't it?' "

On Capitol Hill, throngs had gathered in the halls of the Russell Office Building outside the caucus room where the Watergate hearings took place. Squadrons of television and still cameras packed the room, along with the cream of the writing press, many of whom anticipated Humphrey's announcement of his decision to enter the New Jersey primary. But at 1:40 when the Happy Warrior entered the room, it was obvious from the strain on his face and his wife Muriel's joyous smile that Hubert was not going to make the race. As he put it, "The one thing I don't need at this stage of my life is to be ridiculous."

Joe Crangle, Erie County, New York, Democratic party chairman, told me later that Hubert had waited until the eleventh hour to make his decision, but when Carter swept Pennsylvania (delegates, popular vote, labor, blacks, the elderly, the young) after all Humphrey's efforts there, he knew Carter was unstoppable. The night after the

primary, Hubert's top advisors, including Robert Short, Dave Gartner, Max Kampelman, son-in-law Bruce Solomonson, Fritz Mondale
and Joe Crangle gathered in Humphrey's office to plead with him to
enter the race. Carter must be stopped, they told him over and over
again for hours. Jackson was wiped out, but H.H. could trounce
Carter in New Jersey on June 8 and again in California. For once,
Hubert sat silently, listening, nodding his head in agreement. They
thought. But at eleven o'clock Hubert went home and told Muriel
and his aide, Dave Gartner, that he was not going to run. At 11:30
he spoke to his close friend, Dr. Edgar Berman, who urged him to
make the race, but he told Berman nothing. "I felt sure he was
going," said Berman. "I told him Carter was not representative of
the Democratic party, that people needed an alternative, that the
polls were overwhelmingly in his favor and that he could beat Ford,
so it would be a mistake for him not to run. So help me when I
hung up, I felt sure he was going in."

John Y. Brown, former Kentucky Fried Chicken King and owner
of Lumm's Restaurants, boarded a United flight from Louisville,
Kentucky, the minute he heard about the press conference and flew
to the nation's capital certain he would see his friend announce
under the same crystal chandeliers where John Kennedy announced
he would enter the 1960 race.

But always a master of the dramatic, the eternal crocus kept the
surprise from them all.

After Hubert's tears were shed and the course of the campaign
firmly fixed, his colleague from Minnesota, and Carter's future running mate, Fritz Mondale, stood amidst the shambles of crooked
chairs, cables, newspapers and empty rolls of film, and scratched his
head. "Ya know, this was really quite historic. It was quite something for this guy to say good-bye to us when he still had a real
chance to be President. It was a tough decision. Quite a moment."

Six months later, Humphrey lay in Sloan Kettering Hospital in
New York. His bladder and surrounding lymph nodes had been removed, the surgeons confirmed that his carcinoma *in situ* had spread,
and Humphrey admitted that had he been the candidate he would
have had to step aside.

CHAPTER 25

JERRY BROWN: ENTER AND EXIT THE GURU

EXIT HUMPHREY. Enter the Guru.

Jerry Brown, the Guru-Governor, the priestly pol, who disdains all worldly trappings like briefcases and mansions and limos, and sleeps on a mattress on the floor, stepped from a green Plymouth one May night at the Indian Hill Country Club in Maryland.

"Haven't I met you before?" he asked, shaking my hand. "No," I said, but I would be coming to California to interview him in the next two weeks. "Why don't you come with me all over the country?" replied the Guru, sounding like a member of the Carter staff. I was about to say something about chauvinism, motherhood, the American family and professional journalism, but he was swept away in a horde of pols who had come to glimpse this ascetic ex-Jebbie. He had mean narrow lips and a perpetual sneer. A *New York* Magazine reporter told me later on the bus that Brown was "the coldest fucker I ever met in my life."

Nevertheless Brown had the single ingredient that had been missing from the campaign for four months. The magical ability to turn on an audience regardless of its size.

That night at St. Michael's Church in Silver Spring, they were hanging from the rafters, spilling over into the vestry and out the doors, waiting to hear the young Californian. When he spoke of the "great spaceship earth," an old Adlai Stevenson line, it was as though electric volts charged the audience. No matter what he said they roared approval, even when he told them he couldn't take off his jacket in the stifling heat "because my vest has a hole in it."

They feasted on his banal humor: "We've got one Jerry in the

White House, all I'm saying is, let's put another one there," or "I'm not prepared to offer the Vice Presidency to anyone or accept it. My interest in the Vice Presidency is a little less than Jimmy Carter's," or "I'm not conservative. It's just that I'm cheap."

They sprinted across the lawn after him when he left, reaching for him, calling to him, "Jerry, Jerry," as they used to scream for Bobby during the 1968 Kennedy campaign.

It was the same way wherever he went from Maryland to New Jersey to Nevada to Rhode Island and back to California. The jumpers and shriekers, the touchers and kissers. Enthusiasm extraordinaire. Many were convinced if Brown had started in New Hampshire with everyone else, the nomination would have been his, not Carter's.

One night, dashing from Steelworker's Hall in Baltimore where Democratic functionaries went wild for Jerry, literally bellowing their approval, I rode with Ted Venetoulis and ex-Mayor T. J. Alesandro who had helped organize Maryland for Brown. Venetoulis had not encouraged Brown to become a candidate.

"I told him my professional judgment was that a bachelor from California who slept on the floor shouldn't do it. I told him we had a poll that showed Carter with twenty-four percent and Brown only seven percent. So it all depended on whether he wanted to roll the dice. He called me at two o'clock one morning and told me he was coming in."

Venetoulis and Alesandro agreed that the strategy should be to reach into every nook and cranny of Maryland and to make an impact where no one expected him to, and in a week, Brown was scheduled in all twenty-three counties from the Eastern Shore to Silver Spring.

What they did not anticipate was the tidal wave of interest. The first night he came to Baltimore, the ballroom at the Hilton was partitioned off so that it would accommodate two hundred people, but by six o'clock they were taking down one partition. At seven, they took down another and by eight there were three thousand people in that auditorium. "The organization couldn't turn out that many people if it tried, or even if it could, you couldn't produce that kind of enthusiasm," said Venetoulis.

Much of the Brown phenomenon was curiosity, people wanting to sniff for themselves a politician that prayed, spurned the trappings of office, followed his conscience and slept on the floor. As Perry Smith, the mayor of Cumberland, who came to meet Brown at the airport one cold cloudy day said, "He's very appealing. I just want to see him in person, see what he looks like." There was also the itch to get on the next Democratic Presidential bandwagon early. If Carter faltered in '76, it would be Brown in '80. "He's doing what John Kennedy did back in 1956," said John Coyle, president of the Allegheny County Commission.

Mostly it was an earnest stop-Carter movement that nearly succeeded. As Pat Barry, a Democratic state representative said at an East Baltimore rally, "I think Brown's going to end up as Vice President with Humphrey. This whole thing is going to decide it. Jackson, Shriver, Humphrey and Kennedy are all dumping money into this campaign. They don't think Carter can beat Ford or Reagan. They think Humphrey can."

Brown was, like Carter, a fascination. He was steeped in literature and theology and spouted quotations from profound theologians like Père Teilhard de Chardin with as much ease as he could rattle off the last paragraph of a Camus novel or toss away a line of E. E. Cummings, or discuss Proust, Sartre, Nietzsche, Merton or Thomas Aquinas.

One NBC reporter recalls the end of a grueling day plagued by delayed schedules and frustrations when Brown was frazzled and irritable. It was two A.M. and Brown was standing beside his chartered airplane, scowling, when the reporter approached him and tried to break the solemn mood. "Do not go gently into the night," he began, quoting Dylan Thomas. Brown's ears perked up and the Guru-Gov shot back, "Old age must burn and rage, rage against the dying of the light," finishing the line.

Brown even had an educational effect on his traveling press corps. Many had taken to carrying esoteric works along with their notebooks and tape recorders in order to better question and probe Brown's literary, philosophic, theological mind. A *Playboy* reporter was busy reading Thomas. A *Rolling Stone* reporter was digesting Chardin's *Phenomenon of Man.* A network correspondent was dipping into a volume called *Existential Images,* which Brown paused on the bus to discuss with him one day.

But for all his cerebral acumen, Brown was less polished in human relations. I recall our first interview. Brown slipped into the back seat of his Dodge and stared out the front window for what seemed an eternity. Then he flipped through a few pages of a book on the seat beside him and exchanged a word or two with an aide in the front seat. There was no extended hand, no how-do-you-do's.

Throughout the hours of interviews, Brown split hairs like a theologian, "What does that mean," he would interrupt. When I asked him, for example, who had more influence on his life, his mother or his father, Brown responded, "I wouldn't try to separate it out. It's a very complex question if you think about it. You have to know what my mother is, what my father is, what I am, what you mean by influence, what the causal connections are, the manifestations. I would have to give it a lot of thought."

He was irascible, brushing off questions about programs and specifics like gnats on a summer day. "Look, John Kennedy said during his campaign that we were going to go to the moon, but he didn't draw any organizational charts about how to get there." Then he ripped open a brown leather briefcase with the words "Governor of California" etched in gold. "Look at these briefing papers. Here's my paper on full employment. Read here, and you learn about Humphrey Hawkins." He flipped the page. "Read here, and you learn what my opponent is saying. Running for President is like an I.Q. test, a test of recall, a Ph.D. exam. You're measured on how well you can spew it back." He bristled when asked from whom he was taking foreign policy advice. "Some people say I don't take advice from anybody. No one of note to date. I met with Kissinger for half an hour recently, but he was just passing through. I don't know. Let's see, who will I meet with? Why don't we get Rusk, Kissinger, McNamara and all the architects of disaster of the last ten years and ask them what to do next. That's what candidates are supposed to do. Memorize a little list and every time you buzz a name—Ding! of an advisor, you get a certain response. This foolishness has to be opened up and debunked."

He scoffed at Carter for talking about reforming the tax code. "Candidates are always making grandiose statements. No one's going to restructure the tax code. It's forty thousand pages long. They've been talking about doing it for years. It will never happen. Neither will the closing of the mortgage interest deduction. That's ridiculous. It's not a serious issue."

Brown looked neither like the ascetic they said he was nor like the typical sun-cultivated Californian. Formally attired in a three-piece charcoal-gray pinstriped suit, monogrammed shirt, blue-and-red silk tie twisted into the perfect knot of the affluent, a solid gold Omega watch with lizard band, he looked more like a Wall Street banker. His thirty-eight-year-old face was pasty from lack of sleep and exercise, his cheeks were splotchy from an old razor and it was apparent why he was not given to Jimmy Carter grins. His two front teeth overlapped and one was badly discolored, as though dead at the root.

Asked about his first thoughts of the Presidential race, he was defensive. "When did I start thinking about getting into the race? I don't know. When? Where? The exact hour? I don't know. I mean, I think about a lot of things. I live in the moment. There's an old Jesuit saying, '*Age Quod Agis.*' Do what you're doing." His sister told me he had been "talking about it since he was born."

His campaign press secretary, Fred Epstein, had warned that Brown turned off on personal questions about his life-style, that he found such queries "trivial and silly." Epstein was right. Asked the reason he slept on a mattress on the floor when as Governor he could afford a regular bed, Brown said sarcastically, "So what did you expect, a four-poster?" Then he called to his aide Leroy Chatfield (an ex-priest and then married father of four girls), in the front seat. "Hey, Leroy. This is going to make the difference in whether America survives. The human species faces extinction and we're worrying about why my mattress is on the floor. Look, I lived a certain way before and I still live that way. It's not uncommon among people of my generation."

Brown skirted the subject of the supposedly strained relationship with his father, former Governor Edmund G. "Pat" Brown, but admitted he had gone against his father's wishes when he entered the Jesuit Seminary ("He said not to go, to stop fooling around, to go to school or get out and work"), that he had ignored his advice not to run for the Presidency except as a favorite son and that he never told his father of his decision to run until he had already made his public announcement. He also admitted that growing up, "I got a little less attention than I would have cared for."

Brown still seemed to be groping for who he was through Zen and a variety of other means. "I'm just trying to understand life and myself. There's a saying that in the beginner's mind there are many possibilities. In the expert's very few. People whose minds have been ossified by the same thoughts, the same patterns of mind, miss a great part of the world that's in front of them."

And yet, at thirty-eight, he seemed irretrievably sunken into a workaholic's existence. He rarely read anymore, even the newspapers, or saw a movie or a play. He listened to music only at his Los Angeles house where he would sometimes turn on Gregorian chants. Even eating was a chore. Food did not interest him. Breakfast was a cup of black coffee, lunch a sandwich at the office (when we stopped at an airport cafeteria for lunch, he had a Granola bar and a glass of orange juice), dinner was something light at Shakey's Pizza Parlor or a health food store. He had not had a meal at home since he became Governor. There was little time at the end of a day for dating, although he claimed he wanted to marry someone who would sew his buttons on some day. And in spite of various unproven rumors about his sexuality, he seemed reasonably comfortable with women. When Brown popped out of the shower, wrapping a towel around his nude body, and inadvertently stepped into a room where I was talking to his aide, he did not bolt for cover. "Hey, how ya doing?" he said, pausing to talk—much to the horror of ex-Christian Brother Leroy, who shooed him back into his dressing room.

It was also noteworthy that this new breed of politician, who spurned the perquisites of office and spent years on his knees in a Jesuit seminary, seemed as much at home in the world of Mammon as any other pol. He had no trouble mingling with the sophisticated set of models and writers in New York's brownstones, or the machine pols and bosses of East Baltimore. Of his acquaintance with tough-looking thuglike men with questionable ties, he told me, "That doesn't mean I adopt their philosophy. We have to work in the world. Even Christ preached among sinners. How can I get nominated if I don't?"

Brown turned the tables on Jimmy Carter in Maryland with the help of Governor Marvin Mandel's organization (Mandel hated Carter because Carter reneged on his pledge to support him as conference chairman at the National Governor's Conference in 1971). Brown won 48 percent to Carter's 37 percent. Democrats like Joe Crangle, chairman of the Erie County Democratic Committee and Representative Paul Simon of Illinois cranked up the Draft Humphrey movement again, claiming Carter had stopped growing in the polls. They compared the situation to the Kefauver-Stevenson battle in 1952 when Kefauver succeeded in the primaries but Stevenson won the nomination anyway. They claimed to have two hundred to three hundred delegates ready to go for Humphrey on the second or third ballot.

CHAPTER 26

FROM HELTER-SKELTER
TO VICTORY

BY THE FIRST WEEK OF JUNE, Carter had been soundly licked in Rhode Island, Oregon, Nevada, Montana, Maryland and Idaho by Senator Frank Church of Idaho and Jerry Brown.

Helter-skelter was setting in. Jody Powell got left behind by the press bus and had to take a cab to Los Angeles Airport to catch up with Carter and lost his briefcase in the process. Carter and his press cortege got lost getting to the airport and were twenty minutes late for his press conference.

"We really got our asses whipped in the small towns," Jody told me en route to the airport, since I got deserted too while I was last in line paying my hotel bill. "Ironic, isn't it," he said, lighting up a Kool, "that we came from a small town to get beat in small towns." What disturbed Powell about the Rhode Island loss was Brown's emergence from nowhere. "He isn't even a serious candidate for the Presidency, yet he tells the people of Rhode Island to pull an uncommitted lever to vote for him and they do it. Not only that, but it was a complex vote. There was no beauty contest. Those who wanted to vote for Carter had to vote for his entire slate. Those who wanted to vote for Brown had no 'Brown' lever at the top of the column to pull. They had to vote for individual delegates." What worried Powell was that it was going to be easier in New Jersey where Brown's name would be on the top of the ticket. "Brown's uncommitted-for-Humphrey slate stands a better chance of winning there." What Powell couldn't understand was the fact that Carter had an organization in Rhode Island for over a year, yet it had no effect. Only eight percent turned out to vote, and the majority of that small percentage voted against Carter. What was going wrong? "Just two new fresh faces, I think," said Powell.

Sam Donaldson of ABC stormed into the press conference leading the late troops behind him. "When it comes unraveled, it really comes unraveled," Donaldson spluttered. "It's been my theory all along that the simple Carter plan, the magical, mystical, trust-in-me thing wasn't enough. The more people saw of Carter the less they saw was there. First they bought the big smile, now it's all catching up with him."

Carter was smiling, but his eyes were rimmed with red, his face collapsed with fatigue. With five major losses just behind him, he was down, yet acting the perfect, self-deprecating gentleman. "In the minds of the voters, Church and Brown are much more attractive than I am," he said, playing the underdog even though polls showed him strongly favored in Ohio. "I don't know about next week. I've got some pretty strong favorite sons running against me in Ohio." He backed off his promise of a first-ballot victory. "I feel more confident of a second-ballot victory than a first. There's a good chance to win on the first, but nothin' sure about it."

I asked Carter whether he thought it conceivable he might end up like Kefauver did in 1952. "No," he replied. "Kefauver didn't have the all-pervasive support I have. He had also antagonized a lot of people in the party and he only won eleven primaries. Besides, in those days the delegates were selected and controlled by party leaders and there could not be the personal commitment between the delegates and the candidates that there is today."

Yet to observers it looked as though a loss in California, New Jersey and Ohio all on June 8, would be the kiss of death for Carter. California was already a foregone conclusion for Brown and Church was strong in Ohio.

Some of the media blamed Carter's sudden loss of momentum on faulty advance. On Memorial Day, for example, Carter's Ohio advance scheduled him for a stop at a baseball game, while only a few miles down the road, 20,000 Democrats were having a picnic he should not have missed.

Besides, the novelty of a Carter candidacy had worn off. Brown and Church were not only fresh faces, they were also riveting orators, who could supercharge crowds, while Carter was turning off audiences like the 10,000 who showed up at lunchtime in front of the Crocker Bank in San Francisco and vanished minutes after Carter began speaking. Carter's primary stump had worked in small intimate settings, but reading prepared texts such as his diatribe about

Lockheed scandals in Japan, delivered to a California rush-hour crowd, was about as effective as a lecture on sobriety in Times Square on New Year's Eve.

A man and woman in front of me had elbowed their way out of the mob. A trickle became a river. "He's just not dynamic. If his kick is charisma, he doesn't have it," said one bystander. Those who remained to listen, listened soberly. When Carter ended his speech with the words, "God bless you," there were groans. "Oh, he gave us a blessing," said one black girl. "Do you think if I brought along my New Testament, he'd read it for me?"

Even when Carter introduced former RFK press secretary and McGovern chairman, Frank Mankiewicz, who had become a household word in California, the crowd began to melt away like snow. The money buckets that were passed through the gathering crowds went unfilled.

I stopped by Carter headquarters on Sansome Street to see state coordinator Ben Goddard, a poodle-haired, turquoise-covered ex-campus radical. Goddard had been in California since April 1 operating on a minuscule budget of $450,000 that was to include two weeks of media. In spite of the paltry sum Goddard had opened thirty-five headquarters around the massive state and enlisted two thousand volunteers, and yet he was resigned to the fact Carter would leave the state with no more than 20 to 25 percent of the vote.

Some were still thinking it might yet be a Humphrey vs. Reagan race.

Frank Church was a formidable candidate, a forceful speaker with a lot of style, and he was making inroads. He had won primaries in Nebraska, Montana, Oregon and Idaho.

With his momentum, Church could have gashed deeply into Jimmy Carter's strength in the crucial Ohio primary. With half a dozen losses dragging Carter down in the last two weeks, an Ohio defeat would have annihilated his chances for a first ballot victory in Madison Square Garden, exactly what Hubert Humphrey, Ted Kennedy, Robert Strauss and company were hoping for.

However, at the last minute, Church's campaign mysteriously screeched to a halt. He spent most of his last week away from Ohio. He wasted one day flying all the way to California, "to boost the morale" of his workers—something he could have done by telephone and loudspeaker hookup. He spent his day in California in bed with an alleged strep throat, although he admitted to me he had campaigned many times with other illnesses. Another day he returned to his home state of Idaho to inspect the results of a bad flood. Another time, his plane mysteriously broke down. He skipped opportunities to shake hands, canceled television ads and finally, on his last day in Ohio, Church spent five hours in his Cleveland hotel room supposedly preparing for a television show, although he told me in an interview, he was used to two, three, or four television shows a day and never boned up, unless he was shaky on the issues. He was familiar with the Ohio issues, he admitted.

One would have suspected if Church were serious about stopping Jimmy Carter in the all-important Ohio primary he might have cuffed him around a bit when he had the opportunity. Instead he complimented his opponent. On the last day in Ohio, at a noontime Columbus rally, a question was posed to him from a member of the audience: "What constitutes competency in a candidate running for President?" Church responded, "Well, if the President were viewed as the Governor of the fifty states, I would say anyone who has served well as Governor, as Mr. Carter has, honorably and well, would be excellently qualified."

Coincidentally, the first word that sprang to Church's lips in an interview on the plane that afternoon was "Vice President." Yes, he would very much like to be Vice President, provided that the circumstances were right, that is, if the Vice President had a major foreign policy role to play. And he just happened to have eighteen years of experience on the Foreign Relations Committee, knew world leaders on a first-name basis from his trips around the world, and was eminently qualified to be a balance to the Secretary of State. He also had twenty years of Washington experience, which Carter lacked and needed on the ticket; besides he would provide geographical balance. Carter was weak in the West and needed a Westerner, Church alleged.

Interestingly, the Carter staff members I checked with thought Church had the best shot at the second spot on the ticket. Even Carter was echoing Churchlike refrains on his campaign plane. The day after the Ohio primary he was saying he wanted a Vice President who had experience in foreign relations, and could play a major foreign policy role, and one from the West would help since it was his weakest suit.

But the deal fell through.

Three days later on June 5, Carter had regained the image of a winner. At least 10,000 people squeezed inside a massive glass-domed shopping mall in Cherry Hill, New Jersey, knocking over plants and palms and people trying to cast one glance at the peanut farmer.

And Carter turned on to it, first climbing to the roof of his station wagon to wave, jumping down into the mob to let them paw at him, then whipping them into a frenzy with his stump speech. It was Carter's 2,051st and last speech and he gave it his all. "This is the year of the people," he said, promising intimacy with the voter, a fair income tax structure and welfare reform. "President Carter, we love you," they cheered as they mobbed him on his way out, leaving a tidal wave of fans behind. Once again he sprinted into the mob, positively ebullient from the mood of victory. It was the first time I had seen him really loosened up by a throbbing crowd. He let go a little and it was appealing. Many felt it was his best crowd.

Carter didn't. "No, I wasn't exhilarated by the last rally," he told me later on that night, squelching any thought that he might have gotten carried away. "It was good, sure it was good. But there've been others just as good or better. San Francisco was good [that's where 10,000 melted away from his speech]. Akron was good. This one was dangerous. I got enthusiastic and that's not good. People get out of control. People can get killed that way. Babies get crushed. I hurt my hand. Look," he said, offering a purple paw. "Nearly broke my finger."

How was Amy I asked. "Fine," he said, "except for the first time she cried when we left home. School's over and she has nothing to do, she's home all day alone and she has time to think about us. It's hard on her now."

The next night Carter lost New Jersey, but he won the critical state of Ohio. And that was enough to guarantee him the nomination. In Atlanta, after Carter had greeted his fans in the ballroom of the Hyatt Regency (the hotel with the elevators that look like lighted bullets ascending and descending on the inside of the tower lobby in full view), he flew to Plains for his mother's street dance in his honor. It was well after midnight when the Carter contingent in a fleet of Lear jets took off and there had been some thought of canceling the party, or postponing it for a day. "Try that and you and me'll both be floating out to sea on a shitlist. You don't mess around with Miz Lillian," Jody Powell had told the aide who suggested it.

Landing at the Americus airport at one A.M. in those small sharp-nosed jets on a cracked and broken tarmac without benefit of either control tower or runway lights seemed like landing in the jungles of Vietnam. When we hit the runway, thirty or forty members of the press spilled out of the bellies of the planes, running for cars and camera positions, like GI's heading for cover. At 1:45 we pulled into Plains.

Sure enough, Miz Lillian was still standing at the head of the crowd on Main Street. What were her thoughts tonight a reporter asked her. She must be overwhelmed now. Jimmy was almost the nominee. "Oh, shut up," she told one newshen. Then she noticed the reporter writing in her notebook. "Why . . . I'm so happy. This is a great night. I just want him to come, that's all. I'm tired."

After kissing his mother, Jimmy Carter bounded up the rotting wooden steps of the newly white-washed depot to the stage while his kinfolk mixed with strangers, blacks and whites, at his feet. "I think we'll get the nomination on the first ballot. I'll be very surprised if we don't . . . There are a lot of secrets of our success. We surprised a lot of folks as you know . . . literally thousands were not friendly to me. . . . But I had a lot of people tell me, 'Jimmy we didn't know what kind of person you were till we went down South and met your folks . . .' There's no doubt in my mind the next President will be from Plains, Georgia."

A minute later, as he hugged and kissed his kith and kin someone stuck his head out the door of the depot and shouted to Carter: "Governor Wallace called. He said call back as late as you want to. The phone is by his bed."

"I feel good, man. This is like a vacation." Carter smiled and sprinted inside to return his calls. First California. Carter talked to 2,500 supporters in Los Angeles by speaker hookup. "There's no doubt in my mind now that I'll win the nomination on the first ballot and be the next President," said Carter, sitting on the edge of a desk in his shirt sleeves.

Miz Lillian stood beside him in her blue polyester pantsuit, her hand on his shoulder.

"Tell 'em how much I care about 'em," said Carter, his voice high-pitched with excitement. "You'll be my friends for life." When he hung up, he took a deep breath. "Whew. Happy days are here again."

His phone call to George Wallace was made privately. He would have no comment until the next day.

Carter's aunt, Sissy Dolvin, who had campaigned in thirty-nine states seeking votes for her favorite nephew, was standing outside when Carter slipped into his car at 2:15 A.M., having been up since 5:15 the morning before. "Ever since he was a little boy, everything has always fallen into place. His life is like a jigsaw puzzle."

The next day, the old kingmaker, Mayor Richard Daley of Chicago, and the man from whom he stole the South, George Wallace, endorsed him.

Although Wallace had indulged in bitter diatribes against Carter during the campaign, and at one point threatened to endorse Gerald Ford, political reality brought him to Jimmy Carter's side. "He finally realized that Carter was going to make it," explained a Carter aide. Wallace understood that he was no longer the dominant figure in the South and that for his own political future, although it was a bitter pill to swallow, it would behoove him to let bygones be bygones and be the first in line to congratulate the victor.

Scoop Jackson then freed his delegates and Church and Udall followed suit. Although Governor Jerry Brown of California still remained in the race, essentially, one month before the 1976 Convention at Madison Square Garden, Jimmy Carter was the Democratic nominee. And, in a Democratic year, facing a weak President burdened by a failing economy, there seemed to be practically no way he could lose.

Most Democratic party leaders were dumbfounded by the astonishing Carter victory. They still could not fathom how a virtual unknown had pulled off such a political coup.

But Carter's nomination had been made possible by certain historical changes. It was no longer feasible to make Presidential deals in smoke-filled rooms at the Convention. The nomination had to be won in the primaries. McGovern had been the first dark horse to benefit from the increased number of primaries instituted in 1968. Carter was the second. Although he was an outsider, Jimmy Carter entered and ran in thirty of the thirty-one primaries, taking his case directly to the people, gaining name recognition, national celebrity and media attention through a dazzling chain reaction of early primary victories. The domino theory worked for him. Iowa established him as the candidate to watch and gave him a leg up in New Hampshire. New Hampshire placed him first in the pack of contenders and gave him the necessary momentum to win Florida. Florida established him as a dragon slayer and laid the groundwork for Illinois. The surprising Udall upset in Wisconsin offset the Carter losses in Massachusetts and New York and sent Carter into Pennsylvania doused with the sweet smell of success.

Victory in Pennsylvania and the elimination of Udall and Jackson (and therefore Humphrey) as major contenders virtually assured Carter of the nomination.

The stop Carter efforts of Senator Frank Church and Governor Jerry Brown had proven ineffective.

Carter had outfoxed the entire Democratic party with a very uncomplicated formula. He had studied the new federal election rules and knew the ropes. He formulated a Grand Strategy. He announced first. He hit the hustings long before his competition. He worked longer and harder than the others. Over a two-year period he traveled more than 400,000 miles and made over two thousand speeches. A lonely candidate, he walked the streets looking for votes. He shook hands in barber shops, labor halls, factory shift lines. He made himself known through sheer ubiquity. And where he couldn't be, members of his family and his Peanut Brigade of Georgians went for him.

He budgeted his funds carefully. While other candidates were squandering their cash, Carter asked members of his staff to work for practically peanuts. He relied heavily on volunteers. He hired crack campaign tacticians like Chris Brown and Tim Kraft to organize his efforts in critical states such as Iowa, New Hampshire, Florida and Pennsylvania. He worked from a carefully mapped out strategy that he adhered to faithfully. He had the added plus of a close, dedicated staff unburdened by internal strife or competition for access to him. He possessed magnetic Southern charm coupled with a mesmerizing influence on small crowds. One on one he was irresistible. He was a new face without Washington connections. In the wake of Watergate, his attraction was not only his political purity, but his strong Christian faith. And he looked like a Kennedy.

His candidacy became the rallying point for Southerners who longed for a place in the political sun once again. His victory would mean not only vindication for Dixiecrats, but the end of the Civil War as well.

A peanut farmer, who toted his own garment bag and wore blue jeans and spoke of easing the tax burden and correcting the welfare mess, he became the people's candidate. He gave hope to the little man who for so long had felt disenfranchised, cut off, and disregarded while privilege ruled.

By an extraordinary political balancing act, he carefully peeled off stigmatizing labels and was able to sell himself to a broad spectrum of voters—conservative and liberal, black and white, Christian and agnostic, rich and poor, young and old. He was Everyman. He offered something to all.

But the most important commodity he promised in a time of disillusionment was political medicine to heal and unify a divided nation, and hope to uplift it.

Lastly, luck was on his side. Or was it fate?

PART

VII

FIRST
VICTORY

CHAPTER 27

THE CONVENTION

JIMMY CARTER ARRIVED in New York City with the 1,504 delegate votes needed to nominate him. Although the old guard had planned on the convention being a smoke-filled back-room bargaining session stacked in Hubert Humphrey's favor, it was simply a matter of going through the conventional motions to hand Carter the Democratic crown on a silver platter.

The only real news to emerge from the Americana Hotel and Madison Square Garden was Jimmy Carter's choice of Walter Mondale as running mate, a choice that finally turned a less than enthusiastic convention into a love-in, made the delegates who felt queasy about Carter comfortable, and even settled the feelings of some of the traveling press who until then had pigeonholed Carter somewhere between Mussolini and Che Guevara.

Since the Democratic National Convention was for the most part procedural, most convention goers decided to have a good time attending cocktail parties or partying at Elaine's or "21." Billy Carter, who hated New York ("I plan to see it in as much time as it takes to see Plains.") spent most of his time in the NBC office of the Americana drinking beer. Chip and Caron Carter went on boat trips around Manhattan. Jack Carter spent three out of five nights drinking until dawn at P. J. Clarke's and at Elaine's, watering spots for literati, sophisticati and the beautiful people of Gotham. Laughed number two son, "I got poured into more taxis than you ever saw." Amy fed the monkeys in the zoo, climbed statues in Central Park and read comic books in her room. Miz Lillian went to the theater to see Shirley MacLaine.

Jimmy Carter stayed behind double-oak doors on the twenty-first floor of the Americana Hotel, meeting with staff members, labor groups, Chicanos, VIP's and potential Vice-Presidential running mates.

The nominee-to-be arrived with a plane full of Georgians at La Guardia Airport Saturday around 3:30 P.M. and scrambled for a motorcade of cars, limousines and buses. His relatives, including Billy, Hugh, Sybil, and even superstar Miz Lillian (whom Carter inadvertently left behind in Plains and returned at the last moment to collect) rode in a bus marked "Carter Family Only." Carter, Rosalynn and Amy rode silently in a blue Chrysler. Barreling down East River Drive in front of the bus was a staff station wagon. One sneakered foot belonging to Jody Powell hung out the rear window. Powell had injured his foot playing football in the parking lot of the Best Western Motel in Americus, Georgia. In his three-piece banker's-gray pinstriped suit, one white sneaker and one black shoe, he looked like a cross between David Rockefeller and Donald Dell.

The Welcome Carter rally at 52nd Street and 7th Avenue outside the Americana Hotel was not a crowning moment for the conquering hero in coronation city. The Queen of England had fared better. So had the Tall Ships. The rush-hour crowd consisted of about 1,500 curious New Yorkers, delegates, alternates and newsmen. The Carter advance had painted the streets and sidewalks of New York with signs: "Come see Jimmy Carter, Rally July 10, 4 P.M." and *The New York Times* had carried an ad on the political page. There was not much of a turnout, or much enthusiasm, for "the Goober." Mainly, the mob was a stream of New Yorkers trying to get home from work. "I didn't come to see Carter, I'm just trying to get to Penn Station," growled one man with a shopping bag clutched to his bosom. Many who had come to witness The Man were delegates who became irate that Carter was invisible to all except the television cameras. Carter's speech on the problems of the cities lost his audience, and his one gag bombed. "I would like to announce my own personal choice for Vice President." Jimmy smiled. There were ooohs, ahhhs, ohhhs, shhhs, cheers. Then Carter continued, barely able to keep a straight face, "As soon as I'm sure who the choice for President is going to be." Boos and catcalls.

There were a few enthusiasts. "At least he'd get rid of the Lone Ranger [Kissinger]. Isn't that good enough?" said one man. "He'd do something for the city. Clean it up, get the bums off the sidewalk and stop all the alcohol," said another. All around were the signs of a quiet resignation to a Carter Presidency. As one woman delegate said, "If you don't like him, swallow him."

The candidate and his family were ensconced on the twenty-first floor of the Americana Hotel, so the button to that floor was disconnected. Even VIP's had to get off on the heavily guarded twentieth floor and walk up a flight to get near Carter's suite. Outside the double-oak doors with the gold-eagle knockers that led to the Carter inner sanctum, the blue-carpeted area was bustling with activity. Amy was playing in the hall, barefoot as usual and pigtailed. Miz Lillian opened the portals to beckon her rambunctious granddaughter. Inside the blue living room filled with pseudo-antiques and two large French murals, two television sets were blaring the news. Rosalynn and Jimmy were "in conference" leaving Miz Lillian in charge. "I just love New York, I've been coming here for twenty years. My husband and I used to take the train here from Plains for baseball games. I love the theater, and the pace . . ."

Saturday night the convention hadn't yet begun, but the merry-making had. Just down the hall from Carter's suite, Betty Rainwater, Carter's deputy press secretary, was decked out in red polyester pajamas looking vampish. "I'm all dressed up for the biggest moment of my life." Vicki Rogers, Carter's chief scheduler, who had rarely been seen along the campaign trail in anything but sartorial distress, was redolent with perfume and resplendent in a slinky saffron sheath. "I'm going to have fun for the first time in six months."

Fun was the staff party downstairs in the Americana, where one was struck by the youthfulness of the Georgia mafia. Carter represented a new hope to many younger people in the U. S. who grew up during the Vietnam, Johnson, Nixon and Ford years. They remembered Kennedy only as a blurred figure of their youth. The average age on the Carter staff was twenty-six; the average voter is forty-three. Also, half the room was female, a major change from the Kennedy, Nixon and McGovern staffs of the past.

The atmosphere was jubilant. These people had been working hard, and much to their surprise, were prevailing. One woman, in a black lace dress, said that in the beginning many of them had gone to work for Carter because they were committed to the man, but deep in their hearts didn't really believe he had a chance. "But now . . . My God!" she squealed. "We're winning. What have we done? It's so exciting."

Jimmy Carter, his head bowed practically to his knees, began his Sunday in New York in the Fifth Avenue Presbyterian Church listening to a stinging sermon on rat-infested apartments. An hour later he was mingling with the denizens of Fifth Avenue and Beverly Hills at New York's most exclusive restaurant, "21," at a lively luncheon hosted by a martini-sipping Democratic party chairman, Robert Strauss.

Carter, who normally attends services in the Plains Baptist Church, chose to go to Fifth Avenue Presbyterian in a spirit of "ecumenism," his staff pointed out. The sermonizing was performed by two black Baptist ministers, Samuel S. Simpson of the Bronx Baptist Church, and Dr. Kenneth L. Folkes, pastor of Mt. Carmel Baptist Church.

Both clergymen offered prayers that the Democratic convention be given "divine guidance" in choosing its nominee, but also hammered home to Carter the need to pay attention to the devastating problems of the deprived.

In his prayer, Reverend Simpson said, "We ask you to guide them [the delegates to the Democratic Convention] in their deliberation in the decision they will make. Give a clear mandate to those who lead. We present you with New York City, not the way others see it from outside, but as those of us who see it from within. The people of New York feel the squeeze of unemployment, poor health, burned-out hopes, dreams and aspirations, from rat-infested apartments. Grant that new bridges may be built . . . that new and courageous leadership be inspired."

Reverend Folkes told the congregation he believed "President Carter" would go on to victory in November, but "One of the reasons we are praying" is the fact that "You must change the picture . . . The day of prosperity for the privileged few must end. And a piece of action, as they say, for those in the streets must become a reality for us all. We all want to enjoy a piece of the pie."

A few minutes later Carter was snacking on smoked salmon, giant prawns and Virginia ham at "21" where a martini costs $2.50, a bottle of Dom Perignon champagne forty dollars, and a vegetable plate $9.25. Mingling with the elite, such as Henry Ford, Mrs. Eugene Wyman of California, the R. Peter Strausses and Mrs. Robert Wagner, were an assortment of Democrats ranging from Peter J. Camiel, Democratic chairman of Philadelphia and Arnold Miller, President of the United Mine Workers, to former Democratic candidate Fred Harris and Mickey Griffin, chief political operative of Governor George Wallace.

With the exception of some disbelieving New Yorkers like Sam Bloom who were shocked to hear an orchestra playing "Dixie" and "Way Down Upon the Swanee River" in this exclusive Eastern Establishment eatery ("I never expected to hear that here."), a mood of exuberance and unity prevailed. " 'Yankee Doodle Dandy' and 'Dixie' seem to go together now," said Philadelphia's Pete Camiel. "I haven't seen such unity in thirty years," announced Louisiana finance chairman Ed Carmouch. "It's just one big social occasion," said Vincent McDonnell, New York State mediator. "Just one big party," said Tom Boggs, son of convention chairwoman Lindy Boggs, downing a Bloody Mary.

"I've known Jimmy since 1974," said Mrs. Eugene Wyman, whose late husband had contributed substantially to Democratic candidates over the years. "We had dinner in California after the Democratic telethon and he told me about his plan to run for President. He said he had analyzed the last twenty elections and had a tremendous group of men around him and he was going to win. I told him he couldn't run without having a base as Governor to run from, but he said 'That's O.K. . . . I'll be free to go around meeting people. None of the other candidates who are Governors or Senators will be able to. I'll go all out and win New Hampshire.' And everything he said has happened. It's incredible."

Carter was more relaxed than observers had seen him in months. He took to New York City as though he had lived there all his life, striding down Fifth Avenue, jaywalking on his way to the NBC studios. Once he was in the dressing room for his appearance on *Meet the Press* he never looked in the mirror until he was finished. Frances Kolar, an NBC makeup artist, dabbed Carter's face with some M-1 Ben Nye natural creme foundation, then brushed his brows with a touch of darkener. His makeup was completed in three minutes. Carter refused hairspray and combed his own hair.

"He wanted to look natural," Ms. Kolar explained. "He has a very strong face, good structure and very good natural color. There's enough red and warmth in his skin that he doesn't need much makeup. I just blended a little into his skin because it's a bit flaky and blotchy. This just evens it out." Ms. Kolar found Carter very relaxed too. "He seems to be a very peaceful person. I felt very much at ease with him."

Bill Monroe, moderator of *Meet the Press,* was to pounce on Carter with some tough questions, but off camera just before the show started Monroe was telling him how much he liked his staff.

"Your press people have been very helpful and fair. It's been a very nice experience working with them."

"I hope to keep it that way," said Carter. "If they get arrogant or proud I would be very upset."

Carter was better than usual that morning. He was so pleased he could barely contain himself when Monroe introduced him as the man who had won all the primaries and was most certainly going to be the nominee.

Carter answered even the toughest questions without flinching. When asked why members of the press found it so difficult to understand him, Carter replied, "I'm no more enigmatic or mysterious than any other person . . . I may be hesitant to tell jokes because one out of a hundred might accept it as a serious statement. I think I'm sensitive, tough, a good planner, searching for answers to complicated questions."

He spoke with the air of a man confident of capturing the White House. He would deal with the amnesty question "the first week" in the White House. He said he had already discussed tax reform with the leaders of Congress and found them "ready and willing" to take action on the problem. He reconciled his liberalism on human services and his conservatism on spending by explaining that he ran Georgia as well as any corporation, but also found that the "best investment the country can make is in human beings." He thought it inadvisable to predict government would be smaller at the end of his administration, but he promised he would spend wisely, "in an optimum fashion," to deliver services.

As usual, he waffled on right-to-work laws. When Lawrence Spivak asked why other Southern states except Georgia had voted to repeal right-to-work laws, he retorted, "That principle suits me fine if the states are for it. I grew up in a right-to-work state, but as President if the Congress repeals 14 B, I would sign it into law. I have mixed emotions about it. I don't have any strong belief on one side or the other, I never felt strongly about it one way or the other." He was firm on the need for a strong defense, closing bases overseas, and opted for a "simple, more muscular fighting force with the capability to fight." He would consider a future Arab oil embargo cause for "economic war." He would simply end all shipments of arms and equipment to the Arab states . . . "No weapons, no arms, no nothing."

Rosalynn had been seated in the first row of the audience. As we left she told me that the realization her husband was going to be President finally hit her two weeks before. "In the middle of the campaign I had been so busy, I hadn't had time to think about what was happening. Although it's been a month since we realized Jimmy had the nomination, the overwhelming realization did not set in until the middle of a speech I was making in Greenville, South Carolina. I just broke down. I really believe now that Jimmy is going to be the President and I suddenly realized the tremendous responsibilities he will have to carry as a result."

Sunday night Carter threw a beer-and-fried-chicken bash on the docks of New York for all the delegates and alternates at the convention, but he himself bypassed the beer and merrymaking. It was his avowed purpose to personally greet every delegate. And, feet planted eight inches apart, he stood at attention in the receiving line until every hand had been shaken and his own right paw was crimson. In two-and-a-half hours his only extraneous motion was to wipe lipstick smudges from his cheek or to rock back and forth to relieve the pressure on his bad knee. Amy Carter stood beside him, a copy of *Children's Express* tucked under her left arm, offering a limp hand to a few delegates, but dropped out after fifteen minutes. Miz Lillian spent ten minutes meeting and greeting, but fell by the wayside and sat in a chair guarded by Carter aide Kevin Gorman for the rest of the evening. Only Jimmy and Rosalynn persisted with military discipline. By 8:30 they had pressed two thousand hands, by 9:30, three thousand. The minute the crowd thinned at 9:35, they split.

As Barbara Howar put it, "Success is having half the town screwed up over a party."

Rolling Stone magazine gave a little by-invitation-only supper on Monday night for the Carter campaign staff and half the guests ended up on the streets of New York fighting tooth and nail for entrée. It was to be a little midnight soirée at Automation House at 49 East 68th Street designed to give *tout* New York a glimpse of the staff that created the miracle of Jimmy Carter. But by 1:30 A.M. most of the honored guests themselves gave up trying to wedge their way through the mob at the front door and went back to their hotels. Even the most celebrated members of New York journalistic society were locked out by their own colleagues. Elegant *New York Post* publisher Dolly Schiff, in gray chiffon and pearls was sitting on the fender of a Cadillac while the editorial board of the *Washington Post*, Phil Geyelin and Meg Greenfield peered over the crowd. Ted Kheel, the labor negotiator, who owns the house, was standing across the street craning his neck to see what was going on. Pat Caddell and Jerry Rafshoon arrived by taxi, took one look and drove on. "Is Jimmy Carter in there?" someone yelled.

The cause of the melee, as usual, was political prankster, Dick Tuck. Tuck's convention newspaper, *Reliable Source*, had printed the invitation. Consequently so many crashers showed up for the exclusive bash that the invited guests and even the owner of the house couldn't get any closer than the other side of the street. Governor Pat Lucey of Wisconsin, Bill Vanden Heuvel and the R. Peter Strausses had left an omelette party at the Robert Wagners to come, but departed without getting near the door. "I'm going back to the Wagners'," said Pat Lucey. Mary McGrory of the *Washington Star* and Jules Witcover of the *Washington Post* who were being bounced around in the crowd like corks, gave up and went home. Warren Beatty and Bella Abzug, mangled in the maelstrom, finally climbed hand-in-hand into a yacht-sized limousine and departed.

"I just directed traffic and split," said Bella. Kennedy sister Jean Smith had been inside once, but forgot her housekey and had to stand in the crowd almost an hour before she could reenter. Only Walter Cronkite managed to slip like greased lightning through the throngs, past police, bouncers and the crowd of several hundred blocking the door of the three-story brick building. Was the feasting worth the waiting? Carter issues man Stu Eizenstat elbowed his way outside and said, "I'm not sure it was." "Forget it," said another Carter staffer. "It's the dullest party in town." Cronkite, who finally emerged at two A.M., wasn't impressed. "It was just a lot of elbows and shoulders."

Then why did he stay so long? "It's the first convention since 1956 that I've been able to get out of the anchor booth and go to a party. The town's well enough laid out, the convention broke up early enough, the evening was thoroughly organized so I finally got to have some fun."

At 10:30 Wednesday night in Madison Square Garden as the balloting was ready to begin, I made my way across the teeming floor to the Georgia delegation where Hamilton Jordan was at the vortex of excitement. Bodies were being crushed, feet stomped on and newsmen were falling into the Georgia delegation's pit. Governor Busbee was being bobbed about like a dunking apple. Tom Pettit of NBC tried to maneuver his cameramen into position to be ready to interview Jordan on the spot when the big moment came. When it did, it was one of the first belly-to-belly TV interviews I've ever seen. I found myself wedged against a tall microphone and thought my ribs would be broken. Phil Wise pried people away from me. At 10:45 as the balloting began, an incredible hush fell over the Garden.

At the last New York convention in 1924, the final vote came on the 104th ballot. This time it was obvious the Carter victory was going to be swift and sweet. By 11:10 the delegate tally was up to 919½ for Carter. For a young man who had directed the entire last three years of his life toward this moment, Hamilton Jordan seemed remarkably calm. Standing there in his shirt sleeves and cowboy boots, tie askew, Jordan was his usual wisecracking self. At 11:15 as the count reached 1,134, only 370 votes short of the magic number, Jordan quipped, "It's going to be awfully close." At 11:16, when New York "cast the largest vote of any delegation for the next President of the United States," with 209½ votes, Jordan joked, "Hell, we're runnin' thirty seconds behind."

Between the fever pitch of anticipation and the press of Southern bodies, the temperature must have reached one hundred degrees. "Send out for some Cokes or something," Jordan shouted, locked in place by a solid block of flesh. "Massachusetts passes." Ohio was next. The Garden was silent. "Ohio will do it," said Jordan. It did. Suddenly a convulsion of ecstasy rocked the entire Georgia delegation. The Carter staff burst into a swaying, stomping, hollering, back-slapping, hair-mussing, kissing, hugging, weeping mass. The South had risen again. The Civil War was over. Red-faced with emotion, Jordan raised a clenched power-to-the-people fist, let out a blood-curdling, full-bodied rebel yell and kissed a weeping Jerry Rafshoon. The Carter staff, Jordan, Wise, Rafshoon, Vicki Rogers, and Pat Caddell, were melded into one giant embrace that waxed ever larger as Jordan called for his workers. "Where's Christie? Where's Caroline? Where's Vicki?" Before Jordan knew what was happening, the jubilant Georgia delegation had hoisted him onto their shoulders like Muhammad Ali. "Go Ham Go! Go Ham Go!" they chanted.

Back at the Carter trailers, dozens of Robert Burn cigars were lit and the popping of beer-can tops reverberated like machine-gun fire. Jordan mounted to the top of the steps of a trailer and told his army of workers, "There's no one who did any more than I did." They cracked up.

Thursday noon I lunched at "21" with Pat Anderson, Carter's speechwriter, his wife, Anne, and Terry and Bill Robinson, friends and neighbors of Walter and Joan Mondale's. Anderson was so thoroughly imbued with the populist tone of the acceptance speech he had spent the last one hundred hours writing with Carter, that he was making cracks about "the idle rich" around him. Jackie Kennedy Onassis, who had been attending the convention, her first in twelve years, was sitting with a man directly across from us, and someone teased Anderson that he might go over and ask her what she thought of Carter. Anderson puffed with mock hubris. "She can come to me!" Ethel Kennedy was lunching not far from Jackie with Art Buchwald, Governor Hugh Carey and brother-in-law Steve Smith, master planner of JFK's and RFK's quest for the Presidency. Teddy was missing.

Ted Kennedy had left town after his offer to nominate Carter was flatly rejected. The complexion of Democratic Presidential politics which had intimately involved Kennedys for six conventions over the past twenty years had changed drastically. For the first time, Washington's most celebrated family was experiencing a taste of the medicine some said they too had spooned out during their regime.

Continuing his charade of mystery around his Vice-Presidential choice, Carter marched a steady stream of decoys through his hotel suite—Scoop Jackson, Peter Rodino and Frank Church. Each meeting would be followed by a formal press conference which the media dutifully filmed and recorded. But campaign aides Pat Caddell and Greg Schneiders confided that Carter had already chosen someone with whom he had shared the intimacy of his home in Plains. I assumed that it would be Mondale since Joan Mondale had told her house painter before leaving for New York Sunday that the garage had to be completed by Thursday for the Secret Service.

Ed Muskie's name surfaced at the end as the number one choice because he was Catholic and a Northerner with foreign-relations experience. There was considerable lobbying by Muskie supporters, as well as headlines in the New York *Daily News* trumpeting the strong possibility of his selection. However, close Carter friends whispered that Muskie imbibed too many martinis for the disciplined Carter liking, and was considered lazy because he had not campaigned hard enough in 1972. Besides, the entire Jane Muskie episode that resulted from an article I wrote in *Women's Wear Daily* during the 1972 election was likely to cause problems for Carter if he chose the Maine Senator. The article had quoted Jane Muskie as saying to reporters, "Let's tell dirty jokes," and calling her husband "Big Daddy." Although the article went on to praise Jane Muskie for her knowledge of the issues and her extraordinary campaign ability, only the sensational excerpts were reprinted in *Newsweek*, and appeared in hundreds of newspapers around the country. As a result, Jane Muskie received thousands of letters accusing her husband of being unfit to serve as President because he was married to her. When the Manchester *Union Leader* carried the *Newsweek* excerpts during the New Hampshire primary, Muskie, standing on the back of a flatbed truck, broke down and wept publicly. A display of emotion that some say lost the election for him. These factors made me feel Carter would choose another man.

Senator Frank Church of Idaho, who had won four out of the five last primaries, seemed a likely V.P. prospect during the Ohio primary in June. Two high-ranking Carter staffers also held that opinion, but retrospectively he seemed too anxious for the job. Besides, Carter was advised against Church by many who felt a Humphrey-backed candidate would be better.

John Glenn seemed like the only other strong possibility for veep. But his military image, coupled with Carter's, would cause most liberals to shudder, especially in a post-Vietnam era. He had also fared poorly in business. If there was a glimmer of hope for Glenn it dimmed when he made his crashingly boring keynote address before the delegates at Madison Square Garden.

With the necessity of a liberal on the ticket and the need to assuage the bitter feelings of the Humphrey wing of the party, coupled with admiration for Mondale among the Carter staff and family, the Minnesota Senator seemed the obvious choice; nevertheless, Carter made the veep game the best played one in town. Not even his mother, Miz Lillian, his wife, his children or his staff claimed to know what was on his mind until Carter called Mondale at 8:30 Thursday morning and asked him, "Will you run with me?"

Jimmy Carter had never planned to pick Senator Walter Mondale as his running mate. He considered the Minnesota Senator far too liberal for him. Besides he had almost no name recognition. In May when Pat Caddell and Hamilton Jordan ran a poll on fourteen names from a special list of twenty-four potential running mates compiled by Carter's staff, the results showed that Church, Muskie and Glenn finished near the top for name recognition while Mondale's name was near the bottom. Only 30 percent had ever heard of him.

By July 2, Carter had pretty well narrowed his choice to Senator Frank Church. In fact staff members told me as early as the first week in June that Carter was strongly leaning toward Church. Church had what Carter needed. He was from the West and had run well there. He was a liberal from a conservative state, he had Washington connections and extensive foreign policy experience as a member of the prestigious Foreign Relations Committee. But many Carter advisors did not rate Church as highly as Carter did. Kirbo, for example, wanted Scoop Jackson at first until other advisors warned Carter that his hawkish views and conservative streak might work against him. For a while Senator John Glenn's name was prominent in the Vice-Presidential sweepstakes. Carter at one point favored Glenn.

But on July 8, when Mondale and his wife, Joan, went to Plains, the boyish minister's son won Carter's heart and mind. During their three hours of discussions Carter discovered to his surprise that his views and Mondale's were surprisingly compatible. On busing, for example, Carter learned that the liberal Mondale favored the approach that Carter had taken in Atlanta as Governor. Then too, Carter liked the fact that Mondale had done his homework. He had obviously come prepared for the session and had thoroughly thought out what he was going to say, thus the presentation of his views was crisp, concise and articulate, just the ingredients Carter appreciated.

Moreover, Carter admired Mondale's record in caring for human needs. Like Carter he had been a strong advocate of social programs, particularly for the disadvantaged, the elderly and youth. "I remember very distinctly that when I was a Governor," Carter said, "and faced with termination of Title 4 (a) funds and a problem with revenue sharing, that Senator Mondale was the one with whom I worked most intimately." As Chairman of the Subcommittee on Children and Youth, Mondale had led investigations and worked on legislation in child care, adoption and foster care, and other issues affecting children's health and well-being. He was the original sponsor of the Child Abuse Prevention and Treatment Act, enacted in 1974, and of the Sudden Infant Death Syndrome Act. He was the author of the Day Care Bill. He authored legislation for automatic cost of living increases in the Supplemental Security Income Program and he sponsored the Tax Reduction Act of 1975, which provided major tax savings to small businesses. And like Carter, he was a strong conservationist.

Said Carter, "He has a great feeling of understanding and comprehension and compassion for people who need the services of government most."

An added attraction to the devout Carter was the fact Walter Mondale was a minister's son, and his wife a minister's daughter. The two men found they had more in common than just politics. When they emerged from the house they seemed almost like two old friends, jovial, relaxed and ready to banter with the press.

Another plus for Mondale was the fact that Rosalynn had liked him the best of all the visiting Vice-Presidential contenders and as always, made her views readily known to her husband. Most of the staff found Mondale a likable, personable fellow with a good sense of humor too.

But aside from his congeniality, Mondale was the correct political choice. "A one hundred percent bona fide liberal," as one spokesman for President Ford called him. That label to Republicans was pejorative. But to the disconcerted liberal wing of the Democratic party concerned that the pragmatic centrist Mr. Carter might be too conservative, it was healing unction.

Mondale had an outstanding liberal as well as labor record. His 1975 ADA rating was 94 percent, while his 1975 rating by COPE, the political arm of the AFL-CIO, was twenty-one correct votes out of twenty-two. He was, more importantly, the protégé of Hubert Horatio Humphrey. As a twenty-year-old college student, he had worked in Hubert Humphrey's first Senate Campaign in 1948, and the two had maintained a kind of father-son relationship ever since. Humphrey told me frankly the night of the Mondale selection in New York that he had been pushing his old friend hard for the number two spot. He had advised Carter that he would give his all to the campaign if Carter chose "Fritz." So, by selecting Mondale, Carter not only placated Humphrey and won his support, but he offered an olive branch to the entire Humphrey wing of the party, disillusioned and disgruntled that their man was forever eliminated from the goal of a lifetime.

Mondale was also Carter's symbolic bow to the Washington Congressional establishment that had developed a distinct fear and aversion to the thought of a total outsider running the country. With twelve years in the Senate and membership on seven committees— Budget, Finance, Intelligence, Labor and Public Welfare, Nutrition and Human Needs, Small Business and Aging, as well as a chairmanship of the Subcommittees on Children and Youth and Social Security Financing, Mondale was considered one of the brightest lights in Congress and although he was not reputed to have arm-twisting ability, he knew the right people who did.

As Carter said the morning of July 15 in the press room of the Americana Hotel when he introduced Mondale, "I made an early decision that it would be better for our country if I chose someone from the Congress in one of the two Houses. This is particularly important in my opinion because next year we will have a new Majority Leader in the Senate. There will be a complete shuffling because of those two changes in the structure of the Congress.

"I thought that all other factors being equal, that my bringing into the White House with me another person who was completely removed from the Washington scene, either a nonpolitical figure or someone who is a Mayor or a Governor, would not be a good decision."

Another asset was Mondale's farm connections. Representing an agricultural state, he was a good bridge to the farmers of the Midwest who did not tend to like or understand Southerners.

And he was clean. There were no skeletons in his closet. He represented a voice of opposition to the corruption of the recent past. In his book, *The Accountability of Power: Toward a Responsible Presidency,* he had discussed the desperate need for honesty and openness in a post-Watergate, post Vietnam era.

And finally, he was a young (forty-eight, but considerably younger looking), telegenic, fresh face, with an outstanding speaking ability.

During the convention, women seemed genuinely charmed and satisfied by Carter. Bella Abzug, the first to take almost anyone to task, emerged elated from the first meeting with Carter and the National Women's Political Caucus. "I consider this a very important first of a series of meetings he will hold with us. I think women can expect a real commitment from this nominee . . . he took the opportunity to take stands on key issues such as ERA. It will be an important part of his campaign. He will involve women in his campaign and he strongly believes in an active involvement of women in his administration. This is a very important commitment we have never had from any President, candidate or nominee . . . He said LBJ eliminated many of the legal barriers against blacks, and as President he would want to eliminate legal barriers against women."

I ran into NOW founder Betty Friedan at lunch at *The New York Times.* "This is so different than it was eight years ago. I was moved to tears by Carter. He made a commitment to us in such a substantive way that unless he's an absolute liar, he'll do something for women."

How did she know for sure? "I had a feeling. It was the way he spoke about his mother and his wife working . . ."

During his meeting with women, Carter had also strongly stated his personal abhorrence of abortion. Nevertheless feminists were convinced he was on their side. "I'm so pleased we held firm on abortion," said Friedan. "He included language in the platform that said he would not support an amendment to do away with the Supreme Court decision."

Blacks were also charmed by the Southerner. Prominent black leaders emerged from their rendezvous with Carter thoroughly convinced that, as President, he would give them a piece of the action. How did they know? From his "sincerity" of course. "We believe him," said Charles Rangel (Democrat, N.Y.).

The Chicanos and Latinos were happy too. For the first time in a long while there was someone who not only appeared to care, but who spoke their language. (When Carter met with the Latinos, he began by chastizing one man who hogged the rostrum for too long. "You can speak," said Carter, "but I have to leave.") Then he addressed the group in Spanish.

The delegates were thrilled Carter chose Walter Mondale. The Democratic convention turned into a love-in for everyone except the Georgians. Hundreds of Georgians who had flown from Americus, Georgia, to see Jimmy nominated had been unable to obtain a ticket to Madison Square Garden after three days of asking. Connie Plunkett, Carter's Southern coordinator, was fuming. "Ask Mr. Strauss why I only have twenty-five passes to give out," she growled. "There are seven hundred people who flew here from Georgia at their own expense and the DNC has only given us two hundred tickets even though there are dozens of empty rows behind the bandstand every night." "Don't ask me why. Ask Strauss!" I asked Strauss. "That's stupid!" he replied. "I gave the Georgians everything they wanted. They got a thousand tickets. Well, nine hundred. Three times the legal limit. Don't blame me. Ask Mr. Carter!"

At 9:25 James Earl Carter made his way to the microphone in Madison Square Garden. "Hello, I'm Jimmy Carter and I'm running for President of the United States." The impossible dream had come true. The man no one had heard of in January was a folk hero by July, and he was just taking one moment to remind the nonbelievers in the audience, the politicians who had laughed at him and plotted a Hubert Humphrey coronation, that he was their leader.

And they laughed even though they had been grumbling all week.

"I'm still not sold," said Esther Peterson, vice president of Consumer Programs for Giant Foods. "I guess I'll get to like him. I'll help him anyway."

"I guess I'll get to like him," echoed Dick Murphy, a labor delegate.

"I'm not super enthusiastic," said Alberta Lauterbach, an Illinois delegate. "But I have to admit he really put the system to work the way it's supposed to. If there's any visible divisiveness, it's pretty well coalesced."

The acceptance speech itself was simple, but powerful. "Love must be aggressively translated into simple justice," Carter told a captive audience.

"As I have said before. We can have an American President who does not govern with negativism and fear for the future, but with vigor and vision and aggressive leadership—a President who is not isolated from our people, but who feels your pain and shares your dreams and takes his strength and courage from you."

He spoke of big shot crooks going free while the poor go to jail, about the need for tax reform. He denounced "exclusive private schools," and "special influence and privilege" and the "self-perpetuating alliance between money and politics." "Too many have had to suffer at the hands of a political and economic elite." Ethel Kennedy could hardly bring herself to clap. Kennedy pal Claiborne Pell (Democrat, R.I.), the Senator whose constituency includes the rich and powerful of exclusive Newport was stonefaced, his hands folded in front of him throughout the speech. Once only, he patted the back of his left hand with the palm of his right as though he were brushing away a fly.

Mayor Daley was not thrilled either. Carter had swerved away from Daley as he entered the hall. Daley leaned over to his candidate for Governor, Michael Howlett, and shrugged. "Life is full of surprises."

Nevertheless, the evening was a Strauss masterpiece of political unity, a real Hallmark tableau with Coretta King, Daddy King and Barbara Jordan sharing the same podium with George Wallace. Jerry Brown even hugged Carter. Strauss had created a veritable Noah's Ark on the speaker's platform. McGovern, Muskie, Humphrey—they streamed onto the stage to pay their ostensibly cheerful respects to their new nominee. Only Ted Kennedy was absent.

And, as two black Baptist ministers had welcomed Jimmy Carter to New York at the Fifth Avenue Presbyterian Church at the opening of the convention, a black Baptist minister blessed its closing. Daddy King said, "The Lord brought us Jimmy Carter to bring this country together."

As the orchestra struck up "We Shall Overcome" hundreds in the Garden began to sing, disjointedly at first, then swelling into a huge chorus. People in front of the podium joined hands, swaying back and forth as they sang. Bygones were bygones. A feeling of unity swept the auditorium, tears streamed down hundreds of faces. The Democratic Party had nominated a man who could win.

Carter had barely been the nominee for twenty-four hours when he lost his temper. Carl Leubsdorf of the Associated Press had taped to the bulkhead of Carter's United Charter a poster that showed the Democratic candidate with the beard, long hair and priestly robes of Christ. It was captioned, "J. C. can save America." Unwittingly, Carter leaned against it during an impromptu press conference, while a battery of photographers snapped the picture of him with his Glorified Self. Half the press corps were guffawing into their notebooks, but Carter remained thoroughly unsuspecting until Stan Cloud of *Time* brought it to the attention of a Secret Serviceman. "He's going to be furious when he finds out about that," Cloud said.

"He can be mad about that when he gets over being mad about what he's mad about now," answered the Secret Serviceman.

Carter was steaming because his United Charter had been sitting on the runway at La Guardia for twenty-five minutes, delayed by heavy Friday-afternoon traffic, while two thousand people waited in the streets of Plains to greet their hero. He became even more churlish when he was pressed too hard on a point during a casual question-and-answer session and had angrily stomped away. While the plane was waiting for runway clearance, somebody asked if he thought his acceptance speech was liberal or conservative. Carter offered one of his wilder waffles. "I think the speech not inadvertently shifted back and forth between the liberal and the conservative." That caused a ripple of giggles that Carter did not appreciate. He went on to say he thought the speech was "populist" in tone and he then defined populism. "That means there ought to be a melding of the government with the people themselves. The structure of our party, the strength of our party and the strength of our commitment in philosophical terms derives from the concerns and the yearnings of the people themselves . . . that's my definition of populism."

"Are you saying you're a populist?" asked one reporter.

"Yes, I think so," Carter answered.

Another reporter, who had not been paying attention, chimed in, "How do you define populism?"

"I'll let you define it," Carter said. The reporter pressed. "How do *you* define it?" The nominee snarled. "How do you define liberalism? How do you define honesty or love? How do you define compassion or understanding?"

"Yes," said the reporter, oblivious to Carter's sour mood, "but how do YOU define populism?"

Carter's eyes iced over, his right hand went up like a traffic cop's. "I don't want to be in a position where I have to define it." With that he vanished into first class.

When Carter learned that he had been photographed next to himself in Jesus gear, he dispatched aide Kate King to rip away the poster. Kate told reporters, "If you want this plane to be here tomorrow, it had better come down."

PART

VIII

THE CAMPAIGN

CHAPTER 28

ONCE MORE TO THE HUSTINGS

MORE THAN A MONTH had passed since the Democrats' festive love-in in Madison Square Garden. Jimmy Carter had almost completely vanished from public view, having gone home to Plains to relax, recoup, and regroup for the big fall battle. While he was visiting with the folks down home, importing busloads of advisors and VIPs and rejuvenating on a diet of fresh vegetables and Rosalynn's home cooking, the opposition was meeting in Kansas City to nominate their candidate, Gerald Rudolph Ford. Although that convention was rife with division among the Republican ranks, pitting Reaganites who felt the nomination was wrenched from their grasp at the eleventh hour against the White House Establishment, it nevertheless settled on one candidate. And for Gerald Ford it proved to be his finest hour when he delivered the speech of his life and sounded like a President and not a Congressman.

For the first time since Jimmy Carter began his quest for the White House, he faced a single opponent, one who also happened to be robed in the splendor, ceremony and power of the incumbency. To the American viewer who watched the Republican convention and had long since forgotten the Democrats' love fest, Jimmy Carter was vividly portrayed as a big spender, a slasher of the defense budget, and a double liberal with Mondale on his ticket. Suddenly Carter seemed too different, untried, an unknown quantity, while Ford in all his predictability was as familiar as an old shoe, even though that shoe kept stubbing its toe and tripping over itself. Now given a choice between only two candidates, the people had to select between the known and the unknown. Preference registered in a dramatic change in the polls. By the third week in August, Carter's lead in the Gallup Poll dropped precipitously from twenty-three to ten points. The Carter staff had expected some loss, but never one as drastic as this. Suddenly the Republicans, encumbered by Watergate, the Nixon pardon, a failing economy, a divided party and a leader who made headlines by bumping into doors, took heart. Up to now Ford's campaign for the nomination had been as inept as the candidate himself. As part of the old shoe's new shine, he fired his second campaign manager, Bo Callaway, and hired a third, James Baker, a successful Houston attorney who was smart and aggressive and who was the Mandrake behind Ford's squeaky victory over Reagan.

While President Ford teed off in the Rockies, Carter decided to hit the campaign trail early and hard. Playing from his weakness in the West to his strength in Iowa, Carter began in Los Angeles on August 22, two weeks before the traditional Labor Day start, and after eighteen stops in four grueling days, ended up in Des Moines, where his long quest for the Presidency began.

Although his staff claimed not to be worried about the declining polls, it was apparent from the rigorous trip that Jimmy Carter sensed his twenty months of slavery could all be for naught if he did not move first and fast. Campaign Manager Hamilton Jordan confided he was anxious about Ford's new hard-hitting delivery. "I can envision a scenario where everything we've worked for could disappear in a few short weeks."

And in Des Moines, a Democratic county chairman, Harry Baxter, who had worked so hard during the primaries complained secretly, "The guy's going to lose. I have that same feeling in my bones as I did when he was going to get the nomination. Part of it's his staff. It's already grown into a full-scale bureaucracy, exactly the kind of thing he's supposed to reduce. Everything's changed. It's not the same as it used to be."

There were some raw wires exposed, for sure. Minor frays, but nevertheless worrisome ones that seemed to be accumulating. In the last month Carter made an unflattering reference to Alabama's George Wallace. There had been a staff-level put down of CIA Director George Bush, and on this trip, a party guest list that wasn't screened in advance found Carter mingling with unsavory characters. Jimmy Carter was running scared and rusty.

Still, he appeared more relaxed and at ease after his convention victory and his weeks of study and rest in Plains than he had been during the primaries, and even turned to humor in a way that revealed something about his own personality.

In Des Moines he told a shaggy dog story. It had to do with a man who set up a roadside stand. "Every time the vendor rang the cash register he recited a Biblical passage. When the first customer came in and asked for a loaf of bread and a quart of milk, the vendor rang up thirty cents on the register and said, 'The Lord giveth.' But soon the customer was back complaining that the milk had soured and the bread was stale, so the shopkeeper opened the register and returned the money saying, 'The Lord giveth and the Lord taketh away.' Shortly thereafter, a man drove up with a horse trailer attached to a huge Cadillac and asked to buy a horse blanket. The shopkeeper only had a variety of two-dollar blankets in stock, and a two-dollar blanket, the customer claimed, was too cheap for his several-hundred-thousand-dollar racehorse. The shopkeeper kept bringing out two-dollar blankets and raising the price until finally he brought out a two-dollar blanket and said it cost one hundred dollars. The unsuspecting customer was satisfied he had a quality blanket for his horse. As man and horse drove away and the cash register rang up a hundred dollars the shopkeeper was heard to say, 'He was a stranger and we took him in.' "

In Seattle, Carter told a joke from George Wallace's repertoire which Carter claimed Wallace had adopted from him. "There was a young vet who came back from Vietnam to a small Southern town. He was very small and timid and there were no brass bands to welcome him home. He wandered around his hometown all alone and although he wasn't a drinking man, as is the case with most Legionnaires, one night he went to a local tavern. In the tavern was a big loud-mouthed bully who was talking too loud and telling dirty jokes and he began to abuse the little veteran. After a few drinks, he hit the little fellow, who fell right off the bar stool onto the floor. When he got up and brushed himself off and climbed back up on the bar stool, the big bully hit him in the neck, knocked him down again and told the bartender, 'That's a karate chop from South Korea.' After a few more drinks, he slapped the little fellow again and as he picked himself up off the floor, he wiped a little trickle of blood from his mouth. The bully said, 'That's a jujitsu jab from Japan.'

"Finally, the little fellow went hobbling out of the bar. In a few minutes he returned, drew back and hit the bully right between the eyes. The guy flew twenty feet in the air and fell facedown under the counter. Then the little veteran finally spoke. He said, 'If he wakes up, tell 'im that's a tire tool from Western Auto.' "

Carter was even being funny off the cuff for a change. At a DNC steering committee meeting at a Los Angeles hotel introductions were made around the room and Congresswoman Yvonne Burke said, "This is my district. Welcome." Senator Alan Cranston stood up next and announced, "I'm Senator Cranston and it's my district too." Los Angeles Mayor Tom Bradley added, "I'm Mayor Bradley and it's my district too." When it was his turn to introduce himself Carter said, "I'm Jimmy Carter and I hope next year it's going to be my district too."

At rally after rally Carter teased his audience. "This is strictly a nonpolitical trip. I'm just out here to tell all you folks that our campaign's going to start on Labor Day in Warm Springs, Georgia. And my wife Rosalynn's in Tampa, Florida, and my son Chip's in Virginia, and my son Jack's in Tennessee. They're just all out telling the folks that the campaign is going to begin September seventh."

However, by now, Carter press relations began to sour. Almost every reporter had a different story about the Carter camp. Even their friend and supporter, Atlanta *Constitution* editor Hal Gulliver, complained no one ever returned his calls. *New Republic* reporter John Osborne said he'd never encountered such a lack of responsiveness. Jean Cox of *Women's Wear Daily* said she had spent four hours on the phone calling from Los Angeles to Atlanta trying to get Carter's West Coast schedule. "They kept saying they were going to call back in a few minutes and then they wouldn't. Then they'd tell me they didn't know anything. I've never had so much trouble trying to get information. No one had the answers. No one gave you a direct answer. We finally got the information we needed by calling the places he was going. They seem totally disorganized."

On that first campaign trip after the convention, relations seemed to break down further. In Des Moines, at the Iowa State Fair, Carter's advance man had positioned the camera platform directly in front of Carter, blocking much of the audience's view, which resulted in shaking fists, shouts and general complaints. By the time Carter rose to speak, the howling sounded like a din from the depths of Hades. Carter laid the blame on the media. "Since we're all bound in a common purpose, I'd like to ask as many of the TV people as possible to get down." Then, directing his gaze at Sam Donaldson of ABC, Carter said in front of 7,600 people, "That O.K. with you, Sam?"

Carter's trip to California began August 22 with a major confrontation between the media and the Secret Service while the Carter staff lollygagged and pussyfooted around the event and the issue.

Populist Carter spent the first evening of his post-primary campaign in Los Angeles, gliding through opulent Beverly Hills in a long sleek jet-black limousine. From an exclusive dinner at the plush Hollywood mansion of MCA magnate Lew Wasserman, of *Jaws* fame, he drove to a glittering, late-night exclusive reception at actor Warren Beatty's apartment in the Beverly Wilshire Hotel. Ironically, deleted from Carter's prepared speech the next day at the Town Hall Forum luncheon attended by 1,000 businessmen was the following line: "It seems almost inevitable that if political leaders stay in power too long and eat expensive meals in private clubs too long, and drive in limousines they are going to be cut off from the lives and concerns of ordinary Americans." Carter gave up his limousine the next day, telling reporters, "I felt guilty."

The previous night the People's Candidate had caused a bit of a stir when he dined with some rather controversial types. Included on the guest list with a high-powered melange of businessmen— Motown Record chairman Berry Gordy; producer Dino De Laurentiis; David Kass, director of the company that owns the Plaza Athenée and the George V, two of the most exclusive hotels in Paris —were Sydney Korshak, a lawyer recently named in a *New York Times* article as having a connection with reputed underworld figures; and Armand Hammer, convicted in connection with illegal political contributions. Meanwhile, members of the media, including those granted permission to cover Carter in the Wasserman mansion, were hidden away in Mr. Wasserman's "screening room," across the courtyard.

The pool reporters were granted only a few minutes to observe the dinner. When they asked Wasserman for the names of his guests, he insisted he wanted to keep the names private. However, others mysteriously and freely handed out lists to the pool reporters. Questioned on the reason for Sydney Korshak's invitation, Lew Wasserman replied, "He's a supporter of the Democratic National Committee." And Chairman Robert Strauss, who had arranged for the party, told me, "It's a free country. This is a democracy. I certainly wouldn't have uninvited him because of that" (his underworld connections).

Carter greeted Governor Jerry Brown at the door, observed the opulent setting and said, "It reminds me of Plains." How? Someone wanted to know. "The trees," Carter replied.

Meanwhile, outside the gates a small group of reporters, including Helen Dewar of the *Washington Post* and a reporter from the Baltimore *Sun* implored Carter staff man Barry Jagoda for the use of a telephone and a toilet. Since even the pool reporters were cordoned off from the party, why couldn't they use the facilities in the "screening room"? Request denied. Jagoda seemed terrified that an independent, even reasonable move might alienate his superiors.

A real brouhaha occurred shortly after ten P.M. when the networks and their crews were denied permission to film Carter's arrival at the posh Beverly Wilshire Hotel. A tall, surly Secret Serviceman named Horne, the number two man in the Los Angeles office, stonewalled Rick Kaplan of CBS and Sam Donaldson of ABC, ordering them and their crew to remain with the general public across the driveway for "security reasons."

Unaccustomed to being arbitrarily pushed around, Donaldson pressed his case, his eyes aflame, his voice filled with outrage. "Fully accredited . . . traveling with Carter . . . a public place . . . you just want to be obeyed!" When reason would not hold sway, Donaldson turned on his cameras and recorded the clash with the agent. To no avail. Intercession by Carter advance men failed as well. Agent Horne insisted the Carter staff form a human chain on the top step of the hotel entrance thus preventing the print and TV reporters from moving anywhere.

When Carter arrived in his sleek black limo, and unexpectedly crossed the street to greet the crowds, the network crews attempted to follow, but six Secret Servicemen linked arms forming a second human fence and physically blocked them. At two A.M. East Coast time, Mr. Horne was duly reported by the networks to his superiors in Washington for ignoring the dictates of the candidate's own staff, for restraining accredited reporters from covering a candidate campaigning in a public area, for calling Sam Donaldson an "asshole" and Rick Kaplan "a turkey." There were late-night apologies from everyone, including Carter himself, who said he was sorry for the unnecessary ban imposed on TV cameras at the party. Only Warren Beatty was nonchalant. "What the hell," said the blue-eyed star.

Inside the hotel, the bell captain got into the act, refusing to let reporters ride the elevators "unless you have a room key." And on the eighth floor, the NBC pool crew, which had been predesignated to film the party, was summarily banned by Beatty himself who claimed his guests did not wish to be photographed. Even campaign manager Ham Jordan's pleas were useless. Perhaps it was because Louise Lasser, commonly known as Mary Hartman, sprawled out on the floor in pigtails, T-shirt and pants while Carter spoke, or because another guest, George Peppard, told Beatty he would boycott his party "if there were press or politicians."

It seemed a shame reporters were banned from the party because according to observers, Carter made one of his most impressive campaign appearances. This is Los Angeles *Times'* journalist Ken Reich's pool report: Guests at the Warren Beatty reception included George Segal, Carroll O'Connor, Peter Falk, Louise Lasser, Dennis Weaver, Sidney Poitier, Robert Altman, Faye Dunaway, John Voight, Diana Ross, Neil Simon, Alan Pakula, Art Garfunkel, James Caan, Buck Henry, Herb Sargent, Hugh Hefner, Norman Lear, Tony Randall, Lee Graham, Art Buchwald and George Peppard.

Carter spoke movingly about the underprivileged and also seemed relaxed enough to toss off a series of one-liners. When Warren Beatty remarked that coming to his party might help Carter, "a Southern Baptist," blunt the religious issue with some of the people there, Carter responded, "If I come to Warren Beatty's party, it should wipe out the issue."

Beatty, responding in the same facetious vein, told Carter he and his friends "being pinkos, leftists, Commies . . ." had a "rising enthusiasm" for his candidacy and hoped mightily to see Carter make a $30-billion cut in the defense budget, free Huey Newton, do something for the Chicago Seven, and finally, "stop referring to Ronald Reagan as an actor."

"You are a far superior actor," Beatty told Carter. "We think of an actor as someone who can illuminate the truth." He said that after the McGovern campaign and other losing efforts in recent years his little collection of friends was "a battered group with a need to win." Carter responded that Beatty had described his views "as accurately as the Republicans did at their convention." Someone in the audience asked Carter whether this was his first trip to California. Carter replied, "It's the first time anyone ever noticed I was here."

"It is a real thrill to meet the famous people here tonight," Carter went on. "I hope I don't get to know too much about you."

Carroll O'Connor then interjected that while he planned to vote for Carter, he was a little distressed by Carter's criticism of Kissinger. "Most of the people in the country think more of him than, say, Dean Rusk." O'Connor added he was unhappy that "at the moment, détente is taking a beating" and he hated "to see the campaign become a contest to see which side can downgrade it more." No one wants a war with the Russians, O'Connor told Carter. Kissinger, he said, is working hard to prevent one.

Carter responded that he agreed with "almost" everything O'Connor had said, declaring, "I think we ought to proceed aggressively with détente." He objected to Kissinger because he does things in secret and therefore he has lost recognition as a man who speaks authentically for the American people. "His words don't have the force they used to."

Art Buchwald asked Carter if he would name three or four persons he was considering for Secretary of State. Carter refused.

Tony Randall wanted Carter to commit himself to government subsidy of the arts. Carter replied he thought the government already did subsidize them. As Governor of Georgia, he said, "We multiplied state support of the arts by six hundred percent."

But when Randall forcefully suggested the establishment of a national opera and a national theater, Carter said he was making "a good suggestion" but one that he had never heard in all the time he'd been campaigning for the Presidency.

"You've never met with people of this level," Randall said modestly.

"That's why I won the nomination," Carter replied.

Then Jimmy Carter became serious and made some of the more moving extemporaneous remarks of the campaign:

"If you and I make a mistake, the chances are we won't actually go to prison, and if we don't like the public-school system, we put our kids in private schools. The overwhelming majority of the American people are touched directly and personally when government is ill-managed or insensitive or callous or unconcerned about those kinds of problems. When the tax structure is modified, which Congress does almost every year, you can rest assured that powerful people who are well organized, who have good lawyers, who have lobbyists in the Capitol in Washington, they don't get cheated. But there are millions of people in this country who do get cheated, and they are the very ones who can't afford it.

"So there are a multitude of needs. We take transportation for granted. We can go out and get in our Chevrolet, or our Buick or our Cadillac or Rolls Royce and go anywhere we want to. But a lot of people don't have automobiles. I can go a mile from my house, I can go two hundred yards from my house, and there are people who are very poor. When they get sick it's almost impossible for them to get a doctor. In the county where I farm, we don't even have a doctor, we don't have a dentist, we don't have a pharmacist, we don't have a registered nurse. The very poor there have no access to preventive health care. We found in Georgia through a three-year study that poor women who are mostly black, in rural areas, have twenty times more cervical cancer than white women in urban counties, just because they haven't seen a doctor, because the disease has gone so far that it can't be corrected . . .

"There's a need for public officials, Presidents, Governors, Congressmen and others to bypass the lobbyists and the special-interest groups and our own circle of friends who are very fortunate and try to understand those who are dependent on government to give them a decent life. That is what I hope to do to meet needs . . .

"When people organize, there's an almost built-in separation from the kind of people I've just been describing. Doctors really care about their patients, but when doctors organize and hire a lobbyist, the lobbyist doesn't give a damn about the patients. School teachers love their students. They quite often serve at a sacrificial salary compared to what they should get. But when they organize and hire a lobbyist to work with the Legislature, those lobbyists don't care anything about students. The same with lawyers. They really take care of their clients. But when those lawyers organize, get a lobbyist, those lobbyists don't care anything about clients. The same thing with farmers and with people in business.

"So I say, public servants, like me and Jerry Brown and others, have a special responsibility to bypass the bigshots and to make a concerted effort to understand people who were poor, black, speak a foreign language, who are not well educated, who are inarticulate, who are timid, who have some monumental problem. At the same time we must run the government in a competent way, well organized, efficient, manageable, so that those services which are so badly needed can be delivered . . ."

Carter walked out, encountering Randall, who again told him he was "not going to let you forget" the arts, and then encountered Donaldson, Kaplan, et al.

While Carter's Western swing had been ostensibly designed to help the Democratic National Committee raise funds to help candidates like John Tunney get elected, it also served as a forum from which Carter tested the response to his campaign themes. In addition, the trip gave media man Jerry Rafshoon the opportunity to film a new series of five- and two-minute TV campaign commercials.

Carter presented the "themes," not issues, in a thirty-five-minute blatantly vague address to a group of one thousand businessmen, the members of Town Hall, a business club, at the Biltmore Hotel in downtown Los Angeles, an excellent speech that drew two standing ovations from the audience and general praise from individual members afterward.

Carter spoke of restoring "faith," of "doing what is right," of "vision," "competence," "honesty" and "sensitivity." He sounded symbols like "pride," "patriotism," "unity," "optimism," "hope," "love," and "sacrifice." He spoke of the country having "one last chance," and of the need for "new leaders with new ideas," the "changing of the guard," "the improved delivery of services and good government." He attacked Ford for lack of leadership, insensitivity to human needs, government by veto and disastrous economic policies. He called for a time of healing.

"This," said Carter, "is one of our most important elections, this is one of those elections as in 1932 and 1960 when we have a chance to break with the past and make a fresh start in our national affairs." He compared himself to John Kennedy and Franklin Roosevelt as a man for these times of crisis.

Carter said that the campaign would be taking place on two distinct levels. "At one level, and quite properly, there is the traditional debate over such issues as defense, health care, tax policy, and the economy. But . . . the other level of this year's campaign, the less tangible issue, is simply the desire of the American people to have faith again in our government, to want a fresh start. Most Americans are not very ideological. Most Americans share a deep-seated desire for two goals that might, to an ideological person, seem contradictory. We want both progress and preservation."

And as Carter himself admitted, portraying himself as both liberal and conservative was not always as simple as it looked. "To walk the line between progress and preservation . . . is no easy task," but while the task was impossible for "extremists of either side," it could be accomplished "by leaders who are independent and imaginative and flexible in their thinking, and are not guided by closed minds, but by common sense." Namely, himself.

The major partisan issues of the campaign, Carter pointed out, would be jobs, the economy and Ford's vetoes. "It is a record I cite more in sorrow than in anger, for it is a record of political insensitivity, of missed opportunities, of constant conflict with the Congress, and of national neglect."

Carter blamed Ford for a major share of unemployment because of his veto of the Emergency Employment Act, "which would have created nearly two million full and part-time jobs." He charged him with forcing children to go hungry by vetoing the School Lunch Act, and said that fifty-three vetoes in two years "demonstrated a negativism, a dormancy, and a fear of action that can only be harmful to this country." He did not finish the speech without linking Ford's name with Nixon and calling Mr. Ford "an appointed President."

If Carter made a positive impression on the businessmen, he infuriated American Legionnaires in Seattle, Washington, by announcing his plan to pardon draft dodgers. It was a clever speech. Carter told the Legionnaires that his ancestors had fought in the American Revolution, his son Jack had served in Vietnam and he himself was a Legionnaire having served in World War II. He talked about the need for military strength, tough fiscal management of the Pentagon and pledged to end international terrorism. He explained how in his view the bombing of Hiroshima saved millions of American lives. By the time he dropped his own bomb, the paunchy, pug-faced Legionnaires were eating out of his hand and rewarding him with bursts of applause. Then he said, it slowly, steadily . . .

"I do not favor a blanket amnesty, but for those who violated Selective Service laws, I intend to grant a blanket pardon."

The words were barely uttered when the entire Wyoming delegation rose, shaking their fists, pointing thumbs down. shouting "No! No! No! No!" The rest of the audience joined in. Carter continued, "To me there is a difference. Amnesty means that what you did is right. Pardon means that what you did—right or wrong—is forgiven. So, pardon—yes; amnesty—no."

But the booing lasted an interminable three minutes. Through it all, Carter, looking like the Good Humor man in his Legion cap, forced a broad smile, but he was gulping hard, and his eyes darted nervously back and forth as he watched the hostility spread across the floor.

Soon the bellowing like a sudden storm at sea died down, and the ocean of angry faces seemed soothed by his closing words about healing the wounds of Vietnam. Finally the Legionnaires rose to give him a standing ovation, albeit a short one.

The speech had been calculated for maximum media exposure,

designed to present Carter as a candidate with the courage to take unpopular stands and, finally, to dispel the notion created during the primaries that Carter always told each audience exactly what it wanted to hear.

With only two million American Legionnaire votes, it seemed that even to lose a fraction of that number would prove insignificant. The plan seemed to work. Of the Legionnaires I had talked to after the speech, only two out of seven said they definitely would not vote for Carter, and one Republican Legionnaire said, "Don't worry, they'll get over it. He handled it very well." Mrs. Warren Magnuson, wife of the Washington Senator, was surprised the reaction wasn't stronger too. "We had heard the Pennsylvania delegation was going to walk out. But it didn't."

The Carter staff was delighted with the reaction. It wasn't as bad as they thought it would be. It achieved the desired effect, that is, it made the morning and evening news.

But the Republicans were quick to capitalize on Carter's appearance. Right on Jimmy Carter's heels came Senator Bob Dole, the GOP Vice-Presidential candidate. He told Legionnaires, "The President's position is unequivocal. No blanket pardon, no blanket amnesty, no blanket clemency." Dole was cheered endlessly.

Nearly two weeks after Dole's appearance in Seattle, the headlights of ten cars in Jimmy Carter's caravan pierced the blackness of early morning in Plains. Labor Day, traditionally the first day of the Presidential campaign, dawned and the Democratic nominee left the security and solace of his brick home where he had rested and studied for three weeks to begin one of the shortest Presidential campaigns in memory.

Three thousand friends and fans awaited him in the heat of Indian summer at Warm Springs, Georgia, where Franklin D. Roosevelt had summered, and rendezvouzed with his mistress, Lucy Rutherfurd, and where he died. They pumped the air with signs that read, "The Grin will Win," and "Let's Send Miz Lilly's Boy to Washington." Carter snaked his way along a dirt path toward the small white house with black shutters dispensing smiles, loving glances, kisses and hugs while hearing the encouraging words of admirers like the woman in pink who cooed, "I went to the White House in June and I told the guard, 'Jimmy Carter's going to be the next one living here.' "

It had the makings of a splendid kickoff, but it fell flat. Rusty from too many days off the hustings, Carter's style lacked the punch and polish of the primaries. His speech from low ground in front of Roosevelt's front porch, where only those in the first rows could see him, was hardly overwhelming. "Just whelming," as Don Oliver of NBC put it.

Bob Strauss, the Democratic National Committee chairman, was less taken with the import of the occasion than with the historic setting. "This is a great day for me," he drawled. "I've been an FDR fan all my life, read everything about him. So it's really touching for me to be here." Billy Carter seemed singularly uninspired too. Dressed to the nines in a green suit, white starched collar and mint-green tie with screaming yellow stripes, he stood to the side, only half listening to his brother drone on about how John Kennedy had been considered an outsider too, "because he was young and inexperienced and because of his religious beliefs."

When the speech was over, the Georgians sauntered toward their cars like so many picnickers at the end of a pleasant summer.

ABC's Frank Reynolds was surprised at the indifference of the Georgians toward their native son. He recalled that even a Northerner like JFK had been mobbed. "I was here in 1960 and I had to run to get out of the way of the crowds pressing to get to him. They literally tried to tear off his clothes."

Only Rosalynn Carter seemed visibly moved. Eyes rimmed with red, and face drawn with emotion, she said softly, "I was fine till I got here. Then I just broke up. It's a very emotional time for me, especially seeing all our friends here."

"We both got up at five this morning," Carter told me on the plane later, claiming the day had been a difficult one for him too. "I had to finish writing my speech and do some paperwork and get packed. And we'd both been waiting so long and had kind of pent-up emotions, so it was an emotional experience. We had been together three or four weeks and suddenly to be separated five days a week every week was something we obviously were not going to enjoy. We thought earlier that we might be together once or twice a week, but that's just not practical. Rosalynn's a superb campaigner on her own and it would be a waste of her time and the campaign contribution she could make for her to be with me. But we are ready, both of us. And we were eager too, to see this morning come."

Eager and a bit nervous. After Gerald Ford's dramatic acceptance speech at the GOP convention and the unexpected unity of the Republican party, even Hamilton Jordan admitted, "It scares the shit out of me." And with Carter's precipitous drop in the polls, the prospect of a possible loss loomed larger to the Carter mafia than ever before.

So while Gerald Ford held a series of Rose Garden news conferences and hunkered down in the Oval Office boning up for the debates with speech coach Don Penny, the Carter troops hit the asphalt hard, dividing up the states primary-style. Eleven of them set out in different directions. Chip Carter, who had written his own speech from his father's at the kitchen table of his mobile home, handled the Midwest. His pregnant wife Caron went North. Judy and Jack Carter split up the West Coast and Midwest between them. Rosalynn went Midwest and South. Aunt Sissy headed North and South. Jeff and Annette Carter toured the South. Fritz Mondale hit all four corners of the U.S. and Joan Mondale stayed in the West. In one week the Carter blitzkrieg had roared through thirty-seven states and one hundred seven cities.

Carter was swinging back and forth from slum to society, selling himself as liberal and conservative, rural and urban, farmer and scientist, politician and born-again Christian. He strode as if in seven-league boots through an earsplitting, bare-chested and beer-drinking mob of 85,000 at the Darlington, South Carolina, stock-car races where he chewed Dentyne and talked track in his gray glen plaid suit. From the "people" he moved on to the gaudy opulence of Charles Mitchell's pseudo-Tara brick mansion with its bas-relief ceiling cherubs, fourteen-karat-gold moldings and a veranda supported by twenty-seven white pillars. There he mingled with wealthy tobacco-plantation owners, beer distributors and the pols of Florence, South Carolina.

Standing on a Louis XIV chair, he told them, "I'm a race-car fan. I like to get in the infield. Rosalynn and I have been going to the car races since 1946. I kind of regard race-car drivers as heroes."

Praise of that violent sport reminded me of Romans watching and waiting for a Christian to be devoured by a lion, in this case a car and driver by fire. It seemed inappropriate for the select and wealthy group he was addressing. It would have been more appropriate for the good ole boys that meet at Billy's filling station.

Carter moved from beneath the brilliant blue skies and verdant pines of the Norfolk Botanical Gardens where he addressed a crowd of 25,000 bragging, "Every single stock-car racer in the country is a supporter of mine . . . if I'm elected President, I'll invite them all to come to the White House," to the New York City subway below Columbus Circle where he carried a red rose, "My favorite flower," and snowed a Puerto Rican couple, informing them in his poor Spanish, "Yo estoy un amigo de Puerto Rico."

He stalked the red-lined ghetto of North Philadelphia in his new brown wing-tips and his rolled blue shirt sleeves, peering into decrepit dwellings where hunks of plaster hung from the ceilings. He stood on a heap of garbage and glass to denounce HUD as the "largest slumlord in the U. S." And he basked in the elongated shadows of towering skyscrapers in Pittsburgh, telling a crowd of eight thousand in William Penn Square, "After the next few visits here, it will be obvious I'll be the next President of the United States."

He stood in factory shift lines in Scranton and addressed students in Brooklyn. And all along, the message was more conservative than it had been during the primaries ("We must make sure the people control the government, not the other way around." . . . "If you have your choice, always go with private industry not the government." He struck Reagan themes. . . . "Tough, careful management with the goal of a balanced budget" . . . "A minimum of government secrecy") and peddled liberal programs. ("We need national health insurance, complete income tax reform . . . and to do away with the waste and confusion in the Pentagon.")

He blamed Ford for both the highest inflation rate "since the Hoover depression" (an exaggeration since inflation rose 14 percent during the Forties) and the lack of leadership in Washington.

And although the crowds were bigger, the response to Carter seemed just as subdued as it had been during the primaries. He seemed plagued by the fuzzy, all-things-to-all-people image he had created during his campaign for the nomination. As James Reston of the *Times* wrote in his column on September 16, "Governor Carter is not increasing his popularity in the nation, as he did in many states during the primaries. Something is holding him back— the Democratic party leaders are not quite sure what it is—but something about his personality, his manner of speaking, his thin, trailing voice, and his switches on major policy issues, are hurting his campaign."

Many who stood in the crowds vowed to vote for him, but "unenthusiastically." Many echoed a refrain from the 1972 Nixon-McGovern campaign, calling Carter, "The lesser of two evils."

Carter's passionate followers were the street people, the poor, the ethnics, the laborers, the blacks, the forgotten of the world. When he walked through the burned-out slums in Astoria and North Philadelphia, they clung to him, hugged him, blessed him, waved flags and followed him on foot and on bikes as though he were a Saviour, or at the very least, the Pied Piper. As John Underwood, a black from Philadelphia put it, "The spirit leads me to believe that this is the man the United States wants. How do I know? I just feel it."

CHAPTER 29

LUST IS A FOUR-LETTER WORD

DESPITE THE FAMILY'S EFFORT to be everywhere at once, and Jimmy Carter's travels across the country, what had begun as a lackluster Presidential campaign had all the makings of a first-rate disaster by the third week in September. In addition to particularly bad advance work, political mistakes began to accrue and not all were Carter's fault. In a September 18 interview with the Associated Press, Carter was quoted as saying he would shift the tax burden to "those who have the higher incomes, and reduce the income [tax] on the lower-income and middle-income tax payer." The A.P. at first omitted the words "and middle," then corrected the error. The White House seized the apparent blooper and ran with it. Senator Robert Dole, Ford's Vice-Presidential candidate, used it on the campaign trail. Ford press secretary Ron Nessen called it "a major blunder." Treasury Secretary William Simon called the statement "incredible" and James Lynn, Director of the Office of Management and Budget, used the same description in a hastily arranged White House press conference.

The following Monday, September 20, while Carter was on a whistlestop train trip, the rumor spread that *Playboy* magazine would hit the stands October 14 quoting Carter as saying he had looked at many women with lust and had "committed adultery in my heart many times." He used the words "screw" and "shack up" to describe sexual intercourse and extramarital sex. And the following Sunday in a *New York Times Magazine* interview with Norman Mailer, Carter used the word "fuck," although Mailer covered by calling it "a word the *Times* has refused to print for 125 years."

Baptist preachers, Catholics, Democratic leaders, Carter politicians, grannies, and Lester Maddox nearly died.

In that same *Playboy* interview, Carter also referred to Lyndon Johnson as "lying, cheating and distorting the truth." He had to quickly apologize to Lady Bird Johnson, an apology that never really erased the hurt.

Meanwhile, Ford stayed in Washington making easy and uncontroversial daily headlines and evening news programs with a succession of Rose Garden pronouncements. He conserved his energy for the big late October push and practiced for the first debate. Carter, however, never relented. He continued to campaign as if he were still running in the primaries, beginning with plant gates at dawn and ending up at seedy hotels after midnight, hopscotching from city to city and state to state.

Three weeks at home in Georgia had done nothing to polish his speaking ability. Carter was not only rusty, he was monotonous. He changed his effective, from-the-heart, primary stump speech into a tub-thumping, negative diatribe that neither suited his temperament nor matched his low-key style. He memorized lines extolling the virtues of Harry Truman and FDR, which he rattled off machine-gun-style in his high-pitched timbre. It sounded like Donald Duck reciting "Mary Had a Little Lamb," only not as interesting. It was a disjointed speech too. Even his gifted speechwriter Pat Anderson called it a "mishmash," adding, "He's still trying things out to see what he's comfortable with."

Carter aides grew jittery. "I'm nervous," said campaign aide Patty Conway one day when I called Atlanta to inquire about the debate schedule. "There are only forty days left. It's the last shot. We're down to the wire. And everything that Ham and Jody and Jimmy have been working on for the past six or seven years could come apart. During the primaries we always had the next week to recuperate. Now there are almost no 'next weeks' left."

The press was beginning to sniff failure. No one could quite believe or understand what was happening to Carter and his crack organization. One CBS television correspondent declared, "The campaign is dying right under our feet." Lions of the fourth estate like *Times*men Tom Wicker and Scotty Reston were appalled at the political mudslide they were witnessing, but then, Jack Kennedy's and Hubert Humphrey's campaigns didn't turn around until October 1. Closet complaints about Carter long held in check were unleashed. Mass doubt and distrust surfaced across the land. As I traveled I found those who planned to vote for Carter beginning to lose faith. Many who would cast their ballots for the Georgian admitted openly that they had never really believed in him anyway.

A saleswoman in the lingerie department at I. Magnin's in Chicago said, "I'm voting for Carter, but I don't like him. First of all, I can't understand a thing he says. Secondly, I don't like anybody; I distrust politicians. They all say the same things, and what can they do? The country is in an irredeemable mess anyway. Like this store. No one's shopping. No one has any money except the very rich. Even we who work here can't buy anything but maybe a pair of hose. It's too expensive. What's Carter going to do for the working man?"

Nowhere was the roller-coaster ride to disaster more apparent than on the Democratic whistlestop train trip through six states that began on September 20 and ended the next day.

Granted, 6:30 A.M. was hardly the hour to draw thousands to Pennsylvania Station to see Jimmy off, but those few hundred who did come, mainly union members provided by Victor Gotbaum, were disappointingly cheerless. And Carter did little to spur them on. Vince Clephas, assistant to Chairman Bob Strauss, stepped up on a luggage cart, scratching his head as he surveyed the scene. "Little thin around the edges," he said. Victor Gotbaum, head of New York City Civil Service Commission, is a lanky, swarthy man with wavy hair. It was his union members who were supposed to appear en masse. He greeted a Carter aide rather sheepishly, shuffling backward with a nervous grin. "He ought to be embarrassed," said the aide. "Victor didn't do his job. He was supposed to deliver bodies. There weren't any bodies here. I'm going to tell him he did stinky."

A member of the Democratic National Steering Committee who boarded the train at Penn Station to ride in the guest car was pessimistic. "Carter's in big trouble. He's lost the momentum. It's derailing," she said as the thirteen-car train chugged off down the bumpy tracks. "I knew the issues would catch up with him before long. You can't say everything and get away with it forever. People remember. And the American people are a lot more cautious this year than ever before."

The first stop, Newark, New Jersey, proved a bust. The eight A.M. crowds were sparse and silent. A midget in a straw hat tried to break the apathy, playing a kazoo and ad libbing inane songs about Carter to the tune of "Hello Dolly." When Carter appeared on stage, it could have been the local candidate for school board for all the attention he got. To make matters worse, New Jersey Governor Brendan Byrne, who introduced Carter, was booed vigorously. "That's all right," said Byrne. "You don't have to like me. Just vote for Jimmy Carter."

A black TV repairman named Jimmy Jackson stood near the rostrum brandishing a "Jobs-Jobs-Jobs" banner. Jackson had been a volunteer in the Presidential campaigns of John Kennedy and George McGovern. Now he was trying to help Carter, but was having little luck. "I've tried for weeks to get ahold of Carter's people here, but no one seems to know who's in charge. I guess they don't have their act together yet."

Jackson had passed out pamphlets and leaflets in the Newark ghetto announcing the whistlestop but had not been successful in enticing black Democrats to come. "People are at an all-time low of enthusiasm. They have a lot of empty hopes. They say they've heard all these promises before. They don't know who they're going to vote for yet. They say Ford is bad, but at least he has experience. I asked them to consider Carter's record in Georgia, but they're not interested. A lot of them I asked to come this morning just said they wouldn't come because seven-thirty was too early."

The track-side crowd in Trenton was just as small, lackluster and emotionless as in Newark. ("No one has any oomph in Trenton," said one bystander). Governor Byrne, booed more heartily this time, even though the crowd was largely made up of his own state workers whom he had given two hours off from their jobs for the rally. Carter said Truman's unemployment rate was just three percent as compared to 15 percent in New Jersey under Ford in 1976. He talked about the Captain of the Ship (Ford) "hiding in his stateroom" and about the need for a "tough competent President." He told them as he told other crowds all day long, "I owe special interests nothing, I owe the people everything." Even that populist line proved a dud.

In between stops, Carter remained closeted in his private car, meeting with a variety of politicians who came on board to chat with him. The scene was vividly described in Curtis Wilkie's pool report:

Pool Report/Monday afternoon 9–20/Wilkie, Boston *Globe*
Notes on a visit to the sanctum sanctorum . . .
Shortly after 1 P.M. pool delegation ushered into Carter's car for TV and still purposes. Door opened to scene of chef panfrying some

steaks in small kitchen. Proceed along walnut-paneled corridor to room where several Carter staffers feasting on goodies. Did not appear to have been catered by United. Pool delegation diverted when Strauss comes up to Jody Powell and says he needs to talk with him immediately. We are sequestered in Strauss private room, featuring large double bed and furnished in cathouse-style with row of naked bulbs over mirror, sconce lamps, marble lavatory, TV which was tuned to panel show, etc.

After a while permission granted to enter place where populist from Plains rides rails. Room about fifteen by eight, cluttered in rear by sound system. Two long windows on each side and two more in back with glass door looking out on caboose platform. Speedometer on the walls indicated that train hit seventy-six miles per hour. Also ship's clock and barometer. More walnut paneling. Big couch aginst one wall. Three easy chairs. Another couch on side. Curtains rust-colored. Carpet buff-colored. Ceiling composed of alternate one-inch squares of perforated aluminum and gold-colored metal. Whole thing monument to bad taste. So much for fashions, now on to substance.

Carter came into room from more monkish digs just off the sitting room, where there is just one mean couch, a window and lavatory. He had coat off and sleeves rolled up to normal combat position of two rolls of cuffs. Failed to say "Hi, everybody" as well as "Good deal," and spent time feigning interest in Democratic affairs with Strauss for benefit of audio and cameras.

Much inaudible, but Carter said of trip: "I've enjoyed it, man, I'd like to campaign like this all the time . . . it's a lot better for Governors and Congressmen and other local candidates. I think it'll help us . . . I think Rosalynn will enjoy it. I'll tell her tonight." Carter also talked of trip to Chicago and Daley-sponsored procession through thousands of sewage workers and other patronageers and wardheelers. "He had a big picture of me in fireworks," Carter said, and as it went off to cap the display, Carter said, presumably of Daley's satisfaction with the show, "He was just as happy as a baby."

Pennsylvania speaker of the house Herbert Fineman then brought in to meet great man. Carter recalled coming to Penn. for 200th anniversary of Continental Congress when he was Governor. He also said, "I've been looking out here at the farms," out the window and vowed to discuss agriculture, welfare and government reorganization at the next three stops.

Said in passing to reporter that Friday's visit to Miss. "Surprised a lot of liberal reporters" when they saw Eastland and Stennis on same stage with civil rights leaders.

That third Monday in September, Governor Milton Shapp turned out some five thousand state workers under threatening skies in Harrisburg, Pa. The workers jammed most of the street facing the steps of the State Capitol Building where Carter spoke. But according to observers, the turnout was unimpressive. Ten, fifteen and even twenty thousand had lined that street for other celebrities. The sound system was so poor that relatively few in the audience could hear a word. However, those who could agreed that Carter managed to dissipate whatever interest had been engendered by fiery young Bill Green, candidate for U. S. Senate, who roused the crowd with Kennedy rhetoric. And it began to rain.

Shortly thereafter it happened. News streaked through the train like a lit bomb fuse that Bob Scheer's *Playboy* article was out, quoting Carter as saying:

"I've looked on a lot of women with lust. I've committed adultery in my heart many times. This is something that God recognizes I will do—and I have done it—and God forgives me for it. But that doesn't mean that I condemn someone who not only looks on a woman with lust but who leaves his wife and shacks up with someone out of wedlock.

"Christ says, Don't consider yourself better than someone else because one guy screws a whole bunch of women while the other guy is loyal to his wife . . ."

Disbelief descended on an already puzzled press and fanned whispers of impending doom. Sensing the need not to seem defensive or disturbed, the Carter staff nonchalantly Xeroxed and passed out copies of the fatal page. And Carter himself took a casual walking tour of the train. Before he came, however, reporters were ordered over an intercom to "clear the aisles." If Carter found groups waiting to question him he would "turn back," said a voice. "Please, all return to your seats and sit down, or Governor Carter will not come through the cars." When Carter appeared, he seemed insouciant and in control, but moved quickly enough so that no conversation could last for long. When he came to my seat he brushed my cheek with his hand. "What's Mrs. Carter going to say when she finds out you've lusted after other women?" I asked him.

Carter kept walking, but turned around with a grin and responded in his higher register, "She knows!"

Always teasing, Powell called back: "What he doesn't know yet is I'm the centerfold!"

(One woman for whom Carter certainly has lust in his heart is Elizabeth Taylor. Carter tells the story that at a dinner party he was sitting across the table from the voluptuous Ms. Taylor and could not keep his eyes off of her. At one point Ms. Taylor, looking right at him, asked him a question. Carter did not respond, but continued to stare at her. "Well, Mr. Carter?" the actress asked, expecting an answer. Carter was jolted out of his fantasy world. "I'm sorry, Ms. Taylor," he said sheepishly. "I'm sure you were talking to me, but I didn't hear a word that you said.")

Powell seemed totally unperturbed by the *Playboy* article, as he had been with almost any crisis. As the train lurched from side to side, Powell, surrounded by reporters, lit up a Salem and said simply, "Anyone who's never done anything worse than that ought to vote for someone else."

Some reporters had not yet seen the full text of the interview but had heard that Carter had used the words "screw" and "shack up." "Where does 'screw' come in?" asked a reporter?

"Somewhere in the shack, I guess." said Powell.

"What kind of a reaction will there be?"

"Well, I suppose you'll have some Republican committeewoman stand up somewhere and scream, 'Screwers out of the White House.' Other than that, not much."

Told by Jim Dickinson of the Washington *Star* that the Baptist ministers were already spewing fire about the statements, Powell replied, "If they threw all the men out of the Baptist church who ever lusted after women, they'd starve to death . . . I don't think the use of an earthy term is a disqualification for office. On balance, I think the article was one of the more revealing and best presentations of his views, and anyone who reads the interview generally will have good insight into the man. In it, Jimmy sets high standards for himself, but shows he is tolerant of other people." Then he added with a mischievous smile, "Who knows, by putting spiritual quotes in *Playboy,* we may even get more people to read the Scriptures."

Needless to say Johnstown's and Altoona's friendly crowds and even Pittsburgh's fireworks all were eclipsed by "lust" and a cold drizzle—the issue did not go away.

Nor did the Carter whistlestop end on a very positive note. Arriving at the William Penn Hotel in Pittsburgh close to midnight, over fifty of the traveling party discovered there were no rooms in the inn. They had to traipse around town looking for places to sleep.

City Council Member Jim Lally told me of Carter's growing unpopularity in Pittsburgh. He had angered local politicians and organization types by sending in out-of-state advance men. He had sought and won the endorsement of an unpopular mayor, Pete Flaherty. The anti-Flaherty forces hated him by association. Abortion had turned the Catholic vote strongly anti-Carter.

An indication of the disaffection in Pittsburgh was the size of the crowd at the station that night, perhaps two thousand. There should have been more. "Most of them were Right to Lifers," Lally said. A Roman Catholic, he was "flabbergasted" by the *Playboy* article.

Nor did "lust" go away the next day. It dogged Rosalynn and Fritz Mondale on the Westward-bound whistlestop. Rosalynn and Mondale had joined Carter the night before in Pittsburgh where they witnessed a spectacular fireworks display at a rally. They picked up the whistle-stop campaigning where Carter left off. Early Tuesday morning the train moaned and rocked its sleek body through the undulating Pennsylvania mountains into the cool, green, flat Ohio countryside. Back through thirteen joggling cars, through an entire boxcar of Secret Servicemen, through a galley where a chef was frying onions, I finally arrived in a paneled conference car where Rosalynn sat at one end of an elliptical table sipping tea from a blue-and-white china cup. She was wearing a rust-colored gabardine suit with a rust-and-white striped turtleneck sweater, matching lipstick and a little mascara. She looked pale and seemed tense. She had a bad cold. Even heavy doses of Vitamin C, she said, had provided little relief so far. We talked about other things for a while. Yes, she was still advising Jimmy. She had sat in on most of his meetings on health and national defense when they were home in Plains together, and all the interviews with Vice Presidential aspirants. She didn't like the fact that more attention was being focused on her in the campaign and she felt a certain "tenseness" she hadn't experienced during the primaries. But she thought the campaign was going well.

A pause. The rumble of the train filled the silence with rhythmic sound. Her husband had admitted he had lusted after other women. Had she ever lusted after other men? Rosalynn did not blink or move an inch. Her brown-green eyes contained neither animosity nor surprise. She looked directly at me. "If I had I wouldn't tell you." She giggled. Did she think the *Playboy* article was in good taste? "I don't know. I haven't read the article," she said calmly, "but it's my understanding that it was just Jimmy explaining his Christian religion and that it was a very good article. I haven't talked to him about it."

Did she think it showed good judgment to use the vocabulary that he did? Rosalynn shrugged and glanced nervously at her press secretary, Mary Hoyt, who was sitting at my right elbow. "We have a very close relationship. I trust him completely and it doesn't bother me at all."

Carter had said the day before that his wife knew he lusted after other women. Had he told her about those feelings? "He never had to. I never questioned about it. I trust him completely." But is it something that ever came up in a discussion? Rosalynn turned to the window pensively. Tiny white clapboard houses with front porches, and tidy green fields rushed by. Seconds elapsed. "I don't remember," she said softly. Then she giggled again. "If he did it didn't make an impression on me." Had he ever mentioned it? Rosalynn was squirming and shifting nervously in her chair. "I'm not going to tell you about my personal life. I trust him absolutely completely. I've never doubted him. I've never had any reason to, and that article I think was telling people that God does not expect anybody to be perfect— that He knows we're going to sin and He cares for you anyway. And He forgives you for things that you do if you have a personal relationship with God. I think that's what the whole article was about and it doesn't bother me." Rosalynn claimed Carter's discussion of lust was a very personal private conversation that he (Jimmy) was having anyway.

"During an interview?" I asked.

"I don't . . . you've read it—I haven't," she shot back. "I think I'd like to talk about . . . aren't there some other issues?" she drawled, her voice barely above a whisper. "You know Jimmy made . . . I was on a TV talk show last night with two men who said it was a very, very good article."

But how about the political ramifications? Rosalynn shook her head, shrugged and uttered a little whimper. "I'm not worried. I think he's a human being."

Other politicians on board were however. Bob Strauss was not only concerned about the discussion of sex in *Playboy*, but that Carter had accused Lyndon Johnson of "lying, cheating and distorting the truth." Strauss held his head. "I knew Johnson lied, but I would never say it. How the hell are we going to carry Texas now?"

The *Playboy* problem trailed Rosalynn through the train on a hand-shaking tour with the press. Feminist Betty Friedan asked Mrs. Carter if she thought men and women had "equal rights to lust without being condemned."

"Yes, men and women all have rights," she said and skittered away.

Another reporter asked if she had been "embarrassed" by the *Playboy* article. Rosalynn looked momentarily harried. "No," she said and turned to Mary Hoyt for guidance. Hoyt, who was right at Rosalynn's heels, shook her head. "No. Not at all," Rosalynn added and moved on.

For a once painfully shy woman, Rosalynn Carter was not only holding her own but doing better than her husband. And at each whistlestop, never referring to a note, she managed to captivate her audience, while creating a feeling of intimacy. In spite of her cold, she proved herself to be a forceful performer, generating enthusiasm that would put most politicians to shame.

Under brilliant blue skies in Massillon, Ohio, Rosalynn accepted a painting from the wife of Mayor Frank Moss and told an audience of 1,500, "We have a chance to change the government of our country. And I think we need a change in Washington." Through Mansfield, Lima, Ohio, and Fort Wayne, Indiana, she reiterated her populist theme that her family knows what it means to "work for a living." She attacked the President (at one point she forgot protocol and referred to him simply as "Ford") for being a part of the Washington establishment. "Ford has been in Washington since 1948 . . . And we learned when Jimmy was Governor of Georgia that if we stayed in Atlanta, we lost perspective of the whole state of Georgia. I think there's no way you can spend a major portion of your life in Washington and know what it is to live out in the country and work for a living."

Wrapping herself in a Carter-green coat, she stood before a crowd of AFL-CIO rank and file just yards from the Landmark Lime, Salt, Straw, Lawn Seed, Fertilizer and Gasoline store and told her attentive audience how she and Jimmy had "scrimped and saved," to make their now $5 million-dollar peanut enterprise a "success." "And when you do that and when you get into government and see the waste and extravagance and unnecessary expense, it is just unbelievable. Jimmy couldn't stand it when he was elected Governor.

He *completely* reorganized the state of Georgia," she said, slicing the air sideways.

"It is so important, and I don't think there is a person who disagrees with me," she said heatedly. "The federal government needs some management and Jimmy Carter can manage it."

To a cheerful crowd in Fort Wayne, Indiana, she said dramatically: in her soprano drawl, "I've become concerned about things that never really bothered me before. I've read about grain sales to Russia, but it didn't come to me until I went into a farmer's house and talked to the farmers and found their livelihood depends on a market for their products. I had a man approach me in a courthouse a few weeks ago and say with tears in his eyes, 'Mrs. Carter I've got black lung.' He was thirty-six and had six children. 'I'm too far gone for you to help, but please tell your husband to do something for me.' So I'm concerned about black lung. I spoke to a woman in a New Hampshire shopping center on the Saturday before the primary and she made it clear to me that she was not going to vote because nobody cared. I said, 'Jimmy cares for you' and she said, 'I'll tell you one thing, I'm not going to turn my thermostat down and go cold so some millionaire doesn't have to pay income taxes.' The people of our country don't trust the government to be responsive to their needs. They think the government responds to special interest groups and has in the past to large contributors. Jimmy Carter has no obligations. Jimmy Carter was nominated with no strings attached. We have a chance to elect a President of the U. S. with obligations only to the people. We need your help."

All along the rail Rosalynn Carter won the heart of the Midwest. She was controlled, upbeat, dynamic and the crowds responded in kind. Someone said, "If we could only run her against Mrs. Ford, we'd have an interesting election."

Forty-eight hours later, after a brief study and rest session in Plains, a nervous Carter flew to Philadelphia for his first head-on nationally televised confrontation with President Gerald R. Ford. Carter was uncertain as to how he should handle himself. If he were to be aggressive he might seem disrespectful or threatening to a President. Should he call Ford "Mr. President" or "Mr. Ford?" Should he sit or stand? The result of his uncharacteristic uncertainty was defeat. Rosalynn would become livid with Jimmy's performance and chastise her husband for "not being himself . . . they told him what to say."

CHAPTER 30

ROUND ONE:
A PRESIDENTIAL TKO

A CARNIVAL ATMOSPHERE prevailed in the lobby of the Benjamin Franklin Hotel in Philadelphia the afternoon of what Carter campaign manager Hamilton Jordan called, "The Big Casino." The first of three Presidential debates would be held later that evening of September 23 just forty paces away in the Walnut Street Theater. It had been touted for weeks as the deciding factor in the campaign and the excitement of it made everybody slightly wacky with anticipation.

Both Carter and Ford press secretaries, Jody Powell and Ron Nessen, sat down to drink together in the lobby bar. Carter advance man Jim King and Ford deputy press secretary Bill Greener joined them. Powell was announcing to the bar on Jim King's portable loudspeaker that Nessen was buying a round for everybody. Greener was telling Jim King that if Ford lost the debate he would eat at least two metal oranges from the steel trees outside the press room. Greener was preening his political feathers. "No matter what the outcome, our horse is ready."

Hamilton Jordan, Carter's campaign manager, was poking *Washington Post* writer Jules Witcover with his elbow and generally carrying on like a sophomore. "Nervous? Nah!" he said, clicking the heels of his boots on the carpet like a flamenco dancer. "I've been out buying up *Playboy* magazines. I've already bought three thousand."

At two P.M. after a larger lunch than usual—steak, potatoes and salad—he had walked a half block from the hotel to the theater to inspect the set where he would battle his opponent, the President of the United States. Carter was spotted toting a suit bag over his shoulder. "What's in the bag?" a spectator yelled. "My superman cape and overalls," Carter said.

Young, handsome, articulate Jack Kennedy's campaign had soared after his head-on confrontation with the nervous, lip-licking Richard Nixon. And the Carter camp was counting on debate number one to produce a similar effect for their Kennedyesque candidate. Once the viewing public was exposed to Jimmy Carter's Southern charm, saw his piercing baby blue eyes, and full head of hair and witnessed his extraordinary ability to articulate the issues, once they saw him pitted against a rather slow-witted, balding Ford, how could he lose?

Only this time it was different. The Kennedy-Nixon debates were known factors from which lessons could be learned. The same mistakes would not be made twice. Everyone knew it was style rather than substance that had won the heart of America in 1960. Therefore, there would be no darting eyes, no sweating lips, no rumpled clothes in 1976. Both Carter and Ford would look well groomed and act presentably. What Carter had not counted on was Ford's ability to learn quickly. Carter never anticipated that weeks of preparation and working with videotape machines and dummy Carters could polish Gerald Ford into the perfect Presidential debater. Conversely, Jimmy Carter had refused to practice.

Barry Jagoda, television coordinator for Carter, obtained a film of the Kennedy-Nixon debates from the National Archives, which Carter watched with his family and guest Robert Redford one August night when Redford came to dinner in Plains. He also had been given two inch-thick blue books on the issues. Then he was left to his own devices. "My only advice to him," said TV consultant Al Vecchione, "was to be himself. After that, the best thing we could do was leave him alone." There were no stand-ins for Ford, or the panelists. In fact, only two days before the debate did issues advisor Stu Eizenstat fly down to Plains to make sure Carter had his facts straight. Carter once again became the lonely student.

The Benjamin Franklin teemed with the cream of the broadcasting and writing world, arriving from various points in the country— Teddy White, Jules Witcover, Jack Germond, Liz Drew, Edwin Newman, Frank Reynolds, Jack Chancellor, Barbara Howar, Mary McGrory. (McGrory to Howar: "How do you feel about 'lust'?" Howar: "I want to get as close to it as I possibly can.") *Playboy* author Bob Scheer stalked through the lobby handing out Xeroxed copies of his article. "I think it's a very historic piece that could change the course of the campaign. It will have an impact on at least twenty million people," he said modestly.

Upstairs on the twelfth floor, Hamilton Jordan in a tattersall shirt and boots, was padding around looking for his room and lugging his baggage behind him. The severe downturn in the polls, the recent blunders, the disappointing train trip, the sudden loss of momentum, were hardly worth more than a hard chew on a wad of gum.

"Things are going a lot better than people think. Really, people aren't paying attention to the campaign yet," he said, dropping his bag on the red carpet. "That old political axiom, that people don't start getting interested in politics until after the World Series is true." He was not overly concerned about the *Playboy* article. "It will have a lifespan of forty-eight hours. It'll be like ethnic purity. Besides, the debates will wash it over. Tonight is the Big Casino."

In the theater, Carter television aides Barry Jagoda and Kevin Gorman scuttled about, testing lights and microphones for Carter. While they tested for sound, Gorman stood in for President Ford behind one of the barrel-shaped lecterns. Someone filled in at the long walnut-paneled desk where interrogators Newman, Drew and Reynolds would sit.

"Throw him some softballs," Jagoda said. "Go ahead. I've got a twelve and two record," Carter laughed at the mock-reporters, referring to his softball record in Plains. "How are you doing in the campaign?" they said, again testing the microphones that would later "rebel against the message" as Marshall McLuhan put it.

"I'm slightly ahead in some states, behind in others. But the only poll that counts is the poll on election day," said Carter. Then he went back to room 1258 and napped for two hours.

At 2:45 P.M. the President arrived in Air Force One at the Philadelphia Airport, and like Carter, stopped at the Walnut Street Theater to check out the lights and sound. He seemed serenely confident, smiling as he waved from his limousine to passersby on Walnut Street.

One shopkeeper came to his door and peered out as the President passed, preceded by a phalanx of motorcycle police. The man was thrilled. "Hey, Irma, you see him? He's just like the rest of us, 'cept he's got all sorts of people hanging on him."

Just an hour before the debate began, the panelists were assembling in the lobby. Liz Drew clung fiercely to her manila folder, a brown babushka plastered to her head. "Nervous?"

"Oh, noooo." She grimaced, feigning a swoon.

Edwin Newman's palms were cold and damp. "Can you imagine how Carter and Ford must be feeling?" he said. "I hear the viewership is going to be two hundred million worldwide."

It was a perfect evening in Philadelphia. The temperature was cool, about sixty-eight degrees, and the sky was clear blue. But an eeriness crept over the city. In the midst of the quiet, masses of mounted police and hundreds of Secret Servicemen fanned out around the Ben Franklin Hotel. Thousands of demonstrators mingled with bystanders in an orderly fashion, behind yellow barricades. Pro-abortionists brandished pictures of coat hangers dripping blood captioned "Ford, the Bishop's Hit Man," and "Jesus was a planned pregnancy." Pro-lifers were out as well in full tilt, as were members of the Socialist Workers party.

Inside the modernized theater with the blue-carpeted stage and elliptical raised platform, the fever of anticipation and excitement mounted. Seats had been removed from the orchestra for camera equipment, so a small audience of some 470 VIPs and press crammed the balcony. Presidential advisor Bob Hartmann sat front row center, leaning over the railing, with Rita Hauser and Secretary of Transportation Coleman, and former FCC Chairman Newton Minow.

Finally, at 9:20 P.M. Ruth Clusen, the portly president of the League of Women Voters, appeared and set the mood for what may have contributed to Jimmy Carter's poor showing in the debate. "I want to establish some ground rules." She smiled. "Do not applaud. Do not take any flash photos. Do not laugh, at least no inappropriate laughter. Our goal is to establish an impartial climate."

Five minutes later a grinning Jimmy Carter strode jauntily onto the stage, waving a flat right palm. The silent response seemed to perplex him.

He looked disjointed, as though he had dressed too fast. Jimmy Carter, the perfectionist, the Annapolis man, the stickler for neatness, had been too nervous to get his tie on straight. It was knotted off kilter. And somehow, tonight, the bright red of it seemed too gaudy. He looked like a gawky peanut farmer, not like the man who might be running the United States. Freshly cropped, his hair was too short, feathery on top, with a slight bump just to the right of the part, and slicked down near the ears. He looked like Howdy Doody. Carter removed a square-folded handkerchief from his pocket, placed it under the top of the lectern, clasped his hands on the lectern so tightly the knuckles turned white, lowered his eyes and obviously prayed.

An instant later Ford appeared. It was quite obvious he had up-staged Carter. Ford had worn a "vest." You could hear the word whispered all over the balcony. A small thing, a vest, but it con-jured up the image "Executive," "Chairman of the Board," "Presi-dent,"—not "farmer." He was also wearing a gold tie pin—another minute detail, but important in the overall effect. He looked like a President. Carter seemed to sense it. He tensed. When he shook hands with the President he extended his arm stiffly, holding Ford as far away as possible like a snake on a stick. Carter looked small and unimposing next to the massive, athletic body of the President. What had seemed boyish only months ago, now looked badly worn. The skin above his collar was wattled, corrugated like a nun's coif. He seemed old and tired.

Ford exuded composure. A svelte, raven-haired stage manager asked the President to test his microphone. Ford complied. "I'm glad to be here. I'm looking forward to it. You're a very attractive stage manager." That broke the ice. The audience could not help but erupt in laughter. Ford, lusting after the stage manager in his heart. What a way to open a debate.

Due to the flip of a coin, the first question went to Carter. Frank Reynolds asked what as President he would do first to provide jobs. The answer rattled out carelessly like stray honey-coated machine-gun bullets trying to find a target.

"First of all to channel research and development funds into areas that will provide large numbers of jobs . . . Secondly, we need to have a commitment in the private sector to cooperate with govern-ment in matters like housing, for a small investment of taxpayers' money in the housing field can bring large numbers of extra jobs and the guarantee of mortgage loans, the putting forward of two hundred and two programs for housing for all the people, and so forth to cut down the roughly twenty percent unemployment that now exists in the housing industry."

Carter rambled. He was visibly jangled. Nervously, he licked his lips as Richard Nixon had back in 1960. He punctuated his an-swers with "uhh's" and swallowed his voice. No one in the balcony understood a word he said. Everything sounded like one giant rapid-fire Southern drawl. Observers gave him B minus for content, F for delivery. I thought of Carter's class reunion when he told me his most difficult and painful task in high school had been debating. He was always afraid, he had said, and suddenly on the Walnut Street stage where Ethel Barrymore had played, he seemed like the Plains schoolboy again.

For a minute, Ford scrawled copious notes on blue paper with his left hand. Now he was holding both sides of his desk like a Captain at the Helm, intently studying Jimmy Carter. Carter seemed to wither beneath the President's stare. The minute Carter finished a lengthy, detailed answer on how he would provide jobs, Ford parried swiftly.

"I don't believe Mr. Carter has been any more specific in this case than he has been on many other instances. I notice particularly that he didn't endorse the Humphrey-Hawkins Bill, which he has on occasion, and which is included as a part of the Democratic platform. That legislation allegedly would help our unemployment but we all know that it would have controlled our economy. It would have added ten billion dollars to thirty billion dollars each year in additional expenditures by the federal government. It would have called for export controls on agricultural products . . ."

Touché. Then Ford continued. Speaking slowly, clearly, from the diaphragm, he discussed specific proposals he had recommended as President—a tax reduction of twenty-eight billion dollars—three-quarters of it to go to private taxpayers and one-quarter to business, tax incentives for business to move into the inner cities, or build new plants. His answer was short, well prepared and to the point, designed to underscore the fact that he, not Jimmy Carter was the President, that he, not Carter, had suggested actual legislation, that he, not Carter, was a man of action. Expectations had been low to begin with. So far, he exceeded them brilliantly.

The audience expected a leader in Carter. Instead, he was timid and retiring for most of the debate. Spewing information like a computer, talking too fast, swallowing his words, and allowing his sentences to trail off. While Ford used statistics sparingly to underscore points, Carter's sounded like he was delivering an annual report. Statistics can be sharp weapons when applied sparingly, but not when flung at a listener who most likely had just finished a long hard day and was either at home in pajamas ready for bed, at a bar polishing off a fourth beer, or at a dinner party sodden with martinis, wine and too much food. But Carter persisted.

Carter had indeed done his homework, but he managed to put people to sleep. While Ford took notes only at the very beginning,

Carter buried his nose in his papers, writing constantly, filling an entire blue book, and shuffling papers back and forth nervously. He looked more like a reporter than a would-be President. He also began almost every answer with a conditional "Well," which seemed defensive. He came across in the words of viewer Anthony Guzzardo of Rockford, Illinois, a Democrat, as "Too timid . . . He's not fast. There's no fight in him."

An hour had passed before Carter began to hit his stride, to relax more with familiar topics like reorganization. But in his unexciting way, Ford kept clobbering him. The entire evening was an exercise in ennui but Ford was at least exhibiting a few parries and upper-cuts. Carter aides cringed when Ford attacked Carter's record as Governor. When Carter became Governor, Ford pointed out, "expenditures by the government went up fifty percent. Employees of the government in Georgia during his term of office went up over twenty-five percent and the figures also show that the bonded indebtedness of the state of Georgia went up twenty percent." Carter could not defend himself. There were no rebuttals permitted. The format was more like a turgid press conference, with the principals reciting statements memorized in advance.

Ford anticipated that Carter might accuse him of being a veto President and knocked down the idea before it was brought up. "The Governor has played a little fast and loose with the facts about vetoes. The record shows that President Roosevelt vetoed on an average of fifty-five bills a year. President Truman vetoed on the average about thirty-eight bills a year. I understand that Governor Carter when he was Governor of Georgia vetoed between thirty-five and forty bills a year. My average in two years is twenty-six. But in the process of that we have saved nine billion dollars."

But, in spite of Ford's salvos, Carter was gaining in strength. Over and over he reiterated Ford's advocacy of more than $5 billion in tax reductions for corporations, special interest groups and the very wealthy while he ignored "human beings." He hammered at Ford's lack of leadership, the 50 percent increase in the unemployment rate. He was just getting into the subject of illegal break-ins and the FBI when at 10:51 the audio failed completely.

The entire audience was in a state of shock. What had happened? Five minutes became ten. In hundreds of millions of broadcasting hours, nothing like this ever occurred, and yet in the middle of the second most widely watched program in the history of American politics—no sound. If this had happened during the Super Bowl or a

Muhammad Ali fight, a revolution would have taken place.

Yet, for an eternal twenty-eight minutes, in what was to have been the most important event of the campaign, the President of the United States and his challenger were silenced. Jimmy Carter and Gerald Ford stood side by side, never speaking, never acknowledging each other's presence but for one brief glance. Ford folded his hands behind his back in the manner of British royalty. Carter faced the first moments of the twenty-eight-minute gap by smiling at the insanity of the situation, but it soon became apparent he was seething inside at the incompetency, mechanical or human, that had interrupted his audition for the number one job in the land. Crossing and uncrossing his arms, licking his lips, glowering, breathing deeply and puffing out air like his brother Billy emits cigarette smoke, he finally sat down and stared at the wood panel.

At eleven P.M., Edwin Newman said he thought ABC had got things fixed and invited both men to continue. Newman had to rescind the invitation. "I have just been told that what I just said was not heard on the air." In sheer disbelief the audience howled with laughter. John Chancellor watched both candidates through opera glasses. Reporters joked about the incredible situation. "Two hundred million people just went to bed," said one. "Dick Salant [the president of CBS] was last seen chewing on a cable," said another.

After several false alarms, audio was finally restored at 11:19 P.M. A small amplifier, the size of a cigarette butt, had blown. Amazingly, over 40 percent of the television audience had remained tuned in, but the momentum of the debates had been lost. Carter's sensitive closing remarks as well as Ford's cliché-ridden statement were forgotten. Debate number one had been a fiasco.

Back at the hotel, both sides claimed victory, but Carter's team seemed a little less vigorous in their optimism. I saw Carter in the hall as he moved from one reception to another. "After the first five minutes I was much more relaxed and felt at ease," he said. Someone called to him, "You got more specific on the issues too." Carter snapped, "I've always been that way." Rosalynn padded along behind him. "I just thought he was good. He got progressively better. He was in command of the situation the whole time."

Bob Strauss struggled to find complimentary words. Standing at the entrance to the press room he said, "As the debate went on I think Jimmy showed sensitivity. But no one got knocked out. The first half of the debate was pretty close to a draw." The Carter staff was ringed off in various parts of the Garden room by groups of reporters wanting to know how they thought Carter had fared. The identical message emitted from each group. Nervous for the first fifteen, twenty or thirty minutes, better after that. Jerry Rafshoon, Carter's media man, sat grimly in the back of the room drinking beer with his steady companion, Barbara Howar. Rafshoon knew the score was bad. "No win. No loss," he said curtly and stalked away. Hamilton Jordan hedged his bets. "The election is still out there to be won. Ford's side is claiming they won. Only after a few days of analysis it will be obvious Jimmy won."

Only after a few minutes it was obvious that Jimmy had lost. The Roper Poll based on a sampling of 480 people gave Ford an eight-point edge over Carter. The Carter staff took to drinking, not merry-making. At 2:30 A.M. Jody Powell was still belting down bourbon and soda. Peter Bourne stood at the bar comparing notes with White House Chief of Staff Dick Cheney. They were discussing their latest dinner at the home of Katherine Graham, the publisher of the *Washington Post*. They carefully avoided the topic of the debate. The Carter staff studied the Ford people with quiet fascination, disbelief, and momentary resignation.

The next morning the *Today* show talked to a random sample of men and women on their way to work in Houston, Cleveland, Chicago and New York. The sample showed Ford the overwhelming victor of the debate. An Associated Press poll gave Ford the lead. And four days later on September 27, a *Times*-CBS survey based on 1,167 telephone interviews showed that 37 percent thought the President had won, while only 24 percent thought Carter had the upper hand. But more significantly, the President had cut Carter's lead roughly in half, led Carter among independent voters and had taken a substantial lead in the West. With only five weeks to go, the momentum was clearly against Carter.

I ran into Ron Nessen, Ford's press secretary, in the coffee shop of the Benjamin Franklin Hotel the next morning. Nessen had written my editor, Hillel Black, at William Morrow, a letter saying how angry the White House was with the widely advertised title of my book: *How Jimmy Won*, which had been decided on seven months before the election. "You're going to have to eat your book in the White House press room after November," Nessen sneered. "All of our calls, all of our figures show the President way out in front. I went back to the house with him last night and he was very happy. No one had to tell him he had won. He knew. And

Bob Strauss whispered into my ear that it was the closest thing to a tie he had ever seen. When the Chairman of the Democratic party says that you know that's something."

Pat Caddell, wearing his three-piece suit from the night before, straggled toward the elevators, rumpled, and ill at ease. "Yeah. I got figures. But I'm not saying what they are. So far it's a wash."

In Washington, Capitol Hill was making unkind remarks about the Democratic Presidential nominee.

Carter advisors were peppered for twenty-four hours with suggestions from friends and advisors on how Carter could improve his style. Norval Reece, top political aide to Governor Milton Shapp, fired off a memo to his friends Hamilton Jordan and Jody Powell:

To: Jody Powell

From: Norval D. Reece

Re: Debate

Another memo or comment on this subject is the last thing you need, nevertheless, I'm indulging myself for a couple of quick observations:

Debate I: Boring. An honest draw. Ford was perceived as "winning" because the public expectation of Ford the Bumbler was much lower than the same public's expectation of Carter the Efficient. Hence, Ford surpassed the expectation of him and Carter fell short of the expectation of him. Both expectations were unrealistic and the result of that adjustment caused people to assume a Ford victory.

Carter's strongest card was his weakest in the debate: His personal appeal and calm self-assurance. He seemed so preoccupied with the need to demonstrate "knowledge" that he came across as cold and inhuman. Whoever told Carter "not to smile so much and look more serious" should take a vacation until November 2nd.

This Week: Compassion. Forget statistics for awhile. Get Carter into some highly human events—with individuals with names. Farmers. Unemployed men, women and young people. Housewives fighting inflation.

Humanize Carter's schedule. Take the attack to Ford in human terms. Let Carter do something spontaneous. On a walking tour, pop into a small shop and talk to the proprietor for an "unscheduled" thirteen minutes. Let him meet a little old lady on social security on a street corner and become so concerned and involved, he lingers.

Debate II: Carter will probably "win" this, partly because the same public perceives Ford as "far superior" on the issue and they will be surprised with Carter's knowledgeability.

However, Carter must bear down hard on the human factor. He missed a set-up in Debate I on the Nixon pardon-Draft evaders issue by not coming out with an impassioned Carter speech on double standards of justice, disillusioned youth, etc.

For example: "Détente is wrong when it penalizes American consumers and working people unfairly. A farmer in Ames, Iowa—Jack Johnson—told me he lost $63,000 during the Russian Wheat Deal. And the Russians bought cheaply and then resold some of it at an enormous profit. That's not right, etc."

"On imports. We need to review our policy. Working people have told me at plant gates in Pennsylvania, Illinois, Texas, Massachusetts and all over this country that they're afraid they'll lose their jobs due to cheap imports. One lady in a textile factory told me last week that they had laid off 612 workers in the last three months because of foreign imports, etc., etc., etc."

Enough said. Basically, Carter has to build fast to carry the attack to Ford where he's weakest—in human and moral terms on the issues of the economy and cleaning up government.

I'm one egghead who thinks Carter doesn't have to get more specific and shouldn't. That will only open up a wider attack on Carter and he will find he's on the defensive more and more.

He's got to carry the attack to Ford—now and at Debate II.

I know I'm talking style and not substance, but that's where Carter is going to win it here. No one "likes" Ford. Carter can lose only if they decide they don't "like" him any better.

Rosalynn Carter, the Bournes' weekend guest, had the best suggestion. Rosalynn saw the flaws in Carter's campaign speech and debate style. Too much Truman and FDR, too much history and not enough of the present and the future, not enough punch.

Rosalynn, who had been furious for the way Carter had been "programmed" for the debate, called her husband over the weekend and told him she thought he ought to change his style. It would change in round two. But meanwhile Carter's stump style took a dramatic turn as well. On Monday Carter lashed out at Ford. "Change" could not be expected, he told a boffo crowd of several thousand in Portland, Oregon, from a "leadership that has been bogged down in Washington for the last twenty-five or thirty years, deriving their advice, their counsel, their financial support from lobbyists and from special interests."

But there was restlessness within the campaign organization. A black member of Carter's District of Columbia Committee brooded. "As far as Carter is concerned, we don't exist. He doesn't talk to people. It's a completely closed shop. He should get on the phone and talk to some of the old-time Democrats that he's going to need. But no one does. They still think they're running in the primaries. They think they can do it by themselves."

A member of Carter's staff complained that Carter's Atlanta staff was becoming too smug and arrogant, antagonizing long-time party workers in every state in the union.

The Presidential campaign was at its midpoint. Despite his more strident attacks on Ford, the two weeks following his poor performance in the first debate showed no improvement for the Democratic nominee. Carter was plagued with bad crowds, bad press and bad news. The *Playboy* interview had cut deeply. It hurt Carter the same way Ronald Reagan's proposal to turn $90 billion in federal programs and revenues back to the states hurt the Republican candidate in the New Hampshire primary. It put Carter on the defensive and kept him from gaining needed momentum. Carter's discussion of his proposed income tax reforms in an Associated Press interview wounded him as well, just as McGovern's infamous one thousand dollar per person grant had scared 1972 voters with incomes over $15,000 into thinking he would raise their taxes.

The polls worsened. The October 1 Gallup Poll showed Carter's lead over Ford had been reduced from eighteen points to eight, and that the President had pulled ahead of his challenger among independents by 45 percent to 38 percent. On October 4, the Yankelovich, Skelly & White survey indicated that Carter and Ford were tied 43 percent to 43 percent. Carter, like a man trapped, began to lash out at the press, blaming his steady collapse on the media. The press, he said, was giving Ford a free ride by letting him hide in the White

House during the general election campaign. By contrast, Carter said, he was suffering political damage from being constantly accessible.

Although Carter held the advantage in enough states to give him a majority in the Electoral College, his lead in most of the states with the big blocks of electoral votes began to shrink appreciably. According to *The New York Times* survey eleven states were considered toss-ups. Even if President Ford could claim a solid advantage in only eight states with forty-six electoral votes, a small increase in his nationwide support, even three or four percentage points—could tip enough states in his direction to give him an electoral victory. Carter was in jeopardy in New York, Ohio and Pennsylvania, ahead by only five or six points. The polls were virtually tied in the major battlegrounds of California, Illinois and Texas. Virginia and South Carolina were rated toss-ups as well.

Ford was not without his own problems. The President became the vortex of a swirling controversy over whether he diverted campaign funds in Michigan during the decade 1964–1974 to his own personal use. Then the news broke that Ford had accepted the hospitality of four major corporations on golfing weekends while he was a Congressman.

Ford suffered fallout too for failing to instantly fire Agriculture Secretary Earl Butz for blatant racist remarks he had made to singer Pat Boone. Butz declared that all "coloreds" wanted was "good sex," "loose shoes" and "a warm place" to defecate. Butz was finally forced to quit under fire on October 4.

A deep malaise blanketed the country. No strong issue rallied voters to the banner of either candidate. Ford and Carter heatedly trumpeted secondary issues. As one network commentator put it, "We are being nibbled to death by ducks." By October 6, the day of the second debate, it seemed that the election choice had boiled down to the fear of the unknown versus the fear of the known. Voters felt comfortable albeit unenthusiastic about Ford. He was not brilliant or inspiring, but he was predictable, a known quantity. Carter on the other hand was too new, his record too short. He smiled too much. He was suspicious. Even his traveling press conveyed the message of doubt. "I just don't know," many of them said, shaking their heads.

As they had in 1972, voters felt trapped between Scylla and Charybdis. Gary Freeman, a California voter summed it up. "It doesn't make that much difference either way. Carter and Ford are both so phony."

CHAPTER 31

ROUND TWO: THE CHALLENGER ON POINTS

THE SECOND DEBATE, held in San Francisco, was a walkaway for Jimmy Carter. I was at a dinner/debate-watching party in Washington with several Carter people who had been chewing their fingernails all day in anticipation of a second fiasco. "I know I'm going to get ulcers," one said. But instead of gnawing on their knuckles and gnashing their teeth, most of them were thrusting their fists at the television sets, cheering, "Go baby, go," "Sock it to 'im Jimmy." One of them almost fell off his chair when Ford said he thought Eastern Europe was not under Soviet domination. "That's it, gang! He blew it!" shouted one of Carter's financial supporters. "He just lost the entire Polish, Lithuanian, Hungarian, Czechoslovakian, Yugoslavian and Latvian vote." "God," said another. "I didn't know all those countries weren't under Russia. Why haven't I gone to Poland on vacation before?"

Ford's interjection of His Holiness the Pope in his defense of the Helsinki Agreement brought howls of laughter, and Carter's reply, "I'm not criticizing His Holiness the Pope, I was talking about Mr. Ford . . . I'd like to see Mr. Ford convince Polish-Americans that they're not under Russian domination," brought a round of applause.

"God, Ford looks just like Popeye," said another. "He's leaning over the podium like he's going to take a swing at Jimmy any minute." A prominent Washington journalist with a noted dislike for Carter said nothing throughout the entire program. As it ended, he rose to his feet to leave and announced, "It was a decisive victory for your man. I must admit."

And Ford had seemed to sense it. Ford had looked tense, angry, mean and defensive. While Carter listened with one hand casually thrust in his pocket, Ford had gripped the podium tensely. All the pundits had predicted Carter would face defeat in the foreign policy debate. It was his weakest suit, Ford's strongest. Ford had Kissinger and experience on his side. Carter had neither. Ford was fooled and he seemed unsettled that Carter was so in command of his material. It gave the Democratic nominee the psychological advantage. "Carter was determined to bust his ass to beat Ford this time," said an aide. "He put in twice the amount of time preparing."

Without question Carter had made up for his last appearance. He was both aggressive and relaxed. His tie was not as glaringly red. His suit looked neater. His hair didn't look like a six-year-old boy's on his way to a birthday party. He only licked his lips twice and gulped once. He shed his open-mouthed awe of the Presidency. He even sat down while Ford was speaking. He took fewer notes. He smiled and spoke slowly. During the first debate when he glanced at Ford, it was with a look of sheer terror. This time, he faced Ford fully, took notes on key points, and behaved like a man ready for combat with his opponent rather than a boy in his first school play.

The next morning I talked to several Carter aides in San Francisco about how Carter prepared for that debate. Jody Powell said Carter had watched a videotape of the first debate to see where he had gone wrong. TV aide Barry Jagoda said he had not.

Powell and Jagoda each denied making many suggestions to Carter about how to improve his style in the second debate. However, Dr. Bourne said Jagoda and Powell both "talked to Jimmy at great length, mainly to get him psyched up to be more forceful, to attack Ford more, to put him on the defensive. Jimmy had been concerned he would be criticized for attacking the President. They wanted him to act less deferential."

"It was Jagoda's and Jerry Rafshoon's specific advice to Jimmy that he try sitting down," said Powell. "Bob Squire and I were opposed to it. I wasn't sure how it would look in the two shot. I thought it would look like Ford was looking down at him. But I was wrong."

Said Jagoda, "I never made any specific suggestions. None of us has ever been specific about telling Jimmy Carter how he should act on stage. He's natural TV personality." Jagoda said Carter had worked for about two hours with a tape recorder, studied issues papers and spent less time preparing for this debate than he had the first. Not so, said Peter Bourne. Carter had spent twice as much time preparing for this debate, endless hours talking into a tape recorder and listening to the results, more hours with his staff, practicing with mock questions and answers, and a great deal of time with Congressman Les Aspin (D., Wisconsin) and Zbigniew Brzezinski, both foreign policy advisors. Jagoda said Carter spent only about one and a half hours being briefed by Les Aspin. Aspin said he and Brzezinski briefed Carter for three hours in his hotel room the day before the debate. The rest of the day Carter spent in his room studying alone, but he would occasionally page Aspin if he needed additional information. The morning of the debate, according to Jagoda, only four or five people, including Jerry Rafshoon, Jody Powell, Richard Holbrooke and Greg Schneiders sat in on a brief practice session with Carter. According to Aspin, the meeting lasted an hour and included twice that number, Jerry Rafshoon, Barry Jagoda, Greg Schneiders, Richard Holbrooke, Stu Eizenstat, and Charlie Kirbo, Hamilton Jordan, Peter Bourne and himself. "We psyched out most of the questions," said Aspin. "We picked out eleven of the thirteen questions that were asked."

Aspin said his briefings with Carter began Tuesday morning at eight when breakfast was rolled into Carter's sitting room and lasted until eleven. Present at breakfast were pollster Patrick Caddell, issue advisor Stu Eizenstat, Richard Holbrooke, Aspin and Brzezinski. Brzezinski briefed him on foreign policy and did most of the talking. "I briefed on defense," says Aspin. "One of the points I made was that Carter should be prepared to respond to a question about the five to seven billion-dollar Pentagon budget cut he had suggested during the campaign." Aspin said Carter took notes while he spoke, but responded little.

"It was my first long exposure to him," Aspin went on, "I was impressed with him, he was obviously very bright, but it was not easy to tell if he agreed with what I was saying. I would put forward a whole series of tactical points. I would say if such and such question comes up, there are three alternate tacks you can take, a, b and c. You can attack Ford this way, or that way. He obviously understood what I was talking about, but it was hard to tell what point he agreed with. He wouldn't say anything. He would just nod and take notes. He didn't have much of a sense of humor, it was all pretty serious, but I gathered he's the kind of guy who laughs if someone says something funny. The purpose of the meeting was to tell Carter no matter what the question, the idea is to stay on the offensive."

"It was great, really a decisive victory," said Greg Schneiders. "He did exactly what he set out to do. He did everything he had wanted to do in the first debate but had been reticent to do. He had had too much residual respect for the institution of the Presidency before."

Powell said, "I saw him after the debate and I told him I thought it went pretty well. The important thing was even without Eastern Europe, he still won. He felt real good about it. He was a little surprised about what Ford said about the Eastern European countries. He said, 'Why in God's name would he say a thing like that?' What he couldn't understand was when Max Frankel (of *The New York Times*) gave Ford the chance to undo what he had just said why he didn't take it."

Although some newspapers called it merely a "triumph of form over substance," Jimmy Carter emerged victorious from his second debate with President Ford. The Roper-Public Broadcasting System Poll of three hundred persons who watched the debate showed that 40 percent felt Carter had won, 30 percent said Ford was the winner and 30 percent called it a draw. The outcome was almost the reverse of a Roper Poll following the first debate which gave Ford 39 percent to Carter's 31 percent.

Carter was now in a position to move swiftly toward the triumph that seemed to be slipping like sand through his fingers in the past two weeks. Carter not only had proved himself the winner in a foreign policy and defense policy forum in which he was supposed to be at a disadvantage, he showed a lethargic party faithful unable to muster much enthusiasm for their nominee that he could cuff around an incumbent President on what should have been his own ground. He also breathed new life into his Southern campaign, which had been slipping badly. A number of polls taken before the second debate showed Carter slippage in Dixie was substantial. A Gallup Poll released October 12 showed Carter's lead over the President in the South had tumbled from 63 to 28 percent (after the Republican convention) to a ten-point margin of fifty-three to forty-three. Carter assured Dixiecrats that he was their man.

By October 15, a *New York Times*-CBS survey revealed that Carter's criticism of the President's handling of the economy and foreign policy, coupled with his populist themes, had swung the volatile and critical independent vote back behind him. The Gallup Poll placed Carter ahead of Ford nationally by forty-eight to forty-two.

The October 15 Vice-Presidential debate also aided Carter in a moment of need. Seventy-five minutes of partisan bitterness with few if any precedents in modern Presidential history, the debate established Walter Mondale as a far more attractive and desirable veep than his opponent, and proved President Ford's running mate, Senator Robert Dole the "hatchet man" he was reputed to be. His voice heavy with sarcasm and bitterness, Dole went so far as to suggest that partisanship had played a part in American involvement in World War II, and by implication in the withered hand he suffered as a result of the conflict. He also computed that there had been 1.6 million Americans "killed and wounded" in what he called "Democratic wars in this century." By contrast to the snarling, almost sinister Senator, Mondale, after a few hesitant and nervous minutes, appeared refreshing, relaxed, confident, Presidential. Mondale advisors had expected Dole to be a formidable opponent. Instead it was Mondale who emerged more than just a victor. "This was beyond our wildest dreams. It's a complete wipe out," said John Reilly, a veteran of two Kennedy campaigns and Mondale's senior political advisor. Shortly after the debate, a Harris survey reported Carter leading Ford by five percentage points nationwide, 47 to 42, but when voters were asked to choose between the Carter-Mondale ticket and the Ford-Dole team, the spread increased to eight points, 49 to 41. "If we can really make a difference of three percentage points in this election, then everything we've done has been worthwhile," said Richard Moe, Mondale's campaign director and advisor. The debate plucked Mondale from semianonymity and turned him into an instant hero. He began to draw large and enthusiastic crowds that exuded an enthusiasm Jimmy Carter rarely if ever evoked. Mondale moved, in fact, beyond the traditional role of the number two position and became a major force in the national political campaign.

The campaign quickly escalated to epic proportions. Ford abandoned the leafy shelter of his Rose Garden for the campaign battlefield where he lobbed stinging criticisms at his soft-spoken Southern opponent. During an October 14 press conference Ford alleged that Carter advocated higher taxes for middle-income families, elimination of homeowner tax credits, $100 billion or more in new spending programs and a $15 billion reduction in defense spending.

In retaliation, Carter fired off a telegram to Ford accusing the President of "telling the American people things that are not true," and suggesting that he cease making "misleading and erroneous statements" about Carter's spending and tax plans.

"He wavers, he wanders, he wiggles and he waffles and he shouldn't be President of the United States," Ford told thousands crammed along the tracks at the Pontiac, Illinois, railroad station as he began a 220-mile whistlestop train tour on October 16.

Ford was steaming ahead, hard on the offensive, rested from his long White House incarceration, revved up for the three weeks that lay ahead, better-spoken from weeks of speech lessons and ready for the kill. In spite of another gaffe from one of his administration members, this time General George Brown who spoke of the "burden" of being Israel's ally, a statement that quickly became a campaign issue when Ford's only response was a lukewarm scolding, the President was confident that his media campaign was working. And in spite of a campaign plagued with organizational difficulties, Carter was convinced he was winning too.

Both candidates would go to the third and final debate in Williamsburg certain that each had the upper hand.

CHAPTER 32

ROUND THREE: "HE'S NOT WRITING, HE'S COLORING!"

ON OCTOBER 22, the afternoon of the third debate, Hamilton Jordan joined Charles Kirbo and Bob Lipshutz and their wives and families for a leisurely lunch in the dining room of the Williamsburg Lodge.

Southern Gentleman that he is, Kirbo rose when I came over to the table. The wise man was positively buoyant. "We got it. It's in the cards," he drawled. President Ford had never gone beyond his standing of 40 or 41 percent in the polls, and for an incumbent President, Kirbo said less than half of the vote was hardly a vote of confidence. Besides, the independents were moving to Carter, not to Ford. And he was surprised to find that the reports he had been getting from the field were better than the polls he had been reading. Also, the field organization was beginning to come together and that the money was beginning to pour in again. What was his advice to Carter for the last debate? Kirbo smiled, clenched his fist and jabbed at the air. "Knock 'im out. And he will. You can't tell him anything. He's prepared."

Carter was so prepared he was napping. He had had his hair cut, had studied his Blue Books and Kirbo, Cadell, Jordan, Rafshoon, Eizenstat and Powell had grilled him on a variety of issues from *Playboy* to the state of the economy for an hour that morning. There was another practice session at the theater after lunch with Powell playing moderator and Eizenstat, Jerry Jazinoski and Dick Holbrooke playing reporters shooting questions at him. The idea was to get *Playboy* out of the way early, if he had to bring it up himself, and to capitalize on the odious comparison between the Vice-Presidential candidates, Mondale and Dole. Carter was cautioned to be tough but conversational, and to telegraph his warm personality.

"The idea," said media advisor Barry Jagoda, "is to what extent can the debate shape the last ten days. The focus will be on the economy and who can lead the country best. We told him to be aggressive, but not too." While Carter slept his aides huddled outside the staff room, arriving at last-minute decisions on points Carter should make. "God, I'm so nervous!" said Pat Caddell, traipsing through the hotel in white sneakers. "I think I'm going to hide under a desk with my hands over my head until it's over."

While I was having a Coke with Jordan in the bar, Eizenstat appeared and shoved a note hastily scribbled on a piece of paper ripped from a reporter's notebook under Jordan's nose. "Yes. I think that should go in to him right away," Jordan said. "Tell Kirbo."

Kirbo declined to deliver the note. It was too late for any more points. It would only have confused him.

The young campaign manager was completely confident about the outcome of the election. "If you gave me a million dollars today, I'd bet every cent of it that Jimmy will be President." He was rarely worried along the way, he said, except after the late primary losses in Maryland, Nevada and Oregon. But he knew even then from the number of delegates Carter had accumulated "That unless something humongous happened, we had it."

Ron Nessen was downstairs near the press room whistling in the dark about Ford's fate. The Carter people were nervous he said, "Or else they wouldn't be going back to Virginia and North and South Carolina where the polls show we have a chance to win. Besides, Carter has squandered his advertising money whereas we've saved ours for an ad campaign in the last week. We're coming up in the polls, and he's going down." Carter's lead in the Gallup Poll had just increased that day from four to six points.

Nessen tugged on his open vest and glared at me. "Don't forget you're going to have to eat your book at my press conference the morning after the election." A radio reporter approached Nessen and inquired, "Mr. Carter said if he and Ford come out even tonight, the Vice-Presidential candidates' debate will turn out to have been the most significant of the debates." Nessen turned his back on the reporter and stalked away.

The third Ford-Carter debate was by all standards so boring that the most serious journalists were passing notes and jokes back and forth in the audience and giggling like schoolchildren. Watching Ford furiously take notes, a habit he only mysteriously acquired in the last debate, Curtis Wilkie was amazed at the velocity of Ford's scribbling. "He's not writing, he's coloring!" Wilkie's entire row and the row behind him cracked up. When Ford came to General George Brown's defense, charging that Senator Walter Mondale had accused Brown of not being fit to serve as "Sewer Commissioner," notes flew back and forth scrawled in large letters in programs. "Ford for Sewer Commissioner," or "Is Jerry Brown qualified to be Sewer Commissioner?" As Ford droned on about housing starts, half my row had taken to watching the silent TV monitor on the right side of the auditorium which was running a funky black group, boogying and twanging out what was obviously rock music on electric guitars. "Hey, someone turn up that set," whispered Wilkie.

But in spite of the fact the last debate was as uninspiring as burned eggplant, Carter won hands down.

Why? Instead of looking like he had just stepped off a nineteen-hour flight from Calcutta, run an Afro comb through his hair and tied his cravat in a dark closet, Carter appeared relaxed and well put-together. His hair was shined to a patina and combed into place with surgical care. Carter looked like a young man going to his first Holy Communion.

He got his nervous huffing, puffing and lip-licking over with before the cameras turned on. He tackled the *Playboy* issue head on in his second answer and not only dissipated the issue, but did so with a hefty dose of self-deprecation.

"It [the *Playboy* interview] has been of great concern to me," Carter said with a troubled expression. "I don't really know how to deal with it exactly . . . I would not have given that interview had I to do it all over again." Then he tried out his one-liner that got a better laugh at the Al Smith dinner in New York the night before. "If I should ever decide in the future to discuss my deep Christian beliefs and condemnation and sinfulness, I'll use another forum besides *Playboy*." He followed that with an uppercut to Ford's underhanded campaign tactics. "But I can say this, I'm doing the best I can to get away from that and during the next ten days the American people will not see the Carter campaign running television advertisements and newspaper advertisements based on a personal attack on President Ford's character. I believe the opposite is true with President Ford's campaign."

Carter also proved himself above vitriol when Ford mucked his way through two replies to Jack Nelson of the Los Angeles *Times* about his involvement in the blockage of an early Watergate investigation by Representative Wright Patman's House Banking and Currency Committee. Ford said he did not remember talking to anyone at the White House about cutting off an investigation. Besides, he continued, he had been cleared by two Congressional committees and confirmed by the House and the Senate, which established his innocence beyond all doubt. When Nelson pressed him again on the subject of the White House tapes, which contained conversations between Richard Nixon and staff members about enlisting Ford's help, Ford dodged the question saying that he had answered all the questions during his grilling by the House before he became Vice President, and that he had been given "a clean bill of health." When Carter was asked for his response, he took the high road. "I don't have a response."

Carter let Ford stew in his own juice. For the rest of the debate Ford was labored, halting, dull, and at one point almost juvenile. He not only defended General George Brown, who had called Great Britain's defenses "pathetic," and Israel's army "a burden," but described him as a "great, great man, an outstanding military strategist in the country today." Then he attacked Walter Mondale for saying General Brown "was not qualified to be Sewer Commissioner." From that point on, the field was Carter's.

Members of the Carter staff were drinking beer and celebrating in the press room after the official TV interviews and replies were over. "Everyone is convinced that the debate turned the trick on the uncommitted votes," said Kevin Gorman. "It gave them what they were looking for. I think it cinched the election. Ford just bathed himself in mud. And why in the name of God he ever brought up the Sewer Commissioner, I'll never know. How stupid. Carter was smart to bring up the Mondale-Dole debate and to insinuate Ford chose a hatchet man. Ford's response was so weak. I can't imagine what he was thinking about, he was so stupid."

Stu Eizenstat was finishing a beer and packing up his heavy blue issues books, from which four thousand loose sheets of paper protruded. "We reassured the voters about Jimmy Carter. People needed reassurance and tonight they saw a guy who was deep, substantive, poised, Presidential, a person they felt comfortable with and someone they knew would get the country moving. Yes, the admission of the *Playboy* mistake was our collective idea. We talked about it for a long time. We think it was a relief for a lot of Americans that he said it was a mistake, let's go on. He was at ease and at peace, we did away with any sense of harshness, and yet he was tough on the issues."

"Exactly what the doctor ordered," said Pat Caddell. "I'm glad I'm not in Ford's shoes tonight."

CHAPTER 33

SEEDS OF DEFEAT

WHAT WAS PERCEIVED on the air as victory did not translate to the streets. The Carter campaign was fast losing ground. Atlanta, which served as central headquarters, was now a breeding ground of strife and internal dissension. Too many new faces were now introduced into what had once been a tightly woven fabric of close friends and associates. Furthermore, the staff failed to abandon the technique that proved successful in the limited arenas of the primaries when facing a campaign that had to be conducted simultaneously in all fifty states. Also, Carter as a television performer was entirely different from a street campaigner. He could captivate millions of people in their living rooms through the medium of television just as he had done in person in the primaries when he appeared before small intimate audiences. Somehow Carter on the soapbox speaking to several thousand lost his magical person-to-person presence. He became cold, statistical and difficult to understand. Even those audiences who cheered his arrival were soon turned to stone by the soft-spoken Southerner.

Washington, which had long provided the sinew of previous campaigns, was being ignored or used only for marginal campaign purposes. The advice of the Democratic establishment was not sought and because no one in Carter's headquarters bothered to call on weathered campaign veterans an air of disillusionment and hostility began to permeate the campaign itself.

On a cold and rainy late October afternoon the Averell Harrimans had a little intimate gathering of four hundred. They smudged their muddy feet on Pamela's decorator zigzag carpeting in her peach-colored living room and trudged through the green-and-white-striped tent erected over the boxwoods, and downed gallons of Pamela's homemade caramel ice cream. They came in one of the worst downpours in recent Washington memory, obstensibly to honor Jimmy Carter and Fritz Mondale, the Committee for 51.3 Percent (comprising women all over the country who had aided Carter's campaign) and the Democratic National Committee. But many secretly came to gawk at the real Degas dancer with the disintegrating tutu now incarcerated in a plexiglass cage in one corner of the salon, and to ogle the Monets and Pissaros and other members of the Impressionist School amply sprinkled from room to room. Many of the traditional VIPs who attended the last Harriman Democratic fund raiser were absent. Ted Kennedy, Lloyd Bentsen, Birch Bayh, Hubert Humphrey, Bob Strauss and other superstars were nowhere to be found. And some who were there working for Jimmy Carter had their doubts about Carter and about his election. "I'm working on the transition committee," said one woman, well connected in the Democratic party. "It's just like working with the Nixon bunch. It's very closed."

Said another, in the Washington office, "Fritz is the only one with the organization. It's just superb. Our organization is absolutely terrible. I'm horrified by what I've seen." For example, he said, a high-ranking member of the Atlanta organization had called Carl Yastrzemski, the baseball player, and asked him to campaign for Carter. Yastrzemski said he was going to campaign for Tip O'Neill. The Carter aide had to ask him if Tip O'Neill was Republican or Democrat! When Yastrzemski told him O'Neill was a Democrat, the aide said, "You'd better tell Mr. O'Neill he should get on the Carter bandwagon." Yastrzemski fired back, 'You'd better tell Mr. Carter to get on Tip O'Neill's bandwagon,' and hung up. Now Yastrzemski's going to the Republicans.' "

Many were disgruntled with Atlanta headquarters and furious with Hamilton Jordan and political director Landon Butler for hiring incompetents, failing to tap the best minds in the Democratic party and continuing to run a primary campaign in the middle of a general election.

One high-ranking campaign staff-member complained that the campaign was well run prior to the convention because states were organized individually and organizers did not have to rely on directions from Atlanta. Tim Kraft, for example, had organized Iowa and Pennsylvania on his own, "It didn't matter that there was an Atlanta," the aide said. Kraft specialized in guerrilla warfare, blitzing a state with outside volunteers. But Kraft had been superpromoted from guerrilla to general and his expertise was better suited to the field than to coordinating fifty states. Atlanta as the seat of power was proving to be ineffective, poorly organized and administratively inept. "They hired people off the streets, secretaries, friends, wives and brothers. Stuart Eizenstat is the only one who has an incredibly good campaign staff. He hired high-caliber people from all over the country. There were large numbers of people, lawyers and competent Democrats who would have gladly given three months of their time to go down to Atlanta and help, but they didn't want them. They were concerned about competition. Jordan wanted people they could control. The Jordan bunch are incredibly insecure people who are easily threatened."

Few were making any prediction about the outcome of the campaign. Jayne Coyne, a wealthy Washington Democrat, said she would vote for Ford. A woman journalist said she had just come back across the country and it looked bad for Carter wherever she went. Another woman thought things had gone downhill for Carter since the euphoria of the convention because he peaked too soon.

By the last week of the 1968 Presidential campaign the election had gone the same way. The gap closed between Nixon and Humphrey. Humphrey picked up steam. I remembered mammoth crowds in Long Island and New Jersey screeching for HHH at the top of their lungs. His staggering campaign surged ahead. It looked as if it might go over the top. This October it was Ford who was gaining rapidly on his Democratic opponent, slashing his enormous lead of thirty-three points to ground zero. And in the final days of the campaign, even some of Carter's better moments were marred by poor staff work and television reporting of the disasters rather than the triumphs.

On October 27, a week after the Harriman fund raiser, Jimmy Carter filled the streets of New York with 160,000 people. They flooded past the N.Y.P.D. barricades and spilled onto Fifth Avenue running after the long sleek silver-gray Cadillac where Jimmy and Rosalynn waved from the sun roof, reached out for him calling "Jimmy! Jimmy! Jimmy!"

From the back of a flatbed truck where reporters rode in the twenty-nine-degree cold, I could see myriads of signs: "Greek-Americans for Carter," "Put Jimmy and Rosalynn in the White House," "Peanuts for the Oval Office," "Shalom, Carter," "Ford to City: 'Drop Dead.'" New Yorkers said they would vote for Carter because they wanted something different.

Take Filomena Proccione, a member of the ILGWU Golden Ring Club. "We want a change," said Filomena. "We're tired of the same thing. We've gotten nowhere with the GOP." Filomena usually split her ticket. This time she was voting straight Democratic. But Filomena did not applaud when Jimmy Carter spoke to the crowd of 25,000 at 38th Street and 7th Avenue. She said her hands were cold. Neither did the other fifty or sixty Golden Ringers around her. They said their hands were cold too. But on that same street corner at the same rally for Bobby Kennedy in the early part of 1968 they clapped and screamed and hollered so loud I had to put my hands over my ears.

The other New Yorkers I spoke to along the 7th Avenue barricades said they were voting for Carter too, not because they loved the man, but because he was "a better alternative to Ford."

At the Volunteers-for-Carter rally in the Gold Ballroom of the Statler Hilton Hotel only a few hundred workers appeared. Jerome Rindler, an account executive at WBTB-TV and a public speaker for Carter, explained that the "thousands and thousands" of Carter workers were all "at their jobs," or "out on the street handing out pamphlets," adding, "Besides, they've seen Carter before." But dedicated volunteers want to be thanked by the man they've slaved for, and want to bask in his presence, hoping he'll recognize them, or offer them a job.

Worse, although Carter's top advance team, headed by Richard De St. Phalle out of Atlanta, had been brought in to make the New York rally a success, it was in many ways a disaster.

Advance backfired. At the airport, television cameramen and producers who wanted to get to the rally site ahead of Carter to set up equipment were told to travel on Bus Four. But Bus Four turned out to be a staff bus, and the staff refused to let the TV types board.

En route to the city Jim King told the writing press to board a flatbed truck if they wished to follow the candidate in his motorcade down Fifth Avenue to the Garment Center rally. ("It has a fresh load of sheep shit that has just been scraped off it," King said, "and some is left, but just ignore it.") King tried to joke when he admitted that a one hundred square-foot flatbed truck would have to accommodate over one hundred members of the press. "We'll all undress and be sprayed with a light blue lubricant and we'll all slide right in together." But it was no laughing matter. No one could move, much less make a note or even turn around to look for the candidate. To complicate matters, the candidate's car was at least seven cars behind. No one could see whether New Yorkers were tossing rose petals or spitballs at him. The camera truck was so far ahead of Carter the networks could not film most of Carter's parade. ABC's camera crew finally jumped off and ran alongside of the candidate's car.

It did not help when we pounded on the cab of the truck that was driving at breakneck speed down Fifth Avenue. Nor did our angry shouts. Even Carter staff orders were ignored. The Secret Service commanded police to pay no attention. When Jody Powell leaped onto the press truck's running board and told the driver to slow down, he was yanked off by police and shoved into the crowd. Blue eyes flashing anger, Powell stepped in front of the truck, slowing it down to a two-miles-per-hour crawl, but the police nabbed him again. "That agent will end up transferred to Siberia," Curtis Wilkie yelled. Relentless, Powell climbed back on the truck to argue with the driver. This time, a plainclothesman hit him on the back of the head. "If he slows that truck again, I'll arrest him," he said.

When we arrived at the rally site, the driver refused to stop and allow reporters to descend. The truck careened around the corner well out of sight of the candidate's platform. When it finally came to a stop, halfway up a side street, reporters began to step down, but the truck suddenly lurched forward again, spilling half a dozen journalists onto the street. A shouting match ensued with a large member of the local fuzz who grabbed one reporter by the hair and accused him of kicking him in the shins. Regardless of a dozen press passes dangling from our necks, we were barricaded by a human phalanx of two-hundred-pound police and held more than forty feet away from the speaker's platform.

A major brouhaha developed between the Carter staff and network correspondents because the "MULT" box that allows TV and radio men to plug into a central sound system and record the candidate's voice never arrived on the scene, so TV correspondents had plenty of pictures of Carter with moving lips but no sound. Carter's finest hour in New York hardly received the coverage it merited.

At 3:15 that afternoon of October 27, we flew to Pittsburgh. Pittsburgh was not as cold as New York when we landed, but the reception was. No large crowd and no huzzahs from the group of several hundred at the airport. Teddy White, who was riding the bus for a few days, had little good to say about the cooperation he had had from the Carter staff. He explained that this simply meant the emotionalism of the Sixties had dissipated, that people had become more cautious. But City Councilman Jim Lally said the situation for Carter in Pittsburgh had deteriorated to a very serious stage. "I think he's going to lose."

Advance had been a disaster again. Carter had lost his appeal. Even Lally's eighty-seven-year-old mother, a staunch Democrat all her life, was switching to Ford. "She doesn't trust Carter." City Councilman Dick Caliguiri said he was shocked the other day when he received a desperate call from a Carter staff worker asking for last minute help. "He didn't even know who to call. He was calling me when he should have been calling the county chairman. The problem is they brought this guy in from Connecticut to coordinate things and he doesn't know who's who."

"They've breached all protocol," said Lally. "The Carter staff has completely ignored the local political establishment. They think they can run it alone, but they can't. I'll tell you. The only reason we're voting for him is he's a Democrat."

Norval Reece, special assistant to Pennsylvania Governor Milton Shapp, a long-time political operative and a close friend of Jody Powell and Hamilton Jordan, had to fly to Atlanta to "throw some chairs." He was incensed with the way the Pennsylvania campaign was being run.

"I spent the summer in Cape Cod," Reece said, "and when I came back I thought Carter would be all set up here, ready to come out shooting blazing pistols. Instead, nothing was done, and when he came out, he was shooting water pistols instead. When he came here in September, no one even knew his schedule. His advance men and coordinators didn't touch base with anyone. I didn't even know it until I read it in the paper the day before he came. Jim Mahoney, the head of the state AFL-CIO, didn't know he was going to a Scranton plant gate till the day after he had been there. Mahoney could have turned out hundreds. As it was, Carter only shook ten hands. Some county chairmen didn't even know he was coming into their areas at all. The Carter people didn't know how to handle Philadelphia Mayor Frank Rizzo either. I told Ham, you just handle him the same way you handle Daley. You can afford to be on the same platform with him if you've got a Bill Green and a Milton Shapp, but they were schizophrenic about it." (As it turned out Carter advance invited leaders of the Recall-Rizzo movement to appear on the platform with Carter at a Philadelphia rally the week before the election. Rizzo refused to come. He met with Carter privately on his airplane.)

Reece continued, "When you fight tough primaries, the political rule is you keep the primary theme in general and broaden your campaign to include the people who you beat in the primary. Carter did the opposite. He broadened his theme and narrowed his organizational structure. He also started sounding like Hubert Humphrey, talking about the great traditions of FDR. On the DNC whistlestop train trip I went to Jody and said, 'For God's sake, get him off that. He's not in the tradition of FDR. People like him because they think he's different.' He finally went back to the old primary theme that he was good at, but it may be too late."

Back at the Pittsburgh Hilton around eleven P.M., I found TV advisor Al Vecchione alone and dejected sitting on a couch sipping a beer. It was ironic, Vecchione said, that in a post-Watergate year, with a President appointed by Richard Nixon, that the American people were equating not Gerald Ford but rather Jimmy Carter with Nixon.

"The problem is the perception of the man. People don't see Carter for what he is. At close range, he's great, but we haven't been able to package him right. He comes across to so many as strange. He's so complex. It's difficult to project him the way he really is. So people don't trust him. Another irony in a year in which people are fed up with Republicanism and all it's stood for, is that they don't want a change. Ford is benefiting from all the ironies. You know something? If you asked me tonight where we stand, I wouldn't be able to tell you. It's so damn close. Just five or six points!"

That moment a reporter walked by and told Vecchione the bad news. The national polls showed Ford and Carter down to 1 to 2 percent points apart. Vecchione shrugged, took another long swallow of beer and talked about the new job he would start with Public TV in two weeks.

On the eleven o'clock news, pollsters Harris and Gallup, speaking at the Press Club in Washington, called the election "too close to call." Said Harris: "If Jimmy Carter loses, he will have booted by far the biggest lead in modern political history."

The news was preceded by a five-minute "man on the street" Ford commercial. It showed average Americans saying they liked Ford because there was trust in the White House again, and things were getting better, because he was a good and decent man. Then a forceful Ford appeared on the screen telling an audience that having the trust of the American People meant "earning it." The commercial cut to shots of a friendly Ford talking with old people and down on his knees speaking with groups of children. It also capitalized on Ford's finest hour—his outstanding speech at the convention in Kansas City. It was an excellent commercial. Jimmy Carter did not have one on the air.

CHAPTER 34

INTO THE STRETCH:
FORD CATCHES ON

THE NEXT MORNING CARTER STOPPED to chew out CBS reporter Ed Bradley for his report on the New York Garment Center rally. Bradley had described the turnout on the evening news the night before as mostly a "labor crowd" made up of union members from the Seafarers Organization and the ILGWU, and cited staff snafus for bollixing the visit. "I thought it was crummy," Carter snapped and stormed off. Other staffers were testy. Twenty-six-year-old Rex Granum, a Carter aide, charged at an older journalist like a red-eyed bull for appearing a second day on Peanut One without his permission. Pointing his finger threateningly at the reporter Granum growled, "Don't you tell me not to be mad! I'll be good and goddamn mad if I want." Jim King, the ever friendly advance man, shrugged. "He's just tired."

Carter's rally at a park in Erie, Pennsylvania, that morning of October 28, although well attended by some three thousand, was populated with lookers, not leapers, watchers, not screamers, and some said it was the worst speech they had heard Carter give so far.

Paul Montagne, a stubble-bearded man in overalls and a plaid shirt, was one of many silent observers. "Yeah," said Montagne, a builder, "I think he's pretty good. I guess it's time for a change anyhow." Later that morning, in Cleveland, 10,000 turned out for Carter at the intersection of 6th and Euclid. A small crowd by Presidential standards of the past and many of them had been bused in by labor. Back in 1972 more than 100,000 appeared to hear Richard Nixon speak at Terminal Square in downtown Cleveland.

Stu Eizenstat was cautiously optimistic as we walked to the plane.

"I'm encouraged by what I hear from Pat Caddell. He tells me we're ahead in California." Greg Schneiders echoed the same thing. But a field poll the next day showed Carter six points behind. And Jody Powell unloaded a batch of Caddell findings at an impromptu press conference at the airport, all of which the Ford staff and the latest field poll soon disputed.

"It's a close race in Ohio," Carter's press secretary said. "We're up just a couple of points. In fact, using a very tight screen, we're in a dead heat." Caddell's polls showed Carter 47, Ford 44 in Ohio. In a just-completed poll in California, Carter was ahead 48 percent to 43 percent "a conservative estimate." And according to a variety of news polls, Ford and Carter were dead even in Michigan, Carter was 4 percent ahead in Texas, and had gone from minus two to plus five in St. Louis and from minus two to plus three in a Portland, Oregon, poll. Powell grinned. "What I take to be speculation and rumor that is rampant on the plane is that we are sliding in the polls." One foot was planted on a chair, a filter cigarette protruded from his mouth. "It is my avowed and express goal for my friends in the press to avoid embarrassing themselves in the last few days."

When I linked up with the Ford campaign in Cleveland, Presidential aides were singing the same tune as Carter. Driving in from a rally on board the press bus, White House aide John Carlson, parroting Chief of Staff Richard Cheney, told me Ford was ahead in California "by a very slim margin," ahead in Michigan, only two points behind in Texas, even in Ohio.

"We're not giving out any figures," said Carlson. "The point is we've got two hundred seventy-one electoral votes plus. We're winning because the more you get to know Carter, the more you don't know about him. But Jerry Ford is a known quantity. We've also been careful to save our media money to the end, so we now have statewide shows that are awfully effective. Basically, we've just got the better candidate. Carter is coming across as very harsh, very liberal, and backing off the statement he made the other day about a tax reduction in his first year really hurt. You can't say you're going to lower taxes but increase spending. People also know that closing loopholes on the rich alone does nothing, just raises a few billion dollars, and if you raise taxes on business, they just pass the cost on to the consumer. Carter was a fresh face in the beginning, but now people are wise to him. The momentum and the enthusiasm are on our side."

Why the tide seemed to clearly be running with Ford perplexed even veteran campaign reporters. "This is the closest election I ever covered," said columnist Charles Bartlett. Bob Novak, of the Evans-Novak team, claimed to have polled a bellwether precinct in Ohio that always gives an accurate indication of voter preference, and found the poll score fifty-fifty, a dead heat.

"We're all going strictly by vibes," said Helen Thomas of U.P.I. "I have to keep calling in to my office to ask them who's winning." Bob Pierpoint of CBS, and a group of reporters gathered on the press bus the Friday before the election, puzzling over the outcome. "Ford might win the popular vote and lose the electoral vote, but then, it could be the other way around."

The Ford staff seemed supremely confident and relaxed.

New York Times man James Naughton had played a prank on President Ford by appearing at a press conference dressed in an elaborate chicken head, so when the traveling Ford party arrived in Cleveland, a few jokesters, under the aegis of deputy press secretary Bill Greener, a jovial, cherubic-faced man with a whiskey baritone, decided to rent a live rust-colored rooster and place it in Naughton's room. They also placed raw egg under his pillow, on the towels, in the ashtrays. Naughton sensed what was going on, found the rooster and while Greener was out to dinner, transferred the rooster to Greener's room. When Greener discovered the rooster, he shooed it out into the hall and told the house detective who inquired about the ownership of the bird, now hiding behind the Coke machine, that it belonged to Mr. Naughton. Eventually the rooster ended up at a happy new farm with a farmer who raised organically grown chickens.

The incumbency was still helping Ford. Voters were impressed by Air Force One for instance, a giant, sleek silver-and-sky-blue 707, that looked transparent in the morning sun as it landed, like some powerful spirit, floating onto the runway. Conversely, its takeoff into the piercing blue sky with its roar and thrust, carrying the world's most powerful executive in its belly, was in the words of one Rockwell mechanic, "almost better than sex."

In Cleveland, watching Ford round the corner at the intersection of Fleet Avenue and 53rd Street in the long, sleek Presidential limousine surrounded by a battalion of squad cars with flashing lights seemed to stun onlookers. "It's the thrill of a lifetime," said one woman who had brought her children to see the President.

And there seemed to be a genuine excitement about Ford not seen for Carter, and more significant, an outpouring of crossovers. Standing in the crowd at East 53rd Street next to Karlin Hall in an ethnic section of Cleveland, waving a "Ukrainian for Ford" placard (which had been handed to her by a Ford advance man), Mary Ann Bubena, a Democrat, called Carter "spooky" and Ford "more realistic." Along with her parents, she was voting Republican for the first time in her life. They were angered and upset by the *Playboy* interview, which they found "inappropriate for a candidate." Sue Spillman, twenty-three, another Democrat, had voted for McGovern in 1972, but this time she liked Ford's "honesty and credibility." Sophie Sarnowski, a fifty-year-old Polish "disgruntled Democrat," was voting for Ford "because Carter doesn't stand for anything. If he were my next-door neighbor, I wouldn't vote for him." And even twelve-year-old Chris Kovalcik, a student at St. John's Nepomucene School, disliked Carter because he's "sneaky, a nut, and he's got too many plans for the U. S., but Ford just says what he believes."

Chris's seventh-grade class had had a mock election the previous day. Thirty-five class members voted and Ford won twenty to fifteen. The eighth grade was voting for Ford too, Chris reported, and a student from the Maple School in North Olmstead, Ohio, interjected that her school had voted two hundred fifty for Ford, fifty for Carter.

Encapsulated on the Ford plane reporters were convinced Ford had the edge. Ford aides were secretly gloating over Jimmy Carter's latest gaffe. Carter was having to back away from a statement he made during an interview on a Pittsburgh radio station that a tax cut was "inevitable" during his first term as President. The next day at a Cleveland rally, he was saying maybe, with a good rate of economic growth and lowered inflation and unemployment, there could be some tax cuts. "But I am very careful not to promise that for sure," he waffled. (Greg Schneiders, Carter's closest aide, had told me in an interview the week before to expect a tax cut during Carter's first year.) Stu Eizenstat, Carter's issues director, explained to me that Carter backed off the statement, because "the press was interpreting it as a last-minute political pitch, so we advised him not to use the word 'promise.' " But incalculable damage was already done.

"You heard what Carter said about taxes," said Bob Peck, an airplane mechanic and father of two who planned to vote for Ford. "He said he was going to give a tax cut, then he said maybe, then he said no. You want to vote for a man like that? I'm hostile about a lot of things this year, but I'm more hostile when you don't know when to believe somebody. I'm voting for Ford. At least he's trying."

In Milwaukee, Presidential press secretary Ron Nessen, wearing a "Polish-Americans for Ford" button on his red sweater set, strutted casually backstage at Mecca Auditorium while Ford addressed a warmly receptive audience of some four thousand teachers. "Why are we going to win?" Nessen said. "I just sense it. It's really come down to the character of the two men, there's no really big issue moving people to vote one way or another. It's which man the voters feel more comfortable with. People are uneasy about Carter. He's raised a lot of doubt in their minds about his essential character. Also, we're better organized and we've held to our strategy." That strategy, designed in Vail with a new campaign manager, Jim Baker, was to win the convention, pick a good Vice-Presidential candidate, deliver an exceptional acceptance speech, remain in the Rose Garden and appear Presidential, and to combine an all-out personal and media blitz during the last ten days of the campaign.

And even the press admitted the Ford media blitz was having an effect. Ford had saturated the air waves with $10 million worth of advertising.

While Ford stepped up his cross-country tour to hit over one hundred cities and travel over 100,000 miles, "The Joe and Jerry Show" was playing to TV audiences. Joe was Joe Garagiola, who used to be on the *Today* show and used to play baseball for the St. Louis Cardinals, then the Pittsburgh Pirates, then the Chicago Cubs and then the New York Giants. His lifetime batting average was .257. When he was traded to the Giants, his friend Stan Musial was reported to have said, "Why don't you quit?" When he did he embarked on a successful radio announcing career and finally joined the *Today* show. Jerry, of course, was Jerry Ford. Night after night Garagiola and Ford were on TV stations in six different states appearing on a paid political commercial that cost $400,000.

Garagiola played the part of the guy in the bar, confused by all the conflicting things he had heard from the Presidential candidates. "Carter makes a lot of claims, and so do you, Mr. President, and it's hard to know who to believe. Why you?"

This gave Ford the cue to spell out the differences between himself and Jimmy Carter in the economy, national defense, foreign policy.

Gradually Garagiola would become convinced that Ford had the right answers. Consternation cleared from Garagiola's brow as the light dawned. His expression registered, "Oh, I get it." The difficult had become simple.

The first TV show was presented in California, the next in Illinois, then Pennsylvania, New York, Ohio and Texas.

This is the way it worked. When Mr. Ford came into a big state in the morning, his arrival was filmed and so were his campaign appearances up until mid-afternoon. Then he, Garagiola and prominent Republican figures repaired to a local television studio where they puzzled over the issues in a *Today*-showlike setting, with Garagiola pitching the questions.

I caught the Ohio "Joe and Jerry Show." Garagiola's face came on screen first. "Hi. I'm Joe Garagiola in Ohio and I've been on the campaign trail today with the President and I want to share some of the moments with you."

At that point a film clip of Betty Ford appeared on camera, gracefully descending the steps of her airplane to receive flowers from a small child. Betty was followed by Mike Ford, the President's minister son, munching hamburgers at McDonald's, followed by a zillion balloons pelting the sky as Ford shook hands with adoring crowds and bands played the "Michigan Fight" song.

Cut to the studio. "Gee, Mr. President, my hands used to get pretty sore playing baseball, but what happens to yours? They must get pretty banged up shaking all those hands!" (Ford is warm, friendly, smiling.) "No, Joe. I really enjoy shaking hands with the people."

The rest was a boring, dreadfully long segment on the difference between Ford and Carter, with Ford telling a puppy-dog Garagiola how *he* had experience with serious problems, that *he* sat down across the table from Soviet Party Leader Brezhnev "and so many others," how we are coming out of a recession, how inflation has gone from twelve percent to six percent, how crime "makes a lot of elderly people unhappy," and how he was going to make sure the crooks got caught, and "We're going to put 'em behind bars."

As I listened to the President in St. Louis, his voice was so gravelly that he sounded like Nelson Rockefeller, but his message was still effective. "Confidence has been restored in the Oval Office," he told seven thousand fans packed into a block-square park in the shadow of the impressive 638-foot stainless-steel Archway to the West. "Quick fixes and phony programs are not the solution . . . I promise you that President Jerry Ford will not be satisfied until every person that wants a job has a job. . . . Not a single young American is fighting or dying on foreign soil. We're at peace because America is number one militarily. . . . One day my opponent says he might give a tax reduction. The next day he changes his mind, but you can count on President Ford to reduce taxes in 1977."

"FOUR MORE YEARS . . . FOUR MORE YEARS!" the crowd responded, chanting the Nixon slogan for 1972.

But Ford was also plagued with last-minute problems. The week before the election it was discovered that the producer of his highly successful television ads was also the producer of hard-core pornographic films. He was fired immediately.

Rejoining Carter in St. Louis it was apparent that when push came to shove the momentum was shifting to him. Carter the underdog seemed to bring out the Democrats and the enthusiasm. The more Carter slipped in the polls the more determined Democrats grew to regain the White House and the bigger the crowds became.

In St. Louis, for example, which Ford and Carter both visited the same day, a crowd of seven thousand turned out to see the President, but only a few hours later, twenty thousand stood in the damp cold at the Northwest Shopping Plaza, one of the largest shopping centers in the country, to cheer Carter. It was the most upbeat crowd I had seen for Carter since the day before he won the last primary, but twice as large and loud. Carter sensed the enthusiasm, playfully batting at balloons that floated near him on the podium, and laughing heartily at his own sudden abandon. "WE WANT CARTER . . . WE WANT CARTER," the crowd roared. "Ya got me," smiled Carter.

"I lust for that man," said Emma Naucher from Alton, Illinois. Said another woman, "He's the greatest religious person. Just what we need."

Two thousand people waited two hours in the freezing rain at the airport in Tulsa, Oklahoma. Fifteen thousand greeted him in the seventy-four-degree heat of McAllen, Texas, later that afternoon, and fifty thousand jammed the streets of New Orleans Vieux Carré for an old-fashioned Mardi Gras parade down Bourbon Street. The New Orleans stop was most impressive in a state which the morning St. Louis *Post-Dispatch* reported leaning toward Ford.

Here the press became part of the Mardi Gras-type parade. Led by Jim King and his trusty bullhorn, members of the fourth estate donned colorful Mardi Gras beaded necklaces and marched down Rue Royale in front of Carter's limousine and behind King. "Please try and keep your ranks," said King. "The National Guard recruiters are up ahead. They'll pick the best. . . . Applause for the national press please. . . . There is a large truck bearing down on your rear flank." Turning to the mobs lining the streets, King announced, "These are the direct descendants of those who were here with the British Army."

If Carter was behind in the polls, it was not obvious here. The wrought-iron balconies of Bourbon Street were jammed with tourists toasting Carter with Dixie beer, and waving to him and his Rosalynn as they passed. The Olympia brass band added to the carnival gaiety and Carter seemed in high spirits when he saw Cathedral Square packed with signs that read: "Don't Sweat the Weirdos Jimmy, We Love Ya!" "The Forgotten Americans Support Jimmy Carter." "The Houma Indian Tribe Supports Carter for President." In the spirit of Mardi Gras, Carter scooped up handfuls of silver doubloons and heaved them into the crowds, went back for more and pitched them up toward people in the balcony, stepped to the rear of the platform and tossed some more, smiling and laughing.

Rosalynn was on hand to make her forceful stump speech on Carter's behalf and today it seemed more effective than ever. They cheered her when she told them, "Jimmy's background is so important. He's a farmer and I think we need a President who knows what it is to work for a living." Carter raised his fist in the "Right On" sign.

There were rebel yells for Carter, and a girl climbed up on her boyfriend's shoulders waving a placard that read, "I lust after Jimmy Carter for President." Today Carter was even enunciating and speaking more slowly. At an earlier meeting the staff told him to reduce his rapid-fire staccato pace. He had heeded their advice.

The town of McAllen, Texas, a lush tropical green oasis in the Rio Grande Valley near the Mexican border, is known for its citrus and vegetable industry. McAllen turned out its overwhelmingly Mexican-American population for Carter at 4:40 P.M. Mariachis were playing, the sky was a pointilistic arrangement of colored balloons, and the Latin spirit spilled over in earsplitting chants of "Viva Carter" and "Arriba con Carter."

Carter had had problems in Texas ever since he had called Lyndon Johnson a liar in his *Playboy* interview. He took pains to tell reporters at an impromptu airport press conference that he thought the most serious mistake of his campaign was "making a statement that distorted completely my feelings about President Johnson. And if I had everything to do over again, that's the one thing I would be much more careful about."

When he spotted Luci Baines Johnson Nugent awaiting his arrival at the airport with Robert Strauss, Carter also made certain to plant a huge meaningful kiss on her left cheek. Luci was not about to let bygones be bygones. She made it plain to me that all was not forgiven. "I'm a veteran of the political process, but it [the *Playboy* interview] was very difficult for me. However I've learned you have to look at the overall picture. What's important for the needs of the people and the Democratic party." Lady Bird was conveniently absent. "She's on a little vacation in Mexico," said Luci.

And at a rally of some twelve thousand under a crescent moon by the historic Alamo, Luci went to some trouble to stick it to Carter, opening her remarks by acknowledging "my good friend Governor Dolph Briscoe . . . and Governor Carter." Then she launched into a monologue on the greatness of Lyndon Johnson. Luci was polite but frosty to Carter, and told me later that she wished to impress the Georgia Governor with the fact that LBJ was a bigger man than he. "There were circumstances in the state that were very difficult and made it necessary for me to speak out. It was not the first time that Lyndon Johnson came under attack, but it has been understandably difficult for me and those of us who loved Lyndon Johnson. He was a great man who created a great many social programs and made life better for other people."

"There are sometimes disappointments and sometimes disagreements within the party," she told a rally of twenty thousand Texans at a chicken box lunch at Tarrant County Convention Center. "But Lyndon Johnson supported the Democratic party to the day he died," she said, turning and glaring at Carter. "I remember the last thing he told me, 'The Democratic Party is more important than Harry Truman, or JFK or even Lyndon Johnson.' "

She told the audience that her mother, on an absentee ballot, had voted the straight Democratic ticket, but without mentioning Jimmy Carter's name. When she sat down next to the Democratic nominee, she turned her back to him and faced the podium. Carter squirmed, and yet after he had addressed the audience he called to her, "Luci," and she consented to join him as they waved from the lectern. Finally she kissed him good-bye.

Saturday was, in the words of Carter aide Phil Zeilman, "The most perfect day I've seen so far." "Three good rallies," said Rex Granum. And in spite of Sunday morning's front-page story in the Dallas *Times Herald* that showed Ford to have narrowed Carter's lead even further no one on the staff seemed more sanguine.

CHAPTER 35

IN HIS GUT HE KNEW HE'D WON

CARTER'S LAST CAMPAIGN NIGHT with the press was a far cry from the endings of campaigns past. In 1972, George McGovern's traveling press had thrown an anniversary party for the candidate and his wife, Eleanor, on the top floor of the Biltmore in New York the week before the election. Dick Stout of *Newsweek*, the emcee, introduced Adam Clymer and David Murray of the Chicago *Sun-Times* and Jim Naughton of *The New York Times*, who huddled around the podium at the front of the room and read funny imaginary leads that dealt with a McGovern victory. They also presented the McGoverns with a Tiffany silver bowl, for which everyone on the two planes had chipped in. It was inscribed with the words McGovern had called out to the crew of his shot-up bomber in World War II. "Resume your stations. We're bringing her home."

There were no inscribed silver bowls for Carter. And no press party planned in his honor. United Airlines, grateful for the millions it had made from the Carter charter, threw the only farewell fiesta on board Peanut One en route from California to Albany, Georgia, via Flint, Michigan, where Carter had his last rally. United laid on a chef, complete with white hat and purple *ruban*, formal menus, and a five-course dinner featuring giant New Orleans prawns, gazpacho soup, filet mignon and chocolate mousse, not to mention champagne and all the free booze one could guzzle. They also brought an electric organ on board.

Jim Wooten of *The New York Times*, an accomplished pianist, volunteered his services and spent over two hours at the keyboard, while Curtis Wilkie of the Boston *Globe*, Stan Cloud of *Time*, Carl

Leubsdorf of A.P., Betty Ann Bowser of CBS, Marty Schram of *Newsday,* Jim King, Eleanor Randolph of the *Chicago Tribune* and about twenty others gathered round for choruses from *Carousel* and ballads from the Thirties, Forties, Fifties and Sixties. Jody Powell requested "Goodnight Irene" and Baptist hymns. He knew all the words. In the midst of the singing, Carter unexpectedly appeared. He said not a word, but climbed up on the back of a seat and listened intently for the better part of the two hours, watching the reporters who, unlike him, knew the lyrics to most of the songs. He did join in the singing of "We Shall Overcome," and "The Battle Hymn of the Republic" and he seemed to get a special pleasure out of the oldie but goldie, "You Are My Sunshine." He wanted to hear it again. "Can you play it slower?" he called to Wooten, who had played it at regular four-quarter time. Carter wanted a more romantic version, which Wooten rendered.

For all the time he remained perched on his seat, there was little interaction between Carter and his traveling companions. He acted a bit awkward to be sharing in the festivities of a crowd he felt had contributed to his declining public popularity.

The only fun and games of the evening was the reading of the results of a survey that had been passed out to reporters asking them to name the worst hotel in their ten months of travel, the worst and the best Secret Service agent, the worst police department, most obnoxious person, best softball player, and so forth. There were twenty-six categories in all which jolly Jim King turned into a mini-Academy Awards, that had Carter convulsed with laughter.

"O.K." King began—"Best softball player. Ah! You all remember the softball field, the gnats, the cuts, the scrapes and sprains. Nominees—Rick Kaplan, Jimmy Carter, Billy Carter, Sam Donaldson and Carl Leubsdorf. The winner: Billy Carter." "I'll drink to that." Jimmy Carter laughed.

"Now we come to a category that will be close to all of you. *Women's Wear Daily* is waiting breathlessly for our landing. The Best Dressed! Nominees are—Ed Bradley; Curtis Wilkie—every twenty-third day; Sam Donaldson—the only man who sleeps in a hanger; Jim King as a bag of galoshes."

The winner was Ed Bradley, the black CBS correspondent whose clothes are custom-made and who can look elegant in a blizzard. The next category, King said, required "athletic prowess, coordination and courage tied in with certain fleetness of foot or wit." The Best Jump Into a Moving Vehicle! The winner was network cameraman Bob Sheehcy whose foot was broken when the pool car ran over it as he was trying to leap into it.

King continued, "The Best Drunk and Most Memorable Scene": Sam Donaldson won the award for biting a girl in an unsober moment.

Next category was: The Worst Single Event of the Campaign. "There were one hundred and six nominees," said King. "We cut it down to five. The nominees: New York Garment District—One hundred and sixty thousand people suffered through this one! Scranton—we all remember Scranton! Some said Campaign '76, others said, West New York and the New Jersey walk, and finally, Rochester. Let us look quickly around. Stan Cloud [*Time* magazine] could probably read this better than anyone in America, having done more worst events in his magazine than any other person in the place." The winner: Scranton, where the press found themselves in hotel rooms with hot and cold running rust, where advance failed to build a crowd for Carter at a plant gate and he only got to shake ten hands, and where he attended a round-table discussion at which his advance person forgot to provide microphones so the press could hear.

The next award was for The Worst Hotel. The press was clamoring to change their ballot to include the El Mirador Hotel where we had slept the night before. The rooms had either 110° heat or NONE at all and the showers spouted ice water. "Now wait a minute," said King. "We're not going to have a recount. Remember the JFK International Hotel with sewer gas? Or the Scranton Hilton where they screamed and had an elevator run by mice? Or the Biltmore Towers in Dayton, Ohio? And then Dearborn, Michigan, where we stood on the green and didn't know whether to cry or riot? And then the place we just left where everyone who took a shower ended up with goosebumps on their feet?" The winner: Biltmore Towers, Dayton.

Carter laughed at most of the awards, then added his own at the end. "I just hope the worst day of the campaign is not tomorrow."

Carter stayed for the singing of "Auld Lang Syne" and "Happy Days are Here Again" until the plane landed. Then he left as he had come, quietly and unnoticed. Wooten never did play "Hail to the Chief."

The last few days of the campaign were plagued by two sticky problems that had Jody Powell smoking more Kents than usual,

and most of the staff avoiding the press. Not only did the Gallup
Poll find Ford in the lead for the first time during the campaign,
but his one-point advantage was dramatic. Gerald Ford had more
than come from behind. He had reduced Carter's lead, the largest
in the history of Presidential politics, to ashes. Besides, only two
Presidents in history had ever lost the popular vote and won the
Electoral College, one *New York Times* man was saying, so if Carter
were behind in the popular vote now, it was curtains. And at the
coffee-and-Danish table in the press room of the El Mirador Hotel
in Sacramento, a reporter who heard that the title of this book
was *How Jimmy Won,* just threw back his head and laughed hys-
terically. "You're going to have to change a three-letter word to a
four-letter word—L-O-S-T." He guffawed.

To complicate the disastrous Carter slide, a problem developed
in Plains when a black minister named Clennon King from Americus, Georgia, decided to ask for membership in the Plains Baptist
Church, and was denied by the deacons, who decided to suspend
all Sunday services rather than admit King. King, it just so happened, was not only a rabble-rouser from the past, but a Republican
to boot, and the brother of a man who had once opposed Carter in
his race for the Governorship. Politically motivated perhaps, yet the
incident pointed up the segregated nature of Carter's own church,
and Carter, in spite of the suggestions and urgings of black leaders
such as Coretta King, refused to withdraw his membership in protest.
To make matters worse, when the Reverend Bruce Edwards held a
press conference in Plains to disavow the tactics of the deacons and
the sinful nature of the 1965 resolution barring Negroes, he told
reporters that the wording of the original resolution (which Carter
opposed) had banned "niggers and civil rights agitators."

The words hit the air with the percussion of a hydrogen bomb,
and the incident played the front page of almost every major newspaper. All three networks carried it on the morning and evening
news.

Carter was forced to devote his last press conference of the entire
campaign to that one subject alone. He was "very sad" about it,
he said. But he would not resign from the Plains Baptist Church.
"I can't quit my lifetime of worship . . . I'll do all I can to eliminate the last vestige of discrimination . . . but I'm not going to
resign from the human race because it discriminates. My best opportunity is to stay in the church and try to change its attitude."

It would be a different story if it were a country club that discriminated. Then he would resign. (Carter had belonged to an all-white country club in Americus for over ten years, but dropped out when he was elected Governor.)

Speechwriter Pat Anderson tapped his fingers on his yellow pad. "Well, we're ending this campaign just like we began, in trouble." Jody Powell and Greg Schneiders kept their cool. "We've been through this before."

Jimmy Carter ended twenty-two months of campaigning deep in the heart of his opponent Gerald Ford's home state, Flint, Michigan, on a serious, somber note. He spoke before an audience of ten thousand cheering fans who had been revved to the point of frenzy by his running mate Walter Mondale. But after a three-hour-and-forty-five-minute flight on Peanut One from California and a long campaign day, Carter poured ice water on a hot audience with his stock campaign speech.

On the plane en route to Flint from Los Angeles, the press corps had hoped Carter would appear for a few philosophic thoughts on the campaign. He did, briefly. But he strode purposefully, brushing past reporters standing in the aisle toward the CBS seats to inquire after John Smith, a network cameraman who had filmed Carter for the past two years and had been clobbered by a Secret Serviceman when he attempted to enter a pool area. When one reporter wandered back to where Carter was standing, he interpreted the newsman's presence as an attempt to overhear his conversation or to begin one, and he vamoosed. Before Carter reached his first-class compartment, where he remained in isolation for the remainder of the flight, he paused to chat with Hal Gulliver of the Atlanta *Constitution,* and his seatmate, Dick Lerner of U.P.I. He perched on the edge of a chair, leaned over the back of it, arms folded, and talked about the campaign. For a moment he seemed serenely confident, smiling and laughing.

It had been a good campaign, he said. He was not tired. "I feel good." And he was confident of victory. "My gut feeling is that I'm going to win." Carter still felt plagued by the *Playboy* article. He had called it his most serious mistake twice during the past forty-eight hours. He said he was going to try to retrieve the tape of the interview. "I can't believe I ever linked Richard Nixon and LBJ in the same tone of voice . . . it was just a complete lapse of mind." He wanted to listen to the tape of the interview because he was certain his tone of voice must have been less harsh when he mentioned LBJ.

He spoke of Eugene McCarthy. "You just can't sit back and be cute for twenty months. The system is there. You can make the choice not to go by the system and bitch about it or you can go by the system and win. I didn't get twenty-one million dollars for nothing."

As for his spectacular plunge in the polls, Carter said, "People didn't know me," and he also blamed Ford's negative portrayal of him.

One of the reasons he was glad the campaign had ended was the "tedium," having to repeat the same thing day after day. "I'm glad it's over," he said.

PART

IX

FINAL
VICTORY

CHAPTER 36

THE ELECTION

ELECTION MORNING, November 2, was biting cold and clear. The blue skies of Plains, Georgia, were brilliantly dappled by orange and gold leaves. It was, as Carter's best friend John Pope put it, "A good day to win an election."

Carter and his traveling party had arrived in Plains at three A.M., but the Georgia peanut farmer wanted to vote early. At 7:10 A.M. Jimmy Carter arrived at the polls with Rosalynn. He was wearing a brown open-collared shirt, tan sweater and khaki pants. "Where's Chip?" he asked someone in the crowd of about one hundred newsmen and friends. They had come to see him cast his ballot through the open door of a concrete block structure set on the highway connecting Plains and Americus. Chip and his wife, Caron, were already in line to vote, behind a group of black women, many of them toothless and in rags. Chip was the first of the Carters to cast a ballot. His wife took an unusually long time behind the charcoal-gray curtain of the metal voting machine and when she emerged Jimmy Carter gave a whoop. "Yea. Hooray. Here she comes." Carter voted at 7:29 A.M. He spent five minutes in the booth.

Seemingly relaxed, except for biting one fingernail, Carter talked with Jimmie Wallace and Tellis Jackson, two black laborers. "Jimmie and I used to plow a mule together," he said.

Rosalynn appeared at the door when she finished voting. How did she feel knowing that her husband might be elected President in a few hours? "It's something I've waited for a long time and worked for. It's been a great experience. I would not have missed it for anything. It was long and it was hard work but I really think Jimmy's going to be President." Now she was going to go home, get Amy off to school and then put her suitcase in the attic for two months. Then she added wistfully, "I had my last press conference in Illinois yesterday. I was kind of sentimental about it."

Looking at the blue skies, Rosalynn commented: "I think it's going to be a big turnout. I've never seen such excitement and enthusiasm all through the campaign as I saw this past week. I guess I could really see the difference after the debates."

She never even had a moment of doubt when she heard the Gallup Poll the day before, putting her husband one point behind President Ford for the first time since the campaign began. "No, because the Gallup Poll was old. It had been embargoed until yesterday. Before we even heard about it very early yesterday morning we called the headquarters in Atlanta and everybody there was so excited. The excitement there was unbelievable. Everybody had just seen Pat's polls and everybody said, 'We're winning,' so when we turned on the TV and saw the Gallup Poll it didn't bother me at all. It really didn't. I don't know why. It should have. But I think it just made everybody work harder. And then I saw the Roper Poll and that put us four points ahead, so I didn't worry."

With that Carter stepped out into the maze of reporters and friends. "Let's not get anybody strangled." He had just voted for the Carter-Mondale ticket and he was "very satisfied." Walking swiftly over to his family warehouse for his usual coffee klatch with his brother, Billy, Carter seemed cheerful. "I think we have a good chance to win, and I'm glad the campaign's over. I feel relieved. It's been a good one. I feel good about it. I feel like I've done my best."

And then as though it were just any other day, Carter got himself a cup of black coffee, and perched on the counter, propping one foot beside him to reveal his white good-ole-boy socks carefully rolled down around the top of his brogans. And while the cameras fired away through the window, Carter watched the CBS *Morning News* with Billy and his friend John Pope. "You're gonna win, Jimmy," Pope told him. "I know," said Carter. "Thank you." He told Pope, who complimented him on his election eve commercial, that he "didn't see a thing" and that he was going home to nap. "I didn't get home until three and then Rosalynn and I talked."

ELECTION NIGHT

I talked to Gloria that afternoon. She was just sitting in the kitchen "taking the day off." She was never concerned about the polls, although she had been momentarily concerned about the flap at the Plains Baptist Church thinking that the refusal of the deacons to admit the Reverend Clennon King from Americus might cost her brother some votes. "But it had a positive effect on red-necks. It changed a lot of undecideds for Jimmy. I've gotten a lot of calls about it."

She had no plans for after the election except to "clean up the house and go to Garden Club on Thursday."

That evening Carter bade farewell to his townspeople from a stage erected in the middle of Main Street just outside his cousin Hugh's worm-farm office, telling them how "You made me feel rested when I was tired," and how he would try and serve them in such a way as President that they would never be disappointed.

But on the plane, flying to Atlanta where he would await the returns, Carter was in a less charitable mood with reporters. Stalking back to the press cabin to momentarily chat with a select few, Carter said he had felt good all day. "I expected this turnout, but the press never really understood the enthusiasm . . . the press underestimated our organization."

Jody Powell echoed his sentiments. Riding the press bus, Powell told reporters if Carter won, the editor of the *Atlanta Constitution* was going to fire a cannon all over the city. And if he lost? "We'll fill it full of old nails and bits of metal and wadded-up pieces of copy, and just turn it on the press."

In Atlanta, Carter and his staff disappeared to the fifteenth floor of the Omni International Hotel, while the press was sent off to the World Congress Center supposedly on shuttle buses that never appeared.

Election night was surrealistic. The World Congress Center, a gigantic auditorium the size of NINE football fields, swarmed with close to thirty thousand Southern folk, mostly young and black, who consumed volumes of beer, listened to earsplitting rock and watched returns on a giant screen. Mostly they gathered around near the stage and stood, waiting to catch a glimpse of history. By three-thirty A.M. Dave Brammer, a twenty-seven-year-old camera store manager, had been standing in one spot for almost nine hours. He had arrived at the Congress Center at six-thirty in the evening, got his place in the front row to the left of the stage by eight and never budged until Carter came down at four A.M. Strangely enough, his long-suffering was not out of any great fealty to Carter.

"I voted for Carter because I just didn't like Ford." And he came to the World Congress Center because he thought Carter was going to win. "So it would be worth it . . . Besides, we heard they were going to have free dinner here, and beer," he said, producing a handful of tickets which he never got to use because he was wedged into position by the mob around him. Jack Wasson, a youth minister who works with children involved in cults, came "Because I was in the area wandering around and history is being made here, so this was the place to be." Wasson had voted for Ford in the Texas primary, but found him to be an uninspiring person, trying too hard to be President, while Carter was not only "tremendously refreshing, but he acted like a President. I voted for him." Bonna Whitten-Stoval and medical student Richard Whitten-Stoval were not watching the returns. Bonna was reading fiction. Richard was perusing *The Dialectic of Sex*. "We don't care who wins," said Richard. "It's just a thrill to be here." Bonna had not voted for Carter. "I didn't like his stand on abortion."

Upstairs in the press room where there was a free buffet, members of the staff and press gathered around four television sets stationed in four areas of the massive room nervously watching the staggeringly close returns. Every time another state fell in the Carter column, the screaming and hugging erupted. By 12:45, when New York with its forty-one electoral votes went to Carter, the nail-biting had ceased and a sense of relief prevailed. "I know we won," said Casey Cornell, Jody Powell's blond assistant. "I just want commentators to tell us so I can cry and get it over with." "I feel kind of numb," said Patty Conway, director of scheduling. "I don't know if I should scream, cry or yell."

Meanwhile in 1522—the Capitol Suite of the Omni Hotel—a two-bedroom apartment decorated in tones of beige, brown, navy and gold with a garish red monstrosity of an abstract painting, the Carter family was tightly secured. Press and even pool reporters Dick Dudman of the St. Louis *Post-Dispatch* and Saul Pett of the Associated Press were kept in a holding room for most of the evening and only allowed in for brief five-minute glimpses of the Carter family in their most historic moment.

Carter, who had slept only four hours out of the last forty-eight, was sprawled on a couch, feet on a coffee table, jacket off, his red "good luck" tie loosened, intently watching the returns. Next to him on the couch sat his sister Ruth, her husband, Bob Stapleton, and Rosalynn. Two large tables were set up along the wall, one with coffee and tea, the other with a grizzly-looking yellow cake topped with a sugar map of Georgia and the name of the hotel spelled out in large letters—OMNI. Amy, who had decided to keep the map as a souvenir was on her way to the bathroom to wash the icing off it when she tripped and fell, dropping the map on the coffee table. Georgia lay in smithereens near her father's feet and Amy collapsed in tears. Rosalynn successfully pacified her.

Down the hall where the staff was watching, a roar went up when Massachusetts fell to Carter. Charlie Kirbo downed a Jack Daniels-and-Fanta, and Jason, the Carter grandchild, wailed now and again while phones jangled off the hook. Amy flitted from room to room followed by her friend Laura.

At 3:28 Carter was still watching NBC when Mississippi gave him the Presidency. Carter leaped to his feet, clapping his hands. "All right!" said the first President-elect from the Deep South since 1848. "All right!" Twenty-two months of pumping hands and beating the bushes and four years of work had finally culminated in the most spectacular victory of the decade. Hamilton Jordan let out a bloodcurdling rebel yell and with that the entire room erupted into a tangle of arms, war whoops, kisses, spilled drinks, rubbed heads, tears, hysterical laughter, "Thank you man" and a whispered litany of "Hello, Mr. President." Amy, who had fallen asleep, was brought in from the bedroom for a hug from her father before settling drowsily into her mother's lap.

At 3:40 Carter called his running mate, Walter Mondale. "I just love Mississippi." Carter laughed.

Jody Powell was one of the last to congratulate Carter, the President-elect put both hands on Powell's arms, stared into his eyes with tender fatherly love and embraced him warmly. Through all the hugging and kissing, Carter kept a watchful eye on the television sets.

It was just four A.M. when Carter arrived to give his victory address to the bedraggled mob in the World Congress Center. Many had fallen asleep on the floor by then, surrounded by a sea of beer cans and plastic glasses, but rose to their feet, eyes half glazed, to release eight hours of pent-up cheers. For all the time they had patiently waited, an exhausted Carter gave them only five minutes.

He called Gerald Ford "a good and decent man" (the same

phrase Ford had used to describe his Agriculture Secretary, Earl Butz, when he resigned in disgrace). He prayed he would live up to their confidence and that he would never disappoint them. He told them it was time to "tap a sense of brotherhood and sisterhood," and to make the nation "great once again." He spoke of unity and a sense of purpose and the government belonging to people.

And he was gone, followed by his groggy disciples who trooped out of the hall behind him to the sounds of earsplitting soul rock. There were few tears of joy and little rejoicing. The Carter group looked shell-shocked. "Get the band to play a victory song for the President," Jody Powell commanded an aide. The guitarist kept right on strumming out his two-note primitive rhythm and glared at the aide for making the suggestion. "This is a victory song, man!"

Hamilton Jordan's eyes were glassy with fatigue. "We couldn't do it the simple way. We had to screw around," he told me as he left the hall.

Outside there was a mad scramble for the press buses. "Here we go Carter Press, Carter Press, Carter Press!" Jim King bellowed on his bullhorn. Carter wanted to go to Plains immediately to greet his family and friends who had been waiting in the street all night. He was fuming when one press bus showed up at the Atlanta airport twenty minutes late, having turned off on the wrong exit behind a lost police car. Carter ambled back into the tourist section of the plane searching for Jody Powell and Greg Schneiders. "O.K.," he snapped, looking at his watch. "The forty minutes are up." Carter wanted to take off instantly and leave the rest of the press behind, but Powell and Schneiders hee-hawed him into waiting.

At one point Carter made his way up the center aisle of the plane passing through sleepy reporters. I heard few congratulations offered. There was no jubilation, no celebrating, no champagne. The press simply hunkered down and slept all the way to Plains. "Jesus Christ," said Gregg Jackson, a producer for Paramount films. "You'd think the guy lost. If you took someone who didn't know the outcome of the election and put him on this plane and asked him to figure out what was going on, he'd say, 'Too bad, he lost.'"

November 3 dawned with serenity and peace and a sense that something had been fulfilled according to a Master Plan. At five-thirty A.M. the sky was clearer than usual . . . pure blue and cloudless. And the sun was just beginning to rise. Its shimmering edge formed an aura behind the western-movie setting of the storefronts.

Slowly it began to take the bite out of the chilled morning air, warming the four hundred or five hundred kith and kin who had waited all night long in the street to share the victorious return of their hometown boy, the President-elect of the United States of America.

Carter, his face sunken with exhaustion but exuberant with victory, darted up the rotting steps of the old depot. Behind him stood his sister Ruth, the evangelist, his brother, Billy, barely sobered up for the occasion, Rosalynn and Miz Lillian. Carter embraced the portly Maxine Reese who had run his Plains campaign office, wrapping both arms around her sizable waist and squeezing hard. Then, smiling, he turned to the crowd. They cheered with all the energy they had reserved for the momentous occasion, and more. The war was over. The Civil War. His smile widened and his eyes glistened with warmth. It was the genuine Carter smile. The tenseness of two years of campaigning had vanished. He was relaxed and easygoing, and the humor he had been afraid to reveal for so long appeared. Jimmy teased them. "From now on, you're going to have to call Billy 'Mr. Carter.' "

The scene that followed was one that will be indelibly etched on my memory forever, for it said more about the real Jimmy Carter we had all been searching for than any other moment.

"I told you I didn't intend to lose," he said softly, and the multitude burst into whoops and hollers and applause. But the sight of this haggard band of hometown friends who had waited all night was too overwhelming. His eyes moistened as they searched the crowd. He saw Joyce, the waitress from the Best Western Motel, who had to be at work in half an hour, and he saw Bob Muenscher, a Republican county chairman from the state of Washington who had become enthralled with Jimmy in 1973 when they met at the Spokane World's Fair. Muenscher had driven 3500 miles to be in the street for Jimmy's return. He saw his old friend, John Pope, and Maxine and Charlie Wiggins, who had been up twenty-six hours awaiting Mr. Jimmy's return. He saw the old buildings freshly painted and hung with red-white-and-blue bunting. He saw the remnants of the all-night vigil in the street, and he wept, openly, with a sense of comfort only a man who knew those people very well, like family, could have. He could not have cried, and would not have, anywhere else in the country. "I came through twenty-two months and I didn't get choked up until . . ." Carter wiped away one tear with his crooked index finger, bit his lip hard and turned to his right where he found Rosalynn dissolving too. He stepped away from the lectern, threw his arms around his wife and wept on her shoulder for a long moment while his friends screamed, cheered and laughed with tears streaming down their faces. John Pope's face flooded with emotion. "If my nose had been turned around I surely would have drowned," he said later.

"All the others who ran for President didn't have people who would stay up all night in Plains, Georgia . . . It was a long night, but I guarantee you it's going to be worth it to all of you," Carter continued.

His words were reminiscent of John Kennedy's.

"There is a need in this country for us, each individual person, to look and say what can we do to make our country great. What can we do to make our future brighter. What can we do to return laughter to the United States. And I hope and I believe that we are ready to do it. These next couple of months I'll be doing the best I can to prepare myself to be a President of which this country can be proud . . ."

And in his moment of triumph, humility. "The only reason it was close last night was that the candidate wasn't quite good enough as a campaigner . . . But I'll make up for that in the next four years."

Then for the first time, Carter allowed his sense of the moment to surface. He looked off at the rising sun bathing the storefronts in gold.

"The sun is rising on a beautiful new day and there is a beautiful new spirit in this country, a beautiful new commitment to the future. I feel good about it, and I love every one of you." With that, Jimmy Carter sprang off the platform into a swarm of adoring arms, dispensed a deluge of hugs and kisses, and went home to bed.

While the band played "The Star-Spangled Banner," and the choir sang "God Bless America," Miz Lillian was already busy planning a breakfast at the Back Porch Café and was congratulated as "First Grandmama." Sister Ruth told me she could still not fathom what had happened. "Coming into Plains was like riding in a motorcade in a football rally. I couldn't believe what was happening. It hasn't hit me yet. We campaigned until midnight night before last and I'm just numb. I have to go home and get some rest."

In the half light of morning, Maxine Reese was on the depot platform cutting a giant cake in the shape of the White House, and press secretary Jody Powell signed autographs on an oil drum on the corner of Main and Church streets. "Hey, how we doin' in Ohio? I'm afraid some Northern state is going to secede, or something will go wrong."

Bob Muenscher wrapped his denim jacket tightly around him against the cold and shook his head as he surveyed the scene. "I came thirty-five hundred miles just to see this. Coming to this community has been the biggest thing in my life. To see Plains and to see the whole Carter family every day just walking the streets like everybody else, to be able to meet them and talk to them and get to know them is a thrill. I can hardly believe it. This place, this family, this community, is what Jimmy Carter is all about. This is how Jimmy won."

EPILOGUE

WHY JIMMY WON

THE PEANUTS-TO-POLITICS-TO-PRESIDENT tale of James Earl Carter, Junior, is the most astonishing political story of our decade. The Carter victory was an unexpected coup that happened with such lightning swiftness that many still shake their heads and ask how an unknown rural Southern "born-again" peanut farmer with no traditional Washington ties could have left the Establishment flattened in the red Georgia dust. The odds were all against it. Had it been a novel, even a fairy tale, few would have been willing to suspend their credibility to listen.

And yet, "Jimmy Who" became the thirty-ninth President of the United States.

Why did Jimmy Win?

It was neither a miracle, nor a fluke, nor a master stroke of political genius. In fact, he barely made it.

Carter won 51 percent of the popular vote; Ford 48 percent. Carter received 40,278,840 popular votes, Ford 38,536,990; 297 electoral votes made Carter President, 241 went to Ford. Had Carter been given 29 less electoral votes, Ford would have remained in the White House.

Basically, Jimmy won because he offered the hope of something better. What counted in his twenty-two-month drive to become the thirty-ninth President of the U. S. was not so much promises as promise. He also won because he had in his corner the history of Watergate, the geography of the Confederacy, the reality of the economy and the magnetism of running-mate Senator Walter Mondale.

Simplistically, he was the right man for the right time.

He was first a Democrat and in the eight-year cycle of political history, 1976 was ripe for a Democratic victory. As one high-ranking Democrat told me at the outset of the campaign, "We could run an aardvark this year and win." From Maine to California, the American sentiment was the same: It was time for a change.

Carter was not just any Democrat. He was an engineer, peanut farmer, Sunday-school teacher, businessman, scholar, a new breed of Southern Governor without the taint of racism, a fresh face without the stigma of Washington. He was, in short, something for everybody—and something different.

As Judith Michaelson, the outstanding political reporter of the New York *Post,* put it, "By accident of birth, Jimmy Carter shattered Richard Nixon's Southern strategy." As a native of deep Georgia Carter was able to return the fallen-away South to the shattered catholicity of the Democratic fold. Georgia had voted Republican two out of the last three Presidential elections, as had much of the traditionally Democratic South. Carter was able to revive the faded coalition.

Carter was a Southerner the South could be proud of. He brought the South into the twentieth century. He was not a Maddox or a Wallace who represented the lowest common denominator of the South. "There's no doubt Wallace paved the way for us," said campaign aide Peter Bourne, "but Wallace was the freaky edge." Carter was white-collar Wallace. He telegraphed the same populist message to the man who feared government, higher taxes, big business, and snooty liberalism. But he did it in polished euphemisms and his solemn low-key, evangelical style. He spoke to our hopes and dreams.

"Isn't it time we had a President without an accent?" he teasingly reminded Southerners from Maryland to Mississippi. Dixie had been cut out of the Presidential heartland since the Civil War. Now for the first time in a century it was being recognized as a serious part of the political landscape.

"His election," said campaign aide Peter Bourne, "will be the ultimate resolution of the Civil War that took one hundred years to get resolved." Along with Southern pride in a native son and a burning desire for reentry into the political mainstream, came a solid base of 129 of electoral votes. "All we had to do was build on twenty-seven percent of the electoral vote," said campaign manager Hamilton Jordan. "If we could hold that base steady, there was an infinite combination of ways we could put together the rest of the states," said issues director Stu Eizenstat. "We could even be in trouble in a few of the major industrial states and still win. We had flexibility." With that unshakable base, there was almost no way Carter could lose.

His roots were Old South, his family had been in Georgia for 210 years, but his politics were New South. Although his 1970 gubernatorial campaign smacked of vintage red-neck, he had been able to live up to the words of his 1971 inaugural address:

"I say to you quite frankly the time for racial discrimination is over. No poor, rural, weak or black person should ever have to bear the burden of being deprived of the opportunity for an education, a job or simple justice."

By accident of faith, Carter's salvation was the evangelical and black vote. The blossoming evangelical movement, now the major religious force in America both in numbers and impact, found a common bond with its born-again brother, Jimmy Carter. Many evangelicals worked hard for Nixon in 1960, trying to save America from a Catholic President, but they worked even harder to support one of their own sixteen years later. The numbers of evangelicals in the United States are estimated between 68 and 80 million people. If one were to estimate the evangelicals of voting age at 40 million, that would make up more than a quarter of the electorate.

According to Garry Wills, Carter came by this massive vote naturally just as John Kennedy inherited the Catholic vote. Wills adds, "But the real measure of Carter's advantage is that large fringe of well-disposed people around the evangelical movement. Take, for instance, the black vote, so heavily tilted toward Carter in this year's primaries." Ninety-three percent of the black vote helped to elect him. Not only did his Southern heritage guarantee him a unique electoral position that included 3.5 million blacks registered to vote in the eleven states of the Old Confederacy, but his religious heritage provided him a pulpit from which to address a 50 percent Baptist black population. His appeal was unique for a white politician. One had only to watch the reception Carter received in black churches. They called him "Brother Jimmy," they interrupted his speeches with "Amen," and "That's right!" and "Yes, suh!" They listened when Daddy King told them as he told me, "I see a sincere man. Carter loves people, and that means all people. I know the man's heart and his intent." They listened when Daddy King ended the Democratic National Convention calling Carter a man sent from God.

Blacks saw God in Carter. Some claimed to see an "aura" or a "halo" around him. Vonnie Belle Johnson, a nurse, told me, "The minute I saw Carter's picture on TV I said, 'That is the man God sent us to bail us out.' I could see a halo around his head. I've prayed over it and I believe. I would stand on top of the monument and shout, 'Jimmy Carter!' He's a Jesus man."

And Robert Hill, a pecan farmer from Hawkinsville, Georgia, said, "I like him because I come from the same region, because I'm a Democrat and because he's an honest man. He's done more for black people than the Republicans. But mostly I like him because he is governed by God and has no other alternative than to do what is right. I believe that because I stand close to God myself. God's going to straighten things out through Jimmy Carter."

Still, both his Southernism and his Bible-toting Baptist background weighed just as heavily against him as it did in his favor. Fear of the unknown made his soft Georgia accent seem even more alien to the Northern ear. Many claimed they could not even understand him. Liberals suspected an underlying Southern conservatism and racism. Labor suspected a Georgia right-to-work ethic. Jews were troubled by his ostentatious Christianity. Catholics and Protestants feared his Baptist rigidity. It was little surprise that Carter spent the latter half of his campaign explaining how John F. Kennedy was misunderstood because of his Catholicism, yet how Georgia gave him a larger plurality in 1960 than his home state of Massachusetts.

Carter sensed the mood of the country early. America was turned off, and turned out. About the only event that captured the minds and imaginations of the American people in the year 1976 was the arrival of an armada of Tall Ships. Sailing ships from around the world, multimasted schooners that represented a pirate past, a swashbuckling history at sea, a romantic era of John Paul Jones, Moby Dick, Britannia rules the waves, and the discovery of America. Eyes were focused on the sea, not on our land.

Not even the two hundredth anniversary of the nation's birth caused as big a stir and sensation as the arrival of those majestic vessels into Boston, New York and Baltimore harbors. Hundreds of thousands of Americans made their way to the sea like so many lemmings for a brief glimpse of the flotilla. Newport, the bastion of the idle rich, opened its sprawling, weathered summer mansions to the sailors from foreign lands. Few could resist the call of the Tall Ships.

But the Bicentennial came and went as just another good-natured celebration. There were no riots, no mass demonstrations, no inordinate damage. Nor was there any great national participation or patriotism. The biggest Bicentennial cities, Washington and Philadelphia, ached with empty hotel rooms on July 4th, the Birthday itself. It seemed few felt like celebrating America this year. There was not that much to celebrate. America was in a fugue state, passing through a night of the spirit.

Buffeted by a divisive war, three assassinations, riots and demonstrations, the fall of a President and a Vice President in disgrace, the exposition of CIA and FBI horrors, U. S. participation in government overthrows and assassinations, the discovery of Capitol Hill sexploitation, Congressmen paying mistresses from the public till, Congressmen soliciting prostitutes and consorting with strippers, Senators, doctors, nursing-home operators, all on the take, a faltering economy, a soaring crime rate, an increase in drugs in the schools, a further disintegration of the family, and a host of other ills, the American spirit waxed cynical and turned within.

Doubt, gloom, pessimism and suspicion clouded and colored the collective thinking. No one was to be trusted. Not the mailman, not the family doctor, not the policeman, not the lawyer, not the press, and certainly of all people, not the Washington politician.

The massive constituencies of ex-Governor Ronald Reagan and Governors George Wallace and Jerry Brown bore testimony to that fact. America wanted someone besides a slick Washington Senator with bonds to the special-interest groups, someone besides a Washington lawyer who wined and dined with lobbyists at fancy restaurants. America was searching for the Holy Grail, a symbol of purity, decency, honesty, truth, and even sanctity. America wanted someone to lead, inspire, uplift and manage. Bureaucracy was running away with itself, engulfing all it touched in red tape. It was time for the biggest business of all—government—to be governed.

Morris Udall, Scoop Jackson, Sargent Shriver, Birch Bayh, Lloyd Bentsen, Fred Harris, all represented the Washington Establishment. In the eyes of the voters they were traditional politicians, ambassadors from a corrupt hill-top congregation promising purification.

The White House no longer symbolized integrity, monarchy and the divine right of kings. The American people equated 1600 Pennsylvania Avenue with Richard Nixon, Spiro Agnew, John Ehrlichman, H.R. Haldeman, John Mitchell and a cast of corroded political characters. They associated Capitol Hill with Wayne Hays and Wilbur Mills, Fanne Foxe and Elizabeth Ray. They associated Gerald Ford with both Washington institutions. Ford was not only a twenty-five-year veteran of the Capitol Hill society, he was the appointed handmaiden of Richard Nixon, and his mortal sin was pardoning him. Had Gerald Ford not pardoned Nixon, an act that abruptly ended one of the sweetest Presidential honeymoons in history, he might have been elected President instead of Jimmy Carter. But voters across the land sniffed "a deal."

"A good and decent man," Carter said of Ford at the close of their final debate, and he echoed much of the nation's point of view, but in spite of the fact that Gerald Ford staged the most remarkable comeback since Harry Truman in 1948, the image persisted of an accidental President who fumbled his words, tumbled down ski slopes, bumped his head on helicopter doors and forgot where he was and what he was supposed to say. For all his elocution lessons from Don Penny, his noticeable improvement in speechmaking, particularly his outstanding performance at the Republican National Convention, Ford was perceived as a negative President. He vetoed rather than initiated, did little to uplift the minds and spirits of a depressed people and danced at White House dinners rather than nursed a nation back to health. Gerald Ford did little to help himself by selecting Robert Dole as his vice-presidential running mate. Dole, another Nixon handmaiden and Capitol Hill crony, suffered guilt by association with Watergate and the reputation of a hatchet man which he lived up to during the campaign.

But Carter came from the outside. As he said, "I owe nothing to special interest groups. I owe the people everything." Even Republicans responded to his message. Terry and Carol McLean, conservatives who voted for Goldwater and twice for Nixon, sat on the grass at a Carter rally in Bloomsburg, Pennsylvania, last April, brandishing a Carter banner. "Ford just isn't the caliber of man we need. We've had professional politicians for a long time. But Jimmy doesn't seem like one. He has the intelligence and capacity Ford lacks and he's a refreshing person who's defined himself outside of politics."

Carter struck the right note of optimism in a battered nation. He understood that 1976 was the year of the nonissue. After a heavy diet of political news emanating from the nation's capital, the American people wearied of tedious subjects like energy, taxes, budgets and nuclear proliferation. Although Sargent Shriver prepared the most extensive and complete issues papers offering practical solutions to problems, no one cared and no one read them. Voters wanted charisma, dynamism and leadership. They wanted a hero to worship again. They warmed to the Carter-Kennedy smile and liked his strong physical resemblance to both John and Robert Kennedy.

The people responded to his message. With piercing blue eyes, a soft Georgia drawl and a crooked finger, he offered an America not as it is, but as it ought to be—in Bob Dylan's phrase, "Busy being born, not busy dying." Like a pastor, Carter offered absolution to a country plagued with guilt for its sins. "I want a government that's as truthful and honest and decent and fair and compassionate and filled with love as the rest of the American people." With dancing eyebrows he called our "system" of government "still the best on earth." To a people divided he said, "God has given us a great country. We can bind ourselves together and search for a better life."

To a nation walled off from Washington, he offered intimacy and participation. "This is the ye-uh of the people. We've got a great country. You can determine the kind of government you have."

To a nation alienated by an imperial Presidency, he offered himself as a common man without the baggage of pseudosophistication. He stayed in the homes of little people as he traveled and he made his own bed. He could tote his own suitbag, forsake limousines for sedans, shovel his own peanuts and change from the gray flannel of the executive to the blue denim of the laborer without affectation.

Carter said often, "I have never claimed to be better or wiser than any other person. I think my greatest strength is that I am an ordinary man, just like all of you, one who has worked and learned and loved his family and made mistakes and tried to correct them without always succeeding."

He was just plain "Jimmy." He could roll up his sleeves, stalk through farmers' markets, slog through mines, or fox-trot with senior citizens with as much ease as he could mingle with the stars of Hollywood or the millionaires of Manhattan.

Millie Vincineri will never forget the September day Carter strolled into her husband Charley's corner market on Ditmars Boulevard in Astoria, New York. "I couldn't believe he took the trouble to stop in here. We're only a little store. I've never been that close to anyone so important. I was scared to death, but he was very warm and human. He stayed and talked to us and he hugged me when he left."

"He's common, down to earth, he's for the workingman," said Tina Walker, a Pennsylvania housewife. "We need him more than we need them high-society types."

Although Ford called him someone who "wavers, wiggles, wanders and waffles," Carter established a broad-based appeal by selling himself as both a liberal and a conservative, straddling issues with the agility of a tightrope walker: for and against abortion, for and against bussing, for and against prayer in the schools, for and against right-to-work laws, for and against big business. Pummeling his audiences with statistics he convinced them he understood complex issues well enough to be President. But with his talk of compassion and decency and truth and love, he conveyed he cared first and foremost for what touched human beings.

He started sooner than his opponents. Unlike candidates like Birch Bayh and Sargent Shriver who struggled with their decisions to run until the last minute, or Hubert Humphrey who hid in the wings sending surrogates to campaign for him, Carter began plotting his strategy eighteen months after he became Governor of Georgia.

I asked him once how it felt to have come so far so fast and Carter replied, "Well, from our perspective, it's not coming so fast. It is coming far, but we've been working on this campaign now for a solid four years! We worked at it, thought about it, planned it. What we did then is not apparent, so it's a much more rapid evolution from the perspective of an outsider than it is for us."

As Peter Bourne said, "The whole campaign was like a play written in 1972." And Carter began memorizing his lines immediately. In a seventy-two-page memo his campaign manager, Hamilton Jordan, etched out the necessary steps Carter should take and Carter followed the checklist with utmost care.

Carter not only started sooner, he went everywhere. While most of his opponents carefully targeted key states, Carter entered thirty out of thirty-one primaries, running harder and longer with more sheer physical energy and endurance than any who challenged him. He went to shopping centers, labor halls, livestock sales barns, beauty parlors, and barber shops. While Mo Udall napped, Carter pressed on, using solitary moments on the plane as rest. While Scoop Jackson waited for reporters to finish phone calls and arrived at his next rally forty-five minutes late, Carter abandoned stragglers and arrived twenty minutes early. While Frank Church would languish in a hotel room nursing a strep throat, Carter would forge on despite a 104° fever. The peanut farmer who knew what it was to stay up thirty-six hours at a stretch during drying season knew how to endure.

Carter's own family contributed greatly to his success. They were of enormous news value. Almost everyone in the family was a source of intriguing and colorful copy that created interest in the Carter clan—a mother who joined the Peace Corps at age sixty-eight, an evangelist sister with a large following of her own, another sister who rides motorcycles, an irreverent, beer- and bourbon-drinking brother with a penchant for cowboy books, a cousin with the world's largest worm farm, and an eight-year-old daughter with a lucrative lemonade stand. Most of them plunged into the campaign with as fierce an intensity as the candidate himself. At any given point in the campaign up to thirteen members of Carter's family, including his sons and daughters-in-law—Chip and Caron, Jeff and Annette, Jack and Judy— aunt Sissy Dolvin, brother Billy, sisters Ruth and Gloria, mama Lillian, and wife Rosalynn, were on the road seeking votes. The family fanned out separately across the country, sometimes hitting 107 cities in one week's time, covering ground the candidate could not and seeing more people than he had time to see. Rosalynn, in fact, was in as great demand as the candidate. Often, if Carter was unable to make an appearance they'd say, "O.K., send Rosalynn."

Larry Belair, a New Hampshire legislator, had been a Birch Bayh supporter until Caron Carter converted him in December 1975. "She came to see me four different times," says Belair. "She wouldn't give up and I wouldn't give in. Finally she came a fifth time and asked if I wouldn't at least come and hear Carter speak." Belair went. Halfway through the speech Belair decided to switch his allegiance to Carter.

"She and Chip were the strongest campaigners of all," says a Carter friend. "They appealed and related to a larger number of people."

Carter's friends and associates played an active role in getting him elected. Almost six hundred Georgians, most of whom knew him personally, some who had never met him, and some who traveled from as far away as Hawaii, paid their own way to campaign sixteen to eighteen hours a day for their native son. Chartering a plane, the group that came to be known as the "Peanut Brigade" blitzed almost all the primary states with Carter leaflets, literature, peanuts and Southern charm. The first brigade, one hundred strong, walked the snowy streets of New Hampshire braving 19° below zero weather, chilly New Englanders and a few "killer dogs" to spread the gospel according to Jimmy Carter.

While more than a dozen Democratic hopefuls littered stoops with campaign literature, "None of them bothered to ring the doorbells or call the occupants by name and spend time talking to them. Ours was a whole new approach, a very personal approach," says Betty Pope, whose husband, John, has been a close Carter friend since 1953. "Instead of just getting a phone call asking them to vote for someone, they were pleased that someone actually took the trouble to come and visit with them. Many of them told us, 'You've got to be crazy to do this. If you do this for someone you believe in, he's got to be someone special. I'm going to vote for him.' " Others were impressed with the caliber of campaigner they met. "They were used to meeting college kids hired to hand out literature for the weekend, who had gone campaigning just as an excuse to party and drink beer, but with us, they were meeting mature people of all ages [fifteen to seventy-eight] and all walks of life who were not giddy and silly, but serious people who cared enough to talk to the waitresses and the garbage men as well as executives."

At first, the approach was three-pronged, a personal greeting, "Hi, I'm from Americus, Georgia. I'm a friend of Jimmy Carter's. I know him real well and have most of my life. I'd be glad to talk to you and tell you the truth about him and answer any questions you might have about him."

Step two was a visit with the person or family to explain Carter's record on issues and positions. "Most of them didn't give a darn about the issues," says John Pope, who served as a Peanut Brigade captain. "They mostly wanted to know whether the man they saw on TV was real. He looked too good to be true."

Step three was "follow up." If the person listened and said, "That's my man," they were coded number one on an index card. If they requested literature or a Carter position paper, they received a number two beside their name. "Open minded," rated a number three, and "disinterested" a number four or number five. Ones, twos and threes received immediate "follow-up." Within forty-eight hours a personal thank-you letter arrived.

"We took notes on what was happening while we were talking to them, what the dog did or what a child said, or if someone were ill. Then we would write: 'We so enjoyed meeting your sweet daughter, Kathy,' or 'We hope your husband, Bill, is getting better.'" "The follow-up really paid off handsomely," says Betty Pope. "They knew they weren't getting a computer-kicked-out letter. Jimmy said he could see a fantastic effect. He'd go to a factory and someone would say to him, 'Oh, Mr. Carter, one of your pretty Southern girls came to my door,' or 'I got a letter from one of your friends in Hawkinsville.' He said the personal touch really made the difference. It was why he won. As little known as he was there was no way he and the family alone could have appealed to that many people in a state so far removed as Georgia."

Later, during the general election campaign, peanut brigaders abandoned their casual parlor campaign for a fast-moving media blitz, two hours in a town. While some were interviewed on local TV and radio, others passed out literature in shopping centers. "The idea was maximum media exposure," says Pope.

Carter's campaign was a clever mix of the old-fashioned one-to-one approach with carefully cultivated media exposure. As Charles Kirbo said, "Jimmy probably had more interviews and went before more editorial boards than anyone ever before in a Presidential campaign." It seeemed as though Carter appeared on a different magazine cover every week. As one leading Pennsylvania Democrat grumbled: "If Carter is the next President, it will be the media's fault. Every time he even walks in the front door of his church, he's on TV."

The personal touch went farther than New Hampshire. The Popes, among others, also took it upon themselves to distribute autographed copies of Carter's autobiography, *Why Not the Best?* They gave several hundred copies for Christmas and continued to give them as gifts throughout the year. John often rode over to Carter's house early in the campaign and had him sign batches of forty books at a time. "Friends would write back and say, 'Please send five more copies.' One judge asked for six copies every two weeks," said Betty Pope. "It was a very personalized campaign."

Betty Pope conceived the idea that all five hundred Peanut Brigaders should write ten people and ask each of those ten to write another ten. She wrote eight hundred letters over a period of eight months. "As a result, people would often call us and say, 'I want to start a campaign headquarters in my town, how do I do it?' or 'When Carter's in town tell him he can use my WATS line.' People really wanted to help. They just wanted to be invited."

Anne Robbins, a Rockville, Maryland, housewife who has worked in several Presidential campaigns, penned close to a thousand letters for Carter to labor leaders, columnists, politicians, movers and shakers, explaining Jimmy. "I started back in 1975 when no one knew who he was," says Ms. Robbins. She was assigned to bed for four months of her pregnancy, "So I had the time to do it. I wrote letters tailored to the individual person. If it were a Jewish person, I'd discuss Jimmy's recent trip to Israel; if it were a friend of mine from Kennedy days, I'd discuss how much he valued words and literature, and how much he had restored my faith in politics."

Rosalynn Carter herself papered the country with notes. She also scrawled messages on the bottoms of postcards Carter volunteers sent to people who expressed an interest in the Carter campaign. One she wrote went to a small Mexican-American child in San

Francisco. "Word spread like wildfire through the Mexican-American community that Rosalynn Carter had taken the time to write the child of an ordinary working person," said a campaign aide. "That one personal note was invaluable."

Carter was a pro with the personal touch himself. One friend called it "hustling with a heart." One Maryland couple who had met Carter only a few times, sent him a birthday card the October before the election. When Carter was campaigning in Maryland, he spotted the couple standing outside the 4-H Center in Chevy Chase behind a rope in the rain. He was late and the Secret Service were moving him quickly past the crowd, but Carter stopped to thank them. "Got your birthday card and I really appreciated it," he said.

When daily campaigning consumed him, Carter switched to the telephone. He often called a hundred to two hundred delegates on a Saturday afternoon sitting on a couch in his study.

He asked those to whom he spoke at rallies to make the "sacrifice" and call one hundred people a day just as he had. Many of them did.

The domino theory worked to his advantage. Carter's early victory in the Iowa caucuses and in the New Hampshire primary were essential to the Carter win, in that they provided the element of surprise and catapulted Carter into national prominence. Although Carter's Iowa victory was slim—he only won 27 percent of the vote—it brought him immediate media attention and proved that he was more than a regional candidate—and a winner. The New Hampshire primary, always a bellwether, was key, insofar as no one who ever lost the New Hampshire primary has ever been elected president. His victory over George Wallace in Florida, which Wallace won heavily in 1972, established Carter as a dragon slayer of major proportion and gave him momentum to go on to defeat Wallace in the important Illinois primary. Victory in the early and crucial cluster of primaries and caucuses propelled Carter toward triumph in Pennsylvania. By that time, in spite of Humphrey-generated Stop-Carter movements, Carter was the inevitable nominee. Even substantial showings by Frank Church and Governor Jerry Brown and "uncommitted" in the California, Rhode Island, Idaho, New Jersey and Maryland primaries had failed to stop him.

The debates proved a helpful tool to Carter. While expectations ran high that Ford, a lawyer and Congressman for a quarter century, with the information and aid available to him as President, would be a more informed and practiced debater, Carter proved a steady, aggressive, equally knowledgeable opponent. While Carter began on the defensive, Ford ended on it. While Carter grew in stature, Ford diminished. "Jimmy became increasingly comfortable," says Charles Kirbo. "He found he could 'handle' Ford. What I was fixin' to say was that there was a perception that the public had that Ford wasn't too smart. The debates proved that. The situation was right. The questions came just right. So even if no one won or lost exactly, they were helpful to us politically." Mainly, the debates provided broad national exposure that the relatively unknown Carter desperately needed. Carter intimates were positively gleeful that Ford insisted on a series of debates. It brought Jimmy Carter into 200 million homes for free.

The Mondale-Dole debate unexpectedly turned out to be an asset to the Carter campaign. It catapulted Mondale into national prominence as a dignified, serious, knowledgeable potential President rather than the flaming liberal he had been portrayed by Republicans. Conversely, the debate established Dole as a snarly, immature, slippery, Faustian character who slashed at Carter with such statements as "I suggest George Meany was his makeup man," and at Democratic foreign policy with such an outrageous remark as "You know I figured out the other day, if you added up the killed and wounded in Democratic wars, the figure would be one point six million lives." Dole also defended the man who appointed him chairman of the Republican National Committee, Richard Nixon. "I know it strikes a responsive chord to kick Richard Nixon around, whose wife suffered a serious stroke when he stepped from office . . . " Fritz Mondale responded: "Senator Dole has richly earned his reputation as a hatchet man tonight by stating that it was partisan to fight Nazi Germany. Was it only partisanship that got us into the war with South Korea? Mr. Nixon promised to get us out of the war in Vietnam, but it was Congress that finally ended the war."

Mondale's presence on the ticket was more beneficial to Carter than even he had originally anticipated. With his almost perfect voting record in the view of labor and liberals, the Senator from Minnesota helped reinforce the support that organized labor planned to give to the Democratic nominee. In fact, the extent to which the unions labored in Carter's political vineyard proved monumental. In contrast to the previous election when only the United Automobile Workers and a few other unions rallied to the McGovern standard, almost the entire brotherhood turned on and out for Carter.

The statistics are mind-boggling. According to figures provided by the Committee on Political Education (COPE), the political arm of the AFL-CIO, COPE alone supplied more than 120,000 volunteers, set up thousands of phonebanks that made over ten million calls during register-and-vote campaigns and distributed more than eighty million pieces of literature to union members. As a result an enormous outpouring of union voters appeared at the polls, 70 percent of whom cast their ballots for the Carter-Mondale ticket.

Leonard Woodcock, the president of the UAW, who saw another Kennedy in Carter, personally campaigned for the Georgia peanut farmer as early as the Florida primary, long before any other labor mogul came on board. Later, George Meany, the cigar-smoking Mahatma of the AFL-CIO, raised his gnarled hands in blessing, hands that had the clout to make the difference between four years in the White House and a lifetime in Plains. As Meany observed shortly after the election, "When you look at the Ford Administration, which came on top of the disastrous administration of President Nixon, you will find a complete lack of compassion—a lack of compassion for people who are out of work; a lack of compassion for the growing number of people who are living below the poverty level, and a complete refusal to recognize the condition of America's great cities."

What Meany neglected to say was that this time around what organized labor wanted more than compassion was a winner.

Carter's smooth staff work, at least during the primaries, contributed in large part to his victory. Other staffs were plagued by infighting, backbiting or incompetence. Mo Udall told me during the Massachusetts primary, "Staff problems are the biggest headache I have. It's just endemic to the whole campaign way of life. Scoop Jackson has a lot of internal strife too. Bentsen's guy quit and Birch Bayh has a lot of personnel changes. So did Ford. It's extremely unpleasant to me. I always have to be refereeing fights and ego disputes." Ford went through three campaign managers. Bo Callaway was fired for conflict of interest, Rogers Morton was fired for lack of know-how, and not until the bitter end, when James Baker took over, was there the slightest semblance of order or direction in the Ford campaign.

Carter's inner circle had worked together for six years or more. They were very young, enthusiastic and fiercely loyal to Carter. Jody Powell, Hamilton Jordan, Peter Bourne and Landon Butler were in their twenties when they started with Carter back in the late Sixties and early Seventies and had grown up together. They were more like brothers than staff members and because all had equal access to Carter there was little jockeying for position.

Aside from an occasional tease (Jody Powell called Carter an "arrogant little bastard" once during a softball game) they never indulged in derogatory conversations about their candidate as the McGovern staff and Muskie staffs had in 1972.

"Jimmy has the capacity to attract people who stay with him and people who are loyal to him," said Kirbo. "That's because he's both tough and compassionate. He's very considerate with people, especially when they make mistakes or fall short. There was one young woman on the staff who had been with us for a long time and was in a tough job in the primaries. As the campaign began to blossom, it got too much for her. She just wasn't doing a good enough job, so some people tried to move her out. Jimmy told her to come and see me. He felt sorry for her. She had earned her salt in the past, so he told me to try and find a place for her.

"He takes chances on people. He'll gamble on a young person when he ought to get an old pro. He feels like maybe they've got potential and he likes to give people opportunity."

The staff was also willing to work for little or no pay. Many were paid on an "as needed" basis. While Robert Keefe, Scoop Jackson's campaign manager, was paid $45,000, Hamilton Jordan and Jody Powell struggled along on a little better than half of that. There were times in fact that there was no money in the till to pay them. When that happened, Jordan and Powell took a loan from the bank to tide them over.

Money was rarely squandered during the Carter campaign. Every penny was carefully monitored by lawyer Robert Lipshutz, a kindly man with a streak of Scrooge. While Jackson wasted massive amounts of money, for example, by throwing cocktail parties to which only people already committed to him came, and while Reagan's team spent thousands on press rooms and a daily supply of sandwiches, sweet rolls and coffee for newsmen during the primaries, Carter never wasted a dime.

Careful organization was on Carter's side. "You know behind the scenes in Atlanta we've possibly had the best-organized campaign the country's ever seen," Carter told me. "With the computers, careful budgeting, detailed scheduling, superb organizational structure and the unity of the party."

Jody Powell was a bit less laudatory about the organization.

"Everybody thinks the organization and strategy were so brilliant. It's no more brilliant than anybody else's. The only thing that will make it brilliant is if we win. If we lose, they'll just say, 'It was just a bunch of dumb kids who didn't know what they were doing.'"

INDEX